"But after all that has been said by others, or can be said here, no description of Great Britain can be what we call a finished account, as no cloaths can be made to fit a growing child; no picture carry the likeness of a living face; the size of one, and the countenance of the other always altering with time: so no account of a kingdom thus daily altering its countenance, can be perfect."

Daniel Defoe, *A Tour through England and Wales*, vol. 1, author's Preface to the original edition, 1724

THE WELFARE STATE

or before

THE
WELFARE STATE

An Economic and Social History of Great Britain
from 1945 to the Present Day

by

PAULINE GREGG, Ph.D., B.Sc.(Econ.)

author of
A SOCIAL AND ECONOMIC HISTORY OF BRITAIN
THE CHAIN OF HISTORY
FREE-BORN JOHN

GEORGE G. HARRAP & CO. LTD
London · Toronto · Wellington · Sydney

For
Russell
25+

First published in Great Britain 1967
by GEORGE G. HARRAP & CO. LTD
182 High Holborn, London, W.C.1

Composed in Monotype Times and printed by
William Clowes and Sons Ltd, Beccles
Made in Great Britain

PREFACE

The Welfare State is a sequel to my *Social and Economic History of Britain from 1760 to the Present Day*, recounting in more detail than was possible in the final chapters of that book the social and economic history of Britain since 1945. The Welfare State I take to be the whole of the present socio-political-economic organization, and not merely the welfare services provided by the State. As other ages have been described as mercantilistic, or *laissez-faire*, or feudal, or aristocratic, so it seems appropriate to name the present age by its chief characteristic.

I always hoped that the *Social and Economic History* would serve as a practical introduction to the original sources, and commended to the reader the nineteenth-century Blue Books, which, as I said, are so much more exciting than is commonly supposed by those who have never read them. In this book I have again leaned heavily upon what are called the 'official sources': no student of contemporary affairs could fail to do so, and I render cordial thanks to all the anonymous, as well as the named, writers of Government Reports and compilers of official statistics. As before, I would commend the reader to go to these sources himself, and I hope that what he will see of them in these pages will encourage him to do so. Unlike the nineteenth-century Blue Books, he will find them readily obtainable in newsagents and bookshops or at Her Majesty's Stationery Office. He will also find that their cost is low. He will be rewarded by finding himself free of a whole world of information, ranging from statistical summaries of the economy (far more intelligible than the layman generally believes), through Annual Reports of Government Departments and nationalized industries, to particularized statements or Reports on subjects of immediate interest. The Bibliography names a selection of these official documents, and the Appendices reproduce some of their statistics. For permission to use these tables, for other references in the text, and for permission to quote from two of Winston Churchill's War-time Notes to the Cabinet I am indebted to the Controller of Her Majesty's Stationery Office.

I am grateful also to *The Times* for permission to reproduce in the Appendices the diagram "Planning for Growth in the British Economy", to the Advertising Association for figures of advertising expenditure in Table B, XVIII, of the Appendices, to Faber and Faber, Ltd, for permission to quote from W. H. Auden's dedication in *Nones*, to Frederick Muller, Ltd, for permission to quote from Hugh Dalton's *Memoirs*, to Cassell and Co., Ltd, for permission to use extracts from Winston Churchill's *Second World War*, and to the Royal Norwegian

Ministry of Finance for permission to reproduce in Appendix A I part of *The Norwegian Long-term Programme, 1962–1965*.

Mr J. J. MacGregor, University lecturer in the Department of Forestry at Oxford, and Mr Russell Meiggs, Fellow of Balliol College, helped me with the section of the book on forestry, and I am very grateful to them. I am further indebted to Russell Meiggs for giving time to the tiresome task of proof-reading, and I want to thank, also, my mother, Mrs Elizabeth Gregg, for her indefatigable help in reading and extracting from newspapers and journals.

My debt to the Bodleian Library is great, and in particular I wish to thank the librarian and staff of the Faculty Library of Economics and Statistics at Oxford for the efficiency of their library and for the helpfulness which makes working there such a pleasure.

I should like to thank Harrap's Art Department for reproducing graphs and diagrams; my debt to the Editorial Department for their unfailing care is such that only a fellow-author could appreciate. I thank them warmly and sincerely.

Every writer incurs, also, a family debt, which cannot be repaid but can at least be gratefully acknowledged. Writing is a demanding occupation which not seldom conflicts with other tasks and other duties, and I thank my family again for their forbearance.

Nothing is more difficult to write than 'contemporary history'. Like Defoe, publishing his description of England and Wales two and a half centuries ago, "even while the sheets are in the press . . . almost to every part we are oblig'd to add appendixes, and supplemental accounts". But the exercise does at least reveal to the historian how cosy he is within the confines of comparatively fixed data. When he abandons the historical for the contemporary he leaves a well-charted course for rough and strange reaches where currents are treacherous and the main stream by no means always distinguishable. He will be called upon to steer his course and reach his destination to the accompaniment of shouting, altercation, and conflicting advice. I can only hope the reader who accompanies me will make the journey in the spirit of inquiry in which it is intended, that he will enjoy the detours and the occasional dallying, and become not too angry at judgments that do not accord with his own; above all, that he will not expect to finish in a well-prepared anchorage.

PAULINE GREGG

HOLYWELL MANOR,
OXFORD

CONTENTS

APPENDIX A

APPENDIX B

1*

GRAPHS

TABLE

SELECT BIBLIOGRAPHY

PART ONE

THE FIVE SHINING YEARS

" . . . the tremendous changes which we made in those Five Shining Years, from 1945 to 1950. No other five years of peace in all our Parliamentary story saw such a surge forward, on so wide a beach. . . . There will be no great change back from that main advance."

Hugh Dalton, *High Tide and After*,
being vol. 3 of his memoirs

CHAPTER I

The Beginnings

"... the end lies concealed in the beginning ..."

James Stevens,
The Crock of Gold

BY THE middle of the twentieth century the term 'Welfare State' had become a commonly accepted description of British society. Not capitalist or *laissez-faire*, not the much-dreamed-of socialist or communist society —not even social democracy—was the definitive term: but Welfare Society, complete with welfare services, welfare accounting, welfare economics, even welfare citizens. A century earlier capitalist society had been in its heyday; only a quarter of a century had passed since capitalism in decline faced the threat of socialism or communism or fascism. Yet in the event it was not the co-operative commonwealth of Owen nor the Utopian socialism of William Morris, nor the Fabian socialism of the Webbs, nor the intellectual communism of Karl Marx, nor the bastard fascism of Mosley that took over. Nor did the new order spring from any frontal attack upon capitalism. Suitably wrapped in swaddling clothes, the new society had been deposited on the doorstep by the Liberal Lloyd George half a century earlier. In due course it was gratefully accepted as its heir by capitalist society, who thereafter undertook its education, the Liberal and Labour Parties alike contesting the honour of the child's earlier upbringing.

The actual term 'Welfare State' is so recent that not until 1955 was it included in the *Oxford English Dictionary*, which then defined it as "a polity so organized that every member of the community is assured of his due maintenance, with the most advantageous conditions possible for all".[1] Fourteen years earlier, however, it had been used publicly for possibly the first time by William Temple, Archbishop of York,[2] in his

[1] *Addenda*, 1955.
[2] Later Archbishop of Canterbury.

book *Citizen and Churchman*: "in place of the conception of the Power-State we are led to that of the Welfare-State".[1] The *Concise Oxford Dictionary of Current English* in its new edition of 1964 defined the Welfare State by its attributes: "one having national health, insurance, and other social services".

But though the name is new, the conception of the Welfare State occurred some four hundred years ago with the break-up of the social institutions of the Middle Ages. Until then monasteries and guilds, Christian duty and professional loyalty, had together taken the edge off the worst excesses of illness and unemployment. With the dissolution of the monasteries, the decay of guild organization, the development of industry, and the growth of population the problem of destitution became more acute, and the State, enlarging its sphere of influence in many directions, included social affairs within its scope. By the time the law was codified in the Poor Law Act of 1601 legislation concerning poverty, vagrancy, sickness, unemployment, conditions of work, wages, and prices was taken for granted.

Destitution was a major problem in sixteenth-century England, partly because the 'sturdy beggars' who roamed the countryside were a perpetual threat to law and order and formed the raw material of insurrection. Much of the Tudor Poor Law was consequently harsh. Punishment by the stocks or by branding was common, and in houses of correction men and women worked for long hours with little or no pay under the eye of an overseer who was often brutal and made no scruple to use the whip. Yet the Tudors did make an attempt to see the problem whole, and classified the destitute into four groups: the children and orphans; the sick, aged, and infirm; the unemployed who were willing to work; and the sturdy beggars. Children were looked after in orphanages like Christ's Hospital, and when old enough could be apprenticed to a trade. The sick and aged were cared for in hospitals or given help at home. Pensions were given to soldiers, sailors, and the aged poor; free fuel was provided in winter for those in need; dealers in corn were commanded to sell to the poor at less than market price. People who were unemployed through no fault of their own and were known to be good, honest persons were given stocks of material to work up in their own homes. In an effort to prevent destitution the Government inaugurated public works, such as the building of highways; it made loans for the starting of new industries in places where there was much unemployment; it endeavoured to operate a system of wage assessment.

[1] Chapter II, p. 35. I am indebted for the two references to Dr R. W. Burchfield, editor of the forthcoming supplement to the *Oxford English Dictionary*.

Yet though it contained much of the spirit of the Welfare State the Elizabethan code was by no means universal in its application, and while the Privy Council initiated legislation at the centre it was the parishes who interpreted, operated, and paid for the Poor Law. Here the chief administrator was the Justice of the Peace, appointed by the monarch, who was responsible in a voluntary capacity for everything that went on in the parish and whose outlook and sense of duty, as well as the time he was willing to spend on his job, varied considerably. Under him the unpaid overseers and constables, serving, possibly unwillingly, for a year or two at a time, were responsible for the day-to-day working of the Poor Law.

Periods of harshness succeeded those of greater humanity. At the end of the seventeenth century the law of settlement empowered a parish to return to his place of "legal settlement" anyone who became chargeable, a law that was interpreted throughout most of the eighteenth century with great brutality, both in preventing a labourer from making a settlement and in shipping him from parish to parish until he reached one that could not deny liability for his relief—generally because he had been born there. At the same time the punishment of vagrancy became more severe and workhouse conditions more harsh. Yet, with additions and amendments and with varying emphasis, the Elizabethan Poor Law endured for nearly three hundred years, until the Industrial and Agrarian Revolutions brought a degree of destitution that was more than it could stand.

For a while the reaction of society was to do nothing, in the expectation that natural forces and existing arrangements, if left alone, would bring about the best possible results. But this period of non-intervention formed a mere interlude in British social history, comparable to *laissez-faire* in economic affairs and associated with the rise of industrial capitalism. Unregulated social and economic forces were so clearly not acting to the best advantage of society as a whole, and the Elizabethan Poor Law, though stretched and strained to the uttermost, was so clearly not able to deal with destitution on the scale it had then reached, that society was driven to other expedients. The ill-famed Speenhamland system of out-relief, which attempted to correlate parish relief with the wages of the lowest-paid worker and to increase it with increases in family, existed from 1795 until it was blown away with ignominy by the Poor Law Commission of 1834, which clamped upon the country the Poor Law Amendment Act of the same year. This Act not only intended that all relief should be confined to the workhouse, but laid down that workhouse conditions should always and everywhere be "less eligible" to the recipient than those outside. Three paid Government Commissioners with a paid Secretary were to constitute a Poor Law Department under whom, in the localities, unpaid Boards of Guardians elected by the rate-payers were to replace the parish overseers.

It was this harsh, deterrent, and inefficient Poor Law, unconcerned with the reasons that made a man a pauper, which for a hundred years was the chief refuge of the destitute. The fringe which charity was able to relieve became smaller as industrialism spread and the population grew. In the harsh, competitive society outside the workhouse instructions to "set the poor on work", to keep men in work through slack times, to open a factory merely to provide work, to regulate wages according to prices, would have been dismissed as interference. There was no unemployment benefit, no sick pay, no accident compensation, no pension, no relief except that provided by some of the workers themselves through their friendly societies and trade unions.

Sickness, meantime, at once a cause and a result of unemployment and destitution, had for centuries been treated as a sideline of Poor Law policy or else left to private enterprise. The confusion that resulted for a long time obscured the real issues. In so far as sickness was dealt with under the Poor Law there was an attempt at union between a restorative service and a function which was predominantly deterrent—a misalliance which vitiated many attempts at reform. In so far as it was dealt with by private charity there resulted a service often uncertain, frequently disordered, whose relationship to the Poor Law and the local authorities was undefined. Progress was further retarded by the strange dichotomy that regarded illness in a pauper as different from illness in a rich man, or even from illness in a poor man not on parish relief, while many well-meant suggestions for reform were side-tracked by the failure to appreciate the relationship between Public Health and the health of the people—between a healthy environment and a healthy body.

The sixteenth-century statutes that were consolidated in the Poor Law Act of 1601 contained, besides their main clauses dealing with the destitute, instructions to the parish to obtain "competent sums of money" for the relief of the lame, impotent, old, and blind, and, while workhouses of necessity developed sick-bays, overseers' account-books make it clear that the sick poor were also getting medical and nursing attention in their own homes. In due course, seeking some overall method of dealing with the problem that would function without resort to the overseer in each case, parishes turned to one of the favourite expedients of the eighteenth century and farmed their sick to the local doctors. Arrangements varied from parish to parish, but before the end of the century nearly every parish had contracted with a medical man for the care of its sick poor.

In the towns there were voluntary hospitals, some of them dating from the Middle Ages, which kept open door for the sick. St Bartholomew's and St Thomas's in London were refounded in the sixteenth century. Thomas Guy's hospital was founded to relieve the overcrowding of St Thomas's in 1724. By the end of the eighteenth century few towns were without a voluntary hospital, some of which were particularized to certain functions—the Middlesex, for example, to smallpox and inoculation—and there were lying-in hospitals which gave rise to a spate of eighteenth-century bawdy. In these hospitals not only the poor, who paid what they could afford, but Poor Law patients were received, the latter at fixed charges paid by the parish. Voluntary also were the dispensaries where doctors would both see poor patients and dispense medicines for them, and the medical societies urged their members to "give their advice gratis to all their sick neighbouring poor".

But the problem was assuming ever larger proportions. The growth of population, its concentration in towns, the consequent overcrowding, dirt, and disease, the changing ways of life and fluctuating social patterns associated with the Industrial and Agrarian Revolutions, not only magnified the problem of the sick poor and strained to breaking-point the efforts of parish overseers and philanthropists to deal with it, but demonstrated its vital connection with the health of the whole community. At the same time it emphasized the effect of environment on health, a relationship in which the rich were involved as well as the poor. It was the realization by all sections of the community that no-one could walk alone in industrial society that set in train the Public Health Inquiries of the nineteenth century.

That these Inquiries were inaugurated by the Poor Law Commissioners appointed under the Poor Law Amendment Act of 1834 serves to show the confusion that existed. But the Reports, concerned mainly with the sanitary conditions of the big towns, led to the first Public Health legislation aimed at paving the streets, dealing with sewage, providing water and sanitation, pulling down the worst of the slums. Progress was slow. While streets were being cleaned and slums demolished the poor were still becoming sick, cholera epidemics ravaged the cities, the pressure on workhouse sick-bays increased. In accordance with the Poor Law Amendment Act of 1834, which aimed at keeping the numbers inside the workhouse as low as possible, outdoor medical relief was encouraged, and while workhouse sick-bays developed into something like general hospitals an increasing number of parish medical officers dealt with the sick poor outside the workhouse walls and local authorities began themselves to provide hospitals for the destitute sick. By the end of the century responsibility for the sick poor was divided between local authorities, voluntary organizations, Poor Law Guardians, and the district medical officers, while Public Health was in the hands of some 1800 local authorities of various kinds, using nearly a thousand isolation hospitals and other institutions, employing some 1380 full-time Medical Officers of Health, several thousand sanitary inspectors, and many other officers. There was "an admitted overlapping of work, a chaos of authorities, a startling lack of uniformity between district and district, an absence of any generally accepted principle by which the action of the Local Authorities should be guided".[1]

Slowly there came into being a social-reform movement of wider scope than anything that had gone before. It was partly the result of working-class agitation and organization, partly the work of great humanitarians, including factory-owners like Robert Owen and John Fielden, aristocrats and landowners like Lord Shaftesbury, medical men and administrators like John Simon and Edwin Chadwick. It covered Public Health and factory legislation, Poor Law reform and conditions of work. It included the suggestions of a Church of England clergyman, the Reverend William Lewery Blackley, who, in the last quarter of the nineteenth century, advanced the notion of basing social security upon an insurance principle. His scheme was startlingly simple. There would be a compulsory levy on all wage- or income-earners from the age of about seventeen, the total amount payable by each person to be assessed according to his earnings by a National Friendly Society or Club. But though the total payment was fixed, the time taken to pay it was at the payer's discretion, with an outside age limit of twenty-one, and there might be a reduction for rapid payment. It is remarkable how much of the scheme later adopted by the Government was anticipated by Blackley. Arguing that the instrument of the National Friendly Club would need to be present in every parish, he seized upon the Post Office as the executor of his plan. Going to the source of income, as the National Insurance Acts do, he put the onus on employers to deduct the instalments of the national tax from wages, and he made proof of payment depend upon stamps stuck upon a card. The amount paid was thus readily ascertainable, and when a card was fully stamped the holder was

[1] Sidney and Beatrice Webb, *The State and the Doctor*, p. 11. The figures are for 1910.

exempt from further payments. In return for the sum of £10, which Blackley tentatively suggested as an average amount of levy, claims of something like 8s. a week for sickness and 4s. a week as pension over the age of seventy were proposed. Not only would his scheme take away the stigma of Poor Law relief from the old and the sick,[1] but, since the rich would be paying higher contributions and would not claim benefits, funds would accumulate and the National Friendly Club remain permanently solvent. In anticipating the actual words 'National Insurance' in the title of one of his articles in *The Nineteenth Century Review* in 1878 Blackley was in some doubt. "I have long hesitated", he wrote, "before fixing on such a title as I have chosen for the present writing, from a knowledge that its very sound may induce most readers to pass it over as a matter so extravagant, impracticable, and Utopian, as to be unworthy of serious consideration."[2]

Whether or not this was the reason, nothing came of Blackley's schemes. But other people in other ways were concerning themselves with the same problems. In 1889 Charles Booth published the first of a series of volumes concerning *The Life and Labour of the People of London*. In 1901 B. Seebohm Rowntree published a survey of the town of York: *Poverty, a Study of Town Life*. Both attempted an evaluation of the extent of poverty, and though statistically both studies were feeling their way over new ground they reached similar conclusions—that between 25 and 30 per cent of the population was living in absolute poverty. Meanwhile the socialist societies were growing. The Democratic Federation, founded in 1881, changed its name to *Social* Democratic Federation in 1884 to draw attention to its work among the unemployed. In the same year the Fabian Society was founded. William Morris was writing in 1883 that the contrast of rich and poor was unendurable and that the whole basis of society was vicious; unskilled workers from match-girls to dockers were following the example of the skilled workers and organizing themselves in trade unions; the voices of Sidney and Beatrice Webb began to sound, urging the duty of the State to organize, regularize, initiate Poor Law reform; the voices of the workers themselves were raised—in 1889 when the dockers went on strike in the heart of London, in 1892 when three working-men were returned as Members of Parliament, in 1900 when the Labour Party was born.

No Government could fail to hear. The first step was made in a new direction by a Conservative Government in 1897 when a Workmen's

---

[1] Blackley does not mention unemployment.
[2] *The Nineteenth Century Review*, November 1878. See p. 370 for a note on Blackley and his works.

(Compensation for Accidents) Act made provision for one kind of calamity in the form of weekly payments or a lump sum in case of accident or death in certain dangerous industries. In 1905 it appointed a Royal Commission to study the operation of the Poor Law and tentatively inaugurated a number of labour exchanges of a kind that were already established in several European countries. These were designed to help the able-bodied destitute who would be self-supporting if they could find work. They were to be pools of information for employers requiring workmen and workmen wanting jobs; they would check the validity of unemployment and, where necessary, provide the means of travel to seek work.

The following year, while the Commission was still sitting and the labour exchanges were only beginning to prove their worth, there was a dramatic change of Government, the Conservatives being swept from power by the Liberals, who had been out of office for over ten years, in a reversal of party balance comparable to the changes that followed the Reform Bill in 1832 and the Second World War in 1945. Owing much to the working-class vote, realized fully for the first time under universal manhood suffrage, this decisive verdict against the sitting Government expressed dissatisfaction with the old order and looked to a new era or reform.

The series of social measures then initiated by the Liberal Government have their parallel only in those inaugurated in 1945 by the Labour Government. Like the Labour Government, the Liberals were to some extent carrying on the work of the previous administration augmented and extended by their own reforming zeal; and as the Labour Government was influenced by the Beveridge Report, so the Liberals were influenced by the Reports of the Royal Commission on the Poor Laws that appeared in 1909. But a year before this the Liberals' Old Age Pensions Act had been passed. This was revolutionary in providing as of right, by the State, pensions of from 1s. to 5s. a week, subject to a means test but without the stigma of Poor Relief, for people over seventy years of age. Twelve months after the Act began to operate, over 500,000 old people were receiving these pensions from the State.

The following year Winston Churchill, President of the Board of Trade, encouraged by the undoubted success of the labour exchanges already established, and supported by the Minority Report of the Royal Commission steered through Parliament a Labour Exchanges Bill which provided for a network of exchanges over the whole country. The man appointed to organize them was W. H. Beveridge, afterwards Sir William and later Lord Beveridge. Two years later five or six thousand persons a day were being registered in the exchanges, and more than two thousand vacancies a day, as well as some five hundred casual jobs, were being filled.

The Majority and Minority Reports of the Poor Law Commission were meanwhile being widely read, particularly the Minority Report, which was published separately and eagerly popularized by the Webbs and their friends: Beatrice Webb had been one of the Commissioners and the Minority Report bore unmistakably the stamp of the Webbs. Both Reports emphasized the futility of expecting the Poor Law to deal with all forms of social service or social distress. The Minority Report, in particular, urged the break-up of the Poor Law so that health, education, and other services which had grown up over the years could be dealt with by specially constituted bodies and not by the Poor Law— however poor the recipient might be.

Both Reports had schemes for relieving unemployment, the Majority recommending some form of insurance, particularly among unskilled labourers. It suggested that the voluntary insurance work of the trade unions and Friendly Societies might be extended to this end and, while not advocating a State scheme, went so far as to suggest that, in certain circumstances, public funds might be used as well.

Lloyd George, the Chancellor of the Exchequer, was also thinking in terms of insurance. He rejected the Royal Commission's suggestion of extending the voluntary insurance work of the trade unions and Friendly Societies, but was working on a plan of his own. He visited Europe, and in Germany studied the social-insurance scheme, covering pensions and sick benefit but not unemployment, which Bismarck had there introduced. Hounding on a team of brilliant civil servants and other experts to work out the details with speed, he completed his own National Insurance Bill by 1911. Part I provided for a system of compulsory contributory insurance against loss of health, Part II for compulsory contributory insurance against unemployment. Neither was comprehensive, but both differed from any earlier scheme in being both contributory and compulsory, in expecting contributions from the State and from employers as well as from the workers, and in being State-organized: the Bill was the direct forerunner of the health and unemployment legislation that lies at the heart of today's Welfare State. Perhaps it was the Celt in him that enabled Lloyd George to look even farther ahead when he wrote to his private secretary on March 7, 1911: "Insurance necessarily temporary expedient. At no distant date hope

State will acknowledge a full responsibility in the matter of making provision for sickness, breakdown and unemployment."[1]

Part I of Lloyd George's Act, relating to health, covered on a compulsory contributory basis all, male and female, between the ages of sixteen and seventy in manual employment and all in non-manual employment earning not more than £160 a year. It also offered insurance on a voluntary basis to anyone else wholly or mainly dependent for his livelihood on some regular occupation subject to an income limit of £160 a year. Contributions from compulsorily insured workers were 4*d.* a week, from employers 3*d.* and from the State 2*d.* "Ninepence for fourpence!" was one of the slogans which dealt with opposition. Voluntary contributions varied according to age at entry, and were paid entirely by the contributors. In return, any contributor was entitled to enrol on the 'panel' of any doctor who agreed to take part in the scheme and to receive from him free medical attention. He would also receive a sickness benefit, varying from 5*s.* to 10*s.* for men and from 3*s.* to 7*s.* 6*d.* for women, which ran for twenty-six weeks and would be followed, if necessary, by disablement benefit which normally amounted to 5*s.* a week. A maternity benefit of 30*s.* was given, but apart from this the medical service and medicine allowed under the insurance scheme covered only the insured worker and not his family.

Hospital services were free in the case of real poverty, but entailed an assessment of means and payment accordingly. Medical benefits were administered by newly created Insurance Committees in each county and county borough. Sickness payments were made by Approved Insurance Societies who were to run the insurance side of the scheme. These Societies were to be self-governing, distributing surplus money among their members in the form of increased benefits or reduced contributions and bearing any deficit which might occur. Any group who would guarantee to operate the National Health Insurance part of its business on a non-profit-making basis, and would allow members democratic control of these affairs, could become an Approved Society, and in this way the Friendly Societies and trade unions were brought into the scheme.

Part II, the unemployment section of the Act, was experimental in the sense that it applied at first only to those industries, such as building, shipbuilding, mechanical engineering, and ironfounding, in which severe fluctuations of employment were known to occur, and it covered only about 2¼ million workers—one-sixth of the industrial population.

[1] *Lloyd George's Ambulance Wagon*, the memoirs of W. J. Braithwaite, edited by Sir Henry Bunbury, Introduction, p. 24.

The State was required to add one-third to the total contributions of employers and employed, which at the outset were fixed at the weekly rate of $2\frac{1}{2}d$. each. Benefit was to be 7s. weekly for adults, its duration being limited to one week for five weeks' contributions, with a limit of fifteen weeks in any twelve months; it did not extend to dependents.

Lloyd George presented both parts of the Bill to the House of Commons on May 4, 1911. "I do not pretend that this is a complete remedy," he said. "Before you get a complete remedy for these social evils you will have to eat in deeper. But I think it is partly a remedy. I think it does more. It lays bare a good many of those social evils, and forces the State, as a State, to pay attention to them."[1]

The National Insurance Bill became law in December 1911 to the accompaniment of much opposition outside the House. Workers and socialists complained that the poor should have to pay a contribution to either health or unemployment insurance, but it was the Health section of the scheme that created most uproar. The medical profession hotly contested the issue—"Lloyd George had a far livelier and longer struggle with the Doctors before the First World War than ever Aneurin Bevan did after the Second one"[2]—but the doctors finally agreed to a capitation fee of 9s. for each insured worker registered with them, irrespective of the amount of work done. Realizing in the end that in many areas this would increase their income and in the poorest districts would double it, they abandoned opposition, and the Insurance Panel did, in fact, prove to be "the salvation of many a practice in working-class districts".[3]

The violent campaign launched by the *Daily Mail* and the whole Northcliffe Press directed much of its attack to the mechanics of the scheme—the insurance card with its stamps, now so familiar, but in 1911 quite new. The *Daily Mail* warned mistresses that inspectors would invade their drawing-rooms to see if their servants' cards were stamped, and told servants that their mistresses would dismiss them directly they became sick. The Servants' Tax Registers Defence League was formed, and 20,000 women in and outside the Albert Hall shrilled, "We Won't Pay!" and "Taffy was a Welshman, Taffy was a thief", as well as applauding one of their speakers who told them that the Chancellor of the Exchequer was seeking to do what the worst kings in English history had failed to accomplish, and which their own forefathers

---

[1] Hansard, fifth series, vol. 25, c. 644.
[2] Frank Owen, *Tempestuous Journey: Lloyd George, His Life and Times*, p. 208.
[3] Malcolm Thomson, *David Lloyd George*, p. 202. See also Alfred Cox, *Among the Doctors*, p. 97.

would have died to prevent![1] Lloyd George laconically referred to the day "when the domestic servants drove up in their limousines to the Albert Hall to protest against their mistresses paying 3*d.* a week",[2] and Health Insurance was successfully launched on July 15, the Appointed Day. But the Liberal Chief Whip remarked that if an election had taken place at the end of 1911 the Liberal Party would have been defeated.[3]

Health Insurance was extended by the Act of 1919 to workers earning £250 a year, though still not to their dependents: it covered less than 14 million people. In the same year a Ministry of Health was established under a Minister responsible for "promoting the health of the people throughout England and Wales". His function was to embrace all the various health and medical services that had grown piecemeal, some of which had hitherto lain with other Ministries or organizations, and would include the control of the Health Insurance organization. Ten years later the Local Government Act attempted to deal with the anomaly of unpaid Boards of Guardians administering an ill-defined Poor Law by abolishing the Guardians and giving power to deal with destitute persons to the local authorities. At the same time it took all hospital functions away from the Poor Law and gave them to the major local health authorities.

Part II of the Act was also extended in the following years, and in 1920 a new Unemployment Insurance Act covered nearly 12 million workers, including non-manual workers earning not more than £250 a year. At that time contributions were 4*d.* each for an employed person and his employer, and benefit was about 15*s.* weekly, but civil servants, local-authority employees, railwaymen, domestic workers, agricultural labourers, were all outside the scope of the Act.

But the attempt to cut the administrative tangle of help to the destitute came at a time when destitution was rising. A temporary boom after the War of 1914–18 was succeeded by one of the worst depressions the country had seen. Overseas trade fell, profits declined, wages dropped, unemployment mounted. Left-wing opinion advocated the raising of spending power by increasing pensions and benefits and starting public works, but the Government pursued a deflationary policy of cutting unemployment and sick pay, and firms reduced labour costs. The years between the Wars were grim. By 1922 there were over 1½ million people unemployed in the United Kingdom, many of them outside the scope of the Insurance Acts. For a decade the figure remained well over a million,

---

[1] Frank Owen, *op. cit.*, pp. 208–209.   [2] Frank Owen, *op. cit.*, p. 209.
[3] Thomas Jones, *Lloyd George*, p. 41.

rising over the 2 million mark in the middle of 1930, reaching nearly 3 million in the course of 1932. In coal-mining, iron and steel, ship-building, cotton and textiles, among dock workers and harbour work-ers, in public works and contracting, from 20 to over 30 per cent of labour was unemployed. The figures ran to hundreds of thousands among miners and textile workers and in the heavy industries.[1] Large areas of Wales, Scotland, and the North of England, where these industries were concentrated, stagnated and fell into decay. Only London and the South showed any signs of vitality.

Unemployment on such a scale was quite outside the scope of the 1911 Act and its subsequent amendments, which had been intended to help in a temporary crisis, not to support an unemployed man and his family for an indefinite period. The Act was stretched in various ways. In 1921 benefits were paid in advance of contributions, and a supple-mentary scheme covered benefits for an adult dependent and for child-ren. By 1930 a person was qualified for seventy-four weeks' insurance benefit if he had paid thirty contributions in thirty successive weeks. If he exhausted this benefit, or did not qualify for it, he could still get 'transitional benefit' from the State if he had paid eight contribution immediately before claiming or had paid thirty contributions at any time. By 1930, with about 12 million workers insured and unemploy-ment benefit costing some £110 million, contributions amounted to only £30 million. As Sir William Beveridge said, the system had become neither insurance nor a spreading of wages, but out-relief financed mainly by a tax on employment.[2]

For those who had exhausted transitional benefit, as for those who were still outside the scope of the Insurance Acts, there was no recourse but to private savings or private insurance, to charity, or to a Poor Law still governed by the harsh principles of the nineteenth century. "It is a general Poor Law principle that in determining what relief should be afforded, income and means from every source available to the house-hold must be taken into account," declared the Royal Commission which was appointed in 1930 to study the question of unemployment.[3] So, though the Poor Law Board became the Public Assistance Authority

[1] Mining: 233,000 average unemployment between 1927 and 1931; cotton: 123,000 average unemployment between 1927 and 1931; building: 155,000 unem-ployed in 1931. See *Final Report of the Royal Commission on Unemployment Insurance,* 1931, Cmd. 4185, pp. 83, 89, and *passim,* and *22nd Abstract of Labour Statistics of the United Kingdom (1922–1936),* 1937, Cmd. 5556.

[2] Percy Cohen, *The British System of Social Insurance,* p. 135 and note 4.

[3] *First Report of the Royal Commission on Unemployment Insurance,* 1931, Cmd. 3872, p. 19.

and the 'less eligibility' of the nineteenth century became the 'destitution test' of the twentieth, the result was the same: an applicant was expected to exhaust his savings before getting relief; the earnings and savings, however small, of 'liable relations' were weighed in the balance when considering public assistance; and a 'household means test' brought the income of a whole household into the scale to assess the claims of one of its members.

In the widespread indigence that resulted whole towns in the industrial North were destitute. Jarrow, in particular, became a symbol of the total collapse of capitalist society. Hunger marchers came to London to demand work or maintenance, there were demonstrations against the Government, clashes with the police. Life on the 'dole', the indignity of the 'means test', the failure to provide homes for the working classes, the squalor of the slums, the embittered relations of labour and capital, a series of strikes, including the General Strike of 1926, built up a revolutionary atmosphere in which the working classes seriously talked of insurrection and the Left wing of the Labour Party saw itself as the spearhead of revolution. The General Strike, above all, left behind a legacy of bitterness, not least against the man, Winston Churchill, who led the Government's opposition to the strikers in a campaign that called up troops and reservists as well as special constables, students, and 'blacklegs' to man the services left abandoned and subdue the strikers.

Throughout this inter-War depression the working classes in the Labour Party and the trade unions were fighting hard for better conditions and a larger share of the national resources. The whole conception of welfare as it then existed was, it was clear, limited, partial, and totally inadequate to meet the problem of unemployment or destitution in modern society. The benefits given reached only the fringe of destitution, the redistribution of resources hardly touched the incomes of the rich, and benefits were no more than a feather's weight in the scale that weighs riches and poverty. An extension of welfare benefits was one way of helping the working-man. Yet in those years it was less the extension of welfare than the overthrow of the whole capitalist system that he envisaged. Private enterprise was the enemy, and an integral part of the Labour Party programme was the nationalization of the means of production, distribution, and exchange. The grim years of depression brought it support, and at the General Election of 1923 it formed, for the first time, the Government of the country—although it was a minority Government and existed only with Liberal support. It lasted a few months, but in the 1929 General Election, again helped by national distress and unemployment, 258 Labour Members were returned to Parliament and Labour became the largest single party in the House, though it had no clear majority over all others combined. The second Labour Government was brought down in the world financial crisis of 1931. Thereafter attention was focused increasingly upon Hitler Germany. By the end of the decade unemployment was declining as the world prepared to meet the Nazi menace, organized Labour was willing to sink the fight at home in the interests of the struggle against Nazism and Fascism, and when on September 3, 1939, Britain declared war on Germany, who had invaded Poland two days earlier, it was with the full concurrence of all parties. Eight months later, with German armies invading Scandinavia, the Low Countries, and France, the Labour and Liberal Members of Parliament agreed to support a Coalition Government, provided there was a change of Prime Minister. Neville Chamberlain, whose conduct of the war was considered too dilatory, consequently resigned. He was succeeded by Winston Churchill, in whose Coalition Government Clement Attlee, the leader of the Labour Party, took office as Deputy Prime Minister, Ernest Bevin, the trade-union leader, became Minister of Labour, and other Labour men took lesser office. With Labour sharing power at a time of national crisis the whole concept of government, of the relation of the working classes to the State, underwent a change. The two earlier Minority Labour Governments had been ineffective, disheartening, in their fight against the Establishment. Now the Labour leaders stood shoulder to shoulder with the traditional governing class and were not damaged by the comparison. On the contrary, Attlee and Bevin were outstandingly successful at their posts. Their achievements played an important part in preparing the country for Labour rule.

CHAPTER II

"*Walking with Destiny*"

"What noble opportunities have the new Government inherited! Let them be worthy of their fortune, which is also the fortune of us all. To release and liberate the vital springs of British energy and inventiveness, to let the honest earnings of the nation fructify in the pockets of the people, to spread well-being and security against accident and misfortune throughout the whole nation, to plan, wherever State planning is imperative, and to guide into fertile and healthy channels the native British genius for comprehension and good will."

Winston Churchill, the House of
Commons, August 16, 1945

WHEN THE first shock of war had passed, the Government, in spite of its preoccupation with winning the war, found time to remember the depression that followed the First World War and began to think of reconstruction. When a Minister without Portfolio was appointed whose roving commission included the chairmanship of a Committee on Reconstruction Problems, it was a Labour Minister, Arthur Greenwood, who took office. He it was who on June 10, 1941, announced in the House of Commons that a Committee had been appointed to make a comprehensive survey of existing schemes of social insurance and allied services and that its Chairman would be Sir William Beveridge. It would be, said *The Times*, the widest social survey yet undertaken.[1]

Sir William Beveridge had served at the Board of Trade before and during the First World War; he had played a part in the formation of labour exchanges, was the first Chairman of the Labour Exchanges Committee and Director of Labour Exchanges from 1909 to 1916. He had served in the Ministries of Munitions and Food during the First World War and been concerned with food-rationing in both Wars. He

[1] June 11, 1941.

had been a leader-writer of the *Morning Post*, sub-warden of Toynbee Hall, a member of the Royal Commission on the Coal Industry in 1925, and Director of the London School of Economics. Something of his spirit is displayed in a sentence of an informal talk he gave to the Cosmopolitan Club of the London School of Economics: "Happiness is doing, not enjoying. Happiness is doing what one can do; misery is either wasting faculties in idleness or straining at tasks beyond one's powers."[1]

Sitting on the Committee with Beveridge were the Departmental chiefs and other civil servants concerned with the social services. Civil servants are by tradition expected not to participate publicly in policy-making recommendations. When it was perceived, therefore, that issues of high policy would undoubtedly arise it was decided, not without misgiving and in face of questioning in Parliament, that the civil servants on the Committee should be regarded as advisers and assessors on the various technical and administrative matters with which they were concerned, and that the Report, when made, should be signed by Beveridge alone.

On November 20, 1942, only seventeen months after the appointment of the Committee, it was ready and signed. On December 2 it was made available to the public, and seen at once to go even beyond the expectations of *The Times*. Though called, simply, *Social Insurance and Allied Services*, it was an eloquent cry to end poverty, disease, and unemployment, and purported to supply the means of doing so. Its appeal was instantaneous. Queues besieged the Stationery Office in Kingsway. Not only the Press but BBC news bulletins summarized the Report. Brendan Bracken, the Minister of Information, needed only a few hours in which to perceive its enormous propaganda value, and soon it was being trumpeted across the world in many languages. At the cost of 2s., the then normal price of a Government White Paper, it immediately became a best-seller at home and abroad, the subject of leading articles, letters to the Press, speeches and discussion at every level of society. Beveridge himself explained his Plan to millions on the radio and on the cinema screen, as well as addressing countless meetings. In twelve months 256,000 copies of the full Report were sold, 369,000 copies of an abridged edition, 40,000 copies of an American edition. Permission was given for translation into Spanish, Portuguese, and German. Translations were published in Argentina, Brazil, Portugal, Mexico, and

---

[1] "My Utopia", published in *Planning under Socialism and other Addresses*, p. 142.

Switzerland. Parts I and VI were translated into Czech, the abridgment into Italian and Chinese.[1]

The Trades Union Congress and the Co-operative Party gave it their blessing. The National Council of Labour, representing all the bodies of organized Labour, called for the legislation necessary to implement the Report at an early date.[2] The Liberal Party supported it, and through Geoffrey Mander welcomed the general principles of "that momentous report".[3] A group of young Tories tabled a motion in the House of Commons requiring the Government "to set up forthwith the proposed Ministry of Social Security for the purpose of giving effect to the principles of the Report".[4] "We believe", said Quintin Hogg, who sponsored this motion, "the keynote of the restatement of political controversy after the war to be practical idealism."[5] The Beveridge scheme, said another Tory Member of Parliament, "touches the individual life of every man, woman and child in the country and reaches deep down into the homes of the people".[6] The Labour Party made the Report peculiarly its own. "It expresses", said Sydney Silverman at its Conference in 1943, "the basic principle of this Party, the only thing which entitled us at the beginning and entitles us now to regard ourselves as fundamentally different from all other parties." The Report, wrote *The Times*, had changed the phrase "freedom from want" from a vague though deeply felt aspiration into a plainly realizable project of national endeavour. "Sir William Beveridge and his colleagues have put the nation deeply in their debt, not merely for a confident assurance that the poor need not always be with us, but for a masterly exposition of the ways and means whereby the fact and the fear of involuntary poverty can be speedily abolished altogether." The Report, it concluded, "is a momentous document which should and must exercise a profound and immediate influence on the direction of social change in Britain".[7]

The Plan which thus struck fire was basically an enlargement and extension of the existing unemployment and sickness insurance. Yet, when enlarged to become all-inclusive of persons and all-embracing of contingencies, it took on a new dimension and became not merely an insurance scheme but a plan for social security that not only guaranteed

1 Mr Assheton replying to Mr C. Davies, House of Commons, November 30, 1943 (Hansard, fifth series, vol. 395, c. 221). And see Janet Beveridge, *Beveridge and His Plan.*

2 Hansard, fifth series, vol. 386, c. 1615.

3 House of Commons, December 2, 1942 (*ibid.*, vol. 385, c. 1193).

4 *Ibid.*, vol. 386, c. 1613.

5 February 10, 1943 (*ibid.*, vol. 386, c. 1615).

6 Mrs Cazalet Keir, February 17, 1943 (*ibid.*, vol. 386, c. 1790).

7 December 2, 1942.

security, but gave it as a right and gave it equally. The Report itself was not particularly easy reading for the general public, nor were there many colourful passages to remember, except, perhaps, Beveridge's description of the five giants on the road to reconstruction who must be overcome—Want, Disease, Ignorance, Squalor, and Idleness. But the abridged edition was available, and Beveridge gaily told the public that they need read only the first and last chapters of the Report.

His Plan dealt primarily with want and disease. A scheme of social insurance against the interruption and destruction of earning power and for special expenditure arising at birth and death, it would guarantee the maintenance of a family's income at a minimum subsistence level in health and sickness, work and unemployment, maturity and old age, and so eradicate the spectre of want. It was coupled with a family-allowance scheme that would prevent the standard of living falling with the size of the family, and complemented by a national health-service scheme for the prevention and cure of disease and disability and for rehabilitation. With a few exceptions all benefits would apply to all citizens, regardless of income, and all would pay the insurance contributions. The project was consequently free of stigma, free of discrimination, and would result not only in freedom from want and a greater measure of freedom from disease, but in freedom from fear and freedom from servitude. There would be unemployment pay, which would last as long as unemployment lasted, subject to attendance at a work or training centre after a certain period; widows', retirement, and old-age pensions; there would be family allowances, payable to all dependent children after the first, industrial-injury and disablement pensions, maternity and funeral benefits[1]; there would be sick pay and medical treatment.

Family allowances would be directly payable from the national exchequer. Other benefits, including a comprehensive health service, which would be separately administered, would be covered by compulsory social insurance by the individual, supplemented in most cases by the employer, and added to by the State, with national assistance as a subsidiary aid if necessary. Every citizen of working age, including employers and the self-employed and those of no occupation, would pay a single weekly security contribution to which the employer, where there was one, would add his share, married housewives being covered by payments made by their husbands. The contribution would be represented by a single weekly stamp on one insurance card which would

[1] Based on the work of Eleanor Rathbone. See her *Disinherited Family*.

cover all contingencies for which provision was made. Benefits would be uniform, except that employers, self-employed, and those not gainfully occupied could not receive unemployment benefit, and the last could receive no disablement benefit, and they would be paid at subsistence level: it was important to Beveridge that in establishing a national minimum of aid his Plan should still leave room for voluntary action by each individual to provide more than that minimum for himself and his family. A Ministry of Social Security would be responsible for operating the Plan, and would take over, where necessary, the existing work of other departments in these fields.

The concept of the Beveridge Plan was present in the Lloyd George Act,[1] but by making it universal, comprehensive, adequate, and normal Beveridge was doing more than enlarging its scope. As the proposed name of his new Ministry implied, the concept of social security was being written into the machinery of State. Moreover, apart from its ethical desirability, Beveridge hoped the Plan would help to maintain spending power and therefore to reduce the incidence of trade depression and unemployment. The social-insurance fund might even, Beveridge suggested, be used as an instrument of economic management, the accumulated contributions paid into it in good times being disbursed in bad.

Beveridge put the Plan in its historical perspective when he broadcast on the day his Report was laid before the House of Commons. "The Plan of my Report", he said, "is a completion of what was begun a little more than thirty years ago when Mr Lloyd George introduced National Health Insurance, and Mr Winston Churchill, then President of the Board of Trade, introduced Unemployment Insurance. The man who led us to victory in the last war was the Minister responsible for health insurance. The Minister who more than thirty years ago had the courage and imagination to father the scheme of Unemployment Insurance, a thing then unknown outside Great Britain, is the man who is leading us to victory in this war; I should like to see him complete as well the work that he began in social insurance thirty years ago."[2]

But Winston Churchill did nothing beyond making his position clear to his colleagues in a note circulated to the Cabinet on January 12. He was worried at the "dangerous optimism" that was growing up as to what the country would be able to do after the War. He knew Britain's foreign investments had almost disappeared; he foresaw the dangers of inflation and its effect on the people's 'nest eggs'; he was mindful of

---

[1] *Supra*, p. 12.   [2] *The Listener*, December 10, 1942, vol. 28, p. 743.

post-War difficulties in placing exports and maintaining British shipping-lines; he was afraid of raising false hopes like the 'homes for heroes' of the previous war. "It is because", he concluded, "I do not wish to deceive the people by false hopes and airy visions of Utopia and Eldorado that I have refrained so far from making promises about the future."[1]

But the Report had been in the vote office of the House of Commons since December 1, and on February 16, 1943, Arthur Greenwood moved in the House that the Beveridge Report be welcomed "as a comprehensive review of the present provisions in this sphere and as a valuable aid in determining the lines on which developments and legislation should be pursued as part of the Government's policy of post-war reconstruction". It was a curiously lukewarm and non-committal resolution that reflected Churchill's views but was at variance with the enthusiasm that the Report had raised over the country—and, indeed, with the mover's own words. "No document within living memory", said Mr Greenwood, "has made such a powerful impression, or stirred such hopes. . . . The people . . . have made up their minds to see the plan in its broad outline carried into effect, and nothing will shift them. The plan for social security has struck their imagination. They feel in their hearts . . . that it is their due on grounds of social justice. . . . Where is a Member of the House who would dare to vote against the general proposals ?"[2] Certainly no Member would vote against the general proposals. But when it came to a division only a minority voted for immediate legislation to implement them.

The debate continued in the Commons from February 16 to February 18. But it was a debate on the Report, not on the Government's proposals based upon the Report, for there were none. The House wanted to know where these were, what they were. On all sides came the feeling that action was needed. In the end, of all the amendments put forward, it was a Labour motion, sponsored by James Griffiths, that was selected for debate; it simply called for the early implementation of the Plan as a test of Parliament's sincerity.[3] Churchill was prevented by illness from attending the debates, but on February 14 he circulated another Cabinet minute dealing with the Beveridge Report. "This approach to social security," he wrote, "bringing the magic of averages nearer to the rescue of the millions, constitutes an essential part of any post-war scheme of national betterment." He wanted the

---

[1] Winston Churchill, *The Second World War*, vol. IV, Appendix F, p. 861.
[2] Hansard, fifth series, vol. 386, cc. 1615–16, 1618.
[3] *Ibid.*, vol. 386, c. 1965.

measure to be produced as an "integral conception", and suggested, therefore, a Committee or Commission that would work until the end of the War "polishing, reshaping, and preparing for the necessary legislation". He was firm, however, that legislation could not then be initiated nor the Government committed to the expenditure involved. That could be done only "by a responsible Government and a House of Commons refreshed by contact with the people". "We must not forget", he wrote finally, "that we are a Parliament in the eighth year, and we have been justified in prolonging our existence only by the physical fact of the war situation and for the purposes of the war. We have no right whatever to tie the hands of future Parliaments in regard to social matters which are their proper province. I could not as Prime Minister be responsible at this stage for binding my successor, whoever he may be, without knowledge of the conditions under which he will undertake his responsibilities."[1]

This was true. The political situation could not be left out of account; nor the fact that the War was not yet won and the war effort must continue unabated. Yet perhaps the Prime Minister did not rightly gauge the heartening, stimulating effects of the Beveridge Report. To refuse its immediate acceptance, to refuse to make public any plan for its immediate post-War implementation, even if not for its implementation then and there, was to the people betrayal, whatever and however cogent the reasons. You cannot refuse to welcome a saviour without being suspected of not wishing to be saved—or, at best, of being so blind that you do not know salvation when you see it! And Beveridge by this time was certainly regarded as something of a saviour. Here, after all, was a prophet who could not only dream and express the people's desires but could put them into concrete shape. Nor was he ignorant of the dismal science that too often had been quoted against them. If he said it would work, it would! He was Robert Owen and Adam Smith rolled into one. And he understood the great bugbears of working-class life. They understood the Plan too! For even if they had not read a word of it, Beveridge himself had broadcast and appeared on their cinema screens, and there had been much BBC and Press discussion. Beveridge and his wife had become popular figures. At their marriage at Caxton Hall a fortnight after the publication of the Report the future Lady Beveridge, approaching by car, thought that some kind of popular demonstration was taking place. There was. It was for her and Sir William.[2] A little later, when she

---

[1] *Op. cit.*, vol. IV, Appendix F, p. 862.
[2] Janet Beveridge, *Beveridge and His Plan*, p. 126.

was seeking a taxi in the war-time black-out in London, a vehicle miraculously pulled up at the kerb beside her, the driver not only recognizing her but refusing to take any payment from the wife of the Beveridge Report.[1]

Meanwhile the Labour amendment was put to the House of Commons. "The Beveridge Plan", said James Griffiths, moving it, "has become in the minds of the people and the nation both a symbol and a test. It has become, first of all, a symbol of the kind of Britain we are determined to build when the victory is won, a Britain in which the mass of the people shall be ensured security from preventable want. Almost . . . every comment that has been made in the Press and on the platform since the Report was issued, the widespread interest taken in it and in its proposals, and the almost universal support given to it, are clear indications that the Report and the plan meet a deep-felt need in the minds and the hearts of our people."[2]

But the effect of calling upon a Labour amendment was to unite the Tories against it, in spite of their own speeches, and Griffiths' amendment was lost by 335 votes to 119, leaving the original non-committal motion to stand. It was a regrettable position. After the welcome and the publicity given to Beveridge's proposals, and the high hopes raised, the Report was accepted but then sent to another Committee at Whitehall, who spent nearly two years considering it. Further consideration of details had, indeed, been assumed by its author. But the impression given was of shelving the Report, of wriggling out of its proposals. "This", said Griffiths after the counting of the votes in the House of Commons, "makes the return of the Labour Party to power at the next election an absolute certainty."[3]

Perhaps realizing something of this, Churchill broadcast to the nation on Sunday March 21, 1943, a little over a month after the Parliamentary debates on the Beveridge Plan. He was "very much attracted to the idea" of a Four Year Plan of his own which included "national compulsory insurance for all classes for all purposes from the cradle to the grave", a national health service, a policy of full employment in which private and public enterprise both had a part to play, the rebuilding of towns and a housing programme, and a new Education Act. He envisaged "five or six large measures of a practical character", but did not specify them, leaving the assumption that no advance would be made until the defeat of Germany had "removed the danger now at our

[1] *Op. cit.*, p. 119.
[2] February 18, 1943 (Hansard, fifth series, vol. 386, cc. 1965–66).
[3] Janet Beveridge, *op. cit.*, p. 146.

throats", a new register of civilians and serving men had been compiled, and a new House of Commons freely chosen.[1]

In several respects Churchill was better than his words. Within twelve months of his broadcast the Fleming Report on the Public Schools and the General Educational System was published, and an Education Act in January 1944 took up and strengthened a Bill abandoned in 1939 at the outbreak of war.[2] By September 1943 the Committee under Sir William Jowitt which had been considering the Beveridge Plan had finished its work, and the Government's proposals were published in the form of four White Papers—one in February 1944 dealing with a National Health Service,[3] one on Employment Policy in May,[4] and two in September dealing with Social Insurance[5] and with Industrial Injuries.[6]

About this time Beveridge himself entered the House of Commons as Liberal Member of Parliament for Berwick-on-Tweed. He made his maiden speech on November 3, 1944, when the White Papers on Social Insurance were before the House. "One of the sad incidents of war", he said, "is the separation of parents and children. One of the pleasant foretastes of impending, if not imminent peace, is that children and parents meet again. I hope I may without impropriety regard this occasion as, in one sense, a meeting of a parent and a child, because it is nearly two years ago since I laid on the doorstep of His Majesty's Government in Whitehall a Report on Social Insurance—a large and rather noisy baby. But most kindly the Government took that baby in, and cared for it, and I lost sight of it. It is true that the separation in this case took the slightly abnormal form of keeping the child where it was and evacuating the parent from Whitehall. Nevertheless, the separation was very complete. But today, by one route or another, we meet again; that baby has found itself moved from Whitehall to Westminster, and I also have moved from another place to Westminster.

"The admitting of paternity is always a slightly delicate operation; perhaps it is a particularly delicate operation in a maiden speech. I can only say that I think this plan of the Government's is the baby which I left on their doorstep two years ago. I think it is, substantially, the same as the plan which this House debated a year and a half ago, improved in some respects, disimproved in other respects, but, on the whole, so little altered that every now and again, I do rather wonder just what that

---

1 *The Listener*, March 25, 1943, pp. 347–348, 363–365.
2 *Infra*, p. 31.
3 *A National Health Service*, February 1944, Cmd. 6502.
4 *Employment Policy*, May 1944, Cmd. 6527.
5 *Social Insurance, Part I*, September 1944, Cmd. 6550.
6 *Social Insurance, Part II (Industrial Injuries)*, September 1944, Cmd. 6551.

baby was doing, how it filled in the long time that it spent in White-hall."[1]

The House unanimously welcomed the Government's scheme as out-lined in the White Papers for an enlarged and uniform system of social insurance, and a week later Clement Attlee, the leader of the Labour Party and Deputy Prime Minister in the Coalition Government, rose to propose the second reading of the Bill to establish a Ministry of Social Insurance to co-ordinate and operate these proposals. The House, being agreed on the principle behind the Bill, spent much time in discussing the name of the proposed Ministry. 'Social Insurance' did not mean anything, said Mr Petherick. "I dislike the word 'social' intensely," said Dr Russell Thomas, "I have always associated the word with those people in and outside the House who are concerned with the welfare of all men of all nations but seem to have no friends themselves." Sir Frank Saunders associated 'social' with one section only of the community; Mr Mander thought it comprised the whole nation; some thought it spelt 'socialist'. 'National Insurance' was thought to be better because the term was known; 'social insurance' would not be understood. Aneurin Bevan wanted 'National Insurance' because 'social' implied the whole world. Commander Agnew thought 'social' connoted volun-tary activity. Someone said that if the scheme were to be compulsory 'national' should be the word used. When 'Social Security' was suggested the answer was that it was not a security measure but an insurance scheme. With a motion to amend 'Insurance' to 'Security' and another to amend 'Social' to 'National', Mr Peake pointed out that if both were carried they would have a Ministry of National Security![2]

When Beveridge rose to speak he restored the spirit of the proposal. 'National Insurance' and 'Social Insurance' were as inaccurate as 'National Security'. 'Insurance' did not at all cover the scope of the Bill. It was security they were aiming at. And while 'Social Security' did not cover every kind of security it did cover the kind of security pro-posed by the Bill.[3] But the remarks of the author of the Beveridge Re-port went unheeded, 'National' was carried, and the issue of 'Security' versus 'Insurance' never came up. The Ministry was to be the Ministry of National Insurance.

There the matter rested for a while. The War was still to win, and Churchill, in so far as he turned his mind to home affairs, was disturbed at the unrepresentative nature of the House of Commons. Speaking to

---

[1] Hansard, fifth series, vol. 404, cc. 1121–22.
[2] *Ibid.*, vol. 404, cc. 1659–1710 *passim*, cc. 1829–1918 *passim*.
[3] *Ibid.*, vol. 404, c. 1850.

it a fortnight earlier, moving the routine annual Prolongation of the Life of Parliament Bill, he had reminded it that no-one under thirty years of age had ever cast a vote at a General Election. He wondered whether the end of the German War would not be a convenient time to choose a new House; "... it would be a wrongful act, unworthy of our country's fame," he said, "to break up the present governing instrument before we know where we are with Hitler's Germany". On the other hand, if the German War ended in the spring and "some or all the other parties in the Coalition recall their Ministers out of the Government, or wish to bring it to an end from such dates. That would be a matter of regret, both on public and on personal grounds, to a great many people, but it would not be a matter of reproach."[1]

All that autumn and the following spring "the odour of dissolution was in the air". But in the first months of 1945 attention was riveted upon the drama being played in Europe. In January the Russians entered Warsaw and pushed on westward to the Oder. In February British forces attacked on the Rhine at Nijmegen; later in the month American forces drove on Düsseldorf, in March they crossed the Rhine, closely followed by the British forces under Montgomery. Yet even as the war in Europe swept on to its triumphant conclusion the party sniping was beginning. Statements were circulated covering arrangements for releasing candidates and party agents from the forces for a General Election. The 1943 Prolongation of Parliament Bill had been accompanied by legislation governing the conditions of a future General Election, and now questions were asked concerning its conduct. To provide a more than usually long interval between dissolution and an election, so Attlee told the House of Commons in January 1945, the King had agreed that the date of dissolution should be known three weeks before it actually happened.[2]

Ralph Assheton on February 18 at Leeds warned his hearers against nationalization and bureaucracy and spoke of the Conservative Party standing for the betterment of the people.[3] At the end of March Herbert Morrison told the London Labour Parties there was no longer agreement between the Conservative and Labour parties on economic and industrial issues.[4] On April 7 Ernest Bevin attacked the Tories at a Yorkshire Labour Conference at Leeds: one of the great issues of the election would be the vexed problem of public ownership. Their oppo-

---

[1] October 31, 1944 (Hansard, fifth series, vol. 404, cc. 662 ff.).
[2] January 17, 1945 (*ibid.*, vol. 407, cc. 166–167).
[3] R. B. McCallum and A. Readman, *The British General Election of 1945*, p. 11.
[4] *Ibid.*, pp. 11–12.

nents had nailed to their banner free enterprise and the rights of monopolies.[1] Brendan Bracken retorted at a meeting in Holborn on the 9th: "Britain would never accept the sort of totalitarian State desired by the Socialists. . . . Britain has prospered by daring. What sort of future lies ahead of us if under State control risk-taking is abolished or controlled by that excellent body the Public Accounts Committee of the House of Commons?"[2] "The battle between the parties is a real fight" announced Arthur Greenwood on the same day.[3]

On May 7, 1945, the Germans surrendered unconditionally. On Sunday May 13 the nation gave solemn thanks for its deliverance, and in the evening Churchill came to the microphone and told an heroic tale that was necessarily familiar. It was the sum of all his hearers' lives since 1940.[4] On the 15th he made his Victory in Europe speech in the House of Commons, and the country celebrated with bonfires and rejoicing a resounding victory after five and a half years of total war.

It is typical of the atmosphere of those spring days that, while from Europe a drama on Wagnerian scale was assaulting the senses and from England an irritating twitter of party bickering mocked the heroism that had gone before, the British Government, expecting shortly its own demise, should introduce the first of its measures of practical social reform. The Family Allowances Bill was given its first reading on February 14, and on March 8, 1945, Sir William Jowitt, the first Minister of National Insurance, introduced its second reading.[5]

Yet neither the German surrender nor the Government's demonstration of good faith could prevent the public mind, in Churchill's words, from turning swiftly "from national rejoicing to party strife". Churchill would have wished otherwise, but in view of his own suggestion could do little. Yet now he wished heartily to keep the Coalition till the Japanese war was ended: "Was this too much to ask of a nation we had not served ill?"[6] On May 18, eleven days after the German surrender and two days before the Labour Party Annual Conference at Blackpool, he wrote to the leaders of the other two parties suggesting the continuation of the Coalition until the end of the Japanese war or else its immediate termination and a July election. He suggested the possibility of a referendum to see if the nation would agree to the renewal of the Parliament until the Japanese were defeated.[7]

But the Labour and Liberal leaders alike were opposed to a referendum—"so alien to all our traditions". The Labour Party after full

---

[1] *The Times*, April 9, 1945. [2] *Ibid.*, April 10, 1945.
[3] *Ibid.*, April 10, 1945. [4] *Ibid.*, May 14, 1945.
[5] Hansard, fifth series, vol. 409, cc. 2259 ff.
[6] *The Second World War*, vol. VI, pp. 511, 512. [7] *Op. cit.*, p. 516.

discussions at Blackpool suggested an October election, when a new register of voters would have come into existence, and Attlee wrote accordingly to Churchill on May 21. A rushed election in the summer, he said, would be "utterly wrong", while the differences between the parties on questions of economic reconstruction were too acute for the Coalition to continue until the end of the Japanese war. Only a Government united in principle and policy could take the decisive action necessary to deal with reconstruction problems.[1]

On May 18, the day Churchill proposed continuation until the end of the Japanese war, the Houses of Parliament adjourned for the Whitsun recess. Churchill was "deeply distressed at the prospect of sinking from a national to a party leader" when there was a settlement to make in Europe, the Japanese war to finish, the difficult problem of demobilization to work out, and social issues of all kinds to resolve. Yet, a break in the Coalition and a General Election being certain, he decided on a June rather than an October election: "The worst of all solutions of our problems seemed to me an October election. This was too short to give any effective relief to the political tension, which must increase with every one of the four or five months that were to pass, and must vitiate our thoughts and work at home and abroad. If there must be an election in 1945, the sooner it came the better."[2] So, during the Whitsun recess, on May 23, 1945, Churchill tendered his resignation to the King and asked for the dissolution of Parliament. The House reassembled on May 29 with a new Government. The Conservatives having a majority of a hundred over all parties combined, Churchill had formed from them a Caretaker Government to take over until the General Election results were known.[3] The atmosphere of the House of Commons had certainly changed. When the question arose of making special voting arrangements for holidaymakers Ernest Bevin asked, amid interruptions, "Would it not have been better if the Prime Minister had taken this into account before rushing the Election and had accepted Labour's offer to go on until the Autumn?" "All these difficulties would have been removed to a later period," retorted Churchill, "if the representatives of the Labour and Liberal Parties had consented to go on until the job was finished."[4]

On June 15 Parliament was dissolved, with Polling Day fixed for July 5. To give time for the votes of soldiers and others overseas to be

---

[1] C. Attlee, *As It Happened*, pp. 158–159.   [2] Churchill, *op. cit.*, p. 512.
[3] With the addition of certain non-party men who had served in office during the War.
[4] Hansard, fifth series, vol. 411, c. 33.

returned and counted the declaration of poll was fixed for July 26. In its brief life of little over a fortnight Leslie Hore-Belisha, the new Minister of National Insurance, on June 11 steered into law for the Caretaker Government the Family Allowances Act whose second reading had been approved the previous March while Hitler's Empire was crashing to its doom.[1]

Under the leadership of the Coalition Government, in which the Conservatives held the majority and of which a Conservative was the inspiration, the country had triumphed over such frightful odds that on this ground alone the Tories might have laid claim to a vote of confidence from the electorate. But it also had contrived to tend the flame of social reform and had produced a social programme of which any peace-time Ministry might be proud—a survey of the whole field of the national economy and social services, present and future, which surpassed in breadth and authority anything that had been previously attempted.[2] It had set on foot the Beveridge Committee, a Committee on the Coal Industry, and a Population Commission.[3] It had published four White Papers on social and economic affairs.[4] It had put in preparation and was about to publish a new voting register; it had established the Ministry of National Insurance, whose name alone sounded a new note, and had passed two further Acts of major importance—an Education Act and the Family Allowances Act. It had, moreover, devised a scheme of demobilization which was already beginning to operate.

It was all the more surprising that as the Coalition broke and the parties swung apart the Labour Party should have commanded so much attention. It was clear that Churchill was still adored as the war-leader. But the German war was over. Domestic issues were uppermost in people's minds—the events of 1918–39 rather than of 1939–45. The Election was a challenge to all the Governments of the past unhappy twenty years—a period in which the Tories had held office almost continuously. So, although Churchill appealed to the electorate to "let us finish the job", the unspoken rejoinder was that he had almost finished the job for which he had been chosen but that now other things were afoot. For post-War security they turned to the Labour spokesmen, most of whom they had known as leaders in the pre-War depression and

---

[1] *Ibid.*, vol. 411, c. 1422.   [2] *The Times*, May 24, 1945.
[3] June 10, 1941, reported November 20, 1942, Cmd. 6404; September 1944, reported March 1945, Cmd. 6610; March 3, 1944, reported June 1949, Cmd. 7695.
[4] *Supra*, p. 26.

many of whom now spoke with the added authority of war leaders. These Labour spokesmen stressed the necessity of returning a Government who could be *trusted* to deliver the society the people craved. While both parties offered Food, Work, and Homes, a comprehensive system of National Insurance based on the Beveridge Report, a new National Health Service, the development of education; while both parties recognized that British industry must be made more efficient in order to ensure a high standard of living for all; while both parties spoke of planning as an integral part of the future British economy, it was to Labour that the British people looked to implement these promises: the Tories were too involved with private enterprise and vested interest to make a clean sweep and implement a wide plan.

When it came to details the Labour proposals were more succinct than the Tories'. Their Five Year Plan, given in *Let Us Face the Future*, their chief election manifesto, envisaged the retention of many of the war-time controls and the nationalization of Fuel and Power, of Coal and Mining, of Inland Transport, of Iron and Steel, and of the Bank of England. It was a clear, unrhetorical, and straightforward document. The Tories' Four Year Plan, given in *A Statement of Policy to the Electors*, was much less explicit. They would retain controls as long as necessary, but spoke of them as dangerous impediments. They were, on the whole, against nationalization. They referred again and again to Churchill, who would implement his party's promises. So it came back to a question of trust. Would the people trust the beloved war-leader to give them the life after the Second World War that his party had previously denied them? Or would they trust the leaders who had fought with them on the domestic as well as on the war front? The issue was clinched in the cartoon which the Labour Party flaunted on hoardings and sent in leaflets all over the country—*Under the Counter!*—the war-time story of scarce commodities being kept for favoured customers. It put the issue in a nutshell and expressed the fears of hundreds of thousands of people who still admired and loved Winston Churchill.

Yet Churchill might still have swept the electorate with him in the train of his great prestige and their loyalty and affection if he had not in his first Election broadcast abysmally misjudged the situation. Coming to the microphone on June 4, 1945, he said: "My friends, I must tell you that a Socialist policy is abhorrent to British ideas of freedom.... Socialism is in its essence an attack not only upon British enterprise, but upon the right of an ordinary man or woman to breathe freely without having a harsh, clumsy, tyrannical hand clapped across their mouths and nostrils. A free Parliament—look at that—a free Parliament is odious to the Socialist doctrinaire."[1] The *Daily Express* followed the next day with banner headlines: "Gestapo in Britain if Socialists Win". Neither speech nor newspaper did justice to the sober maturity of the electors at that time.

When Clement Attlee broadcast in reply on June 5 he pitched at once upon the right note and, while gently deriding Churchill and questioning his ability to lead the nation in peace, raised his own prestige higher than it had been before. "When I listened to the Prime Minister's speech last night," he said, "in which he gave such a travesty of the policy of the Labour Party, I realized at once what was his object. He wanted the electors to understand how great was the difference between Winston Churchill the great leader in war of a united nation and Mr Churchill the great leader of the Conservatives."[2]

In the Election campaign practically all the important issues were economic and social—housing, employment, pensions, social insurance, the control of industry, food-rationing, agricultural policy, the overall question of plan or no plan. Audiences were keen not only to listen but to question speakers—like an adult education class according to some observers.[3] *The Times* reported that their "refusal to suffer quietly the more irresponsible flights of electioneering oratory" disclosed "a sober search for the best in policies and persons".[4] It was inevitable that Churchill's strange behaviour at the time of the Beveridge Report should be remembered against him. His Four Year Plan and his Government's White Papers could hold no candle to Beveridge.

While the Labour Party had always stood four square for the Beveridge Report, the Liberals not only went into the Election under the banner of Beveridge, but with the author of the Beveridge Report himself as one of their candidates. They might have been expected to win more support than they did. But the electorate seemed unprepared for what they were afraid might be half-measures. If the Beveridge Report was to be implemented the Labour Party was a better operator than the Liberals, and Beveridge himself was misguided not to see this. The Liberals "Clean Hands" plea was a good one, though their slogan "Freedom through Security" was a little too intellectual for people to whom the promise of security was itself sufficient. And if it came to clean hands, Labour's hands were cleaner than anybody's!

So, while everything the Coalition had done was regarded by the people as too little or too late or performed under duress, on the Labour

[1] *The Listener*, June 7, 1945.   [2] *Ibid.*, June 14, 1945.
[3] McCallum and Readman, *op. cit.*, p. 151.
[4] June 18, 1945, quoted by McCallum and Readman, *op. cit.*, p. 151.

Party fell the hopes of a century and a half of working-class struggle. A deep and fundamental instinct told the people that the ballot-box was their revolution. They would effect a social revolution as surely by returning Labour to power as if they had by force unseated the capitalist class. The issue, of course, was by no means as clear as this. Yet their reasoning had an elemental quality that had nothing to do with the war or victory but reached back as far as their memories—and their parents' and grandparents' memories—went. And it rejected Churchill, the great war-leader. That he was still the most popular man in England did not alter the case.

Polling Day was to be on July 5, when an electorate of nearly 33 million would exercise its right to go to the polls in the United Kingdom, about a quarter of them for the first time, nearly 3 million of them serving men and women for whom special voting arrangements were being made. The election campaign was real enough on the hustings and at the public meetings yet strangely unreal in relation to the grim struggle still proceeding and the momentous world-wide issues being decided while party conflict waged. The Japanese war continued, with the Japanese fighting heroically—madly—their suicide squadrons of bombers taking toll of British and Americans while they destroyed themselves.

Churchill found the month hard to live through. He made three or four speeches a day. He gave four "laboriously prepared broadcasts". At night the election candidate changed to the war-time Prime Minister who worked far into the night. "The incongruity of party excitement and clatter with the sombre background which filled my mind was in itself an affront to reality and proportion. I was glad indeed when polling day at last arrived and the ballot-papers were safely sealed for three weeks in their boxes."[1] This interval of three weeks while the votes of those service men and women who had not voted by proxy were being counted added an additional element of the bizarre to an unprecedented situation. The boxes closed, Churchill and Attlee each left the scene for a short holiday. Churchill, in Bordeaux, strove to put party politics out of his head, yet "the mystery of the ballot-boxes and their contents had an ugly trick of knocking on the door and peering in at the windows".[2]

World events, meantime, could not wait to be summoned by the British electorate, and the Russian, British, and American zoning of Europe was being worked out. To the Potsdam Conference of the heads of these states Churchill arrived with Attlee, explaining to his wondering allies that although a new British Parliament had been elected the re-

[1] Churchill, *op. cit.*, vol. VI, p. 528.   [2] *Ibid.*, p. 531.

sults were as yet unknown, so it seemed right that his possible successor should be present. On July 17, with the boxes still sealed and Britain's Government still unknown, news came to Potsdam of the explosion of the first atomic bomb in the American desert. On July 25, the day before the ballot-boxes were due to be opened, Churchill flew home. The Conservative Central Office was of opinion that they would retain a substantial majority, and Churchill went to bed "in the belief that the British people would wish me to continue my work". But the first results were unfavourable to the Conservatives. By noon of the 26th it was clear that the Labour Party would have a majority. Churchill wasted no time. The verdict of the electors, he afterwards wrote, "had been so over-whelmingly expressed that I did not wish to remain even for an hour responsible for their affairs". At 7 P.M. he asked an audience of the King and tendered his resignation, advising the King to send for Mr Attlee.[1] On the same day an ultimatum to Japan was published.

When all the votes were counted Labour and Labour supporters had 399 seats, Conservatives and supporters 213, the Liberals and others of the centre 28. The Labour Party alone received nearly 12 million votes, the Liberals 2·2 million. Churchill's appeal to the electorate had been answered directly and affirmatively only by the 8·7 million people who voted for his party. "British history", said The Times, "affords no such example of the reversal of national leadership on the morrow of a crowning victory."[2]

Comparable swings had occurred only twice before—in 1832 after the Reform Bill, when the Whigs achieved a majority of 307, and in 1906, when the Liberals turned a Conservative majority of 134 into one of 356 for themselves. Yet all parties and persons stood behind the tribute that The Times paid to Winston Churchill: "Even though the electorate has exercised its right to declare yet once more that gratitude belongs to history, and not to politics, no shadow can fall across an achievement and a name that are for ever national possessions."[3]

There were contributory reasons for the Conservative defeat: the swing of the pendulum after virtually twenty years of Tory rule; the propensity of new voters to exercise power by voting against the sitting candidate; the conduct of the Election itself, when, as The Times re-minded its readers, "Mr Churchill himself introduced and insisted upon emphasizing the narrower animosities of the party fight"[4]; the feeling

[1] Ibid., p. 583.
[2] July 27, 1945. Yet the total pro-Labour vote was only about 12 million; the total anti-Labour vote 11·9 million (McCallum and Readman, op. cit., p. 252).
[3] July 27, 1945.   [4] July 27, 1945.

that Churchill's power was too great—"the one-man business Churchill was running".[1] But, above all, there was suspicion of the forces behind Churchill and fear of betrayal when peace succeeded war. Yet for a brief spell social reform was suspended as giant forces, already determined, brought the Japanese War to a close: less than two weeks after the results of the British General Election were announced the first atom bomb fell on Hiroshima. The final terms of the Japanese surrender were made public on August 14, the day before the new Parliament assembled for the first time. So it was with military victory on all fronts that the Labour Government began its task of social rehabilitation.

The Labour Members of Parliament included 168 'workers', 165 professional men and women, 31 businessmen, 4 agriculturists, and 3 Members too young to have had a profession before the War. One hundred and sixty-seven of them were Trade Unionists, 173 had seen public service in local government. Teachers were the biggest single group, journalists next, with barristers close behind. They were not young: of those whose ages are known only 6 were in their twenties, 13 were over seventy; of the rest 54 were in the thirties, 163 in the forties and fifties, 51 in the sixties.[2] But, whatever their age or profession, all were bound by a common feeling of exultation. They were the executors of the British working-man come at last into his inheritance. As, one by one, they were sworn in by the Speaker their forebears in the Labour Movement might have been answering the summons too—Samuel Hartley and John Booth, the Luddites; Elizabeth Bentley, the "little doffer"; Margaret Hipps, the "quite beautiful" little coalminer; George Loveless and Thomas Muir; Francis Place and Tom Paine; William Lovett and George Shell; jolly old Cobbett and fiery O'Connor; Keir Hardie and George Lansbury—they filled the House many times over. When Hartley Shawcross exclaimed, "We are the masters now!" he was speaking for them all. "There was exhilaration among us, joy and hope, determination and confidence," recounted Hugh Dalton. "We felt exalted, dedicated, walking on air, walking with destiny."[3]

[1] Clement Attlee in *A Prime Minister Remembers*, conversations with Francis Williams, p. 8.
[2] McCallum and Readman, *op. cit.*, pp. 273–274.
[3] Hugh Dalton, *High Tide and After*, being vol. 3 of his memoirs, p. 3.

CHAPTER III

Social Security

"... a nation with a high power of production would not have solved its problem if it included any appreciable section of people who were in want, whether through loss of individual earning power, due to ill-health, unemployment or old age, or through inability to provide properly for their children. Only when this problem is also solved has a community achieved genuine social security."

White Paper on Social Insurance, September 1944, Cmd. 6550

IF IT could have controlled events more closely, July 1945 was perhaps not the time the Labour Party would have chosen to begin its first period of government with power. It came to office, however, possessed of certain assets, not least of which was a corner of the mantle of victory draped round its shoulders. But also its clear majority over all parties in the House, combined with its voting strength in the country, gave it a definite mandate for the measures of nationalization and social reform upon which it had fought the election. It had a record not only clear of responsibility for pre-War distress, but of devoted service to the cause of the people. It had the experience of successful participation in the Coalition Government and the benefit of contacts with the Governments and civil servants of other countries. It inherited not only the social legislation of the Coalition, its White Papers upon social policy and its inquiries into various aspects of social and economic life, but it came into a legacy of controls, direction of labour, rationing and savings campaigns that had made familiar the idea of planning. The War had wiped out unemployment, the bugbear of pre-War Governments, and an orderly demobilization, based upon the plans of the Coalition, had already started. In some ways, too, the War had wiped the slate clean. It was easier to rebuild than to convert, and the mood was for action. Moreover, as Attlee readily admitted, the Labour Government was in the unique position of being faced by an Opposition pledged to carry out many of the measures that the Government would propose.

Yet the Labour leaders, when the election fever had died down and their opponents had left the field, may well have regarded their balance sheet with solemnity. Ranged against all the assets they could muster were the devastation and confusion of five years of total war in which manpower and resources of all kinds had been diverted from the uses of peace to those of conflict. Nor was it a mere reorientation that was required. Worn and torn by the efforts and strains of war, the whole British economy and the whole British nation needed repair and rejuvenation. Nearly 400,000 persons had been lost in the War. Enemy bombing had destroyed or damaged 4 million houses, apart from factories and offices. Parts of the big cities had been razed to the ground and many people had lost their homes and all their possessions. Their maimed and wounded were still being tended in their hospitals, their children were often far away—evacuated from the towns to safer country areas or overseas—or were but recently returned after years of separation. Strict rationing and shortage of food and clothes, the constant queuing for anything beyond the meagre ration, the blacked-out houses, the unlighted streets, the weary nights in air-raid shelters, had all left their mark. Demobilization was too slow for those longing for reunion; all could not come home at once, and many were still needed to finish the war against Japan and to occupy the defeated countries for the Allies. In all its assessments of post-War needs the Labour Government would never be able to forget that it was dealing with a nation which had suffered and borne hardship for more than five and a half years and whose wounds were not yet healed.

Moreover, the war-time controls had a double edge: they were useful aids to a planned economy, but they had generated an atmosphere of restriction and resentment. This was true in high degree of commodity controls, raw-material allocation systems, and licensing devices—they were useful aids and precedents, but the longer they remained the more irksome they became and consequently the more damaging to a Government whose programme was associated with plan and control. To an even greater degree this was true of consumer rationing—of eggs, butter, cheese, cooking-fat, meat and bacon, sugar and sweets and chocolate, tea and cakes, of soaps and washing-powders, of clothing and petrol, coal and coke. The people who still endured strict rationing in the interests of fair shares for all might be said to be half-way to socialism, but they would not for long support a peace-time Government that could not rapidly end it. Furthermore, they would not for long countenance an embargo on spending the savings that they had accumulated in the thrift campaigns of the War.[1]

The full picture in 1945 did nothing to encourage optimism. In spite of some demobilization there were still 5·2 million men and women engaged directly in the armed forces, compared with 0·6 million in 1939. Four million more were still employed on munitions and other military production, compared with 1·4 million in 1939. This meant that about 42 per cent of the nation's manpower was either in the armed forces or directly engaged in supplying them. Less than 8 per cent were supplying and maintaining the country's capital equipment. Only 2 per cent were producing goods for export[2]—there were neither ships to carry produce overseas nor people nor materials to make it. In general, Britain's exports at the end of the War were only enough to finance one quarter of her pre-War volume of imports.[3] An average balance of payments for the years 1936–38 gave an estimated debit balance of £43 million; for 1946 the estimate was about £750 million. An Index volume of exports of 100 for 1938 had by 1944 dwindled to 30.[4]

In ships the nation had lost more than half its tonnage, and only part of the loss had been made good by new building and acquisition: at the end of the War United Kingdom and Colonial merchant shipping together amounted to less than three-quarters of the pre-War fleet.[5] Much industrial plant had been destroyed by enemy action. Over and above this, plant and machinery had been deliberately run down and starved of all but the most vital repair and maintenance. This domestic disinvestment—apart from enemy destruction and the running down of personal consumer goods of all kinds—was to the tune of £885 million.[6]

It would have been impossible for the United Kingdom to keep going during the War if she had not sold her overseas capital assets. This she had done to a total of over £1000 million. By the end of the War her net

---

[1] About 25 per cent of disposable incomes had been saved during the War, compared with about 5 per cent before it (G. D. N. Worswick and P. H. Ady, *The British Economy 1945–1950*, p. 22).

[2] *Economic Survey for 1947*, p. 9; *Statistical Material presented during the Washington Negotiations*, December 1945, p. 7.

[3] *Economic Survey for 1947*, p. 11.

[4] *Statistics Presented to Washington*, p. 8.

[5] *Ibid.*, p. 8.

[6] *Ibid.*, p. 13.

annual income from overseas investments was less than one half the 1938 figure. But not only had Britain sold her securities to pay for the materials of war and realized what assets she could, she had also incurred a heavy debt, amounting at June 30, 1945, to well over £3000 million.[1] Until March 1941 she had also had to pay for all she took from the United States: the Lend-Lease legislation of that year saved her from piling up additional debt at the time, though the settlement was due later. But in August 1945, a month after the Labour Government took office, Lend-Lease came to an abrupt end and precipitated one of the many exchange crises of the post-War years. Britain's normal pre-War economy was built upon the import of two-thirds of her foodstuffs and the bulk of her raw materials, except coal, all of which had to be paid for by exports. With exports only about one-third of the pre-War volume, even rationing and the strictest import control could not provide sufficient to keep the economy going without the aid of American dollars. In December 1945, therefore, one of the Labour Government's first tasks was to approach the United States Government with a full statement of Britain's position[2] and to negotiate a new dollar-loan agreement. By this the United States agreed to lend Britain $3750 million and to settle outstanding debts under Lend-Lease by chalking up a further loan of $650 million, Britain's indebtedness then being to the tune of $4400 million.[3]

The Labour leaders were well aware of the gravity of the situation. "For Britain those early post-War years were desperately difficult," wrote Hugh Dalton. "Some of our problems, arising directly from the war, notably that of the gap in our overseas trade balance, were, on a short view, quite insoluble. Nothing which could have been done would then have closed that gap."[4] In this knowledge, but with the determination to proceed immediately with the programme that had been set out in their Election manifesto, Attlee chose his Cabinet. There were disappointments, some private sparring, but the chief Ministerial posts were filled within a few days of the Election results. Hugh Dalton, who would have liked to be Foreign Secretary, became Chancellor of the Exchequer; Ernest Bevin, who fancied the Exchequer, became Foreign Secretary—an unexpected but highly successful appointment: nothing could have been more expressive of the change that had occurred

---

[1] *Statistics Presented to Washington*, pp. 4, 9, 10, 11.
[2] *Statistics Presented to Washington*, December 1945.
[3] *Financial Agreement between the Governments of the United States and the United Kingdom*, December 6, 1945.
[4] *High Tide and After*, being vol. 3 of the memoirs of Hugh Dalton, p. xi.

than the appointment of a working-man and prominent trade-union leader to the Foreign Office, the Citadel of the Establishment. Also unexpected, in view of his rebellious history, but significant of Labour's unity in its moment of power, was the appointment of the fiery South Wales miner Aneurin Bevan as Minister of Health.

At 11 A.M. on August 15, 1945, the new House of Commons assembled in St Stephen's Hall, the Commons' Chamber having been destroyed by an enemy bomb during the War. Having been to the House of Lords to hear the King's Speech, they were addressed by Attlee at 4.5 P.M. His first speech to the House as Prime Minister was auspicious: "Mr Speaker, at midnight last night the terms of the Japanese surrender were announced to the world. . . . Thus the long, grievous war is at an end. . . . I think, therefore, that the House will wish forthwith to go to the Church of St Margaret's to render thanks." The Speaker with the mace led the procession of Labour Ministers, members of the late Coalition, and the former Prime Minister from the House.[1]

Later that day the Speaker read the King's Speech to the Commons. It provided for the nationalization of the Bank of England, of the Coal Industry, of Civil Aviation, of Public Transport, of Electricity, of Gas, of the Iron and Steel Industry. It outlined more social-security measures, including a National Health Service. It promised a food-production drive and financial provision for the rapid reconstruction of industry and the essential services, and an immediate start on the building programme, including houses.[2] According to custom the first to rise in the new House was a Member of the majority party making his maiden speech in the form of an Address in reply to the Speech from the Throne; on August 16 it was a young soldier, fresh from the wars, wearing several ribbons on his service jacket.

"The country is conscious", said Major John Freeman, "of the seriousness of the years that lie ahead; but our people are not depressed by the outlook nor are they overwhelmed by their responsibilities. On the contrary, on every side is a spirit of high adventure, of gay determination, a readiness to experiment, to take reasonable risks, to stake high in this magnificent venture of rebuilding our civilisation, as we have staked high in the winning of the war."[3] Later in the afternoon Attlee

1 Hansard, fifth series, vol. 413, cc. 48–50.
2 Ibid., vol. 413, cc. 53–57.
3 Ibid., c. vol. 413, 73.

took Freeman to the smokeroom of the House of Commons and introduced him to Churchill. "Looking on this young soldier, the old man wept."[1]

It was a heavy programme the Labour Government had before it. "The legislative programme on which the 1945 Labour Government embarked", wrote Attlee, "was much more extensive than that launched by any peace-time Government and it undoubtedly made a heavy demand on the House of Commons. It would certainly have astonished Members of Parliament of the days before the First World War, when one major measure in a session was thought to be quite enough. The verdict of the electors had, however, been sufficiently decisive to prevent the Opposition from indulging in obstruction."[2] The Labour Government therefore went ahead, producing almost simultaneously Bills for social reform and for nationalization, finding time also, early in 1946, to repeal the obnoxious Trade Disputes Act of 1927. "I have been waiting twenty years to do this," said Ernest Bevin, speaking to the second reading.

The Coalition Government had established a Ministry of National Insurance[3] and passed a Family Allowances Act which was steered into law by the Caretaker Government.[4] One of the first actions of the Labour Government was to announce in October 1945 that the payment of Family Allowances would begin, in advance of other benefits, on August 6, 1946. That gave the new Ministry only ten months in which to devise and set up the machinery of certification, record, and payment and all which that involved. Civil servants had, of course, been thinking in such terms for some time, but the Ministry itself was less than a year old, and the Family Allowances Act had become law only four months previously.

It was decided to establish the payments branch of the Ministry at Newcastle. A nucleus of staff was drafted from the Blackpool offices of the Ministry of Pensions, where contributory and war pensions had been handled, and the recruitment and training of some 2000 more people began. Early in 1946 they moved into temporary premises at Newcastle, working in hutments, living in hostels, and more local labour was enlisted.

Millions of explanatory leaflets and forms were printed and distri-

---

[1] *The Fateful Years*, being vol. 2 of the memoirs of Hugh Dalton, p. 482.
[2] *As It Happened*, p. 191.
[3] *Supra*, p. 27.   [4] *Supra*, pp. 29, 31.

buted. It was announced that claim forms, together with envelopes addressed to the Newcastle office, would be available at post-offices from April 1. By the end of April 1,400,000 claims had been received, by August 6, the Appointed Day, 2,300,000, and most claimants had received their Family Allowances Order books ready for payment at their local post-offices. Three index slips were made for each claimant for record purposes, and the whole scheme slipped quietly into operation without a hitch. By July 1949, 4,700,000 family allowances were being paid to nearly 3 million families. As Beveridge had urged, they depended upon no contribution but were a direct grant from the Exchequer. Beveridge had wanted them to be at the rate of 8s. weekly for each child after the first, but the Act had fixed 5s. as the amount, taking into account the free school meals and milk received.

Before the Family Allowances Act was operating the Labour Government had implemented the other two proposals intended to give substance to the scheme for a comprehensive system of social insurance. When James Griffiths, the Minister of National Insurance introduced the second reading of the Industrial Injuries Bill on October 10, 1945—a Bill "to make compensation for industrial injuries a part of this country's social services"[1]—he made full acknowledgment to the Coalition Government, who had outlined the general principles of the Bill in the second part of their White Paper.[2] The Bill agreed also with the Beveridge Report in financing industrial-injuries benefits by compulsory weekly contributions from employers and employed, and it accepted the principle that incapacity caused by industrial injury should qualify for a higher rate of benefit than ordinary sickness. It rejected, however, the recommendations of the Report that this higher rate should depend upon the workman's contribution record and that it should be paid only after thirteen weeks of incapacity. It proposed instead that the higher rate of benefit should be paid from the outset and be replaced by an industrial pension if the disability was likely to be permanent or prolonged, and that its amount should depend solely on the degree of injury suffered. This, as Griffiths said, was the essential difference, not only between his scheme and that of Beveridge, but between his scheme and the old Workmen's Compensation Acts. The new Bill rejected, also, the suggestions of the Beveridge Report that fatal cases should be dealt with by the payment of a lump sum to the workman's dependents rather than by a pension or weekly allowance, and that there should be a special levy on employers in hazardous industries.

The National Insurance (Industrial Injuries) Bill was read a second

1 Hansard, fifth series, vol. 414, c. 268.   2 Supra, p. 26.

time on October 11, 1945, and became law on July 26, 6. Pressing on with speed, the Government had by this time given a second reading to its main National Insurance Bill "to establish an extended system of national insurance providing pecuniary payments by way of unemployment benefit, sickness benefit, maternity benefit, retirement pension, widow's benefit, guardian's allowance and death grant". "This Bill", said Griffiths, introducing its second reading on February 6, 1946, "is the culmination of half a century's development of our British Social Services." He recalled Keir Hardie in 1895 standing up in his place in the House of Commons and demanding the acceptance by the State of the principle of work or maintenance. He recalled Asquith on May 10, 1908, introducing his Old Age Pensions Bill, and Lloyd George, who piloted the Bill through the House and whose name was so strongly associated with the scheme that the old-age pension was in many places referred to as "my Lloyd George". He recalled also some of the comments made in both Houses at the time. One noble lord feared that "A scheme so prodigal of expenditure might be dealing a mortal blow at the Empire"; another feared they "would weaken the moral fibre of the nation . . . and diminish the self-respect of our people".[1]

The Prime Minister, Clement Attlee, speaking later in the debate, fully acknowledged the debt to Beveridge: "This Bill is founded on the Beveridge Report"—but he pointed out how necessary it had been to devote a considerable amount of time to the examination of the Report before publishing the Coalition White Paper: an interesting comment on the delay which, by angering the public, had helped to put him in the position he then was. Earlier legislation, he said, had been "concessions to misery", "the provision for Lazarus of some crumbs from the rich man's table". This Bill, he went on, "is designed not for one class but for all, and it is a point to be noted how the emphasis of social provision by the State has rightly moved from the conception of doing something just for one class . . . at the bottom of the ladder . . . and seeks to provide equal benefits in exchange for equal payments".[2]

In his very powerful speech Attlee went to the heart of this whole new conception of social insurance and of the completely changed role of Government in employment policy. It was a speech which, for lucidity and unemotional persuasiveness, ranks high among the great contributions to Parliamentary debate. The Bill, he said, took its place as part of a policy of full employment put forward by the Coalition Government. "In that Government's White Paper on employment policy, there

[1] Hansard, fifth series, vol. 418, cc. 1734, 1735.
[2] *Ibid.*, vol. 418, cc. 1896, 1897.

was set forth . . . almost for the first time in a State document, the vital importance to the economy of the country of maintaining a high standard of purchasing power among the masses of the people. We now recognise", he said, "that, to allow, through mass unemployment or through sickness, great numbers of people to be ineffective as consumers is an economic loss to the country. We all now hold the view that we must maintain purchasing power and must have a proper distribution of purchasing power among the masses of the people. The old idea that this could only be done through wages and profits, and not by collective provisions of this sort, is now, I think, dying . . . it is interesting to see how far, in quite a short time, we have travelled from the conception of the panic cutting-down of the purchasing power of the masses, which was employed as a means of dealing with the abundance crisis of 1931. We now realise that we have the backing of experienced administrators and of the economists," he said, in insisting "that it is necessary, in this matter, to have a degree of planning."[1]

He then considered the question of cost. "The question is asked— Can we afford it? Supposing the answer is 'No', what does that mean? It really means that the sum total of the goods produced and the services rendered by the people of this country is not sufficient to provide for all our people at all times, in sickness, in health, in youth and in age, the very modest standard of life that is represented by the sums of money set out in the Second Schedule to this Bill. I cannot believe that our national productivity is so slow, that our willingness to work is so feeble or that we can submit to the world that the masses of our people must be condemned to penury. After all, this is really the payment into a pool of contributions from employers and workers and the products of taxation, and the payment thereout of benefits to various categories of persons. It is a method of distributing purchasing power, and the only validity for the claim that we cannot afford it must rest either on there not being enough in the pool, or on the claim that some sections of society have a priority to take out so much that others must suffer want."[2]

There was little opposition to the Bill. In fact, so far from opposing, the Opposition claimed credit for the principles involved; "we on this side of the House", said Richard Law, "welcome this Measure . . . are entitled to credit for this Measure."[3] "We regard this as a fine scheme. . . . We are proud, on this side of the House, to have played a part, an

1 Cf. Beveridge, *supra*, p. 22.
2 Hansard, fifth series, vol. 418, cc. 1897, 1900–01.
3 *Ibid.*, vol. 418, c. 1904.

mportant part, even . . . in the preparation of this plan," asserted Mr Peake.[1] The Bill was carried without a count on February 11, 1946.

Family allowances were straight payments by the State, involving no direct contribution by the recipients. Other benefits, including sickness benefit, rested, however, on a somewhat fragile basis of so-called insurance. As in the schemes already in operation, payment was made by deduction from wages or salary and certified by means of a stamp upon a card. Employers would buy for themselves and for their workpeople; self-employed and independent persons were left to buy their own stamps from a post-office. As before, the employer contributed to the cost of the stamp, except in the case of the independent or self-employed person, who paid the full amount necessary to the cover he received. One stamp covered all aspects of insurance—unemployment, pension, health, and industrial injury. The money went to the Ministry of National Insurance, who then allocated to the Ministry of Health the amount due in respect of Health Insurance.

All parties emphasized that the 'insurance' aspect of National Insurance was very small. Let it be well remembered, said the White Paper on the subject, "that the contributions from insured persons and their employers cover only part of the ground. They will not contribute directly to family allowances nor, of course, to National Assistance; and their contribution to the National Health Service will be relatively small. The balance has to be found from taxation. Towards the whole cost of the services named 54 per cent. at first and, twenty years later, 64 per cent. will have to come from taxation".[2]

Beveridge had assumed that in return for these joint contributions, supplemented by the Exchequer, cash benefits would be paid on a subsistence-level basis, and he had carefully calculated subsistence at 1938 prices plus 25 per cent for the increased cost of living. The White Paper had decided that subsistence rates of benefit were not practicable, and the Act agreed. The right objective, it said, "was to give a rate of benefit which provided a reasonable insurance against want and at the same time took account of the maximum contributions which the great body of contributors could properly be asked to pay". The disadvantage of this was that in times of rising prices beneficiaries would receive a falling real income, and cases of hardship would be driven to the Public Assistance Authority. For Beveridge this would destroy the whole basis of his scheme: "For assistance subject to a means test is assistance on condition of being poor, is discouragement to thinking and saving for one-

[1] Hansard fifth series, vol. 419, c. 93.   [2] Cmd. 6550.

self. Insurance benefit as a right without inquiry as to other means puts a floor below inequalities. Assistance subject to means test puts a ceiling above which no one may rise."[1]

When the Acts had been passed and the Appointed Days had been fixed—pensions, like family allowances, in 1946, but July 5, 1948, for other benefits—the Government departments concerned were faced with the Herculean task of making major changes from the old system to the new at a time when war dislocation and shortages of staff and supplies were still acute. Under the old methods unemployment insurance was administered by the Ministry of Labour and National Service, contributory pensions by the Ministry of Health, old-age pensions by the Ministry of Pensions, National Health Insurance by Approved Societies,[2] while the liability to compensate his worker for industrial injury rested with the employer. In taking away these functions from the bodies concerned and vesting them in the Ministry of National Insurance many questions had to be decided and dozens of regulations, which needed Parliamentary sanction but which had not been embodied in the main Bill, needed to be evolved and approved. Staff had to be recruited and trained, some transferred from existing departments, others completely new to the work. To the existing nucleus of about 5500 from existing Ministries some 34,000 were added as war pressures relaxed. The Ministry of National Insurance was to be at Newcastle, where the family allowances branch already was, and more accommodation had to be provided at once not only for offices but for residence.

The immediate task meant winding up some thousand Approved Societies with membership ranging from 50 to 2,000,000, with some 7000 branch offices over the country and recovering from them the insurance cards of their members. It meant correlating new insurance cards with the records held by labour exchanges, the Ministry of Labour, and the Ministry of Health. It involved giving a National Insurance number to every person directly he became gainfully employed and keeping a card that contained a record of his payments and receipts, his liabilities and his allowances. It involved an enormous amount of printing, indexing, and cross-reference. Vital decisions had also to be made on the degree of decentralization to be practised. Should all work be done by post from Newcastle or should existing local agencies be used? Local offices, it was decided, would give the maximum of personal contact, and would save much paper and postal work, while having the additional advantage of using local labour and premises. Records, however, were to be centralized at Newcastle, while the employment

[1] *The Times*, November 9, 1953.   [2] *Supra*, p. 12, and *infra*, Chapter IV.

exchanges paid unemployment benefits, and post-offices paid pensions as well as family allowances, sickness and injury benefits.

The work depended upon hard and far-sighted work from a nucleus of highly trained civil servants. It also depended upon the public. For this reason it was necessary that they should be fully informed—that the 25 million people who would be affected as contributors or beneficiaries should know about the schemes that concerned them. The Ministry's campaign involved sending to 14 million households between May 24 and June 12, 1948, a 32-page *Family Guide to National Insurance*. There was an edition in Welsh and one—an interesting light on the aftermath of war—in Polish. Gradually more and more leaflets supplemented the booklet, and by July 1949 some 50 million leaflets had been distributed. Lecturers and speakers were supplied by the Central Office of Information who spoke at Women's Institutes, Rotary Clubs, factories, and offices. A special film was shown at over 3000 cinemas. The Press and the BBC publicized and familiarized the new schemes. The whole operation was a task that involved far more than the drafting of an Act and its debate in Parliament. But on the Appointed Day all was ready. Insurance cards were in the hands of the people, post-offices held stocks of the insurance stamps that would be put on them, pensioners had their new pension-books, mothers of families had their family-allowance books, the post-offices and the labour exchanges held sufficient money to meet the demands made upon them. Thus, with a minimum of fuss, the structure of National Insurance upon which the Welfare State proper rests was established within three years of the end of the War. The flow of pensions and allowances each week, the payment of sick and unemployment pay as it is required, the recording and checking of ages and conditions and size of families, of people reaching pensionable age, of young people ceasing to be in full-time education or becoming gainfully employed, of sickness and injury claims, of changes in address, of changes of name through marriage or for other reasons, of changes in pension or allowance rates, which entail not only changes in the amount of money available at post-offices and labour exchanges but printed changes in millions of pension and allowance books, are a tribute to the efficiency of the Welfare State. That the legislation upon which they are based was brought before the House of Commons in part during the War and in part in six crowded months after it is a tribute alike to the foresight of the Coalition Government and to the zeal of the Labour Ministry. But to complete the structure of the Welfare State the cornerstone was needed—the National Health Service, the counterpart and complement of what had gone before.

CHAPTER IV

The National Health Service

"The most valuable asset of the State and of Society is man.
Each life has a determined value. To conserve it intact to the
very end is a duty dictated not only by humanity but in the
very interests of society."

The Archduke Rudolph, *Inaugural
Address to the International
Health Congress of Vienna*, 1887

AT THE heart of the Welfare State lies the National Health Service—
"the very temple of our social security system".[1]

It was early apparent that the Second World War had made the problem of national health both easier and more difficult to tackle. Easier
because it gave the kind of shock to the body politic that caused it to
make a clean sweep and start afresh, gave it the benefit of the rapid advance in drugs, nursing, and medical skill that had developed under
stress of war, and gave it, perhaps for the first time in matters concerning
the health of the people, a sense of driving one way. The problem was
more difficult because, like all other post-War problems of reconstruction, it had to take its turn with others, to face an appalling amount of
sheer physical destruction, and an intense shortage of manpower and
materials of all kinds.

In 1942, during the War, the scope of health insurance had been considerably widened by the raising of the income limit for participation to
£420 a year. But it still covered only about half the population and included neither specialist nor hospital service, neither dental, optical, nor
hearing aids. Mental deficiency was isolated from other forms of illness.
Medical practitioners were unevenly spread over the country—they had

[1] Harold Wilson, the House of Commons, November 2, 1960 (Hansard, fifth
series, vol. 629, c. 190).

been before the War, but now their war-time service had too often disrupted their practices and left their surgeries to run down or suffer bomb damage.

Hospitals were in all stages of development. There were more than a thousand voluntary hospitals in England and Wales, varying from large general or specialist hospitals with first-class modern equipment and with medical schools attended by distinguished consultants, down to small local cottage hospitals. There were some 2000 more which had been founded by the local authorities or had developed from the sick ward of the old workhouse, ranging again through all types and degrees of excellence. Waiting-lists were long; most hospitals came out of the War under-equipped with staff and resources of all kinds; all needed painting, repairing, reorganizing; some were cleaning up after bomb damage; most needed to reorient themselves before they turned from war casualties to peace-time commitments; all needed new equipment and new buildings. Other medical services were only too clearly the result of haphazard development. There were Medical Officers of Health employed by the local authorities, sanitary inspectors concerned with environmental health, medical inspectors of factories, nearly 2000 doctors on call to industry, as well as doctors privately appointed by firms to treat their staff. A school medical service provided for regular inspection of all children in public elementary and secondary schools; local authorities provided maternity and child care, health visiting, tuberculosis treatment, and other services for the poor, which varied widely from district to district. How many people there were of all ages and classes who were needing treatment but not getting it could only be guessed at.

Since it was clear that *ad hoc* improvement would no longer serve, a complete reshaping of the health and medical service marked the only line of advance. The general pattern it would take was indicated by Sir William Beveridge, who laid down in his Report in 1942 the axiom that a health service must be universal, that the needs of the rich and poor are alike and should be met by the same means: "Restoration of a sick person to health is a duty of the state ... prior to any other," a "comprehensive national health service will ensure that for every citizen there is available whatever medical treatment he requires, in whatever form he requires it, domiciliary or institutional, general, specialist or consultant, and will ensure also the provision of dental, ophthalmic and surgical appliances, nursing and midwifery and rehabilitation after accidents."[1]

The Coalition Government accepted the Health Service proposals of the Beveridge Report and prepared a White Paper, which it presented

[1] Pp. 159, 158.

to Parliament in February 1944,[1] saying the same thing as Beveridge in different words: "The Government . . . intend to establish a comprehensive health service for everybody in this country. They want to ensure that in future every man and woman and child can rely on getting all the advice and treatment and care which they may need in matters of personal health; that what they get shall be the best medical and other facilities available; that their getting these shall not depend on whether they can pay for them, or on any other factor irrelevant to the real need —the real need being to bring the country's full resources to bear upon reducing ill-health and promoting good health in all its citizens." The Health Service, it said, should be as water, as the highways, available to all and all should pay through rates, taxes and social insurance.[2]

Ernest Brown, a Liberal National, Minister of Health in the Coalition Government, was responsible for a first plan for a National Health Service which subordinated the general practitioner to the Medical Officer of Health and the local authorities. It was abandoned amid a professional storm. The scheme of Henry Willink, a later Minister of Health, was modelled on the White Paper, but was set aside with the defeat of Churchill's Government in the 1945 Election. In the Labour Government the role of Minister of Health fell to Aneurin Bevan, who produced a scheme within a few months of Labour's victory.

Bevan started with assumptions similar to those of Beveridge and the White Paper: "Society becomes more wholesome, more serene, and spiritually healthier, if it knows that its citizens have at the back of their consciousness the knowledge that not only themselves, but all their fellows, have access, when ill, to the best that medical skill can provide."[3] Few dissented from this belief. Its translation into practice, however, took three years of careful planning, of long, often bitter negotiation with the medical profession, of lengthy discussions with hospital authorities and local authorities; it entailed dozens of committees, formal and informal, Parliamentary questions and Parliamentary debate, the drafting and redrafting of the Bill itself, the discussion of various amendments, and finally the actual implementation of the decisions taken. Six months before the Appointed Day it looked as though the whole edifice might crash through lack of support from the medical profession; but a near-last-minute agreement saved the structure.

At the beginning three problems stood out: first, how to meet the cost of a service that was to be all-inclusive of persons and services; second,

---

[1] *Supra*, p. 26.   [2] *A National Health Service*, pp. 5, 6.
[3] A. Bevan, *In Place of Fear*, p. 100.

how to cut the Gordian knot in which not only preventive and curative functions were tangled but in which local and central government, voluntary work and professional, factories and schools, the Factory Inspectorate, the School Inspectorate, the Poor Law Authorities, the Board of Trade, the Ministry of Education, and the Ministry of Health were involved; and, third, how to incorporate into a public service a medical profession which of its nature and history was personal, individual, and chary of anything that smacked of coercion. Bound up with these problems were those relating to the people, the buildings, the institutions, the methods of procedure which would all be shaken up, changed, abolished, extended, or in some way interfered with by a National Health Service: clean sweeps are stimulating to those who make them, but not always to those who are swept up.

The cost of a National Health Service could be reduced by establishing an income limit for free service. Bevan dismissed this as "the creation of a two-standard health service, one below and one above the salt".[1] His Bill would be all-inclusive of persons, compulsory for all, men and women, whatever their occupation or income or even if they had none. But while not accepting the income limit used in earlier legislation he adhered to the so-called insurance principle of Lloyd George and Beveridge. He made no attempt to disguise the fact, however, that the insurance element would cover only a fraction of the cost involved and that the term 'Health Insurance' was, in fact, a misnomer. It was the Exchequer that would have to meet out of taxation the main cost of the service: "If we are to carry out our obligation and to provide the people of Great Britain, no matter where they may be, with the same level of service, then the nation itself will have to carry the expenditure."[2] This meant that the rich would pay more towards a National Health Service through higher taxation than the poorer members of society, although all would pay the same weekly contribution.

The administrative problem had not even the superficial simplicity of the financial, though in broad outline the new proposals looked straightforward enough. In place of the existing authorities, for all health purposes central to the individual there would be a National Health Service under a Ministry of Health which, in the person of the Minister, would be responsible to Parliament for the health of the nation. A Central Health Services Council would advise the Minister on professional and technical questions and keep under review the general development of the Service. This Council was to consist of forty-one members appointed by the Minister after consultation with the professional bodies con-

[1] *In Place of Fear*, p. 101.   [2] Hansard, fifth series, vol. 422, c. 50.

cerned and include *ex officio* the Presidents of the Royal Medical Colleges. The largest single group in the Council was made up of the fifteen
representatives of the general practitioners. There were nine Standing
Advisory Committees—medical, dental, pharmaceutical, ophthalmic,
nursing, maternity and midwifery, tuberculosis, mental health, cancer
and radiography. Special committees needed, for example, to study
questions of hospital supplies or general practice were to be appointed
as necessary on the recommendation of the Council. All, including the
Central Council, were to be purely advisory, but the Minister was required to lay the Annual Report of the Council before Parliament, thus
ensuring an airing for its views.

The National Health Service itself was to be administered in three
parts: services run by the local authorities, hospital and specialist
services, and the personal practitioner service. They would find a
common meeting-ground in health centres provided by the local
authorities.[1]

The local authorities, which were, in effect, the county or county
borough councils, were still to provide 'preventive' services like vaccination and immunization, would supply health visitors and home
nurses, run maternity and midwifery services and the all-important
ambulance service, as well as being responsible for street-cleansing,
water-supply, prevention of nuisances, and the other services basic
to 'environmental' health. Medical Officers of Health, appointed by
and responsible to the local authority, would exercise the same functions as they had done before the inception of the National Health
Service.

For hospital and specialist services the country was divided into
Regional Hospital Groups—thirteen for England, one for Wales, five
for Scotland,[2] and one for Northern Ireland,[3] each connected with a
university which had, or would be provided with, a school of medicine.
Each Region had a voluntary Regional Hospital Board, appointed by
the Minister, which included members of the universities, the health
authorities, and the Medical Associations of the area. The size of the
Boards varied between 22 and 32; the original members were appointed
for varying periods, but subsequent appointments would be for three
years. While the Boards would be responsible, under the Minister, for
planning, providing, and supervising the hospital services of the Region,

[1] *Infra*, p. 59.
[2] See *A National Health Service*, issued jointly by the Ministry of Health and
the Department of Health for Scotland, February 1944, Cmd. 6502. There was a
separate Act for Scotland, The National Health Service (Scotland) Act, 1947.
[3] The Health Services Act (Northern Ireland), 1948.

the day-to-day running of the hospitals would be in the hands of voluntary Hospital Management Committees appointed by the Regional Hospital Boards, to which each would be responsible for a single hospital or group of hospitals. The teaching hospitals within this grouping were to be administered separately by their own Boards of Governors, appointed by the Minister from nominations which included those from the associated Regional Hospital Board, the dentists and doctors who were teaching in the hospital, and the university with which the Board was associated. These Boards of Governors would act for their hospitals as Regional Hospital Boards and Hospital Management Committees and be directly responsible to the Minister.

Administratively it was feared that the proposed arrangements would result in a hospital bureaucracy whose structure would be too vast or too topheavy to function without rigid control from the top and that individual units would be straitjacketed. There was resentment that the voluntary hospitals, many of them still using the bequests of dead benefactors, should be taken over by the State. In spite of their weighting with medical men, it was feared that the Hospital Management Committees and the Regional Hospital Boards would result in the interference of well-meaning amateurs rather than the guidance of informed professionals. Generally speaking, however, the hospitals were sufficiently in need of repair, reorganization, and money to accept the proposals in the Bill and assist their implementation.

Bevan's biggest struggle, like Lloyd George's, was with the doctors. There was something of David and Goliath in the combat as the Labour man from the Welsh valleys faced the professional body representing high professional skill backed by centuries of independence and public esteem. Not that Bevan was good—or right—all the time or that the British Medical Association was bad and wrong. There was much that was right and good on both sides. And when it came to dialectical skill in argument it was Bevan who was the Goliath. The professional doctor, when he made his protest, turned into the merest amateur politician; the detached clinical observer made wild speeches and wrote hysterical letters. As Bevan noted, the doctors were unable to distinguish between the atmosphere of the mass demonstration and the quite different mood of the negotiating table, and he knew he could discount much of what had been said from the rostrum. In the cooler atmosphere of the conference table he was able, for example, to concede their point, made with much passion, that they would "never be made into civil servants" because he had never intended that they should. He was able to agree that there should be a free choice of doctor because he had always been anxious to insist on this. "They were" said Bevan, "mobilising their forces to fight a battle that was never likely to begin."[1]

It was natural that the doctors should want to feel their way carefully into such a comprehensive service as Bevan proposed. Many were afraid that any Labour Party scheme would be based upon a complete nationalization of medicine in which doctors would be salaried, and badly paid, civil servants under a National Board which would control all services, stifle incentive and research, deny the patient's right to a free choice of doctor, interfere with the delicate and important doctor-patient relationship, and even violate the secrecy of the consulting-room. Undoubtedly these fears were exacerbated by the record of Bevan —firebrand, Left-winger, enemy to every form of capitalist society— and the machinery that it was necessary to establish undoubtedly helped to foster apprehension for the future of a free medical service. But Bevan repeatedly emphasized that there would be no coercion. Doctors, dentists, ophthalmologists, and all concerned would be free to enter the Service or not, as they pleased, and they could take both private and National Health patients if they wished. The public had a similar freedom to receive treatment privately or through enrolment on a panel; they could take one part of the Service nationally another part privately; they could change doctor, dentist, or optician with little formality. With the doctors' fears of a lowering of professional standards, a strangulation by red tape, a subordination of the medical man to the official, an excessive amount of paper work, he was in strong sympathy. Although he could not resist sparring with the doctors Bevan did, in fact, give full weight to the fear of medical men that lay interference might affect professional freedom and come between the doctor and his patient. "Any health service which hopes to win the consent of the doctors", he stated, "must allay these fears. . . . There is no alternative to self-government by the medical profession in all matters affecting the content of its academic life. . . . It is for the community to provide the apparatus of medicine for the doctor. It is for him to use it freely in accordance with the standards of his profession and the requirements of his oath."[2] Bevan, however, held out on one or two real points too long. He could have spared himself and the profession the last angry and wearing months before the Service came into operation. But, overall, the ethics of the profession and the faith of the Minister met on common ground in wanting to make provision for all the sick, whatever their age, profession, income, or circumstances. And on the whole the disputes were subordinate to this end.

[1] *In Place of Fear*, p. 111.　　　　[2] *Op. cit.*, pp. 113–114.

Administratively, the spearhead of the general-practitioner service would be the Executive Councils appointed for each county and county borough to represent the doctors and dentists of the area in all National Health affairs. Each of these voluntary organizations would consist of twenty-four members—twelve lay and twelve professional—and a chairman appointed by the Minister.[1] Of the lay members eight were to be appointed by the local health authority and four by the Minister. The professional members were to be appointed by local Committees of the professions concerned—seven by the Local Medical Committee, three by the Local Dental Committee, and two by the Local Pharmaceutical Committee. All the practical work of the National Health Service was to be done by the paid staffs of these Executive Councils. They would keep the medical record cards of all the National Health patients in the area, would note changes of address and changes of doctor. Payments from the central pool for doctors' salaries would be received here and paid out to the doctors.[2] Dental, ophthalmic, and pharmaceutical salaries, though dealt with in slightly different fashion, would also be paid from the Executive Office. Dentists would be paid in accordance with work done, after prior approval of the more elaborate treatments and of examination and verification of estimates submitted for all the work they had completed; ophthalmologists and opticians also on the basis of work done in accordance with the scales laid down by a Whitley Council[3]; pharmacists in accordance with the number of prescriptions made up.[4]

Bevan had strong views concerning the purchase and sale of medical practices, which was widely current. Doctors regarded the goodwill that they built up over years of medical practice as something saleable, and on giving up a practice would sell it to the incoming doctor. It was generally assumed that the money received was a kind of retirement bonus or realization of an investment and that the doctor was entitled to the best price he could get. Bevan emphatically opposed the whole conception. It did nothing to ensure that doctors settled in the poorer, densely populated areas where they were most needed or that a poor or young doctor got the practice he was most fitted for. It was, moreover, "an evil in itself . . . tantamount to the sale and purchase of patients".[5]

---

[1] See *infra*, p. 61, for the change made by the Act of 1949.

[2] *Infra*, pp. 58, 321.

[3] A joint negotiating body representing both sides of a profession or industry, so called from the reports of a Committee under the chairmanship of J. H. Whitley which in 1917 and 1918 recommended such machinery.

[4] *Infra*, p. 197.

[5] House of Commons, April 30, 1946 (Hansard, fifth series, vol. 422, c. 53).

He proposed, instead, a scheme whereby a doctor needed the approval of a Medical Practices Committee before setting up and a retiring doctor received a pension instead of selling a practice. In this way old practices would not be perpetuated in areas where they were not required, new blood would be made to flow where there was most need, and the most suitable rather than the doctor who offered most money would be installed; the proposals did nothing to encourage the building up of a practice as a personal achievement.

Two Medical Practices Committees were proposed—one for England and Wales and one for Scotland. Each would consist of seven doctors and two laymen and, besides themselves surveying the country, they would work in close contact with the Executive Councils. There was much opposition to the whole concept from doctors who had been accustomed to regard the goodwill of a practice as a nest-egg for retirement, who resented what they felt to be a loss of freedom, and who felt the Government's proposed reimbursement to be too low. But the Minister swept aside all protests and, in consultation with the British Medical Association, earmarked a sum of £66 million to be divided between all practitioners who entered the Health Service at its inception in proportion to their average gross annual receipts for the two years prior to the Appointed Day. This would be paid on retirement or death, whichever was earlier, together with interest expected to be about 2·75 per cent.

The major part of the administrative machinery was completed by the establishment of a central tribunal to deal with disciplinary cases, consisting of a chairman and two members. Since the power of dismissal from the Service would rest with the Tribunal its composition was of the highest importance. The chairman was to be nominated by the Lord Chancellor, one member by the Minister; the other was to be a professional practitioner chosen for each case by the Minister from names submitted by the profession. An appeal against dismissal would lie to the Minister. Like the Medical Practices Committee, the Tribunal aroused intense opposition from the medical profession.

But more bitter, more prolonged, and more dangerous to the birth of the National Health Service was Bevan's struggle with the doctors over the question of their pay. All branches of the profession had been accustomed to getting their income from a combination of private practice, National Health Insurance work, local-government work, and a certain amount of examination for insurance companies and private firms. Nearly all gave some free service to poor patients in their surgeries or in hospitals. There was a wide range of income, varying with age, locality, type of practice, popularity, and skill. A few specialists and general practitioners were wealthy men. Others followed a round in poor districts where reward was measured more by service than by money. Young doctors in hospitals were badly paid, in many cases getting no more than their board and pocket-money. Senior hospital consultants relied on private practice and not the hospital for their incomes.

Three inter-departmental Committees, each under the chairmanship of Sir Will Spens, were appointed to consider the remuneration of general practitioners, consultants and specialists, and of dental practitioners; none reported before the National Health Service Bill went to Parliament. The first, the *Report on the Remuneration of General Practitioners*, appeared in May 1946, when the Bill had been presented to the House of Commons but a month before its second reading. Any estimate of a basic salary at which the Service should aim, it said, was bound to be very general, but, taking an average at 1939—*i.e.*, pre-War—values, the Committee suggested a range of annual income from £1000 to £2500, which the Minister accepted. This, they calculated, could be achieved on the basis of a capitation fee of 15*s.* for each National Health patient on a doctor's books. A central pool was to be established, whose size would be determined by multiplying 15*s.* by the total number of insured persons. From this pool general practitioners would draw in accordance with the number of their National Health patients.[1] The proposals were not ungenerous, and in accepting the concept of the capitation fee the Minister was making use of a device familiar since the inauguration of Lloyd George's scheme. He also suggested that, to help a young doctor with a small practice, part of the salary should consist of a straight payment of £300 each year irrespective of the number of patients on his list.

But the doctors were far from being satisfied. The resultant struggle had barely started when at 3.47 P.M. on April 30 Bevan rose to propose the second reading of the National Health Service Bill "to promote the establishment in England and Wales[2] of a comprehensive health service designed to secure improvement in the physical and mental health of the people of England and Wales and the prevention, diagnosis and treatment of illness, and for that purpose to provide or secure the effective provision of services". "The services so provided", stated the Bill, "shall be free of charge, except where any provision of this Act expressly provides for the making and recovery of charges."[3]

An amendment in the names of Winston Churchill and others, which

[1] Cmd. 6810. And see Appendix, p. 321.
[2] There were separate Acts for Scotland and Northern Ireland (*supra*, p. 53 *n.* 2 and *n.* 3).
[3] National Health Service Act, 1946.

was moved by Mr Willink, voiced most of the Parliamentary opposition to the Bill: "This House," it said, "while wishing to establish a comprehensive health service, declines to give a Second Reading to a Bill which prejudices the patient's right to an independent family doctor; which retards the development of the hospital services by destroying local ownership, and gravely menaces all charitable foundations by diverting to purposes other than those intended by the donors the trust funds of the voluntary hospitals; and which weakens the responsibility of local authorities without planning the health services as a whole".[1]

The first of the points made by the amendment was hotly denied at the time and has not been substantiated in practice: the doctor has always been free to be in or out of the Service, the patient has always been free to choose, or to change, his doctor. The second criticism has hardly been borne out in practice, though there is a danger inherent in the hospital organization. The third criticism was true at the time and is still valid today. Though the Act intended, by the creation of health centres, to go some way towards meeting this objection, all it said was: "It shall be the duty of every local health authority to provide, equip, and maintain to the satisfaction of the Minister premises, which shall be called 'health centres', at which facilities shall be available for all or any of the following purposes:—

general medical services
general dental services
pharmaceutical services
any local health authority services
services of specialists"

and all Bevan said in their support was that he attached "very great importance indeed" to health centres. It is curious that he never used with any confidence the one card in his hand which would have done most to attract the support of the doctors and, at the same time, enormously strengthen the Health Service. On the contrary, he seemed to play down the concept of the health centre.

The amendment was lost, and the Bill was given its second reading on May 2, 1946, and its third reading twelve weeks later.[2] Most of the 113 Members who then voted against it believed in some kind of National Health Service; many were genuinely afraid of a Labour version; some disliked the actual structure proposed; the majority voted on a purely party ticket. By and large, judging from the speeches made in the House,

1 Hansard, fifth series, vol. 422, c. 222.
2 *Ibid.*, vol. 422, cc. 222–313, 356–418; vol. 426, cc. 392–475.

there were very few who were on principle opposed to a National Health Service—perhaps very few who, in view of the temper of the country, *dared* be against a National Health Service.

The doctors, however, were by no means intimidated, even after the National Health Service Act received the Royal Assent on November 6, 1946; and since the general practitioner was the person who was required to turn himself into a National Health doctor his importance to the whole scheme was paramount. He was still beset with fears of a salaried State medical service, which were most irrationally kept alive by the proposed £300 basic salary; he was worried over the liberty of movement of practitioners; he resented the abolition of the sale of practices; he was not convinced that the disciplinary action to be in the hands of the Central Tribunal would not be used as a political weapon; he feared that the Executive Councils would become mere instruments of the Government. A poll of the doctors conducted by the British Medical Association shortly after the passage of the Act gave 8972 in favour of entering into discussions with the Minister and 23,111 against.

Bevan gave a "brilliant display of dialectical skill" in trying to win over the doctors. But he was also conciliatory. He asked for advice, and promised to consider further legislation on the chief points of trouble. Meetings began again early in the New Year and continued throughout the summer. But by the end of 1947 they had broken down once more. "I say that the new service as propounded in its present form is entirely unsuitable, entirely improper for us to accept, and we should endeavour to persuade our colleagues to vote against accepting any servce under the Act in its present form," declared Dr Guy Dain, Chairman of the Council of the British Medical Association and one of the chief organizers of opposition.[1] Dr Charles Hill, the Secretary of the Council of the BMA, told an enormous meeting at BMA House in London that the Act was the first step to the fulfilment of the Socialist programme for a whole-time State Medical Service.[2] Letters to the *British Medical Journal* became more angry, less reasonable, and more abusive of Bevan. Bevan accused the doctors of "organising wholesale resistance to the implementation of an Act of Parliament". In a most reasoned speech in the House of Commons he complained that the whole thing began "to look

[1] At Wimbledon Town Hall, January 4, 1948, addressing members of the profession from Surrey.

[2] January 1, 1948—the largest meeting that had ever assembled at BMA House, according to the *British Medical Journal* of January 10. Dr Hill, created Baron Hill of Luton in 1963, was well known for his broadcast talks as the Radio Doctor, and later became Conservative Member of Parliament for Luton and Postmaster General (1955–57).

more like a squalid political conspiracy than the representations of an honoured and learned profession".[1]

On January 8, 1948, six months before the Service was due to go into operation, a special representative meeting of the BMA unanimously passed a resolution in which they solemnly declared that "in their considered opinion the National Health Service Act, 1946, in its present form is so grossly at variance with the essential principles of our profession that it should be rejected absolutely by all practitioners".[2] A month later a plebiscite of the profession asked the question, "Do you approve, or disapprove, of the National Health Service Act, 1946, in its present form?" In an 84 per cent poll a nine-to-one majority voted disapproval.[3] A month after this a representative meeting of the BMA decided unanimously not to enter the new Service on July 5 unless substantial changes were made in the Act.[4] "Now, BMA, stand firm!" exhorted a correspondent in the *Journal* of the BMA after this vote. "The profession has spoken in no uncertain voice. . . . We are all behind you and expect a lead. Don't give way or compromise—it is too dangerous. . . . Our patients look to us to refuse service under the Act as it stands and to maintain our professional freedom. Think of what public apathy cost Germany in the '30s. We must cling to our liberty."[5]

In April, with the sands running out, Bevan made the concessions which were hardly concessions because they in no way ran counter to the assurances he had repeatedly given to the profession. What they did was to give substance to those assurances. He might have done so earlier. He repeated that a full-time State medical service was not intended, and he agreed to make this clear by legislation[6]; he agreed to revise the idea of the £300 basic salary, which was intended to help young doctors, and to offer it only to those setting up for the first time. On the vexed question of discipline as exercised through the Central Tribunal, he promised that the chairman, nominated by the Lord Chancellor, should be a lawyer of high professional standing. The Executive Councils should, he offered, appoint their own chairmen as vacancies occurred, the Minister then appointing 5 members to each Committee instead of 4 and a chairman.[7]

A third plebiscite was held by the BMA. The results published on May 5 gave 14,620 in favour of the Act and 25,842 against. Of general

[1] February 9, 1948 (Hansard, fifth series, vol. 447, cc. 36–39).

[2] *British Medical Journal*, January 17, 1948.

[3] 43,013 voted; 38,534 voted disapproval. *British Medical Journal*, February 21, 1948.

[4] *British Medical Journal*, March 27, 1948.   [5] March 20, 1948.

[6] National Health Service (Amendment) Act, 1949, section 11.

[7] Hansard, fifth series, vol. 449, cc. 164–169.

3*

practitioners 8639 voted for it, 9588 against. In view of the reduction of opposition and of the fact that nearly 9000 practitioners were willing to man the Service, a BMA meeting on May 28 recommended the profession to participate. "Abject Surrender!" thundered a letter published in the *B.M.J.* on May 29. But it was not that. The medical profession had won certain assurances; the Minister of Health had won their co-operation. "Victory all Round" was perhaps nearer the mark. By July 5, the Appointed Day, a majority of general practitioners had applied to enter the Service. By September more than 18,000 in England and Wales out of a total of 21,000 had decided to become part of the National Health Service.

The Spens Committee *Report on the Remuneration of Consultants and Specialists* had been published in May 1948. The Committee spoke sympathetically of the work of these highly trained people. It wanted them to be relieved of the "stage of comparative penury and hardship" which they endured as young men, and wanted the specialist in later life to be paid "a salary commensurate with the growth in his skill and the increasing responsibility of his work". Moreover, to give him the opportunity to earn an income comparable with the highest that would be earned in other professions, there should be a series of merit awards in the form of higher salaries for a few consultants who distinguished themselves, which would bring their incomes on 1939 prices to about £5000 a year.[1] Most of these men carried on with their work in the hospitals after the Appointed Day as they had done before; within a few years there were more full-time hospital consultants than previously.

The Spens *Report on the Remuneration of General Dental Practitioners*, also published in May, considered that the income of dentists was too low. Seventy per cent of them received incomes below £1000 a year. In the age group 35–54 about 20 per cent got less than £400 a year. A reasonable income, the Committee estimated, would be about £1600 for a single-handed practitioner paid on the basis of work done. There were some who earned more than this; and although the majority, especially of the younger men, stood to gain from the National Health Service the response at first was slow. But demand for dental attention was high, and, with payment in proportion to work done, incomes rose; within three months of the inception of the Service about 75 per cent of dentists had come in; all but about 5 per cent subsequently followed.

The Appointed Day was named as July 5, 1948, by Order in Council issued on January 26, 1948. On that day Lloyd George's Health Insur-

[1] See Appendix, pp. 321–322.

ance scheme came to an end as one of the measures repealed by the National Insurance Act of 1946, and the two functions with which it was mainly concerned—the payment of monetary benefit during sickness and the provision of free medical service—became separated, the Ministry of National Insurance taking the one and the Ministry of Health the other. The public responded with enthusiasm. By the Appointed Day about three-quarters of the population had registered with the National Health Service; by 1952 it was estimated that only about 1·5 per cent remained outside.[1] As the first contributions to the new National Health Service were paid there was a justifiable sense of pride on all sides that in three years from the end of the War so much had been achieved. There was, however, no startling change immediately apparent. The patient who went to sleep in hospital on the night of July 4 noticed no difference when he awoke next morning to his National Health tea brought by his National Health nurse, nor did the doctors or specialists act differently from before. The surgery waiting-rooms seemed much the same, and the doctor who questioned his patients adopted no different manner because he was now a National Health doctor. There was, of course, a sense of experiment, a general questioning on all sides, and the first months were anxious times for all concerned in building the new Service. But overall there was enthusiasm for something eminently worth while, a sense of participation in what its chief architect called "the most civilised achievement of modern government".[2]

[1] P. G. Gray and Ann Cartwright, "Choosing and Changing Doctors", *The Lancet*, December 19, 1953, p. 1308.
[2] Aneurin Bevan, the House of Commons, July 30, 1958 (Hansard, fifth series, vol 592, c. 1398).

CHAPTER V

Nationalization

"To secure for the producers by hand or by brain the full
fruits of their industry, and the most equitable distribution
thereof that may be possible, upon the basis of common
ownership of the means of production and the best obtainable
system of popular administration and control of each
industry or service."

Labour Party Constitution, 1917

ON THE day that the second reading of the Industrial Injuries Bill was
proposed—October 10, 1945[1]—the first of the Labour Government's
nationalization measures was presented to the House.

The doctrine of nationalization, socialization, or common ownership
of the means of production had come down to the Labour Party through
a variety of channels, and since the Party's inception had formed part of
its programme. Long before that, workmen, using tools or machines
owned by their employers, or working on land not their own, seeing
the product of their labour go to someone whose hands no more than
touched the raw material, had associated low wages and bad conditions of work with private property. The communism of primitive
Christianity gave sanction to the goal of common ownership, and
through Wycliffe and John Ball—"When Adam dalf and Eve span, Who
was then a gentilman?"—through the practical attempt by Gerrard
Winstanley and his followers during the Civil Wars to dig the commons,
the concept grew. Using the allied principles of the equality of man and
man and of freedom as man's natural right, Jean-Jacques Rousseau
took the measure of contemporary society and pronounced that "man
is born free and is everywhere to be found in chains". The newly born
United States of America implicitly took upon itself the reversal of this

1 *Supra*, p. 43.

position, proudly proclaiming in 1776 the "self-evident" truths that all men are born equal and are entitled to the "unalienable" rights of life, liberty, and the pursuit of happiness. Thirteen years later the French Declaration of the Rights of Man asserted that all men are born equal and remain equal in rights.

"Equality" has full meaning only when related to economics, but it was a poet who asked the relevant question:

> "Men of England, wherefore plough
> For the lords who lay ye low?
> Wherefore weave with toil and care
> The rich robes your tyrants wear?
>
> . . . .
>
> "The seed ye sow, another reaps;
> The wealth ye find, another keeps;
> The robes ye weave, another wears;
> The arms ye forge, another bears."[1]

About the time that Shelley was writing, Robert Owen was preaching the Co-operative Commonwealth and devising plans for Villages of Co-operation, and half a century later William Morris, poet and craftsman, described in fantasy a community of common ownership and joint service with equal reward. Co-operative trading societies, both wholesale and retail, attempted in a practical way to win control of the means of production; Chartism, though political in its immediate objectives, carried the undertones of a communist society; and the whole concept of common ownership of the means of production, distribution, and exchange was built into a theory by Karl Marx, a German exile working in London.

The British Labour Movement as a whole was deeply imbued with each of these principles, though it shied away from the ruthlessness of the Marxist doctrine, which implied the overthrow of the capitalist class by force. The Democratic Federation, formed in 1881, included nationalization of the land, of the railways, and of the mines in its programme, while the Independent Labour Party on its formation at Bradford in 1893 announced among its objectives the collective ownership and control of the means of production, distribution, and exchange. When the

---

[1] Shelley, *Song to the Men of England.*

Labour Representation Committee was formed in 1900, with the specific purpose of returning a distinct Labour group to the House of Commons, it refused to commit itself to nationalization, but eighteen years later, when the LRC had become simply the Labour Party, it resolved "To secure for the producers by hand or by brain the full fruits of their industry, and the most equitable distribution thereof that may be possible, upon the basis of common ownership of the means of production and the best obtainable system of popular administration and control of each industry or service."

This clause remained part of the Labour Party programme, being given varying degrees of emphasis according to the speaker, the audience, and the circumstances. Labour's two short spells of office without power in 1924 and 1929–31 had given it no opportunity to implement the provision, which appeared again in its Election Manifesto in 1945. Yet when Labour found itself at last a strong Government it was in the strange position of finding that events had in some respects overtaken it. The enclaves of public ownership that had existed in such forms as local-authority water and gas supplies had spread and become larger; there were many forms of municipal socialism and many Public Utility Corporations. Water Boards, roads, sewage and cleansing works were publicly administered. Public Health was accepted as 'public'. Coal royalties—as opposed to the mines themselves—had been nationalized in 1938. The Post Office was a 'nationalized' concern, so was the BBC. The British Overseas Airways Corporation had been run as a public concern during the War, and still was. The London Passenger Transport Board, founded in 1931, was a successful example of near-nationalization, and the Central Electricity Board and the Port of London Authority were imbued with at least some of the ideas of public ownership.

Yet, though public control had in many directions unobtrusively supplanted private, there was nowhere the feeling that the battle for nationalization had been won, nor even that the issue had been decisively joined. The *mystique* which surrounded the term remained, and supporters of the Labour Party were emotionally committed to something they felt was not only wider in scope but different in essence from anything they saw around them. It was nationalization in their sense which, in the hands of a Labour Government, would demonstrably change the relationship of capital and labour, obliterate class distinctions, and raise the standard of living all round. Pledged to nationalization of this kind, the Labour Government had several possibilities open: to proceed further with the Public Utilities; to go for heavy industry and transport, vital to the country's economy; to nationalize the land, for long regarded as the ultimate source of wealth, one of the earliest candidates for nationalization and one which could still arouse impassioned partisanship; to nationalize the big consumer industries, which would be popular in giving the workers an end product easily handled and distinguished: "the mines for the miners" was a fair promise, but more immediately enticing would be the prospect of owning the cars and radio sets which their labour produced. In the event the Labour Government left the land alone, nor did it interfere with the private manufacture of consumer goods. Instead, it went for the public utilities, proposed to extend nationalization from the coal deposits to the mines, to integrate the transport system under a nationalized scheme, and also to thrust well into the capitalist camp by nationalizing the Iron and Steel Industry.

Besides arousing opposition among its opponents, whatever it did was bound to leave gaps, cause disappointment, evoke criticism, and generally fail to measure up to a good many expectations among its supporters. This was inevitable. The Labour Party had held to a doctrine in face of evolution and development for nearly thirty years, and was bound to find the key a little rusty in the lock when the opportunity came for opening the door. It was also bound to be blamed if equality and prosperity did not lie on the other side.

When the candidates for nationalization had been selected and the priorities had been determined there still remained questions of method and form. There were various ways in which nationalization could have been effected: the Labour Party had never made up its mind. It might have chosen a syndicalist form which involved control of the industry from below, built up by a series of committees from floor to management, or any of its variants such as Guild Socialism or Sovietism; but these the Party had consistently refused to advocate. When the actual Bills for nationalization came to be drafted there was no plan by which to shape them. Even the Minister of Fuel and Power in the Labour Government, who had been Parliamentary Secretary to the Department of Mines in the two preceding Labour Governments and who sat for a mining constituency, had done no preparatory work in nationalization and had no knowledge of any plans that had been drawn up. "For the whole of my political life", wrote Emanuel Shinwell, "I had listened to the Party speakers advocating State ownership and control of the coal mines, and I had myself spoken of it as a primary task once the Labour Party was in power. I had believed, as other members had, that in the party archives a blue print was ready. Now, as Minister of Fuel and Power, I found that nothing practical and tangible existed."[1]

When the opportunity came to act, time was short. Six nationalization measures were introduced and passed between 1945 and 1950. Pressure on Bill-drafters, on Ministers, their staffs and Parliamentary Secretaries, on the Cabinet, and on Parliament itself was severe. Before the first nationalization of industry Bill there were only four months of preparation. Bills consequently tended to be short, containing little detail, leaving much to be added in Committee. The mould for all became, in fact, the Public Corporation, an organization consisting of a Board with a chairman and members appointed by the appropriate Minister, to whom the Board was responsible and who was himself responsible to Parliament and people. The Board could institute a policy, but only with the approval of the Minister; in the last resort he could dictate policy to them. There were Joint Consultative Committees to bring together representatives of workers and management in each nationalized concern, but on policy the workers were to have little more influence than Workers' Committees under the old management. The Board had to submit its Report and Accounts each year to the Minister, and committees were appointed from time to time by Parliament to examine and report on the development of the concern. Such accountability is a minimum requirement for a public concern in a democracy and does not imply workers' control or a socialist policy: in the last resort it implies the policy of the Government of the day. Short-term control nevertheless belongs to the Board, whose constitution thus becomes very important. Workers and their organizations were represented on the Boards, and the intention was to appoint local men to the various Regional Boards and Committees. Many National Boards reported, however, that there was little enthusiasm among the workers to take on such appointments. A more clearly cut nationalization policy, more widely known, with draft plans drawn up and discussed over the years, particularly by the trade unions affected, would have made an enormous difference to the first years of nationalization. The War had cut across all such activity, but does not entirely explain the lack of a plan.

In the event it was not an industry but the Bank of England which took pride of place as the first subject of nationalization. High finance had long been regarded by the Labour Party as the power for evil behind the throne, and when the Chancellor of the Exchequer, Hugh Dalton, presented the Bill "to bring the capital stock of the Bank of England

[1] *Conflict Without Malice*, p. 172.

into public ownership and bring the bank under public control" the measure was symbolic to an extent which the outside world could hardly understand. Practically, as Dalton said in moving its second reading on October 29, 1945, the Bill merely legalized an actual situation. "The relations between the Bank of England and the Treasury have long been close, confidential, even intimate. . . . But this relationship has, until now, been factual rather than legal."[1] Churchill had already given the Bill his blessing in the Debate on the Address: "The national ownership of the Bank of England does not in my opinion", he said, "raise any matter of principle. . . . There are important examples in the United States and in our Dominions of central banking institutions."[2]

The Bill was short—"a streamlined Socialist Statute"—containing five clauses and three schedules, and was carried by 348 votes to 153. "We do not intend any day-to-day interference by the Government or the Treasury with the ordinary work of the Bank," Dalton promised; on matters of policy, however, the Treasury might give directions to the Bank after consultation with the Governor. The Directors of the Bank were to be reduced from twenty-four to sixteen, and on the Appointed Day the Governor, Deputy Governor, and Directors would all vacate their offices to make way for the new Governor and his Directors. The whole of the existing stock of the Bank of England was to be transferred to the Treasury and Government stock issued to shareholders in exchange. The change-over was effected with the utmost smoothness.

With this simple, though major, measure behind it, the Government turned to the nationalization of industry. In spite of the years of impassioned controversy which had gone before, the actual process of nationalization, when it came, was not so dramatic after all. As Churchill had taken the wind out of the sails of the nationalization of the Bank of England by remarking that there were central banking institutions in the United States and the Dominions, so the existence of public utilities and controls took the edge off many of the industrial nationalization measures. To only three of the Labour Government's nationalization proposals—Road Haulage, Iron and Steel, and (later) a suggestion relating to sugar—was the opposition more than ideological or more extensive than questions of compensation and personnel.

The British Overseas Airways Corporation had been run as a public concern since April 1, 1940. The British European Airways Corporation, with a mere 7000 employees, slipped easily into line with BOAC, and on August 1, 1946, was vested as a Public Corporation. The coal

---

[1] Hansard, fifth series, vol. 415, c. 47.   [2] Ibid., vol. 413, c. 94.

industry was a far vaster undertaking, with a recent history of depression and industrial unrest. But its very inefficiency reduced the opposition to its nationalization: Churchill had said as early as 1943 that the question was simply whether the State could make a better business of running the mines than private enterprise and competition.[1]

A Committee of mining engineers under the chairmanship of Charles Carlow Reid had been appointed in September 1944, even before the War was over, "to examine the present technique of coal production from face to wagon, and to advise what technical changes are necessary in order to bring the Industry to a state of full technical efficiency", and had reported in March 1945. Since the seven Committee members were all colliery directors or former colliery directors it was difficult not to accept their findings.

They reported that the industry was abysmally inefficient, they analysed the general causes of its low productivity, they showed the difficulties under which the mining engineer laboured, and they made drastic and far-reaching recommendations for technical changes. But, they said, they were forced to the conclusion that these technical changes, which they believed to be fully practicable, could not be carried through by the industry organized as it then was. Only a thorough reorganization on a coalfield basis by a full-time planning staff could hope to implement them.[2]

The Report of the Reid Committee was concise and lucid, and the competence and integrity of its members were beyond dispute. It was also one of the most readable of official Reports. In presenting the Labour Bill "to established public ownership and control of the coal-mining industry and certain allied activities" Emanuel Shinwell, Minister of Fuel and Power, Member of Parliament for the coal-mining area of Seaham, Durham, needed no better ally. When he rose on January 29, 1946, to propose the Bill's second reading his case for nationalization rested on the need for efficiency and for the wellbeing of the miners. The industry was backward compared with its Continental and other competitors; relations between owners and men were soured and embittered. Twenty years of effort, of Commissions, Committees, and attempted remedies—"I can hardly recall a Session of Parliament in that period without either a coal Debate or a coal crisis"—had resulted in failure. Why? Because no comprehensive method of reorganization was possible without cutting across a great mass of private interests and privileges. "In short," he said, "if this coal problem, which in magnitude

[1] Hansard, fifth series, vol. 392, c. 921.
[2] *Coal Mining: Report of the Technical Advisory Committee*, 1945 (the Reid Committee), Section XXV, p. 137: "The Conditions of Success".

transcends all other industrial problems, is to be solved, the Government . . . must prescribe the remedy which the Labour Movement has placed in the forefront of its programme for nearly half a century."[1]

There was emotion in the speeches of many of the Labour Members who followed. Labour organization and industrial struggle among the miners has a long history. It was coalminers who, in the depression following the Napoleonic wars, toured England with their coal-carts and the proud banner "Willing to work but none of us will beg". It was in the North-east, on the moors by Newcastle and at Black Fell, Durham, by Shinwell's own constituency, that Tommy Hepburn led his miners in the early eighteen-thirties to temporary victory. A century later miners had swelled the ranks of the hunger marchers coming from the North to Westminster to demand justice; it was miners who were the occasion in 1926 of the only General Strike the country had known.

Thomas Hubbard, from Kirkcaldy, spoke of the miners' leaders they all remembered—Arthur Cook, Herbert Smith, Tom Richardson, Tom Richards, "and Scotland's own leader, Bob Smillie".[2] Margaret Herbison, representing North Lanark, had known the miner's life from experience: "My father was a man who worked in the mines all his life, and whose body was racked, bruised and torn through that work, while my brother had his lung pierced by an accident caused by a runaway hatch. . . . The tragedy", she said, "is that these are only two of thousands."[3]

The Tory amendment which Victor Raikes moved on January 30 did not object to the Bill on principle, but raised questions of compensation, of immediate action to arrest the decline of the industry, restore the export trade, and recruit labour.[4] Anthony Eden denounced the Bill as a monopoly: "What this Bill proposes to do is to set up a State monopoly for the production of coal, and that is all"; it made no attempt to show how the mines would be run under the *aegis* of the State.[5] But the whole debate was remarkably mild, and the Bill was carried on January 30, 1946, by a majority of 359 votes to 182. It set up a National Coal Board of nine members appointed by the Minister—a public but semi-independent body with a limited responsibility to the Ministry of Fuel and Power. The country was divided into eight Regions, and compensation was paid to the mine-owners on the basis of "reasonable net maintainable revenue".

The nationalization of the mines was an extensive project; but the

---

[1] Hansard, fifth series, vol. 418, cc. 703–704.
[2] *Ibid.*, vol. 418, cc. 929–933.   [3] *Ibid.*, vol. 418, cc. 924–929.
[4] *Ibid.*, vol. 418, cc. 905–916.   [5] *Ibid.*, vol. 418, c. 718.

proposed nationalization of transport was "the largest and most extensive socialization Measure ever presented to a free democratic Parliament".[1] The Bill introduced in November 1946 and presented for its second reading by Alfred Barnes, the Minister of Transport, on December 16, 1946, provided for the nationalization of the railways, of canals, inland waterways, and Port Authorities, of London Transport and some road passenger and goods services. It was intended "to provide or promote an efficient, adequate, economical, and properly integrated system of public inland transport and port facilities within Great Britain for passengers and goods".[2] Compensation to private owners was to be paid on the basis of the market values of the relevant securities on the Stock Exchange at a specified date and amounted to over £1000 million, about seven times the price paid for the coalmines: it would be paid in British Transport stock issued by the Committee and backed by Government guarantee.

A British Transport Commission was to be responsible for the whole system, under which would be five Executive organizations—for railways; for ports, harbours, and inland waterways; for road passenger and goods services; for the London Passenger Transport Service, which, in many ways, with its bright stations, comfortable trains, and general efficiency, was a model; and for railway hotels and catering. No major Inquiry directly preceded the Bill, but Barnes drew on five major Acts of Parliament and twenty previous Inquiries which had been made. It was time for action, he said. The War had taken a heavy toll of the transport services, and a uniform and equitable distribution of the capital resources available for reconstruction was urgently needed. The Minister's sights were set high. He envisaged that integration would enable transport to be taken to sparsely served districts, that buses would link with trains, that railway-stations would be rebuilt to become Centres of Transport in a real sense, and that Britain would have "the most efficient, comfortable, speedy and cheap system of transport in the world".[3]

As with the Mines, the Transport Bill was in principle accepted by both sides of the House, though the Tories took the motion to a division, when it was carried by 362 votes to 204 on December 18, 1946. Two days later the Electricity Bill was presented by Mr Shinwell "to provide for the establishment of a British Electricity Authority and Area Electricity Boards", and the Town and Country Planning Bill by Mr

[1] Hansard, fifth series, vol. 431, c. 1617.
[2] *Ibid.*, vol. 431, c. 1623.
[3] *Ibid.*, vol. 431, cc. 1617 ff.

Silkin "to make fresh provision for planning the development and use of land".

The Electricity Bill came up for its second reading on February 3, 1947. The history of electricity supply was another example of haphazard growth and piecemeal legislation. At one time there had been no less than 635 Electricity Undertakings over the country; in London there were still 75 in 1947. The industry was governed by 243 Provisional and Special Orders and Acts of Parliament; tariffs and voltages differed from area to area, and often in adjoining districts; municipal and company undertakings had never come to terms. Whichever Government had been returned in 1945 would have had to impose some degree of order and rationalization upon the industry. Scotland alone showed some ordered development. In 1941 Thomas Johnstone, the devoted Secretary of State for Scotland in the Coalition Government, had appointed a Committee to consider the practicability of developing the water-power resources of Scotland for the generation of electricity. It was a scheme which would make work for areas which were losing their population besides bringing the great boon of electricity to small townships and scattered homesteads. It was a great tribute to a country at war that in February 1943 it had passed the Hydro-electric Development (Scotland) Act which established a Hydro-electric Board for the North of Scotland.

The Bill before the House in 1947 proposed to establish a British Electricity Authority with full responsibility for generating electricity and selling it in bulk. Local distribution would be in the hands of fourteen area boards, Scotland would still be served by the Scottish Hydro-electric Board, whose jurisdiction was extended to include some 22,000 square miles north and west of a line from the Firth of Tay to the Firth of Clyde—about three-quarters of the total area of Scotland. Again the measure raised only a token opposition and took 165 Conservatives into the lobby against it on February 4, 1947, rather as a gesture against the Labour Government than from real opposition to the Bill.[1]

A similar pattern was proposed for the reorganization of the Gas Industry. On January 21, 1948, the Bill "to provide for the establishment of Area Gas Boards and a Gas Council" was presented by Hugh Gaitskell, who had succeeded Shinwell as Minister of Fuel and Power. It was given its second reading on February 11 by 354 votes to 179. Gas supply, like Electricity, was complicated, disintegrated, inefficient, and controlled by a legislative framework that was a major obstacle to

[1] *Ibid.*, vol. 432, cc. 1404 ff.

improvement. All Reports agreed on the desirability for larger areas of administration and for greater integration, and Gaitskell claimed that the most suitable structure for the industry would be found under public ownership.[1]

The major conflict came with the presentation of the Iron and Steel Bill "to provide for the establishment of an Iron and Steel Corporation of Great Britain and for defining their functions", presented on October 27, 1948, and brought up for second reading on November 15. A Public Opinion poll had found a majority against the Bill, and opposition was strong and well organized. The industry's close and often interlocking connections with engineering concerns of all kinds, its vital importance to almost every other industry in the country, its high contribution, not only itself but through other industries, to the export trade (the steel and the steel-using industries accounted for nearly half the value of Britain's exports), made it not only vital to economic development but immensely rich and powerful. Governments since the mid-thirties had tried various ways of exercising some control over it, and the Labour Government had already set up a Steel Board in 1946 to maintain war-time price controls and supervise plans for expansion. But nationalization was another matter. No case could be made out on grounds of inefficiency nor of price: the British Steel Industry was not inefficient, and its prices were lower than those in most other countries. The Labour Government could speak of development schemes, but there was no reason to suppose that private ownership had not schemes also. Nor was there a long history of labour troubles in the industry. On the contrary, no serious strike had affected it for fifty years. Moreover, the process of nationalization would be very difficult because of the ramifications of the industry. In presenting their Bill the Government had to prepare for a very different fight from the resistance which the more inefficient industries had marshalled.

George Strauss, the Minister of Supply, in moving the second reading of the Bill to nationalize the Iron and Steel Industry accused the steel magnates of bungling pre-War plans for improvement—"the industry was torn with conflicts between producers, the banks, and the Government"—and of delaying or killing schemes which might have saved Jarrow and other towns from the worst of their depression. He taunted them with wanting private ownership tempered by State control and supported by subsidies and price controls—a vital, State-protected monopoly with immense influence all over industry. But by and large

[1] Hansard, fifth series, vol. 447, cc. 218 ff.

his case rested on the fundamental differences between the Government and the iron and steel magnates. "In our view", he said, "it would be madness for a Government determined to build the nation's future prosperity on sound economic foundations to perpetuate in this basic industry a system in which serious clashes on matters of major policy between private and public interests are bound sooner or later to arise, possibly with the gravest consequences. . . . We say in short that the iron and steel industry shall no longer be distracted by two loyalties."[1] Sir Stafford Cripps put the same point less emotionally when he said, later in the debate: "in the light of the historical development of the industry in this country, I believe that it is generally accepted that a large degree of cartelisation or monopoly of control is required in the iron and steel industry . . . we have to decide whether such a large measure of industrial control by private interests is consistent with present-day democratic government. When a private monopoly control reaches the magnitude of that in the iron and steel industry, and thereby the power to influence the strategic requirements of the State and the interests of a large proportion of our main industries, it is not right, in my view, that it should be perpetuated . . . the time has come when the size, importance and structure of the steel industry demands the change from private to public monopoly control." Reinforcing this argument, "now we are seeking", he said, "to have some measure of foresight in our economic activities, we must be able, so far as certain basic matters are concerned, to plan ahead for production . . . we must be able to plan this most important of our economic activities ahead. . . . We cannot allow the steel industry to determine, from the point of view of nothing but its own profitability, the limits of its own expansion."[2]

The Bill proposed to set up an Iron and Steel Corporation of Great Britain, which would own all the securities of the major concerns at the core of the industry. Since some demarcation had to be made, the concerns taken over would be all those that on the average of the years 1946 and 1947 produced more than 50,000 tons of iron ore, more than 20,000 tons of pig iron, or 20,000 tons of ingot steel, including alloy steel, and shaped more than 20,000 tons of steel by hot rolling: this would bring in the larger part of the industry, responsible for 90 to 100 per cent of its basic products. Compensation to private owners would be based on the purchase of securities at Stock Exchange valuation,[3] and would amount to about £243 million.[4]

[1] November 15, 1948 (*ibid.*, vol. 458, c. 57).
[2] *Ibid.*, vol. 458, cc. 319, 321.
[3] Strauss (*ibid.*, vol. 458, c. 69).   [4] Cripps, *ibid.*, vol. 458, c. 311.

Their opponents retorted that the Government had made out no case for nationalization; "the issue to-day is not whether the steel industry met with fair or unfair competition in the 'twenties or 'thirties, or whether it was then efficient or inefficient, but whether there is a case for nationalization to-day, and I say that the Minister made out no semblance of a case", said Oliver Lyttelton. Nor had he proposed any plan of any kind for running the industry. On the contrary, the arbitrary selection of firms for nationalization would create difficulties and confusion. In general, most speakers for the Opposition accepted the Government's view that the case for nationalization rested largely on grounds of policy, and Oliver Lyttelton quoted Mr Cocks: "Once we have nationalized steel, we shall have broken the back of capitalist control of industry in this country". "Let us agree", said Mr Lyttelton, "that, if the nationalization of steel is carried out, a revolution, not evolution, will have taken place, and that revolution at the end of a Parliament."[1]

The Bill was carried on November 17, 1948, by 373 votes to 211, and was in fact one of the last Acts of the Administration and the last nationalization measure to be proposed in the British Parliament for twenty years: and then the issue would be a *re*nationalization measure.

Nationalization, it has been said, was a political and economic revolution, forced through after a generation of waiting.[2] There had been a generation—and more—of waiting, but both the election results of 1945 and the debates in the House of Commons override any suggestion that the nationalization measures were 'forced through'. The myth that they involved "a political and economic revolution" is disposed of on several grounds: the industries concerned (with the exception of iron and steel) were either semi-derelict or in urgent need of such reorganization as could come only from a central authority with large resources to back it; they were all natural monopolies amenable to the advantages of large-scale operation; they were either public services or approximating to such; their public control was in step with a world-wide movement and one which, in Britain itself, was already well established. Banking and insurance all over the world, big power projects like the Tennessee Valley Authority in the U.S.A., the Volta River scheme in Ghana, the Panama Canal Company, the Aswan Dam on the Nile, the Kariba Dam on the Zambezi, afforestation schemes, flood-control, navigation improvement, agricultural development, railways in Europe, America,

[1] Hansard, fifth series, vol. 458, cc. 79–81, *passim*.
[2] R. Kelf-Cohen, *Nationalisation in Britain*.

Canada, Australia—schemes which started before or after and continued at the same time as the British nationalization undertakings—put Britain in the main flood of development, not in any revolutionary situation. For the Labour Party and for their opponents this was a paradox that changed the whole political scene. Who had stolen whose thunder was difficult to determine, but, with the exception of iron and steel, it was unlikely that much party political capital could ever again be made out of the issue of nationalization.

While pressing with unexampled speed its series of nationalization measures through the House the Labour Government was never able to relax its grip on day-to-day issues—how far to loosen war-time controls while still directing resources to essential work; how to build up a favourable balance of trade while preventing the export of goods and materials vital to the home economy; how to mine more coal, produce more power; how to expand production all round while holding back the dammed-up demand for consumer goods until capital and export priorities had been met. In spite of considerable all-round progress the position at the beginning of 1947 was still dangerous. Any external event was liable to throw the machinery of recovery off balance, and the failure of European crops in 1947 was a major catastrophe that increased British as well as European dependence upon America, prolonging rationing and 'making do' at all levels of life. It was difficult for the population to accept austerity in peace as it had done in war, yet the personal example of the lean, ascetic Stafford Cripps, a man with a sense of vocation, first at the Board of Trade, rationing and allocating, and then at the Exchequer, denying money here, refusing it there, frequently at the microphone explaining to a weary population that it could not have its cake and eat it too, epitomized these lean years of peace.

Fortunately American opinion had by this time accepted the fact that European disequilibrium after the War would take more than a few years to level out. General Marshall, the American Secretary of State, speaking at Harvard on June 5, 1947, expressed the view that the "rehabilitation of the economic structure of Europe quite evidently will require a much longer time and greater effort than has been foreseen. .... The truth of the matter is that Europe's requirements for the next three or four years of ... essential products—principally from America— are so much greater than her present ability to pay that she must have substantial additional help". He looked ahead to 1952 as a possible date for establishing equilibrium, and spoke of American dollar aid to all countries who would submit plans for production and trade. In a subsequent clarification of the Harvard speech he mentioned $5000 million or $6000 million a year for several years.

The Marshall Plan was approved by Congress in April 1948 as the Economic Co-operation Act. Its purpose was "to promote world peace and the general welfare, national interest, and foreign policy of the United States through economic, financial, and other measures necessary to the maintenance of conditions abroad on which free institutions may survive and consistent with the maintenance of the strength and stability of the United States". In return for American dollar aid participating countries were to pledge themselves to increase production, to establish monetary stability, and to co-operate with other countries in reducing trade barriers. The Economic Recovery Programme thus launched originally contemplated aid to the extent of about $17,000 million over four years, but the Act as passed provided for appropriations on a yearly basis. The sum of over $5000 million was authorized for the first year, and by the end of 1948 European plans for mutual aid and increased trade were in operation, and boom conditions were already succeeding the depression of the previous years. Britain shared in the general European recovery, and by the end of 1948 her economy was freed of most of the war-time controls on raw materials and commodities. Clothing came off ration in March 1949, petrol in May 1950, and soap in September 1950. Food-rationing stayed longest. Meat, bacon, fats, cheese, eggs, tea, were still on ration at the end of 1950, while an attempt in 1949 to deration sweets and chocolate was not successful and controls were reimposed. Petrol had its own special difficulties, and a Committee under Mr Russell Vick was appointed to investigate the extent of the black market and to suggest remedies.

"It is the duty of any democratic Government to take the people frankly into its confidence, however difficult the position of the country may be," Attlee wrote in 1947,[1] and the *Economic Surveys* which the Government published annually from 1947 onwards were directed to this end. The *Economic Survey* for 1951 was able to claim that by the end of 1950 "the immediate task of post-War recovery was completed".[2] In spite of vicissitudes the general trend from 1945 to 1950 had been upward, employment, industrial production, personal expenditure, volume of exports, and volume of imports having all substantially increased. In 1950 the balance of payments was in surplus, by the end of the year the United Kingdom was solvent,[3] and the Government consequently agreed to the suspension of Marshall Aid from January 1,

[1] *Economic Survey for 1947*, Foreword.   [2] P. 3.
[3] Worswick and Ady, *op. cit.*, pp. 1–2.

1951. While expressing gratitude to America and the Commonwealth it did not forget Britain: "the people of this country should look back on the record of the past five years with some pride. By a steady and sustained effort, by restraint and sacrifice, they had achieved a great and rapid recovery from the effects of war, and achieved it faster than most would have dared to hope."[1] They had also nationalized various undertakings and laid the foundations of the Welfare State in social matters.[2]

The issue now became one of going further with nationalization or of denationalizing the two controversial industries—road haulage and iron and steel—while paring down some of the existing social-service benefits. When, thinking ahead to the end of its five-year term and to the next election, the Labour Party produced in January 1950 *Let Us Win Through Together* it proposed the nationalization of industrial insurance, of the cement industry, of sugar-refining and -manufacturing, of meat distribution, of the water supply. But no-one regarded these issues as vital, and the manifesto displayed none of the practical immediacy that had characterized *Let Us Face the Future*. As Hugh Dalton wrote later: "This list adds up to quite a substantial increase of the public sector. It was the residue of a much longer list of 'possibles' which had been worked over by our National Executive and its Policy Committee. . . . All these items, I think, had more strong opponents than strong supporters. All probably, therefore, lost us votes. None had been the subject of serious or prolonged propaganda. Some antagonised or . . . frightened or alienated the workers concerned. None were persuasively propounded by the general body of Labour candidates."[3]

The Tories published *This Is the Road* a week later. It welcomed the Welfare State, thus identifying itself with the best of the social measures that had been passed and warranting the *Manchester Guardian*'s description of its policy as "Tory Socialism", but it also pledged the party to the de-nationalization of the Iron and Steel Industry and of road haulage.[4] The Tories had been building up their electioneering machinery during the previous five years, the idealistic enthusiasm for Labour had been partly spent, and the Tories had a further ally in a simple little person—Mr Cube. Mr Cube was the creation of the sugar-refiners, their answer to Labour's announced intention of nationalizing the sugar industry. He appeared on hoardings, in newspapers, on packets of sugar—a jolly little man who insisted he was better off, and that the public would be better off, if they left the sugar industry well alone.

[1] *Economic Survey for 1951*, p. 4.   [2] See Chapters III, IV.
[3] *High Tide and After*, being vol. 3 of his memoirs, p. 339.
[4] *Infra*, pp. 131–132.

It was natural that the post-War crises should have told against the sitting Government. Inevitably the progress in reconstruction, particularly in house-building,[1] had been less rapid than people had expected. The austerities that remained were resented. As they had voted against the man who led them to victory in the War, so the electorate began to swing away from the party who had successfully led them in five years of reconstruction following it. After the Election of February 1950 Labour's strength in the House of Commons was only five more than that of all the other parties combined and its voting strength in the country less. It was not sufficient for effective government. Outside conditions continued to be precarious. In the middle of 1950 the United States announced support for the South Korean Government in its war with North Korea and the stockpiling of tin, rubber, wool, and other commodities began, sending prices soaring. Trade boomed in the U.S.A. and in Europe, but rising prices set the terms of trade against Britain. The total import bill for 1951 was over £1100 million higher than in the previous year,[2] and her deficit with the non-sterling world alone amounted to £760 million, of which £600 million fell in the second half of the year.[3] In addition, Britain herself had felt bound to embark on a new and costly defence programme, while inflation brought demands for wage and salary increases to the tune of £765 million between 1950 and 1951, an increase of 11 per cent.[4] At this same time, in the middle of 1951, the Government of Persia took over the Anglo-Iranian Oil Company at Abadan, in which £350 million of British capital was sunk and which had supplied one-quarter of Britain's crude oil supplies the previous year. Alternative supplies were necessary, in spite of a temporary reimposition of petrol-rationing at home, but cost dollars. With prices rising everywhere, expenditure at home was mounting rapidly in all directions, and the Exchequer was faced with heavy deficits.

A Government with a substantial majority could have weathered the storm. But the Labour Government's position was too precarious. On September 19, 1951, Attlee, having tendered the resignation of the second post-War Labour Government, announced a General Election on October 25. This time the Tories had a majority of 17 over all others, though barely as many votes as the Labour Party, and Churchill again became Prime Minister. With the Tories back in office it would seem in some respects that the wheel had come full circle. But there were many differences. The Labour Party, and not the Liberals, were

---

[1] See *infra*, p. 231.   [2] *Economic Survey for 1952*, p. 8.   [3] *Ibid.*, p. 7.
[4] *Ibid.*, p. 41. Taking all personal incomes together, the increase was of the order of £900 million.

established as His Majesty's Opposition, rising prosperity was of a different order—stretching further, penetrating more deeply—than ever before, and the society over which the new Government was exercising its rule was blessed with an extent of social service never before known. It had been the inauguration of this social service which had been the Labour Government's biggest contribution to the wellbeing of the country. Though its impetus was now spent, nothing could detract from the achievements—nor the glory—of "the five shining years" in which the shattered economy was rebuilt, the idle wheels set turning, State control accepted, and a new conception of social service built into the machinery of State. It was an achievement for which all parties and all the nation bore credit. But there was a flame burning within the Labour Party in those years, compounded of the struggles and the sufferings of generations of working men and women, that made the achievement peculiarly its own.

PART TWO

INTO AFFLUENCE

"The problems of an affluent world, which does not understand itself, may be serious, and they can needlessly threaten the affluence itself. But they are not likely to be as serious as those of a poor world where the simple exigencies of poverty preclude the luxury of misunderstanding but where, also and alas, no solutions are to be had."

John Kenneth Galbraith,
The Affluent Society

CHAPTER VI

The Expanding Economy

"Why should we not aim to double our standard of living in the next twenty-five years?"

R. A. Butler, Chancellor of the Exchequer,
October 1954

THE CONSERVATIVE Government took over at a time of temporary crisis, which showed itself in an adverse balance of trade for 1951 of £521 million. Exports were hampered by a fall in world demand for British textile and other consumer goods and for her shipping services. Interest had to be paid on the Canadian and American loans, Britain had to pay for rearming herself after the Korean crisis. Yet essential capital goods had to be replaced and restored, and home consumer demand was straining at the leash. The Government acted by raising Bank rate from 2 to 2½ per cent, the first change for nearly twenty years, apart from a short rise to 4 per cent at the beginning of the War; by cutting imports, mainly of unrationed food but also of tobacco and raw materials; by forgoing a planned increase of rationed foods; by reducing the foreign travel allowance from £100 to £50 and, in January 1952, to £25. The measures were unpopular, spelling a continued dwelling with austerity, but within two years the buoyancy of the economy was restored, the cuts were made good, and 1954 was a year of all-round expansion. Thereafter British and European recovery went hand in hand.

By 1953 Europe had licked her war wounds and, helped by the American Aid programmes, was busy with the occupations of peace. Like Britain, she had much to make up in terms of rebuilding and re-equipment as well as of mouths to feed and backs to clothe. But in Europe, as in Britain and America, the techniques and materials developed during the War were there to be used, and labour was waiting to be employed. With work went wages, with wages went spending power; the more there

4+

was to spend the faster turned the wheels of industry. European recovery stimulated Britain. In the immediate post-War years she had been tied to the U.S.A. by loans and through the dependence of sterling upon the dollar; now she looked to Europe as market, as source of supply, and as competitor. By the middle of 1954 Britain had taken off or relaxed most of her war-time controls of industry, production had risen by nearly 10 per cent since 1952, private saving was increasing and investment developing on a considerable scale.[1] At the same time the retail-price rise was slowing down and dollar reserves were satisfactory.

For years priority had been given to goods for export and to capital construction; now the home consumer had an ever-growing market to choose from. "Why should we not aim to double our standard of living in the next twenty-five years?" asked R. A. Butler, Chancellor of the Exchequer, in October 1954.[2] And the population was determined to try. When the primary need for food and clothes had been satisfied the demand for consumer durables grew—for washing-machines, television sets, vacuum cleaners, furniture and furnishings of all kinds, for refrigerators, motor-cars. In this atmosphere the Tories were returned at the General Election of 1955 with a majority of a hundred and nearly a million more votes than the Labour Members. By this time the economy was so stretched that the Chancellor, as a measure of restraint, raised Bank rate to $4\frac{1}{2}$ per cent, thus introducing a "new policy of economic regulation without direct controls".[3] In February 1956 the rate was raised to $5\frac{1}{2}$ per cent, and in March the Government issued a White Paper, *Economic Implications of Full Employment*,[4] while the new Chancellor, Harold Macmillan, introduced Premium Bonds in his April Budget to encourage people to save rather than to spend.[5] Unemployment at this time was only about 1 per cent of the insured population, having most of the time since 1945 been under 2 per cent. But while since 1946 the national output of goods and services of all kinds had risen by 30 per cent their prices had increased by 50 per cent.[6] There was danger here beyond the immediate effect upon the cost of living.

Cycles of prosperity, like cycles of depression, are self-generating.

---

[1] Capital formation in all industries between 1953 and 1956 rose by 16 per cent, in transport and communications by 26 per cent, in mining and quarrying by 32 per cent, in manufacture generally by 32 per cent, in distribution and other services by 58 per cent (*National Income and Expenditure*, 1960, p. 53; G. D. N. Worswick and P. H. Ady, *The British Economy in the Nineteen-fifties*, p. 31).

[2] At the Conservative Party Conference at Blackpool.

[3] Worswick and Ady, *op. cit.*, p. 33.   [4] Cmd. 9725, March 1956.

[5] The bonds yield no interest, but a monthly raffle allots money prizes to those whose numbers are drawn.

[6] *Economic Implications of Full Employment*.

Before the War too few goods were being chased by too low prices, the goods became fewer, the prices, including incomes, became lower, until the chase ground to a standstill. When the post-War difficulties had been surmounted prices of all kinds started to rise, and kept up such a pursuit that increasing production was never sufficient to satisfy them. In full employment most sections of the community are in a strong position to bargain for wage increases, and as the market produced more goods that they wanted to buy people forced up prices on the one hand by higher spending and on the other demanded higher incomes to keep up with prices. The price rise was reflected not only in goods, wages, salaries, and interest rates but in the increasing cost of the welfare services and in pressure for higher pensions, sickness and unemployment benefits, and larger family allowances. Not only were incomes higher, but the benefits conferred by the Welfare State left more to spend on immediate consumption, required less to be saved against calamity. As prices continued to rise and incomes to rise even faster Mr Thorneycroft, the Chancellor of the Exchequer, issued a warning: "If an attempt were made to take out of the system in money income more than is put in by new efforts and products, the only result would be a reduction in activity and the employment of fewer men."[1]

There was a temporary setback in November 1956 when the "Suez crisis" resulted in the closing of the Canal to British ships for three months and the closure of the Iraq oil line across Syria. Goods normally travelling through the Canal were routed round the Cape, and Britain had to buy oil for dollars and impose a rationing scheme for consumers; but the weather was mild, and the chief setback internally was to the motor-car manufacturers, for purchasers held back while rationing continued. Externally, however, the purchase of oil for dollars and a panic run against sterling caused a severe fall in dollar and gold reserves. Unaffected, the incomes-and-prices spiral continued to rise in the early months of 1957, but a further fall in dollars and gold and a flight from the pound brought restrictive measures in September, with Bank rate reaching an unprecedented 7 per cent, public investment programmes reduced, and overseas credit tightened. This particular crisis was surmounted like the others, but the same forces were still at work within the economy.

The annual average wage per head of those employed, including salaried workers, had increased by 6½ per cent between 1948 and 1958; it rose by a further 3 per cent in 1958 and a further 3½ per cent in 1959.

[1] At the International Monetary Fund meeting in Washington, September 1957. Reported in *The Economist*, September 28, 1957.

One aspect of these increases was the rise in the hire-purchase debt, a high proportion of which is attributable to the personal sector. Even the bigger pay packets taken home each week could not immediately procure all the consumer goods that increasing prosperity made possible, and, in spite of periodic restriction, hire-purchase agreements had been entered into on a scale hitherto unknown, the amount outstanding growing from £556 million in 1958 to £935 million in 1960.[1] Earnings were up again in 1960, imports rising, shortages of labour developing, and there was a general pressure on resources of all kinds. The Bank rate, which had been reduced when the "Suez crisis" was over, was again raised, first to 5 per cent and then to 6 per cent, and taxation was increased. Some incomes were in this way diverted from spending to saving, and the rise in consumption was slightly stemmed, but the position was not held for long. The Budget of 1961 raised profits tax and increased indirect taxation, but higher prices were seriously affecting the balance of payments, and on July 25 emergency measures were announced. Bank rate was raised to 7 per cent, credit restricted, and a pay pause instituted that was intended to postpone wage and salary increases until the crisis was over.

The pay pause was a difficult concept to hold in face of rising prices and labour scarcity, and, with the situation a little easier, in January 1962 the Government agreed with the trade unions that it should end on March 31 1962. At the same time a White Paper on Incomes Policy[2] expressed the view that increases in incomes in 1962 should not exceed $2\frac{1}{2}$ per cent, which was the probable amount of the increase in national production per head. A National Economic Development Council, consisting of representatives of the Government, of management, and of the trade unions, was at the same time established to secure better economic performance. "Neddy" had its first meeting in March 1962, and the following February issued its first Report, a forward-looking appraisement of the economy as a whole which postulated an increase in the growth of national production from $2\frac{1}{2}$ per cent to an average annual rate of 4 per cent between 1961 and 1966.[3] Two months later *Conditions Favourable to Further Growth* pinpointed certain directions in which growth could be encouraged—by education, including adult education, by scientific and technical training and research, management training and the establishment of business schools; by a recognized policy for encouraging labour mobility and, related to this, plans

---

[1] *Annual Abstract of Statistics*, 1964, Table 356, p. 307; and see *infra*, Appendix B XIII(*e*).

[2] *Incomes Policy: The Next Step*, February 1962, Cmnd. 1626.

[3] *Growth of the United Kingdom Economy 1961 to 1966*, February 1963.

for regional development. At the same time the Council emphasized the grave disadvantages to the economy of alternate expansion and restriction, and urged that the only real solution to Britain's difficulties lay in a reduction of the rate of increase of costs and prices.

This was the more important since Britain in the post-War world was no longer in the monopoly position she had enjoyed a century earlier, and would never be able to restore that situation. No longer was she industrially ahead of other nations, exporting widely her manufactured products and her natural resources. She faced a similarly industrialized world where it was a combination of cheapness, quality, and efficient marketing which booked the orders. She was, moreover, provided with few of the raw materials of the new age. Oil was now the leading international source of power, and while British coal exports dropped to a fraction of their former size, the import of crude petroleum and lubricants was her largest item by value. At the same time, in spite of a highly organized home agriculture, she was still dependent on outside sources of food to the extent of about 32 per cent of her total imports by value. She was the world's largest importer of wheat, meat, butter, tea, citrus fruits, and imported about half of her total food supplies. Moreover, in a world now closely and easily knit together by modern transport and communications, the United Kingdom was revealed as a very small part of the whole. Her links with her former Empire, expressed economically by preferential trading agreements within the Commonwealth, only partly redressed the balance.

In shipping services, banking, and insurance Britain likewise faced competition where she had been leader. But one factor was still of prime importance—her currency, sterling, still stood, with the dollar and gold, as a world international currency with a fixed relation to the dollar. This relationship was fixed after the War by members of the International Monetary Fund, the pound then representing $4.03; but in 1949 devaluation by the Labour Government brought it to the equivalent of $2·80. As well as being freely accepted all over the world, sterling is of special significance to the countries belonging to the sterling area, whose currencies maintain a fixed relationship with sterling and whose foreign reserves are kept mainly in sterling. These consist of the Commonwealth and of many developing and newly developed countries who find it convenient to bank in London. To Britain there are advantages of bankers' business as well as prestige, but the price is a greater vulnerability.

The direction of Britain's trade was also changing. Canada, Australia, and New Zealand remained very important, particularly for the import of food. India and the U.S.A. also remained her close trading partners. At the same time British trade with Western Europe was growing fast; trade with Latin America, Eastern Europe, and the U.S.S.R. was small, but growing; trade ties with the Middle East, because of oil supplies, were close; and, on the whole, there was a fall in the amount of trade done with the Commonwealth and with the sterling area.

Britain still paid for her imports largely by the export of manufactured goods—but always in the face of keen competition. Engineering products were the most important exports, and included machinery, electrical equipment, road vehicles, tractors, scientific instruments; chemical exports were also valuable, and the 'invisible' items on the balance sheet, though smaller than they had been, were still important. But it was a situation which was bound to be precarious and in which balance-of-trade difficulties were bound to arise, largely because it left Britain vulnerable to overseas competition, vulnerable to her own inflation.

When Britain looked across the Channel she saw that Western Europe as a whole was in many ways managing its economy more effectively. Europe had been quick to realize that post-War recovery depended upon economic co-operation, and the Organization for European Economic Co-operation (OEEC) had been founded in 1948 for co-operation in the distribution of Marshall Aid and for liberalizing trade. The European Coal and Steel Community, based on the Schuman Plan, led to the European Economic Community (EEC), founded in 1958 on the basis of the Common Market Treaty ratified in Rome the previous year. There were six Common Market countries—France, Germany, Italy, Holland, Belgium, Luxembourg—but the door was open for others to join them. Their object, laid down in the Treaty of Rome, was the reduction and eventual abolition of tariffs and trade restrictions, a common external tariff, and a much freer flow of capital, enterprise, and labour between the member countries. In 1956 Britain had considered joining the Six, but negotiations broke down partly because she wished to exclude agriculture from the agreement, partly because, although she would agree to free trade within the Common Market area, she wished to maintain freedom for each member to decide its own external tariffs. Three years later Britain signed a treaty at Stockholm with Sweden, Norway, Denmark, Austria, Portugal, and Switzerland which established the European Free Trade Association (EFTA), the members of which benefited from reciprocal tariff reductions without losing their rights to establish individual tariffs against outsiders.

Britain, for various reasons related chiefly to her agriculture and her relationship to the Commonwealth, made no further approaches to the European Economic Community until July 1961, when the idea of entry into the Common Market was developed by Harold Macmillan, the Tory Prime Minister. Although not carrying all his party with him, he built up the idea of unity with Europe into a crusade that would further political as well as economic integration. All parties, the professional economists, businessmen, and the country as a whole were deeply divided throughout the whole course of negotiations, which lasted for eighteen months. Macmillan issued a statement explaining his Government's reasons for negotiation: "We knew that such an unprecedented departure from the past was bound to cause genuine anxieties and fears, both at home and in the Commonwealth." Yet the economic ties that bound Britain to the Commonwealth were becoming less strong than those which called from Europe. She was bound to the Commonwealth as to "a flexible grouping of independent nations"; but the people of Britain remained Europeans. By joining the new European Community, "bringing together the manpower, the material resources, and the inventive skills of some of the most advanced countries in the world", Britain would also be part of a new organization rapidly developing the capacity to stand on an equal footing with the great power groupings of the world. Macmillan believed the Common Market had been a powerful stimulus to the economic growth of Europe since the War, and while joining would mean some radical changes in the development of British industry and commerce, it would at the same time give Britain access to a rapidly developing market of some 170 million people. Staying out, on the other hand, would also entail some rethinking. The people of Britain must in either case "make a great effort as pioneers and leaders of the new revolutionary processes such as electronics, automatic equipment, computers, miniaturization and supersonic flight".[1]

The Labour Party was split. Its leader, Hugh Gaitskell, declared that the economic arguments were nicely balanced, but that the terms Britain was likely to get would not be good enough to warrant her joining, while politically she would suffer through loosening ties with the Commonwealth. By October 1962 he was demanding a plebiscite on the question of entry or non-entry, and the Labour Party's opposition was hardening. The Liberals approved, as a general principle, the reduction of any inter-state barriers, but, like the Labour Party, were concerned that the terms should not be to the country's disadvantage.

By the middle of October it was clear that Macmillan had carried his

[1] *The Common Market* (Conservative Central Office), October 8, 1962.

party with him, the Conservative Party Conference at Llandudno giving an overwhelming vote in favour of negotiation with the Common Market countries. But economists and industrialists continued to be worried and uncertain. "The challenge will mean increased efficiency and high investment. If we do not join, the future of sterling will be bleak," said one economist.[1] Others feared that Britain would soon be discriminating in favour of European agriculture at the expense of the Commonwealth.[2] Some businessmen welcomed the shake-up that direct competition would give, and were confident that breaking down trade barriers would offer them a wider European market. Others feared a long period of adjustment, with falling markets for British goods and higher prices for imported European goods. Some would welcome, others feared, a common external Common Market tariff. Workmen were similarly divided, some afraid of falling wages and unemployment, others believing there would be more jobs, wider choice, and higher pay if the European Economic Community were open to Britain.

Over the country as a whole some people welcomed any policy that advanced European unity as a step towards closer world co-operation; others considered it would disrupt the Commonwealth, which was making its own special contribution to world harmony; and there were fears that joining Europe would sap the country's independence, rob it of initiative, and even deny it freedom of action in political matters. The Commonwealth itself was worried, and throughout the Common Market discussions the question of how far increased trade with Europe would affect British imports of dairy produce from New Zealand and Australia remained a burning question. A meeting of Commonwealth Prime Ministers in London in September 1962, while examining the situation warily, decided that final judgment could be made only when the full terms of admission were known. About the same time an economist summed up the position by saying, "What we know suggests that the gain will be small, but there is so much we don't know that it is a case of 'your guess is as good as mine'."[3]

But, while the country was locked in argument, at the conference table in Brussels Britain's chief negotiator, Edward Heath,[4] was having a difficult time: whether for or against entry into the Common Market there was agreement that Britain could go in only on terms that were favourable to her. There were difficulties, one after another, particularly

---

[1] Professor Brinley Thomas in *The Observer*, October 14, 1962.
[2] *E.g.*, Professor E. F. Nash, *idem*.
[3] Professor R. G. Lipsey, *idem*.
[4] Lord Privy Seal with Foreign Office Responsibilities.

on agricultural questions. Repeatedly Heath returned to London, went back to Brussels, went over points again and again with his economic advisers. The feeling began to grow in Britain that, whatever the merits of the case, the Six were insisting upon very hard terms. The final session in Brussels was difficult, exhausting. The prestige of France and the personal influence of President de Gaulle gave her great power in the councils of the Six, and she was clearly in favour of breaking off negotiations. The other five wished to continue. But France refused to accept their proposal, they yielded, and on January 29, 1963, the President of the Assembly informed Heath that negotiations were at an end.[1] There were many in the United Kingdom, whatever position they had taken up, who breathed a sigh of relief that at last it was all over and Britain had only her own familiar house to keep in order. This promised, however, to be no easy task.

Not only were incomes, costs, and prices rising throughout 1962, but before the year was out extraneous factors began to operate, and by Christmas the snow and ice of one of the coldest winters Britain had known set in over most of the country, bringing building and all outside work to a standstill. By the end of the year 600,000 people in the United Kingdom were without jobs. In January 1963 the total unemployment figure rose to 860,000, in February to well over 900,000.[2] Nothing like it had been known since the War. The pinched and anxious faces of the people affected, their convergence upon London, the passionate meetings in Hyde Park, were all too familiar to those whose memories stretched beyond the War. Fear of a major breakdown was widespread. But the Government lowered the Bank rate, the weather improved, and from March 1963 the unemployment figures began to decline. The economic regulation of the economy without direct controls had again appeared to work—this time as an aid to expansion—in spite of "Neddy's" strictures.

The most severe unemployment had been in the North of England, in Scotland, and in Wales, and the Government had extended the duties of the President of the Board of Trade to cover Regional Development as well as Industry and Trade. It also set on foot inquiries into the regions affected, as well as into the South-eastern region, whose growth and prosperity was out of proportion to that of other parts of the country. The Budget of 1963 took as its keynote expansion without

[1] See Hansard, January 30, 1963, fifth series, vol. 670, cc. 941–943, for Heath's own account of the final breakdown of the negotiations.
[2] *Monthly Digest of Statistics.*

CHAPTER VII

Crisis

"A new Labour Government; a new Ministry of Economic Affairs; but the old problem. The continued need to right the balance of payments and to combine this with steady non-inflationary growth is the link between new administration and old."

The Times Annual Financial and Commercial Review, October 26, 1964

In the autumn of 1964 the Tories, who had remained continuously in power through three General Elections, went to the country with thirteen years of unbroken office behind them. Churchill had resigned the Premiership in April 1955: "He gave a leadership to this country when it needed it most, and in history, as one of the greatest of all Prime Ministers, his place is assured," Attlee had said in tribute in the House of Commons.[1] He had been succeeded by Anthony Eden, who resigned through illness in January 1957, to be followed by Harold Macmillan, whose deft touch was well suited to the expanding economy, and in the General Elections of 1955 and 1959 the Tories had won increasingly large majorities,[2] partly induced by the rising standard of living expressed in two phrases current during the period: "You've never had it so good!" and "I'm all right, Jack!"

But the "economic regulation of the economy without direct controls", though it had succeeded in regulating the economy, was rather like riding in an old jerky car when a new and smoother limousine was thought to be waiting at the door. Moreover, there was a growing feeling that although the old car was fit to travel, other people were going much faster. The Labour Party had been preparing for a comeback by opposition to the Stop-Go policy of the Tories, though what it offered

[1] April 6, 1955 (Hansard, fifth series, vol. 539, c. 1181).
[2] See Appendix A III.

instead was not very positive. Generally speaking, it promised a wide-spread increase in productivity based upon the fullest possible use of technological change and a managerial revolution that would vitalize industry and exploit markets to the full. It spoke of the long-term planning of school and university syllabuses, of business schools, management courses, the immediate training of workers to the new skills, and the drying up of the 'brain-drain' that was causing scientists and technicians to take posts abroad at higher salaries and with better research facilities than they had in Britain. There was nothing in this the Tories would disagree with: "Neddy" had already said it, Macmillan had said it during the Common Market discussions. Management studies were being pursued at university and other levels, and business schools associated with the universities were being set up with funds provided by businessmen. Yet when Harold Wilson, leader of the Labour Party since Gaitskell's death in 1963, spoke to the Trades Union Congress at Blackpool in September 1964 in terms of a second Industrial Revolution he created an atmosphere of urgency and novelty. The Labour Party's Election manifesto, *The New Britain*, spoke of "mobilising the resources of technology under a national plan; harnessing our national wealth in brains, our genius for scientific invention and medical discovery"; it promised new Ministries of Economic Affairs and Technology.

While the Labour Party had been seeing itself as pioneer of the second Industrial Revolution the Tories had been suffering a series of internal crises. Their Minister for War had resigned after a sordid personal scandal which had culminated in the lie he told in the House of Commons.[1] Their leader and Prime Minister, Harold Macmillan, had resigned through sudden illness in October 1963, and the party had then played out an embarrassing struggle for the succession in full public view. When the mantle fell upon Lord Home, who needed to divest himself of his peerage and gain admission to the House of Commons before assuming the Premiership, it looked like political *hara-kiri* on a full scale. Yet the Tories delayed a General Election as long as they could, and the Public Opinion polls, which in the summer of 1964 gave Labour a clear lead, showed the parties drawing closer together as Election Day approached.

It was a dull Election, fought as much before the television cameras as on the hustings over ground that had been trodden over for months before, the chief excitement being provided by the fluctuations of the Opinion polls. All parties promised increased social-service benefits and spoke of the technological revolution. The Labour Party pledged itself

[1] *Lord Denning's Report*, September 1963, Cmnd. 2152.

to remove National Health prescription charges[1] and spoke of a capital-gains tax, a close inspection of "expense accounts" and income-tax evasions, and the renationalization of the iron and steel industry. The Tories pointed to the overall progress of the economy during the previous thirteen years. The Liberals opposed the renationalization of iron and steel and spoke of social-service benefits higher than either of the other parties was offering. No talk of a new Britain struck fire. No party raised either itself or the electorate above the humdrum. In the end mistrust of the Stop-Go economy coupled with a worsening of the balance of payments and a general feeling that it was time for a change gave the Labour Party an overall majority of four over all other parties combined.[2]

It was the balance of payments on which the Labour Government's attention was focused as it took office. For some time the worsening of the visible trade deficit had been noted as a danger sign. Fluctuating in 1962, imports increased steadily in 1963, and between 1963 and 1964 rose by 11 per cent in volume, an increase augmented in value by a 4 per cent price rise on imported goods. Exports, which again had fluctuated during 1962, rose strongly in the first part of 1963, but flattened out during the second half of the year and fell throughout 1964.

The imports were of varying importance. Some, such as oil and the raw materials of industry, were an index of expansion; the disturbing feature was the swollen quantities of manufactured and semi-manufactured goods, many only slightly different from those Britain produced herself, which flowed into the country.[3] Imports of manufactured consumer goods, which increased by 8 per cent in value in 1962, rose by 23 per cent in each of the two subsequent years; imports of manufactured capital goods rose by 8 and 2 per cent in 1962 and 1963 and by 31 per cent in 1964. Taking the year 1961 as 100, the index numbers of imports by volume for 1964 were for all imports 119, for food, beverages, and tobacco 104, for basic materials 108, for fuels 120, for manufactured goods 137.[4]

At the side of an expensive import programme stood increasingly large overseas commitments in the shape of aid to underdeveloped countries and military expenditure. In 1952 Government spending abroad totalled £74 million, in 1964 nearly £500 million. The bulk of this in 1964—some £350 million—went in military spending, including the army in Germany and bases in the Far and Middle East. There was at

[1] *Infra*, pp. 206–207.   [2] See Appendix A III.

[3] The import of goods which can be manufactured at home can be justified only if coupled with vigorous selling of goods which can be produced at home even more efficiently.

[4] *Annual Abstract of Statistics*, 1965, Table 265.

the same time a continued outflow of private capital, particularly a large increase in overseas oil investment.

None of this would have mattered so much if the export trade had kept up, but the country's old staples—machinery, transport equipment, metals, textiles—either fell or barely held their own. The position was underlined in the case of machinery, where imports had increased by 30 per cent between 1963 and 1964 while exports remained stagnant. At the same time the invisible earnings by means of which Britain had always balanced her budget were low, shipping, banking, insurance, and other financial services having dropped sharply. A cheering aspect of the economy, although not compensating for other defects, was the growth in Britain's tourist industry, which in ten years rose by 150 per cent, increasing both in terms of foreign tourists and in the amount of money they spent in Britain. In 1965 some 2,600,000 would spend nearly £250 million of foreign currency in the country, besides fares paid to British carriers. Tourism ranks as Britain's fourth largest export industry and her biggest single dollar-earner: in 1963 nearly twice as many dollars were spent in the United Kingdom by visitors as were received from the export of whisky to the United States.[1]

But two ears of corn do not make a harvest, and when international comparisons were made the position was revealed even more starkly: Britain's share in trade in manufactured goods had fallen and was continuing to fall, having dropped in value from over 20 per cent in 1954 to under 14 per cent in 1964. The gainers were France, Belgium, the Netherlands, Italy, West Germany, Japan. West Germany had consistently had export surpluses since 1951, Italy since 1953. Belgium and the Netherlands had had to deal with nothing more adverse than one or two small debit balances, France had seemingly emerged successfully from her balance-of-payments troubles, Japan was forging ahead with export orders on many fronts, notably with shipbuilding, where Britain and Europe had hitherto held the monopoly.[2]

The United Kingdom had surmounted several such balance-of-payments crises by borrowing, raising bank rate and making other adjustments to her rate of development. Such a solution smacked too much of

---

[1] *Reports of the British Travel and Holidays Association; The Times* Supplement on the British Travel Industry, February 18, 1965; *The Times*, leading article, August 28, 1965. The British Travel and Holidays Association claimed, on September 30, 1964, as much as £307 million in total receipts for the British tourist industry in 1963.

[2] *Monthly Reports on Overseas Trade* (Statistical Division of the Board of Trade); *Economic Surveys* by OECD of United Kingdom Trade, July 1963, June 1965; *Conditions Favourable to Faster Growth*, April 1963 (NEDC); *The National Plan*, September 1965, Cmnd. 2764; *Government Expenditure Overseas*: Economic Trends, December 1964, Table 4, p. ix; OECD Yearbook of National Accounts Statistics; and see *infra*, Appendix B V.

Stop-Go to accord with Labour Party policy. It became clear, however, that the deficit in 1964 would be of a very high order—by the third quarter of the year £600 million seemed likely, by September £720 million seemed a truer estimate, and the Labour Government in its first appraisal of the situation estimated a deficit of from £700 to £800 million by the end of the year.[1] The highest previous adverse balances since the War had been the £500 million of 1947 and 1951.

In an atmosphere of crisis the new Government took steps immediately after the Election in October 1964 to deal with the situation. To reduce imports it imposed a temporary 15 per cent levy on all imports except foodstuffs, unmanufactured tobacco, and basic raw materials, later extending the exemptions to include books. To encourage exports it immediately offered tax rebates to exporters in the form of repayment of some of the indirect tax that had entered into the cost of their export goods, amounting to an estimated £80 million for the first year. On November 11 the new Chancellor of the Exchequer, James Callaghan, introduced an emergency Budget which announced an extra 6d. on the standard rate of income tax from the following April and put an extra 6d. a gallon duty on petrol immediately. It forecast a capital-gains tax, which would apply to gains arising from assets wherever acquired, and a corporation tax, which would replace income tax and profits tax on the income of companies. It also announced, to take effect the following spring, extra social-service benefits, paid for partly by higher insurance and partly by the State, and the abolition in the New Year of prescription charges for medicines received under National Health Insurance.

The atmosphere of uncertainty which always surrounds a General Election and which had hung over Britain for longer than customary had no doubt made her situation more parlous. But the international lack of confidence in the pound that developed was more pronounced than was warranted by the balance-of-payments deficit, serious though that was, or by Election uncertainties. The atmosphere of crisis promulgated by the Labour Government, which was anxious to make more than clear that it had inherited an Augean stable, added to the general unease, which the Budget now fed. The Government had met a present situation which its own pronouncements were proclaiming to be catastrophic by a future increase in income tax and an unsettling allusion to new forms of taxation, and for the present by no more than a 6d. petrol duty. It had matched its diagnosis that what was required was increased productivity by wide extensions of social-service benefit such as

[1] *The Economic Situation: A Statement by Her Majesty's Government*, October 26, 1964. In the event the deficit was £745 million.

normally are associated with prosperity. The outside world could not be blamed if it saw in this not Labour's determination to keep faith but an irresponsible attitude to a crisis. The unsatisfactory Budget apart, the Government's efforts to save the pound rested upon the 15 per cent surcharge. And this, rushed through without discussion with Britain's partners of the European Free Trade Association,[1] although it effected them all as exporters to Britain, caused much ill-will and enormous resentment.

By the second half of November lack of confidence in the Government's ability to maintain the pound at its existing ratio with other currencies and fear of devaluation was causing a large-scale selling of sterling by business and commercial houses within the sterling area[2] who were anxious to provide for their future foreign currency needs before the pound lost its value, while holders of sterling everywhere were hastening to part with a falling asset. On November 23 Bank rate was raised from 5 to 7 per cent in an effort to attract funds to London, but this brought only temporary relief. With trade figures running heavily against Britain and her gold and foreign-currency reserves falling as the Exchange Equalization Account strove to support sterling, it was clear that large-scale external help was needed.

The external help to which Britain might look was governed by arrangements made in 1947 with the object of keeping the world monetary system smoothly working. A system of more or less stable exchange rates was then agreed which linked one currency with another. If one currency got out of line with the others it was expected that the Government concerned would try to put it right by coming into the market itself to buy or sell as the case might be. This is what the British Exchange Equalization Account was trying to do at the time of the November crisis. For deeper-seated trouble an International Monetary Fund was established in 1947 to which each member state contributed a quota to form a pool—25 per cent in gold and 75 per cent in its own currency. Against these pooled resources members could draw in case of need, automatically to the extent of less than 25 per cent of their contribution and more at the discretion of the Bank of International Settlements, which controlled the fund. Some time afterwards a group of countries, of which Britain was one, supplemented the resources of the IMF by an additional $6000 million under what was known as the Paris Club Agreement. In addition, informal 'swap' arrangements between countries would help in time of temporary difficulty.

Early in October, before the Election, the British Government had

[1] *Supra*, p. 90.   [2] *Supra*, p. 89.

availed itself of 'swap' facilities with the Federal Reserve Banks of New York and Canada and with six European Central Banks, and had also drawn $1000 million under a 'stand-by' agreement with the IMF. This had all been swallowed up as the crisis deepened, and Britain turned to the Fund for more. There were preliminary delays and difficulties since the IMF was temporarily short of funds and the member countries, still highly critical of Britain's 15 per cent duty, and doubtful whether she was capable of taking strong enough action to support a loan by her own efforts, at first demurred. But when the loan was granted, after Britain had stood before Europe's bankers, it was given in full measure, $3000 million being made available to Britain on November 25 from the Bank of International Settlements, acting for the IMF, and the Consortium of World Central Banks. This was followed in early December by a further $1000 million under arrangements with the ten banks of the Paris Club and an additional $80 million from Switzerland, who was not a member.

It was a massive rescue operation, the largest of its kind ever mounted, and demonstrated an awareness of the mutual dependence of international trade and the need to prevent the devaluation of the pound. But Europe wanted, in return for its aid, an assurance that Britain would put its house in order: the price of support was a deep and continued scrutiny of Britain's economic life by European Committees.[1] This was salutary, and there was much to learn from their diagnosis. Unfortunately, the improvement which followed the loans was shortlived. At the end of the year and into 1965 there were more 'swap' loans, and the spring and summer of 1965 were punctuated with alarums and shocks: alarums as one economic crisis succeeded another, as confidence in the pound was repeatedly checked, as gold reserves fell and talk of devaluation continued; shocks provided by the Labour Government's second and third Budgets—the 'normal' Budget in April and a supplementary 'public spending curb' at the end of July. The April Budget increased the duty on tobacco and alcohol, raised the annual motor-vehicle licence, instituted the promised capital-gains tax and corporation tax, and introduced a tax on expense accounts.[2] "In the first six months of his Chancellorship", said *The Economist*, referring to the first two Budgets, "Mr. Callaghan has imposed more than twice as big a squeeze as any Conservative Chancellor ever did."[3]

[1] Like the *Economic Surveys* by OECD.
[2] The Chancellor of the Exchequer, House of Commons, April 6, 1965 (Hansard, fifth series, vol. 710, c. 244, and cc. 244–391 *passim*).
[3] April 10, 1965.

The July Budget was directed to curbing overseas investment, particularly outside the sterling area, and to reducing public expenditure of all kinds. The defence programme was to be cut by £400 million by 1969–70, the Estimates of Government Departments reduced within a determined limit, expenditure by nationalized undertakings deferred; housing, school, and hospital programmes were to be contained within existing programmes, road, water, and other local-authority work was to be delayed, lending by local authorities for house purchase was to be restricted, hire-purchase expenditure reduced by cutting the period over which repayment could be spread. No further social-service reforms would, for the time being, follow the pension increases and the curiously mistimed abolition of National Health Service prescription charges.[1] It was a Budget for Europe. The second and third Budgets had, indeed, made up for much that observers had thought was lacking from the first. No-one, in fact, at home or abroad, would quarrel with a shaping of the coat according to the cloth, but that badly needed hospitals and schools should suffer showed that the cutting machine was not sufficiently selective. Nor had anyone yet made a convincing estimate of the amount of cloth available.

The balance of payments made a better showing by the end of 1965, but fresh international aid had been necessary at the beginning of September, when a further $1,400,000 was made available to Britain by the Bank of International Settlements and the European Central Banks, with the exception of the French Bank. As 1966 opened it was not yet demonstrable that the Labour Government's version of Stop-Go, or Go-Stop, was any more effective as an instrument of managing the economy than the Tories' version. And the two instruments were strangely alike. The Labour Government in 1964 had inherited a crisis similar to other crises—it was, as an economist put it, the Year of the Seventh Crisis since the War[2]—and it had been dealt with in much the same way as the other six: international finance was underpinning the British economy under a Labour Government as it had done before under other Governments, the only difference being the size of the operation. And, in spite of all it had said about the Stop-Go policy of managing the economy, the Labour Government was treading on the brakes pretty heavily. It was also laying up a further price rise as the various items of the Budgets percolated through the economy.

---

[1] James Callaghan, House of Commons, July 27, 1965 (Hansard, fifth series, vol. 717, c. 229, and 228–241 *passim*).
[2] William Rees-Mogg in the *Sunday Times*, November 29, 1964.

Though necessarily concentrating on the immediate problem of saving the pound, the Government was also thinking of less spectacular measures that would help the export trade and give sterling a more permanent lift. Not only did it remit certain taxation to exporters but, as part of a longer-term policy, it extended the existing overseas co-operative selling arrangements. Area organizations already existed for Europe, the Middle East, Canada, the U.S.A., and Latin America under the National Exports Council. Now there were to be similar agencies for Australia, New Zealand, and other Commonwealth countries under the guidance of a Commonwealth Exports Council. Since it was on small firms, many of whom had not yet ventured into the export trade, that the Government pinned much of its hope for expansion in the overseas market, it directed a great deal of its efforts to them. It offered cheaper and simpler export credits to run as long as fifteen years, it explained the co-operative selling facilities that would be available under the overseas area organizations, stressed the advantages of overseas agents, advertised courses of instruction on market research and selling abroad, while the chairman of the British National Export Council wrote a series of five short, explanatory articles in *The Times*.[1]

In trying to achieve more vigorous overseas marketing the Government had laid its finger on one of the weak spots of the export trade: it was often not so much the quality of British goods as the quality of their salesmen that was at fault. The inefficient follow up of contacts, failure to keep delivery dates, neglect of servicing, failure to provide spare parts for new installations—even an inability to speak the customer's language—provided a cogent set of reasons for failure to capture more orders. But it remained necessary to produce the goods at the right price and of the right quality, making use of every available technique, wasting neither material nor effort. By creating a Ministry of Technology and joining Education and Science in a single Department the Government hoped to produce the men and the means.

Meanwhile, among the business schools and management courses there was by this time some danger of enthusiasm overshooting the mark and leaving the business executive puzzled at the choice of alternatives before him. There had been surprisingly little discussion of what they should teach. How many businessmen really thought in terms of decision theory? Or of discounted cash flow techniques or linear programming? How many would think their time well spent on a course that could "straddle most of the social sciences and a great deal of

[1] Starting on February 1, 1965.

technology as well"?[1] And who, and for how long, and at what stage in his career, should take these courses? "Neddy" had spoken of the education of executives, and to some a post-experience term of training seemed more profitable than a postgraduate course. A Report on Business Schools by Lord Franks had spoken of a year's course for recent graduates and twenty weeks for experienced businessmen.[2] Professor Hague, of the Manchester Business School, thought two years was not too long for anybody. A businessman, J. W. Platt, saying that the whole subject was "in a considerable muddle", called for a union of "the intellectual capacity of the academic and the consuming urge for action of the man of affairs".[3] But the business schools had to run for a while of their own volition. Politicians were absorbed in other matters.

It was bad luck for the Labour Government that, while it was attending to the balance of payments, nursing the pound, and helping exporters, trouble should come to a head at the docks. Trouble, indeed, had been brewing for some time, and a Committee under Lord Devlin was examining the labour position when, as 1964 drew to a close, the Press began carrying pictures of idle congestion at the Port of London. At the same time exporters were writing angry letters to the papers pointing to delays and hold-ups at the docks as a prime cause of the deficiency in the balance of payments: "Leading exporters are already satisfied that the organisation of docks is the biggest single bottleneck in the development of the export trade and that the removal of that bottleneck is becoming a question of desperate urgency," wrote *The Times* on December 8, and it spoke of "orders worth perhaps tens of millions of pounds" being held up. Export firms spoke not only of delays, but of orders cancelled, goodwill lost, and future sales abandoned.

Part of the trouble at the docks lay deep in an organization with bitter memories of labour hardship and capitalist exploitation. Still there were many employing bodies and a system of employment which, although not 'casual', yet implied the re-engaging of labour for every cargo. The first post-War Labour Government had, indeed, enacted a 'dockers' charter' which ended the old system of casual labour fighting at the dock gates for work. The Dock Labour scheme initiated by the Dock Workers (Registration of Employment) Act of 1946 and the Dock Workers (Regulation of Employment) Order of 1947 was operated by a central

---

[1] Professor D. C. Hague, speaking to the Manchester Business School Council, February 10, 1965.

[2] *British Business Schools* (British Institute of Management), 1963.

[3] Speaking at Convocation of the University of London.

Dock Labour Board and at each port by local boards consisting of representatives of the port employers and the employed. Employment was limited to those on a register of dock workers, whose size was controlled by the Dock Labour Board, and the dock worker was guaranteed a minimum wage. About a quarter of the dockers were in permanent employment by 1964; they were usually employed by the week and were known as 'perms'. The rest attended the labour stand for two 'turns' each day—morning and afternoon—and the local Dock Board allocated labour to the employers who wanted it. In many ports there was in addition, a 'free-call', at which foremen were able to pick before the allocation anyone they specially wanted in their gangs. This selection of the so-called 'blue-eyed boys' was an invidious and jarring feature of the scheme.

Those dockers on the register who attended for work but were not called got 9s. attendance money in 1964 at each 'turn'. If they got no work for a week they would receive £4 10s. for ten separate attendances. But there was also a minimum wage, which stood at £9 in 1964, and if a docker's work and attendance money together did not reach this it was made up by the Dock Labour Board from a fund provided by the employers. The docker was not completely decasualized; there were far too many small employers at the various ports to make regulation of employment easy, and many anomalies, yet the docker's position was much improved, and the Dock Boards provided regular amenities such as medical centres and canteen and recreational facilities. But the number of dockers had not kept pace with the quantity of work available, and strikes had been numerous—about 130,000 man-days were lost in 1964 —while time-wasting and restrictive practices were common. There was, for example, the practice of 'welting' in Liverpool docks or 'spelling' in Glasgow, by which members of a gang took turns during a job to absent themselves, sometimes working only alternate hours; there was refusal to work with short-handed gangs, late starting, early finishing. There was also the 'continuity rule', which provided that a gang remained on a job until it was completed, but then returned to the call-stand for re-engagement even if it was in the middle of a 'turn'. There was some fairness in this in preventing one employer from keeping a good gang in permanent employment at the expense of another, but it wasted many hours in waiting for the next 'turn' and often resulted in men refusing to move from hatch to hatch on a ship, or job to job on the quays, without first being paid off and going back to the call-stand for re-engagement. Any work that was lost could easily be made up by overtime. But the best known of the dockers' restrictive practices was the ban on overtime at week-ends at the Port of London which lasted from July 1964 until well into 1965, and it was this which intensified the pile-up about which exporters complained.

The Devlin Committee reported on August 4, 1965,[1] and underlined and emphasized the restrictive practices, the slack discipline, the insecurity that existed in Britain's docks. The large number of employers, the casualness of hiring, were strongly condemned, and in particular the weak hold of the Transport and General Workers' Union, who represented the majority of the dockers and yet left ample scope for troublemakers and unofficial strikes. The regularization of employment, weekly engagements for all men on a register in every port, the cutting down of the number of employers by amalgamation or otherwise, and a determination by the TGWU to restore its authority were the first steps necessary to ensure that the ports functioned as they should.

Much of the trouble, however, was inherent in the construction of the ports. In spite of official Inquiries, notably by the Rochdale Committee, which reported in 1962,[2] and a certain amount of new equipment, in spite of efforts to bring the ports within a nationalized transport plan, with or without giving them greater autonomy, there still had been no overall co-ordination, no planned outlay of capital. There was a shortage of deep-water berths, the rate of turn-round of ships was slow, incoming vessels were kept waiting outside the ports, the inland transport system that fed the docks was inadequate. It was originally adapted to receive and discharge goods inland by rail, but there had been a concentration upon road services without an adequate provision of new roads; meanwhile a railway network which was laid into the heart of the docks was allowed to decay for want of capital improvement. Britain's docks, as *The Times* said, were "a discredit to those who run them, to those who work in them, to some extent to those who use them, and to the nation."[3]

[1] *Final Report of the Committee of Inquiry under the Rt. Hon. Lord Devlin into certain matters concerning the Port Transport Industry*, Cmnd. 2734.
[2] *The Committee of Inquiry into the Major Ports of Great Britain*, September 1962, Cmnd. 1824.
[3] January 9, 1965.

CHAPTER VIII

Introspection

"... it will be for the nation to respond by a fresh outburst of that creative energy which has marked the greatest periods of our history and is vitally necessary in the years now before us."   *Social Insurance*, Part I, p.40
(September 1944, Cmd. 6550)

"... the [Government's] policy will be put in jeopardy if money incomes rise faster than the volume of national production, as has been the persistent tendency since the end of the war."   *Incomes Policy. The Next Step*, p.3
(February 1962, Cmnd. 1626)

"The object must be to increase productivity and efficiency as rapidly as possible in order to raise real incomes and to avoid, wherever possible, increases in money incomes that push up costs and prices."
Prices and Incomes Policy, p.7
(April 1965, Cmnd. 2639)

"What is needed is a shake out which will release the nation's manpower, skilled and unskilled, and lead to a more purposive use of labour ... the whole operation stands or falls on the extent to which we can keep our costs and prices under control."
The Prime Minister, House of Commons,
July 21, 1966

THE PROBLEM of rising prices is common to the whole world, and no country has found a satisfactory solution. Yet other countries have on the whole been more successful than Britain in the search. In Germany, Italy, the Netherlands, and Belgium prices rose only about half as fast between 1950 and 1961 as they did in Britain.[1] And British prices continued to rise unabated throughout 1962, 1963, and 1964, the biggest constituents of the price-rise being incomes of all kinds—people talked of an 'incomes policy' rather than of a 'price policy' or a 'production policy'.

Total personal incomes rose from £22·9 million in 1961 to £27·3 million in 1964. Consumer expenditure rose from £17·9 million to £21·3 million over the same period.[2] Prices of consumer goods and services continued their upward swing, rising by 9 per cent between 1960 and 1964, wages, salaries and profits swinging upward sharply by 12 per cent over the same period.[3] In 1964 there was a further increase of 3·7 per cent in the average level of full-time weekly rates of wages in the principal industries and services, and $9\frac{1}{4}$ million manual workers received an aggregate increase of approximately £$4\frac{3}{4}$ million in basic, full-time weekly wage rates.[4] Incomes of all kinds were still rising in 1965, with increases back-dated to 1964. As *The Observer* remarked, "If an incomes policy is to be more than a form of words, the point will come when someone will have to say 'no' to a pay claim"[5]: it might have included dividends and profits in its stricture.

The alternative to having to say 'no' to a pay-claim at any level of society is that there should be a corresponding increase in productivity. Yet British productivity fails by every test. Between 1950 and 1961 the gross national product of the United Kingdom at constant prices rose by 30 per cent, that of the Common Market countries together rose by 80 per cent.[6] Volume indices of gross national product at market prices with 1958 as 100 show the United Kingdom as 95 in 1955 and 112 in 1962.

The Federal Republic of Germany, having started at 85 in 1955, reached an Index number of 136 in 1962. Close behind her was Italy with indices of gross national product of 87 and 132 at the two dates. Apart from the United Kingdom, Belgium was lowest on the European chart for 1962 with an index of 115.[7]

As important as gross national product itself are the indices of the growth of gross national product per head of population. Again the United Kingdom lagged: with an index number of 109 in 1962 (with 1958 at 100) the United Kingdom was at the bottom of the European

---

[1] A. Lamfalussy, *The United Kingdom and the Six*, pp. 2–3.
[2] *National Income and Expenditure*, 1965, Table 2, p. 4.
[3] *Ibid.*, Table 15, p. 14.
[4] *Ministry of Labour Gazette*, January 1965, pp. 9–11.
[5] January 24, 1965.   [6] Lamfalussy, *op. cit.*, pp. 1–3.
[7] OECD *Statistics of National Accounts, 1955–62* (Supplement), April 1964, p. 7.

chart, Italy with 129 leading the way, Germany following at 127.[1] Over the whole period 1950–61 gross national product per head rose by 26 per cent in the United Kingdom, but by 61 per cent in the European Economic Community.[2] While neither growth nor productivity rates are in themselves the full story—a change from agriculture to industry such as might occur in an underdeveloped country gives a high figure, a high proportion of service industries such as appears in highly developed economies gives a low—there were here sufficient reasons for disquiet. If more were needed they could be found in the fact that while wage costs per hour in the United Kingdom between 1960 and 1962 rose by 15 per cent, output per hour rose by only 1 per cent.

It is not easy to discover why British productivity lags. With the forty-hour week becoming a general average, hours in the United Kingdom are rather less than in Europe, more than in the United States or Canada. The number of working days lost through strikes is high in Britain; there were over 2000 stoppages, more than 1¾ million working days lost, and nearly 600,000 workers were involved in labour disputes in Britain in 1963; in 1965 there were 2400 stoppages, nearly 3 million working days lost, and nearly 900,000 workers were involved.[3] Illness accounts for more. How much time is lost through idleness or restrictive practices can be only guessed. Everyone has seen building workers idle on the site, everyone knows the story of the 'tea-boys' who provide tea for building workers and on whose behalf a 'go slow' was staged so that they might be allowed, with overtime, to earn £42 a week. "After all," said a senior shop steward, "the tea-boys are necessary to the site. Without them we would not work." In March 1966 a storeman at the British Motor Corporation depot at Cowley, Oxford, revealed that he was getting £30 for a nominal 40-hour week, which, he said, was actually only a 30-hour week after tea-breaks and smokes had been allowed for. It was, moreover, he said, "an unskilled job which could be learnt in half an hour", consisting of invoicing components at the stores. "These high wages coupled with restrictive working give me an uneasy feeling," he wrote. "It is a selfish and a short-sighted policy that must inevitably lead to disaster. And high wages plus restrictive working obviously go hand in hand with inefficient and inept management."[4] The storeman was compelled, by pressure from his colleagues, to leave his job at Cowley. We all know of the strike caused because the wrong trade group drove the

[1] *Idem.*   [2] Lamfalussy, *op. cit.*, p. 3.
[3] *Ministry of Labour Gazette*, January 1966.
[4] In a letter to the Liberal Party, reported through television and broadcasting services on March 11, 1966, and in *The Times* and the Press generally on March 12, 1966.

nail or turned the screw or riveted the steel plates. We all know the extended coffee-break, the too-long lunch hour, the chatting shop-assistant, the 'closed' positions in bank and post-office while people queue for attention. The same attitude goes right through industry and business of every kind at every level. How much it lowers productivity is not more measurable than the executive's business lunch, but it seems that a great deal of slack can be taken up all round without trammelling the human element if the right attitude to work is obtained. Leading articles in the Press, letters to newspapers, reiterate the fact that what is lacking is the "right spirit", a "sense of purpose", "responsibility". "The only thing that will solve Britain's problems is the long overdue reawakening of the British people," proclaimed *The Times*. But reawakening to what? Partly our very prosperity hinders us from finding out. So much emphasis is put upon a higher standard of living, so many calls go out to buy so many things, so many needs are created by reiterated advertisement, so little is said about any value save consumption, that the worker forgets he is working for anything but the bigger penny, and everything that happens on the job is but a means to the end of a higher material standard of living.

It is in line with this attitude that we allocate more of what we produce to immediate consumption than we do to sale abroad. We might reasonably argue that this was what we wanted, but the corollary is a reduction of imports: we cannot gain on the swings as well as on the roundabouts. Of the increase in her gross national product between 1950 and 1960 the United Kingdom allocated 59.2 per cent to consumer durables and other private consumption, 11·4 per cent to public civilian expenditure, 6·4 per cent to defence, 26·5 per cent to domestic investment, and 19·6 per cent to exporting goods and services.[1] All other European countries but France devoted more to export, all but France devoted less to consumer expenditure, none spent so much on defence, all but France and Denmark spent more on investment.

So, not only is our production rising more slowly than that of other countries, both absolutely and in terms of population, but we are putting less back into industry in the form of investment. There was an enormous increase of capital formation everywhere between 1950 and 1960, but in the United Kingdom it amounted to only 15·4 as a proportion of gross national product at current prices, whereas in Germany it was 24, in the Netherlands 24·2, and in Norway as high as 26·4[2]; and though British figures have been rising since 1960 British industry still

[1] Maddison, *Economic Growth in the West*, Table II–8, p. 62.
[2] *Ibid.*, Table III–1, p. 76.

remains relatively under-capitalized: the increase in the imports of finished manufactures by an average of about 12 per cent per annum between 1954 and 1964, and of semi-manufactures by about 8 per cent per annum over the same period, itself suggests a shortage of home capacity resulting from inadequate investment.

Under-capitalization means retaining outmoded or outworn instruments of production, whether an office typewriter or filing system, a piece of machinery in a factory, or an accounts department whose work could be done by a computer. It results in a failure to take advantage and make full use of new techniques and new labour-machine relationships, to be bold enough with mechanization or with automation. Mechanization of the production line has raised output enormously, though even on this level there are still many firms where labour-saving could proceed farther, where a new appraisal of existing methods would yield abundant reward, but where custom, inertia, fear of labour troubles and lack of a plan hold back the management: it is part of the function of business schools and industrial consultants to help in this respect. But Britain has reached the stage where an extension of the Industrial Revolution is not enough, where she needs to welcome the techniques of a further Industrial Revolution—that associated with cybernetics or automation. A prime purpose of the new Ministry of Technology and the new business schools is to open its possibilities to industry, and make them alive to the urgency of the situation.

What precisely automation is, how it will help a particular section of the economy, must also be explained. Sir Leon Bagrit, giving the Reith lectures in 1964, endeavoured to define it. Automation, he said, "integrates all the sensing, thinking, and decision-making elements" in man. While man is "extending his eyes with radar; his tongue and his ear through telecommunications; his muscle and his body structure through mechanization", while he "extends his own energies by the generation and transmission of power", he extends "his nervous system and his thinking and decision-making faculties through automation".[1] "Automation," he said, "is really an umbrella term for a complex of related systems. It includes, for instance, data processing and the scanning of information with alarm systems. It includes computation for specific purposes, for accountancy, for switching of information, for all kinds of recording, for observing, recording, and controlling every conceivable kind of activity—industrial, commercial, governmental, and social."[2] At the heart of the system is an electric computer whose distinguishing

[1] Lecture I, *The Listener*, November 12, 1964.
[2] Lecture II, *ibid.*, November 19, 1964.

quality is "a speed beyond human imagination", which will collect data, measure it, process it, and advise on the best action in terms of the data it has assimilated. In air-traffic control, in oil-refining, in chemical processing, in steel production, for accounting, bookkeeping, administration generally, it is already in use, but while Bagrit estimated that no more than a hundred companies were automated in Britain, the United States has accepted automation as necessary to the new age: the United States as an industrial economy was automating, because it had to in order to maintain its standard of living, as an American business-man told a German businessmen's conference. Britain, although she has been active in manufacturing computers, lags behind the U.S.A., and has barely begun to train the technicians who are needed to process them. It is, moreover, still doubtful to what extent British firms will com-puterize in the near future, many being unwilling to make the capital outlay or the staff changes involved, others being genuinely doubtful of their use to any save a very large establishment.[1]

Automation will require men to change jobs; so will other forms of technological change, so will reorganization, so will efficiency drives. If our resources are to be used to the best possible end this is unavoid-able. As Lord Plowden said, while every man has a right to a job he has not got a right to his existing job for ever if it becomes outdated.[2] But while economically the dictum is sound the repercussions in terms of human happiness are wide. The Government and the trade unions are considering various ways of speeding and softening change from one employment to another, and there are already examples in coal-mining and with railways of the problems involved. Even with careful forward planning, a detailed survey of 'natural wastage' due to retirement, a limiting of recruitment, individual interviewing of those required to change, with lump-sum severance pay and wage-related unemployment benefit, the running down of a labour force is certain to cause distress, bound up as it is with personal problems of family, locality, and famili-arity. In August 1965 a Redundancy Payments Act provided for the making by employers of payments to employees in respect of redun-dancy.[3] To meet the expense employers were required to make

[1] See Appendix A VI.

[2] At Eastbourne at the joint conference of the British Employers' Confedera-tion, the Federation of British Industries, and the National Association of British Manufacturers, January 20, 1965. Lord Plowden was Chief Planning Officer in the Treasury and Chairman of the Economic Planning Board, 1947–53. Reported in *The Times*, January 21, 1965.

[3] Redundancy payments are payable at the rate of one and a half weeks' pay for each year of employment from the age of forty-one, one week's pay for each year

contributions to a Redundancy Fund, to which the State would contribute if necessary. Already it has been seen that the employment exchanges can play a big part in re-employment, and that the earlier they are informed of the numbers involved in any reorganization the more effectively they can help.

Retraining schemes are also vitally necessary, and here the methods employed, the attitude of all concerned, the training payments made are all-important. A reassuring example of what could be done was in the recruiting and training from scratch of more than 10,000 workers for the new Ford factories at Halewood, on Merseyside. None of them had been inside a car factory before, training took from eight weeks for the average production worker to three months for those on more complex operations, but by that time, with wages satisfactory and conditions and prospects of promotion good, jobs were "highly cherished".[1] Although Americans have been more willing than the British to follow the money, the magnetizing of workers by some of the more highly paid industries, like Vauxhall's at Luton and Morris's at Oxford, shows that many workers in Britain will move if the conditions offered are good enough. And the whole situation would be made a little easier if the term 'redundancy' were dropped. No-one likes to be told he is 'redundant'—on the scrapheap; emphasis on the need for labour elsewhere is a more effective method of inducing change.

A subsidiary cause of the faster growth of some Continental countries may be found in their tax system. Most Western European countries collect more of their taxation for social-security purposes on the basis of payroll charges, and it was suggested some years ago that German employers more easily dispensed with labour than British since each worker meant not only his wages but also a high national insurance contribution. The British Chancellor actually spoke in 1960 of levying a special tax on the wages bill of each firm, but nothing came of the suggestion until the 1966 Budget, when the Labour Chancellor introduced a payroll tax on labour in service industries and in building. The intention of the Selective Employment Tax was to economize labour in unproductive concerns, but it did nothing to make labour in industry more productive.

Certain facts are inescapable: British productivity lags, British prices

of employment between the ages of twenty-two and forty inclusive, and half a week's pay for each year of employment between the ages of eighteen and twenty-one inclusive. A man who has reached the age of sixty-five or a woman who has reached the age of sixty is not entitled to redundancy payment.

[1] See report in *The Times*, February 4, 1965.

are too high, Britain sells less abroad than her competitors. The reasons are that her investment rate is low, her incomes growth is not related to her productivity growth, she devotes too much of her resources to immediate consumption and to the social services, she is insufficiently automated, she does not make full use, or the best use, of her equipment, she has not mastered the art of redistributing her labour over the economic field as it becomes necessary, she has failed to train it for some of the most urgent of today's requirements, she has neglected the vital cornerstone of her trade—the docks. With income increases being pressed on every side—and this includes dividends and profits as well as wages and salaries—with trade unions claiming shorter hours, resisting dismissals or transfers, with labour of all grades and kinds, from top to bottom of society, slacking in various ways, with the social services inviolable, there is no easy way out.

But, when all has been said, and whatever the state of industry at a given moment, a great deal will always depend upon the attitude of the workman to his job, whether it is programming a computer for an hour a day, serving behind a shop counter for eight hours a day, bricklaying or mining for six or eight, or making a virtually full-time job of teaching, medicine, or politics. In the "beaten and crouching" history of the British working-man there was little place for pride, except in the trade union. With a shortening of the working-day, a lengthening of the week-end, with social amenities at works and offices, with bonuses and share participation, with education widening, with entertainment, culture, leisure activities more generalized, with a standard of living rising all round, with irksome restrictions between 'salaried' and 'wages' staff already disappearing and class distinctions fading, there is every reason for pride in the economy itself—in the economy that makes all this possible. No workman will surrender his independence by abandoning restrictive practices, by doing a week's work without stint. Increasing productivity, on the other hand, will give his union a stronger lever to better conditions. While all that has happened since the War has underlined his right to an increasing share in the national product, the role of his trade union has become increasingly difficult to determine. On the one hand, the machinery for negotiation is wide and, on the whole, effective; on the other hand, the spread of ownership through shareholding and nationalization has partly wiped out the old capitalist-worker dichotomy. At the beginning of February 1965 the appointment of a Royal Commission under Lord Donovan was announced to consider the position of the trade unions in the second half of the twentieth century. A great deal of water had run under the bridge since the previous Inquiry half a century earlier.[1] There would be ample scope for the new Commission to wipe out the ugliness of past relationships and to define the role of the trade unions in terms that would make them proud to further the progress of the expanding economy.

But Britain could not wait either for a Report of a Royal Commission or for a change of heart among her people. The new Government, immediately upon taking office in 1964, had declared its intention of watching prices and in particular the prices of key products like food and those which formed an important element in the costs of other industries.[2] By December George Brown, the Minister in charge of the newly created Department of Economic Affairs, had succeeded in bringing together representatives of the employers' organizations and the trade unions to sign a *Joint Statement of Intent on Productivity, Prices and Incomes*, which signified their agreement to co-operate with the Government in keeping prices under review.[3] In early February the Government published a White Paper on the *Machinery of a Prices and Incomes Policy*,[4] which again had been agreed with the Trades Union Congress and the various Employers' Associations. There would be a National Board for Prices and Incomes, working in two separate divisions—the Prices Review Division and the Incomes Review Division. The Board would consist of an independent chairman, a number of independent members, a businessman, and a trade unionist. In principle, the Prices Review Division would be able to investigate any price or group of prices, and the Incomes Review Division any claim, settlement, or other question relating to incomes, hours of work, or conditions of service. In both Prices and Incomes Divisions the whole range of the private sector, the public sector, and the public services would be covered, and the Government would retain direct responsibility for all references. Although the machinery was intended to work through voluntary co-operation, the Government would have to consider, the White Paper said, using statutory authority if experience showed it was necessary. The agreed policy that would necessarily lie beneath the work of the National Board for Prices and Incomes would be worked out by the National Economic Development Office.[5]

By the autumn of 1965 the Department of Economic Affairs, with the

[1] *Report of the Royal Commission on Trade Disputes and Trade Combinations*, 1906, Cd. 2825.
[2] George Brown, House of Commons, November 4, 1964 (Hansard, fifth series, vol. 701, c. 223).
[3] December 16, 1964.   [4] February 11, 1965, Cmnd. 2577.
[5] *Machinery of a Prices and Incomes Policy*, February 11, 1965, Cmnd. 2577.

co-operation of the National Economic Development Council and various specialists, had prepared a Five Year Plan for British industry. To help implement it Economic Development Councils, consisting of representatives of management and of the trade unions concerned, were being formed for each industry. By September thirteen of these 'little Neddies' were in existence, and twenty were expected by the end of the year, covering between them about two-thirds of the private sector of the economy. This, the most ambitious planning project ever undertaken by a British Government, except in time of war, was published as *The National Plan* on September 16, 1965.[1] Far exceeding the size of a normal White Paper, it ran to 474 pages. Part I (204 pages) was concerned with targets and the pattern of economic production required to implement them. Part II (239 pages) consisted of statements and estimates by the EDCs of their output, their needs for labour, their requirements in fixed investment, their views on the necessary action. There were 31 pages of appendices.

The target of the National Plan was a 25 per cent increase in total national output between 1964 and 1970, which in terms of money was an increase of some £8000 million at 1964 prices, involving an annual average increase of 3·8 per cent. It was estimated that by 1970 there would be a manpower gap of about 200,000 persons, and, taking this into account, output per head would have to grow by an average of 3·4 per cent each year to achieve the target. Since rather more than half the total increase, about £4500 million, was expected to go in increased personal expenditure and a further £1500 million on public social services, the incentive to extra effort was high: education expenditure was to rise by 32 per cent, health services by 23½ per cent, roads by 41½ per cent, housing by 33 per cent, over the five-year period. All this raised the standard of living. Yet the actual yearly targets announced by the Plan imposed a limit to the rise of personal consumption of 3·2 per cent, a limit of 4 per cent on the growth of imports, and an expansion of exports by about 5¼ per cent, which meant that the consumer would take a smaller share (though a larger actual amount) of the increased product. Whether he would be content with this was the crux of the problem. It implied close working with the Prices and Incomes Board and the holding of incomes steady within a closely defined growth rate. By the beginning of 1966 there was little evidence that this had been achieved.

The Plan put on record that it would welcome more foreign investment and, in certain industries, more amalgamations and mergers, and it spoke frankly of the need for large movements of labour from over-

[1] Cmnd. 2764.

manned industries and services to others in need. To ease the transition it would use all the methods already suggested or in operation, and it came down on the side of wage-related unemployment benefit if periods of idleness were unavoidable. Industry was promised more management education and greater efficiency of labour, help with rationalization, modernization, the achievement of 'long runs', and the encouragement of investment. The greater efficiency of labour was the most difficult of these ends to achieve. Whether, and how, the intractable human element could be harnessed to serve the Plan within the limits of a free society was not, because it could not be, made clear. *The National Plan* was a brave and worth-while essay in planning whose success had necessarily to depend upon persuasion. How far any Government could, or would, be forced to introduce another element into the social and economic system remained to be seen. But it was at least clear, allowing for Party differences, that the concept of planning the economy had been accepted: the issue of Plan or No Plan had ceased to exist. When it was discussed in the House of Commons on November 3, 1965, the Members resolved, without a division, "That this House welcomes the National Plan".[1]

A complement to the National Plan was the Government's announcement that it would keep expenditure within the public sector, for which it was directly responsible, to a level "consistent with the needs and capability of the economy as a whole". This involved a decision, in accordance with the National Plan, to limit the total growth of public-sector expenditure to an average of $4\frac{1}{4}$ per cent a year at constant prices for 1964–65 to 1969–70. Within this total there would be an allocation to each of the main public services within which they would need to contain their Estimates. In coming to this decision, the White Paper said, "the essential and novel element was the procedure of deciding first how much the country could afford; then deciding how this could best be deployed; and finally requiring each spending Minister to arrange his expenditure within his agreed allocation".[2] One of the most controversial economies was the cutting of defence expenditure, which it was planned to cut from over 7 per cent of the gross national product to about 6 per cent by 1969–70.[3]

Several wages and prices claims were referred to the Prices and Incomes Board, and at its annual conference at Brighton in 1965 the Trades Union Congress agreed to co-operate still further with the Government by

1 Hansard, fifth series, vol. 718, cc. 1041 ff.

2 *Public Expenditure: Planning and Control*, February 23, 1966, Cmnd. 2915.

3 *The Defence Review*, February 22, 1966, Cmnd. 2901; *Defence Estimates, 1966*, Cmnd. 2902.

5+

operating a voluntary 'early warning system' by which trade unions would notify the TUC of impending wage-claims. Such notification could not sidetrack a wage-claim, but it could at least delay it, ensure that it was backed by a strong case, and give the Board ample time for consideration. Notwithstanding, incomes and prices were still rising. The Index of Retail Prices rose by 4·6 per cent between January 1964 and January 1965 and by 4·4 per cent between January 1965 and January 1966. The Index of Food Prices rose by 4·6 per cent and 2·4 per cent over the same period.[1] Wages and salaries in 1965 were £1300 million up on the previous year, other money incomes were £500 million up, yet productivity rose to the extent of only £600 million.[2] Even so, hire-purchase and other credit instalments outstanding in Great Britain had grown without remission since 1960, and at the end of 1965 stood at £1386 million[3]: to that extent the nation was using goods it had not paid for.

By the end of 1965 the Minister for Economic Affairs was speaking in terms of compulsion, and on February 24, 1966, he gave notice in the House of Commons of a Bill that would not only require notice of increases but would contain provisions for enforcing a temporary standstill in prices or charges or terms and conditions of employment.[4]

In March 1966 the Prime Minister asked for the dissolution of Parliament, and the Labour Government appealed to the country for a more decisive mandate to continue its policy. The General Election of March 31, 1966, gave the Labour Party a majority of 96 over all other parties combined: it was a mandate sufficient for confidence and strengthened them in handling the economic situation.

The first Budget of the new Administration was remarkable for the Selective Employment Tax,[5] and the wide discussion and considerable opposition which followed this had not died down when George Brown introduced the second reading of the promised Prices and Incomes Bill on July 14. The Minister had been facing a mounting barrage of criticism from trade unionists who felt that this was to be a weapon whose sharpest edge would be reserved for wage-earners while other forms of income escaped the axe. Brown promised explicitly that his Act would apply also to dividends. But still the men were not satisfied, and there began to rise the feeling that the very purpose for which trade unions

---

[1] Written answer, House of Commons, February 25, 1966, (Hansard, fifth series, vol. 725, c. 159).

[2] The Prime Minister, House of Commons, July 20, 1966 (*ibid.*, vol. 732, c. 635).

[3] *Monthly Digest of Statistics*.

[4] Hansard, fifth series, vol. 725, c. 634.   [5] *Supra*, p. 113.

existed, the purpose for which they had been founded, was being threatened. Wage negotiations between employers and employed had for centuries ended in the masters' favour: it was unreasonable to ask, now that the men had the upper hand, that they should abandon the traditional form of settlement.

Leading opponent of an incomes policy was the powerful Transport and General Workers' Union. Secretary of the Union was Frank Cousins. He had been given leave of absence to stand for Parliament, was returned as Member of Parliament for Nuneaton, and took office as Minister of Technology. Any stand he made was bound to be effective. On July 3 he resigned his Ministerial post, but not his seat in the House. His trade union approved his action, and his constituency was content that he should continue to represent it in Parliament. Thus backed, he strongly opposed Brown's Prices and Incomes Bill on July 14.

He took the issue back to fundamentals. We were concentrating, he said, on the wages question; yet doctors, judges, generals, Ministers, Members of Parliament all had increases of income too. "The issue is how I explain this kind of thing to the kind of people I represent in Nuneaton and in the Transport and General Workers' Union." "The mistake which we are making", he said, "is in assuming that our problem is to tackle an inflationary situation created by a wage cycle. I do not accept this. Ours is not a high-wage economy in any sense." He silenced an Opposition interrupter by turning on him and retorting: "The Hon. Member's Company gave itself an increase, through its directors, of 15 per cent last year. I also am in favour of that kind of incomes policy." He cut through a great deal of slipshod talk by asserting: "We talk rather loosely about productivity and production; but there are no figures. ... We say that productivity is not rising fast enough. ... 'Productivity is not rising as fast as wages.' Which productivity? Which wages?" Cousins appealed to the Labour Government not to forfeit the support of the trade union Members who put it in office.[1]

Cousins's case lost its edge slightly in view of the fact that since the beginning of 1966, $5\frac{1}{4}$ million workers had had wage increases, $1\frac{1}{2}$ million others had a cut in hours, $2\frac{1}{4}$ million had both; hourly earning in manufacturing rose by 7 per cent in the first three months of the year. Since the Labour Party—*their* Party—took office in October 1964 hourly earnings had risen $2\frac{1}{4}$ times faster than output per man hour. There had been many wage agreements but few productivity agreements.[2] Though both sides of industry were to blame for this the fact

[1] House of Commons, July 14, 1966 (Hansard, fifth series, vol. 731, cc. 1787 ff.).
[2] *The Economist*, July 2, 1966.

remained that the Labour Government had not taken its trade unionists along with it—a fact which had been demonstrated in even more immediately damaging fashion by a seven weeks' strike of seamen in May and June. When the seamen returned to work it was on better terms than the Government-appointed court of inquiry recommended[1] and was a sharp blow to the incomes policy. The strike also adversely affected the balance of payments. The passage of the Prices and Incomes Bill on July 14 by 340 votes to 236 was rather like sewing the wind.

The trade figures for June were known by this time, and were bad enough, coupled with the general situation, to start off the old bogey—a run on the pound. Another Emergency. Devaluation of the pound was considered more seriously. But Britain could not easily change the relationship of sterling and other currencies, and instead the Prime Minister announced a six months' standstill on incomes and prices; increases in purchase tax and duties; a stiffening of hire-purchase contracts; a temporary increase in surtax; a steep reduction in foreign holiday allowances; a deferment of public expenditure and stiff control of building projects.[2] It was a good dose of deflation that might have been given much earlier with excellent results. Its outstanding weakness was its inability to make effective the prices-and-incomes standstill: it would be dependent upon the Unions and the attitude they cared to take—even if it was stiffened by compulsion. Its inherent danger lay in the unemployment that deflation was likely to bring in its train.

One thing was clear. No solution had yet been found to Britain's problem. Perhaps there was no problem? The man in the street, still better off than he had ever been before, enjoying World Cup international football live or on his television screen while Wilson's Cabinet was making its grave decisions, was inclined to regard the whole thing as a case of The Emperor's New Clothes. Another thing was certain. No clarion call that would sound the "re-awakening of the British people" had yet been heard, and nothing better was envisaged than a consumers' society in which titillation was easy and consciences need not prick because the underprivileged were few and all political parties had promised to help them. Nightmares concerning balance of payments, devaluation, and insolvency could be scotched by the story of the boy who cried wolf—it was the boy and not the villagers who was eaten when the wolf actually did appear!

---

[1] *First Report of the Court of Inquiry into certain matters concerning the Shipping Industry* (the Pearson Report), June 1966, Cmnd. 3025.

[2] The Prime Minister, House of Commons, July 20, 1966 (Hansard, fifth series, vol. 732, cc. 627–654).

CHAPTER IX

The Nationalized Undertakings: Principles and Aims

"... an industry's efficiency is compounded of two factors: its success in giving its customers the goods and services they want, and its success in minimising the cost of so doing."

The Herbert Committee on the
Electricity Supply

BRITISH ECONOMIC development was taking place upon the basis of a mixed economy of private enterprise and nationalization. There had been little objection to this, except in the case of iron and steel and road haulage, and with these exceptions the Tory succession had resulted in no call for denationalization.

A British nationalized concern is accountable to Parliament through a Minister and through Parliament to the nation. Although the Public Corporation, which was the statutory form taken by a nationalized enterprise in Britain, was endowed with a considerable measure of independence which covered the day-to-day running of its concern, yet policy matters rested with the Minister. The Minister's relation to the Corporation was delicate: a man holding only temporary office, by profession a politician and only fortuitously a businessman or expert, was responsible for the policy of a Board of highly specialized professionals. He needed men to advise him on technical matters: should these be civil servants? But why should civil servants be good businessmen? Should they be members of the industry concerned? There was then the suggestion of bias. Should the Minister informally seek to learn from and convey decisions to the Board? When a Conservative administration practised too much informal contact Parliament was quick to preserve its rights. The power of the Minister must be open and direct, not informal. The latter means that Ministers are taking policy decisions for which they cannot be made answerable in Parliament and opens the way to "a species of the corporate society more familiar to Italian Fascist principles than to the British democratic constitution", as Aneurin Bevan said in the House of Commons. The responsibility of deciding what was in the overriding interests of the nation must rest openly and completely with the Minister, he said, "because only by it resting with him can it rest here".[1]

The composition of the Boards who ran the nationalized concerns was of great importance. There was criticism that too many industrial tycoons, too many from the employing and management side generally, were being used, yet the new Boards found they needed skill and experience in management and the overall understanding of techniques. As Attlee admitted, it was one of the big problems of nationalization: "You couldn't suddenly create a whole lot of new mining engineers." Moreover, trade unionists were strangely unwilling to come on to the Boards. "We used what we could get," Attlee said ten years later. "They weren't always willing to cross over, nor were their men always willing for them to go in: a curious contradiction, because they talked of Labour running the show and yet when you put a trade unionist in to help run a nationalized industry they tended to regard him as a bosses' man."[2] This feeling among trade unionists that, even in public industry, they should not be involved in management decisions, that this would divert them from their proper role of fighting for the interests of their members, showed how deep-seated was the belief in a fundamental difference of attitude and end between the two sides of industry. It was partly responsible for the feeling that grew up that nationalization meant the same old bosses under different names. As Attlee said, the workers themselves were partly to blame. The Government tried hard, he said, to establish a greater voice by workers in the running of industry, to establish more joint consultation. But many workers still had the old feeling of opposition to any administration; others frankly declared that management wasn't their job; others found that after the establishment of the new Board their existing loyalties were interfered with—this was particularly true of the railways, where there had been a certain amount of pride in being a Great Western man or a North-Eastern man.[3]

The Central Board of the British Transport Commission had two out of five full-time members from the labour side—John Benstead, of the

[1] February 25, 1952 (Hansard, fifth series, vol. 496, c. 818).
[2] *A Prime Minister Remembers*, conversations with Francis Williams, pp. 93, 92.
[3] *Ibid.*, p. 93.

National Union of Railwaymen, and Lord Rusholme, from the Co-operative Union. On the Railway Executive W. P. Allen, of the Associated Society of Locomotive Engineers and Firemen, was the only labour man out of six full-time members. The Docks and Inland Waterways Executive had as their only labour representative out of four full-time appointments John Donovan, of the Docks Group of the Transport and General Workers' Union. The London Passenger Transport Executive drew all its five full-time members from the management side. The Road Transport Executive had one out of five full-time members from a trade union—H. E. Clay, of the Transport and General Workers' Union. The Gas Council consisted exclusively of men with professional qualifications. The Coal Board was at first well served with Lord Citrine, the trade union leader, in charge of manpower and welfare, and Ebby Edwards, of the Miners' Federation of Great Britain, in charge of labour relations—two out of nine full-time members. The British Electricity Authority took as Chairman Lord Citrine, from the Coal Board, and E. W. Bussey, from the Electrical Trades Union, to act as Labour Relations and Welfare Officer—two out of four.

But quite apart from the composition of the Boards neither Labour nor Conservative Governments have doubted the necessity of keeping a strict watch on the nationalized industries, and it has been Government policy to subject them to periodic scrutiny by Parliamentary Committees. There have even been Committees to consider whether the recommendations of Committees have been carried out. In this way a large literature of White Papers and Blue Books has grown up concerning nationalization generally and the development of each industry in particular. This, together with their own Annual Reports and the accountability to the Minister inherent in their set-up, has ensured that the activities of the nationalized industries are public—too much so according to some observers who complain that the Boards of nationalized concerns are made to work in glasshouses subject to pettifogging and uninformed scrutiny.

Accountability implies the recognition of a standard or principle. Yet, beyond the general recognition that public ownership would supersede private and that an enterprise would be managed in the public interest, the aim of nationalization was not made very clear at the time of the legislation and has only slowly evolved since. The Boards were given little guidance as to what constituted 'public interest'; doubtless the question had as many answers as there were divisions in society and would vary with the same person according as he regarded himself as consumer, worker, manager, or taxpayer. There was at one time the feeling that the nationalized industries would be used in a revolutionary sense to manage the economy, and some remarks of Attlee carried this implication. They had to go ahead with "fundamental nationalization", he claimed, "because it fell in with the planning, the essential planning of the country".[1] Fifteen years later a Labour Party Conference approved of nationalization because it would give the community power over "the commanding heights of the economy".[2] In neither case would the criteria of success need to be measured in ordinary business terms. Similarly, if it were decided that the main object of a nationalized concern was to provide the public with a comprehensive service at low cost, then the criteria of private enterprise would have to be abandoned and some other measure of efficiency substituted. In either case the Government might need to think in terms of subsidy rather than of profit. On the other hand, and this fell in with many of the arguments for nationalization and many of the claims made on its behalf, it could be expected of a nationalized concern that it used its position and its size in the interests of efficiency, service, and cheapness. In this case it would be amenable to the standards of the private sector of the economy and be expected to show a profit in the ordinary commercial sense.

The nationalization statutes had met the problem in a very general kind of way which assumed that the object was to provide the best possible service at the lowest possible cost. The criteria which they demanded in practice differed from industry to industry but, on the whole, prescribed a minimum of performance rather than a maximum. They expected that revenues should, on an average of good and bad years, be not less than sufficient to meet all items properly chargeable to revenue, including interest, depreciation, the redemption of capital, and the provision of reserves. None of the statutes gave the Government formal power to fix prices, though the nationalized industries were expected, in deciding these prices, to give great weight to considerations of the national interest and, through their Annual Reports, were accountable to their Ministries for their decisions.

Before ten years had passed it was apparent that by commercial standards the nationalized industries were far from being successful: they were not, that is to say, providing a return on capital invested which was anywhere near as good as that obtainable in the private sector of the economy. With a total investment of more than £800 million, more than half of which came from the Exchequer, it then became necessary to ask whether any balancing of economic and social considerations in the running of the nationalized industries warranted this divergence. In

---

[1] *Ibid.*, p. 88.   [2] In 1959 at Blackpool; and see *infra*, pp. 128–129.

other words, the question had to be asked more specifically whether the criteria applied to the nationalized industries should be the same as those applying to industry as a whole, or whether social considerations were so important as to outweigh the need to show a profit in the conventional sense. If it was considered legitimate, for non-economic reasons, that the public sector should show a return of, say, 5 per cent while the private sector earned 15 per cent, then the community would be subsidized so far as those particular services were concerned, and it would become a question of national policy as to how far this was admissible. There would be the additional danger of stepping up demand for the cheaper, nationalized products, directing too much of the nation's resources to them, and ultimately damaging the whole economy, both by a lopsided development and by increased taxation—for the nationalized industries in this situation would be leaning more heavily upon the Exchequer than was healthy either for themselves, the taxpayer, or the economy generally.

The Labour Party as a whole came down on the side of regarding the nationalized concerns as normal business enterprises. They were to be given every help to stand on their own feet, and to this end Herbert Morrison suggested that the chairmen of the various Boards should establish an efficiency unit as a collective organ of the Corporations to act as a body of industrial consultants advising on problems of management, costing, finance, and organization. This suggestion was not taken up, but Lord Citrine thought that the Corporations should call in industrial consultants if they needed them. Both men recognized that the principles of the business world could, and should, be used to induce efficiency in a nationalized concern. The Conservatives had always believed this, and while they were in power it was openly recognized that the nationalized industries must be judged by commercial standards. In 1958 a Committee examining the Electricity Supply, while assuming that this should be so, raised the secondary question of how to measure such efficiency: "an industry's efficiency is compounded of two factors: its success in giving its customers the goods and services they want, and its success in minimising the cost of so doing. The problem in assessing the efficiency of a monopolistic industry, whether nationalized or not, is how to judge whether its consumers are getting what they want, whether the costs are properly allocated between them, and whether the industry is using the least quantity of real resources for any given level of output."[1]

[1] *The Report of the Committee of Inquiry into the Electricity Supply Industry* (the Herbert Committee), 1956, Part II, Chapter 2, p. 5.

In April 1961 a Government White Paper went further, and devoted itself explicitly to the task of reviewing the manner in which the economic and financial principles inherent in the nationalization statutes had been applied in practice and how they should be interpreted for the future. "First", it said, "the task of government is to ensure that the industries are organised and administered efficiently and economically to carry out their responsibilities, and that they are thus enabled to make the maximum contribution towards the economic well-being of the community as a whole. Second, although the industries have obligations of a national and non-commercial kind, they are not, and ought not, to be regarded as social services absolved from economic and commercial justification." It would not want to alter the basic financial and economic principles which the nationalized undertakings were by their statutes required to observe, yet it would require these to be interpreted more precisely in the form of financial objectives. It suggested that revenue should be made to balance over a five-year period and that the rate of return expected over the period should be agreed between the Minister and the Board of each industry.[1]

Discussions between the Ministers concerned and the various nationalized undertakings accordingly followed, and specific results were announced during 1962. The Electricity Boards agreed to an average gross return of about $12\frac{1}{2}$ per cent on average net assets from 1962–63 to 1966–67; the North of Scotland Hydro-electric Board made a similar agreement. The Gas Board agreed to an average return of about $10\frac{1}{4}$ per cent. The National Coal Board was compelled by its circumstances to make a slightly different provision and agreed to break even from 1963 after paying interest and making proper provision for depreciation, including the earmarking of £10 million a year to help cover the difference between depreciation at historic and replacement cost.[2]

It had taken nearly twenty years to decide that the nationalized industries should be run as commercial, profit-making concerns. Over that period they had, on the whole, kept pace with the improvements in conditions, hours of work, and wages that had been common to the whole economy, but nothing had occurred either in their relations to the economy as a whole, in their role as producer, in their relationship to their staffs or in the staffs' relation to the industry to justify the dreams of Labour pioneers. Herbert Morrison had hoped that the sense that they

---

[1] *The Financial and Economic Obligations of the Nationalised Industries*, Cmnd. 1337, pp. 3, 7.

[2] Mr Barber in a written reply to the House of Commons, March 11, 1963 (Hansard, fifth series, vol. 673, cc. 109–110).

were all working together for the good of the community would develop "a new consciousness on the part of management, technicians and labour" of their role in society that would cause them to "go about their daily work accordingly, deriving pleasure from the fact that they have the privilege of working for the good of the country and the well-being of their fellow citizens".[1] That it was not to be quite like this was made clear by Attlee's remarks. The men had expected more—more in the tangible sense of more money, shorter hours; more possibly in the sense of seeing their work change its nature; more in the sense of becoming personally more important, more than continuing to be the same cog in a similar wheel; possibly just more in the sense of seeing brightness displace the drab of the familiar workplace.

Railwaymen must have felt extraordinarily bitter when they heard the British Transport Commission argue that its statutory obligation to cover expenses precluded it from granting the wage increases demanded by the National Union of Railwaymen. But the Court of Inquiry which was appointed refused to accept this view and enunciated what has become the classic statement of wages policy for a nationalized industry: "The Nation has provided by statute that there shall be a nationalised system of railway transport, which must therefore be regarded as a public utility of the first importance. Having willed the end, the Nation must will the means. This implies that employees of such a national service should receive a fair and adequate wage, and that, in broad terms, the railwayman should be in no worse case than his colleague in a comparable industry. The argument which has been repeatedly used by the British Transport Commission, that they found themselves unable to pay rates of wages which they might otherwise deem proper and desirable, is, of course, wholly inconsistent with such a view. In these circumstances it is plain that there is no substance in the argument that there is an absolute statutory bar which prevents the Commission from paying such rates of wages as may involve them in any particular year in a deficit."[2] The Final Report of the Court of Inquiry explicitly stated how the railwaymen's wages should be determined: "Where (as in the case of the Commission) the employer is bound to keep his business going and can neither show a working profit, nor shift the scene of his operations, nor reorganise his capital structure, nor be wound up by his creditors, then the factors which are understood by all as affecting the

[1] Foreword to *Efficiency in the Nationalised Industries* (Institute of Public Administration).

[2] *Interim Report* of a Court of Inquiry into a Dispute between the British Transport Commission and the National Union of Railwaymen presided over by Sir John (later Lord) Cameron, January 1955, Cmd. 9352, p. 6.

wage rates in normal industry are absent. The conditions in his business are, commercially speaking, artificial and it therefore becomes necessary to fall back on the expedient of relating the wages he should pay to those paid in such comparable industries as may be found."[1] It was good to hear such a pronouncement, but ironic that the nationalized undertaking, so far from setting a standard, was expected to take its standards from private industry.

In their 1950 Election Manifesto the Labour Party had still seen fit, in spite of the fact that the nationalized concerns were not at that period doing particularly well, to advocate the extension of nationalization to a wide range of enterprises. This was commonly held to have contributed to their defeat,[2] and in the period of soul-searching that followed the concept of nationalization and its extension was widely discussed. In 1952 the Institute of Public Administration published a booklet entitled *Efficiency in the Nationalised Industries*, to which Herbert Morrison's *Foreword* was somewhat apologetic. Gone was the crusader zeal of earlier days. "It is clearly thoughtless and unreasonable", he wrote, "to expect that the mere passage of an Act of Parliament and the subsequent transfer of privately owned industries to public will bring about a new order of things overnight." After the Labour Party was beaten again at the General Election of October 1959 it summoned a special Conference at Blackpool to consider the reasons. Hugh Gaitskell, the Party leader, called for the withdrawal of Clause IV, subsection 4, of the Party Constitution which had been adopted in 1918 and which spoke of securing the common ownership of the means of production.[3] Clause IV, he claimed, laid the party open to continual misrepresentation. Nationalization was not the be-all and end-all, the ultimate first principle and aim of Socialism: "we regard public ownership not as an end in itself, but as a means—and not necessarily the only or most important one to certain ends—such as full employment, greater equality and high productivity." Nor did the Labour Party intend to spread nationalization indefinitely. The belief that they did was doing them endless harm. The public were led to suppose they were going to take over everything indiscriminately, right and left, when they got back to power, simply out of a doctrinaire belief in public ownership. The existing nationalized industries were unpopular, and nationalization in general was a vote-loser.

But Clause IV was not amended. Instead a compromise was reached which extended the Clause and was intended to clarify the Party's

---

[1] *Ibid., Final Report*, January 1955, Cmd. 9372, para 62, p. 21.
[2] *Supra*, p. 79.   [3] *Supra*, p. 66.

attitude to nationalization. The social and economic objectives of the Party, it said, could "be achieved only through an expansion of common ownership substantial enough to give the community power over the commanding heights of the economy. Common ownership takes varying forms, including State-owned industries and firms, producer and consumer co-operation, municipal ownership, and public participation in private concerns. Recognizing that both public and private enterprise have a place in the economy, it believes that further extension of common ownership should be decided from time to time in the light of these objectives and according to circumstances, with due regard for the views of the workers and consumers concerned." This addition was approved by the Conference of the Labour Party at Scarborough in 1960. Henceforth the voter might take Clause IV section 4 unadulterated or any variant that the addendum proposed. In the 1964 General Election nationalization was scarcely an issue except that the Iron and Steel Industry still remained a battle-ground for the rival parties.

CHAPTER X

The Nationalized Undertakings: Controversy—Iron and Steel

"... the whole business is controversial from start to finish, whoever does anything."

Herbert Morrison, House of Commons,
October 23, 1952

WHILE THE defeated Labour Party was practising self-analysis on the subject of nationalization the victorious Conservatives had already denationalized one of the industries brought under public ownership by the Labour Government.

The Labour Government's Iron and Steel Act of November 1949 had been passed in the teeth of strong opposition by a Government in the last months of its life.[1] It came into operation against a background of international uncertainty and economic difficulty and to the accompaniment of constant Conservative sniping. Three months after its passage into law the General Election of February 1950 reduced the Labour Government's votes to a minority and gave it a bare majority of seats in the House. Nevertheless, on October 2, 1950, it appointed an Iron and Steel Corporation and announced that Vesting Day would be early in 1951—the earliest date permitted by the Act. As the Korean crisis developed in 1950 the Conservatives argued that this was no time for a major change in British economic policy by a minority Government. Early in 1951 a new White Paper on defence, increasing public expenditure to £4700 million over three years and raising National Service to two years[2] provided an unpropitious background for Vesting Day, which the Government nevertheless fixed for February 15. Only eight months after the vesting of the Iron and Steel Corporation of

[1] *Supra*, pp. 74–76. It took a year to pass from its second reading into law.
[2] Cmd. 8146.

Great Britain the General Election of October brought the Conservatives to power with an overall majority of 17, and while standstill orders were immediately issued to the State Corporation, the King's Speech of November 6, 1951, announced a Bill to annul the Iron and Steel Act and reorganize the industry under free enterprise but with an adequate measure of public supervision[1]: there was, in effect, never any nationalization of iron and steel.

In July 1952 the Conservative Government issued a White Paper announcing its detailed plans. Two bodies were proposed—an Iron and Steel Board to supervise the industry and an Iron and Steel Realization Agency to take over and dispose of the assets held by the State. The Iron and Steel Board would be composed of not more than twelve members, appointed by the Minister of Supply, who would all have knowledge of the industry itself, of the principal industries using iron and steel, or of the trade unions concerned. There would be an independent chairman and some independent members, and all would be appointed for a maximum term of five years and be eligible for reappointment. The White Paper made a strong point of reuniting the nationalized and non-nationalized sectors of the industry: "It is intended that all the main processes which make up the iron and steel industry . . . shall come within the purview of the new Board, thus bringing the whole industry again under the supervision of a single authority and ending the present distinction between nationalised and non-nationalised sectors." On the other hand, certain engineering and extraneous activities which had been brought under the control of the Iron and Steel Corporation because they happened to form part of the activities of the nationalized companies would not be included. In general, the powers and duties of the Board were to consist of "supervising the industry with a view to promoting the efficient, economical and adequate supply of iron and steel". In particular, they were to concern the development of production capacity, prices, the supply of raw material, research and technical training, arrangements for joint consultation between management and employees on matters of mutual interest other than wages and conditions of service, and arrangements for the health, safety, and welfare of employees.[2]

On October 23, 1952, Duncan Sandys, the Minister of Supply, moved in the House of Commons the approval of the policy set out in the White Paper, and thus gave an opportunity for discussion of the intended de-nationalization measure. It would abandon, he said, the "progressive tightening of central control" feared by the steel industry and end the "arbitrary division which was created by the 1949 Act". Consumers

1 Hansard, fifth series, vol. 493, c. 52.   2 Cmd. 8619.

would be more adequately represented on the new Board than they had been on the Corporation, capital development would be supervised by the Board in order that individual schemes should dovetail with the development of the industry as a whole, and the Minister, where no company felt able to undertake schemes of development which in the national interest seemed desirable, would have powers to supply the necessary facilities. The Board would have power to restrain a company and, in view of the importance of iron and steel to the national economy, the Government would have reserve powers over the Board to fix maximum prices if necessary and to ensure an adequate supply of raw material.[1] The Bill proposed by Sandys in November 1952—three years after nationalization, nearly two years after vesting date—was to this effect. Discussion throughout the debates ran along the general lines already laid down: Steel is power! *versus* Iron and Steel—leave well alone! It is "indefensible", said Strauss for the Labour Party, "for the control of this industry—on which depends our economy—the fate of townships and the livelihood of hundreds of thousands of employees—to rest in the hands of people with no public responsibility". It is necessary, said Sandys, to restore the "independence, initiative and enterprise in the iron and steel industry" which is not possible under nationalization.[2]

The Bill was given its second reading on November 27, 1952, by 305 votes to 269. It became law on May 14 in the following year, and came into operation on July 13, when the shares of private owners which had been acquired by the Iron and Steel Corporation were handed over to the Iron and Steel Holding and Realization Agency to sell, offers from previous owners being given priority. The sale was not very rapid, and handing back was even more protracted than acquisition. In 1965 Richard Thomas and Baldwins, Ltd, was still owned by the Agency. One of the lessons of the whole episode was that a change-over is disturbing whichever way it goes.

In its one and only full Report the Iron and Steel Corporation had announced a target output of 20 million tons of steel for 1957. The target was reached and passed with an output of 22 million tons in 1957 and 24·3 million tons in 1960. Taking the period between 1948 and 1960 as a whole, there had been, in fact, a greater increase than in the previous thirty years. But Britain had been much slower in getting off the mark than some other countries, and her progress compared unfavourably with theirs. While United Kingdom crude-steel production increased by

---

1 Hansard, fifth series, vol. 505, cc. 1274 ff.
2 *Ibid.*, vol. 505, cc. 1274–1406 *passim*, and vol. 508, cc. 266–325, 384–426, 643–754 *passim*.

60 per cent between 1948 and 1960, world production more than doubled. The figures for iron ore and for pig-iron give a similar picture: Britain's progress was more than matched by most other countries.[1]

For Western Europe as a whole a period of intensive growth ended in 1960, and steel was no exception to the relative decline that set in over the next two years in most countries. The share of Western Europe as a whole in world crude-steel production dropped from 31·1 per cent in 1960 to 28·3 per cent in 1962, while that of Eastern Europe and Asia increased. In the first half of 1963 the British Steel Industry showed a small rise in output, but was working to only about 70 per cent of capacity. With cuts in production, labour redundancy, falling prices and profits, increased indebtedness and financial difficulties, modernization plans were delayed. In part this was a reflection of Britain's domestic position, for the Iron and Steel Industry supplies, in the main, the big home industries—railways, shipbuilding, motor-cars, engineering generally, big building enterprises, and many producers of consumer articles. In their development can be read her own fortunes, and the depression of 1962–63 was bound to affect her.[2] But, while the British industry was working below capacity, steel imports were rising in 1962–1963. Under Commonwealth Preference, Canada, South Africa, and Australia sent in duty-free many semi-finished steel products; Scandinavia and France, partly to recoup their own falling fortunes at that time, sent bars, rods, sheets, and other steel items. Some were genuinely cheap; some were of low quality but adequate for their price and purpose; others again were highly specialized or of special quality; some were simply sent at the whim of a purchaser who liked to diversify his source. But others were merely 'dumped'

Yet, while this was happening and while previous customers were developing their own steel capacity and reducing their orders, the United Kingdom nevertheless exported 3·2 million tons of steel in 1963, surpassing the previous record of 1961 by 300,000 tons. But she was exporting on a buyer's market and prices were low.

British steel production turned upwards as the general economy expanded from the middle of 1963, helped by the expansionist measures announced by the Chancellor at the end of 1962 and by the Budget of 1963 as well as by financial grants made to enterprises setting up or expanding in Development districts. By the end of the year domestic deliveries of steel were running well above the previous year's figures, and there had been a sharp increase in productivity.

[1] *Statistical Yearbook, United Nations*, 1963, Table 115, p. 283
[2] *Supra*, pp. 93–94.

Although the expansion continued into 1964 there were still questions in some minds as to whether the industry could not be more adaptable—selling more sophisticated, highly finished articles where the market for crude steel was saturated; adopting a more flexible price structure that would bring down prices at home and abroad in times of over-supply; being quicker to experiment with new methods of production and new techniques—in short, improving both its competitive power and its productivity. The Iron and Steel Board's Annual Report for 1963 admitted that there was much ground to be made up before productivity approached that of the best steel industries abroad, but it claimed that the industry had emerged from the recession greatly strengthened by an extensive programme of expansion and modernization which had been virtually completed, that less efficient units had been closed and the industry become more research-minded. By March 1964, although it had been slow in beginning, it was making use of one of the more revolutionary oxygen techniques to a greater extent than most Continental countries. By the end of 1965 continuous casting was in full operation in four works, with sixteen major plants preparing to follow—an achievement which gave Britain a world lead. Research, which was primarily the responsibility of private steel firms, was going ahead generally. There was a new research centre at the Abbey Works of the Steel Company of Wales; there were new research laboratories at Firth Brown, Ltd, costing half a million pounds, new laboratories, costing £650,000, were under construction by the English Steel Corporation.[1]

With unemployment in the industry practically eliminated, with a remarkably trouble-free labour record, with its 300,000 workers among the highest paid and the most respected in the country, the iron and steel industry could feel "in excellent heart and shape" and out to beat all previous records. It asked only that imports should be controlled. Instead, in October 1964, against the advice of many economists and politicians, the newly elected Labour Government, albeit with an overall majority of only four, was preparing for the renationalization of the Iron and Steel Industry—its third major dislocation since the War.

The demands of the economic situation and the Labour Government's small majority prevented the measure being introduced in the first year of the new Parliament. But Harold Wilson was under considerable pressure from his Left wing, and the Queen's Speech of November 1965 again promised the renationalization of the industry.

[1] *British Iron and Steel Federation, Annual Report*, 1963. *Report of the Iron and Steel Board*, 1963; Report on "Research in the Iron and Steel Industry" by the Iron and Steel Board; *Development in the Iron and Steel Industry, Special Report, 1964.*

Again the weight of other business delayed the measure, and it was promised once again in the Speech from the Throne of April 21 that inaugurated the Parliament of 1966.

By that time the full production figures of crude steel for 1964 had shown a record, and those for 1965 a further 5 per cent increase to 27 million tons. Exports by volume and value were up, and imports had fallen by more than 50 per cent. The Iron and Steel Federation, at last admitting, nevertheless, the repeatedly urged need for reorganization, had appointed a Committee to study the future structure of the industry. Rationalization, organization into bigger units, competition, a new pricing system, and preparations for possible entry into the Common Market were among the recommendations it published two days before the renationalization Bill came up for its second reading.

The Bill, which was debated on July 25, proposed to take into public ownership the thirteen privately owned companies and Richard Thomas and Baldwin (which had never gone back to private ownership): these formed the dominant section of the industry. Compensation to existing owners would be paid on the basis of average Stock Exchange quotations on mid-month days. There was no detailed definition of the new structure, but it was intended that a National Steel Corporation would not only control the industry but have power to take over any of the activities of the fourteen companies. As these extended to some 40 per cent of the structural steelwork of the country and included aircraft manufacture, motor-car and vehicle production, the power to be vested in the Corporation and the Minister was enormous. Iron and steel was the only one of the nationalization measures that went beyond a service industry or a public utility, and it was doing it wholeheartedly, embracing a great manufacturing complex at the very core of the economy. Although the Minister of Power spoke persuasively of the need for ever greater efficiency and of the industry's failure to reorganize itself during the years of de-nationaliztion, it was clear that the fundamental question of power underlay the debate. It was given voice by the spokesman who wound up for the Government: "Steel is one of the commanding heights . . ." said Mr Diamond. "We propose", he concluded, "that Britain should occupy that height, and do it now."

The Bill was carried on July 25, 1966, by 81 votes. *The Times*, which had devoted a leading article to the Benson Report two days previously, did not give the news pride of place, nor mention it in a leader.[1]

[1] *British Iron and Steel Federation, Annual Report*, 1965. *Steel Nationalisation*, April 1965, Cmnd. 2651. Hansard, fifth series, vol. 732, cc. 1215–1363.

CHAPTER XI

The Nationalized Undertakings: Transport and Communications

"Industry and business depend on...the intricate and wide-embracing communication links which are essential to their own, and ultimately to the nation's, economic well being."

Post Office Report and Accounts, 1964–65, p.7

THE TRANSPORT ACT of 1947 was intended to provide "an efficient, adequate, economical and properly integrated system of public inland transport and port facilities" for the whole country. But the British Transport Commission soon ran into difficulties. Centralization on such a scale was impossibly clumsy, particularly since the parts of the whole were unlike, with varying problems and differing histories. The five public organizations, called Executives, in charge of the specialized services—the Railway Executive, the Road Transport Executive, the Inland Waterways Executive, the London Transport Executive, and the Hotels Executive—were not partners in an integrated whole but different organizations with separate problems: the formlessness of the title 'Executive' was some measure of the lack of clear thought that had gone into their establishment. True, they all—with one exception—shared the problem of carrying people or things from one place to another, and the more there was of one form of transport the less there should be of another. But it was unreal to lump under one authority institutions so different as a whole railway system and all the ports and inland waterways of the country. Moreover, to give equal status to institutions of such differing importance and size as the railways and the catering provisions made for those railways was fantastic. Problems of railway hotels and catering services at stations and on trains are fundamentally those of the caterer and not of a transport executive; and, as one commentator asked, what have docks and canals in common except water?

In any case it was ludicrous to put the whole railway network of the country into a subordinate position where it had only delegated powers. It could not itself approve expenditure of more than £25,000 (later raised to £50,000), and could borrow no money except temporarily for current business without the authority of the Commission. Moreover, the railways were not relieved of certain statutory obligations concerning carrying which were a feature of their growth and put them at a disadvantage with road carriers. In short, there was nothing in their history, there was nothing peculiar to them in 1947, to imply that being lumped together with other forms of transport and taken over lock, stock, and barrel by the State would make for efficiency. Only a most careful examination of their particular problems would suffice. A Railway Executive could do this. But it was not realistic to believe that subordination to a British Transport Authority on equal terms with a Hotels Executive would be encouraging.

Of the five Executives established in 1947 the London Transport Executive, in charge of a concern already firmly and profitably established, continued to do well. Ports and harbours remained in urgent need of modernization, but the BTC did much to unify inland waterways. It also acquired by agreement two of the three largest omnibus undertakings in the country and almost completed the acquisition of long-distance road haulage, organizing into a public service between 3000 and 4000 separate road-haulage undertakings. It was the Railway Executive, the largest and oldest of the individual units, which gave most of the trouble; "a very poor bag of physical assets" someone had called it shortly after nationalization. "Poor or not," remarked *The Times*, "the bag is of mammoth size."[1] There were 52,000 miles of railway, 20,000 locomotives, 45,000 passenger vehicles, 1,230,000 goods wagons, 50,000 houses, 70 hotels, hundreds of refreshment rooms, 100 ships.

The various private railway lines had been fiercely competitive in their origin and early development. Interest on capital invested, payment to landowners for transit rights, wages to navvies who built them, were high. The adventure and recklessness of the early years, of railway fortunes made and broken, were succeeded by sober amalgamation and State regulation. After the First World War 123 separate companies were by Act of Parliament amalgamated into the big four main-line systems, which carried on the mixture of good, bad, and indifferent lines they had inherited. In the years between the Wars they suffered both from the general depression, from road competition, and from

[1] Leading article, January 1, 1948.

their own loaded-in charges. Railway wages were low, and strikes and labour troubles were a feature of the industry. The companies did remarkably little to meet road competition, but invoked statutory authority to limit their rivals. Motor-bus and motor-coach services were regulated by the Road Traffic Act of 1930, and road haulage by that of 1933—both in the interests of the railways. But the railways still suffered from the disability of being compelled to carry at a published flat rate, which gave their rivals the opportunity of price-cutting and capturing trade. It was, on the whole, a somewhat dismal railway network, though enlivened by the distinctive colourings and uniforms of each of the Big Four.

The railways rose to the occasion during the Second World War, working hard and being worked to the uttermost without any possibility of renewal of equipment. By the end of the War their condition was deplorable, and the severe winter of 1946–47 added to their troubles. Yet they were the Cinderellas of post-War investment, and even the process of nationalization provided them with no capital renewal. By 1955, seven years after nationalization, they had received no share of post-War capital investment, and their financial position was precarious in the extreme—all the more so because it was undisclosed. The global system of accounting which had been passed on, without question, at each fresh stage of railway history had resulted in accounting units becoming larger as companies merged without any offsetting increase in detail; it is difficult to believe that the Railways Executive had anything but the very vaguest idea of its finances. And all the time all railway operating charges were rising against it—wages, national-insurance payments, the price of coal, petrol, oil, iron, steel, wood. Road passenger and goods transport was becoming more competitive, and railway traffic was falling, while fares remained uneconomically low: although the public was receiving railway services at less than cost it was bitterly hostile to any increase. Was there any important unsubsidized commodity or service of importance in this country, asked the British Transport Commission in its Report for 1950, the price of which was quite so low, relatively to pre-War, as the price of transport in the closing months of 1950?[1] The railways were less able to stand the strain than their rivals and provided the major part of the accumulated deficit of the BTC, which by 1950 was £39·6 million.[2]

Some authorities believed that in the circumstances and taking account of their inheritance the railways had not done a bad job and that a few more years should be allowed before further interference.

[1] Pp. 40–41.   [2] *Ibid.*, p. 37.

Some improvement in 1951, 1952, and 1953 supported this view.[1] But the Tories, who replaced the Labour Government in 1951, were pledged to reorganize the Transport Commission in general and the railways in particular. They had also promised to de-nationalize road-haulage. The case for de-nationalizing road haulage rested on its excessive centralization, on lack of co-ordination between road and rail services, and on the elaborate system of depots working under the Road Haulage Executive which gave, so it was claimed by the Tories, none of the speedy, individual, or specialized services which had been afforded by free enterprise.

A Section of the Transport Act of 1953 enacted that road haulage assets should be returned to private ownership by open tender through a Road Haulage Disposal Board appointed by the Minister of Transport. To help them meet the expected competition from private hauliers greater freedom was allowed the railways in the sphere of freight-charging, and they were no longer required to refrain from "undue preference" nor to preserve equality of charging. Contrary to the Government's expectations, however, there was no rush from free enterprise to acquire vehicles; at the same time the Government itself found the trunk service network which the Road Haulage Executive was running to be extremely useful in many ways.[2] Three years later, consequently, a further Transport Act modified the Commission's obligations to dispose of the major part of its road haulage undertakings and permitted it to retain a part of the general haulage fleet not at that time returned to private enterprise and amounting to some 8000 lorries.[3]

The Act of 1953 also intended a reorganization of the whole Transport Commission, and on August 19 the Minister made an Order for the abolition of all the Transport Executives except the London Transport Executive, which would retain its identity. A Board of Management, responsible to the BTC, would be in charge of docks and inland waterways; a similar Board would be responsible for what remained of road haulage; the Hotels Executive was replaced by a Chief Officer, also responsible to the BTC. In place of the Railway Executive were to be 6 Regional Authorities and 28 Area Authorities, the Regions to be fully responsible for the management and operation of their regional railway

[1] 1951: surplus balance on net revenue, £0·1 m.; 1952: surplus, £4·5 m.; 1953: surplus, £4·2 m. (Railways only). £2·9 m.; £8·4 m.; £4·2 m. (BTC).

[2] See, e.g., Hansard, fifth series, vol. 574, c. 573.

[3] The Transport (Disposal of Road Haulage Property) Act, 1956. The Transport Commission was left with three operating companies—British Road Services, Ltd (general haulage), British Road Services (Pickfords) Ltd for special traffics, and British Road Services (Contracts) Ltd, for contract hire.

systems through their Chief Regional Officers. The British Transport Commission was not taken by surprise. It had itself, indeed, already advised a reorganization that would give greater flexibility to the Regions: it believed "that the three-tier organization of Commission, Executive, and Region was no longer suitable to flexible and commercial methods of management" and that it was necessary "to knit transport policy together more closely at the centre on the one hand and, on the other, to decentralise day-to-day management, particularly on the railways".[1]

As well as reorganization the Act of 1953 required the British Transport Commission to prepare a scheme to bring British Railways up to date. By 1954 this was ready. Its basic objective was to "transform the operation of British Railways so as to offer the public a rail service second to none, whilst deriving from the re-equipment the full economic benefits it can provide". The sentiments were only too familiar. Concretely the plan provided for the progressive replacement of steam by diesel and electric traction, for improvements in track and operating installations including signalling and other modern equipment, and for the modernization of freight services with increased mechanization of goods depots and better terminal facilities generally, and for new and improved rolling stock and freight vehicles. The cost, over a period of fifteen years, was estimated at £1200 million; subsequently it was reassessed at £1660 million.[2]

It was expected that the modernization plan would put the railways in balance by 1961–62 and provide a surplus by 1970. From the point of view of comfort and appearance alone the results were good; and the British Transport Commission went on to establish a Design Panel with a small executive staff to advise upon the best means of obtaining a high standard of appearance and amenity in equipment, and it ran a five weeks' exhibition at the Design Centre in London on New Design for the Railways. But schemes like this were a drop in the ocean of rising costs and under-capitalization. The railway plan was excellent as a modernization-of-equipment scheme, but it did not, partly because it could not, envisage any basic changes in the scope and organization of the railways. The three years of surplus were ended with a deficit by the British Transport Commission of £11·9 million in 1954 and £30·6 million in 1955, and the chief contributor to the deficit was British Railways.

The tragedy of the railways was under-capitalization. They were constantly endeavouring to make good past losses, applying capital, when

---

[1] *Report of the British Transport Commission*, 1953, p. 6.   [2] Cmd. 9191.

at last they had it, to repairing losses incurred during and after the War. 'Development' in the sense of expansion by new schemes and general refurbishment was not possible until 1954, and by then it was too little and too late. Any increase in railway fares was bitterly opposed both by railway-users and by those who wanted to retain some measure of competition between road and rail; yet unless fares kept up with costs there could be no solvency: so late as 1958 railway fares were only double their pre-War level, though the cost-of-living index had risen by 270 per cent. Some observers pointed out that all the costs of running the railways, including the cost of the permanent way—the track costs—are regarded as internal railway charges and loaded into the outlay upon which the railways are expected to show profit. The cost of building and maintaining roads, on the other hand, is met by general taxation. True, road-users contribute heavily, but it is not incumbent upon any particular carrier to make any operation financially viable in terms which include the cost of providing and servicing the stretch of road concerned—the contributions of general taxation and of all the other road-users are also involved. If railways and road traffic could be treated exactly equally in this respect, in having the true costs of the permanent way or road attributed to each of them, there would at least be equality of opportunity to both to compete for traffic.

In 1956 a fresh system of accounting divorced the railways from the other activities of the British Transport Commission, and thereafter the development of British Railways was undisguised—a deficit of £27·1 million in 1956, of £48·1 million in 1958, of £42 million in 1959, of £67·7 million in 1960, of £87 million in 1961, £104 million in 1962.[1] In 1960 the Government had again taken alarm: the railway system "must be of a size and pattern suited to modern conditions and prospects," said the Prime Minister in the House of Commons; it "must be remodelled to meet current needs".[2] The means to this end were announced at the end of the year in a White Paper on *The Reorganisation of the Nationalised Transport Undertaking*,[3] which proposed to wind up the British Transport Commission as being too large and diverse for the effective control of its constituents. Instead a separate Board was proposed for each of its main activities, each Board holding its own assets, liable for its own debts, and directly responsible to the Minister of Transport. As a first step towards this reorganization the Chairman of the Commission retired in June 1961.

1 Working deficit before charging interest.
2 March 10, 1960 (Hansard, fifth series, vol. 619, c. 643).
3 December 1960, Cmnd. 1248.

Since the new arrangements were largely in the interests of railway efficiency the personnel of the proposed British Railways Board was of great importance, and on March 15, 1961, the Government announced in the House of Commons that Dr Richard Beeching, a man of distinguished scientific achievements and a Director of Imperial Chemical Industries, was to be its chairman; he would also assume the vacant chairmanship of the British Transport Commission until its demise. Immediately there was uproar. He was being 'lent' by ICI for five years at his then salary of £24,000 a year—"interrupting his career", as the Minister put it, to turn his exceptional talents to reorganizing the railways. It was an "exceptional salary for an exceptional appointment". If they wanted the best they must pay what the best could earn in organizations outside the Government. What about engine-drivers? How much would go in income tax? What would count as expenses? Members shouted. The Minister could only reiterate in various forms the basic dilemma: after thirteen years of nationalization the railways were losing £300,000 a day, and exceptional action was required. But Mr Grimond still wanted the Minister to explain what was meant by his extraordinary announcement that Dr Beeching was "prepared to interrupt his career". "Are we taking the railways seriously or are we not?" he asked. "Can we get no-one in this country who is prepared to make a career of the railways and to stake his reputation on making them efficient, and to treat the matter with a modicum of seriousness?"[1]

The new Transport Act became law in 1962, and came into force on September 1. Vesting Day for the new organization was January 1, 1963, when the British Transport Commission was abolished and five Authorities took over—the British Railways Board, the British Waterways Board, the London Transport Board, the British Transport Docks Board, and a Holding Company. Docks and Inland Waterways were separated, the Holding Company included (as British Road Services) the road carrier services not sold back to private enterprise, two passenger road service groups acquired by the BTC (Tilling Buses and Scottish Omnibuses), certain shipping services and road freight services, Thos. Cook and Son, Ltd, whose large travel organization had been acquired by the BTC, and several other enterprises lumped together as "Other Holdings". All were ultimately responsible to the Minister of Transport.

The British Railways Board directed the general policy of six Regional Railway Boards, but each of these was fully responsible for the management and operation of its railway system. The names were the old names

[1] Hansard, fifth series, vol. 636, cc. 1400–13 *passim*.

only slightly altered—there were even suggestions for reviving distinctive uniforms and colours for each region—the Eastern Railway Board, the London, Midland Railway Board, the North-Eastern, the Scottish, the Southern, the Western Railway Boards. Their chairmen, appointed by the Minister of Transport, sat on the British Railways Board; the catering for their trains and stations, Pullman cars and hotels, was in the hands of British Transport Hotels, Ltd, responsible to the British Railways Board.[1] Dr Beeching took up the chairmanship of the British Railways Board towards the end of 1962, when the BTC and the BRB existed for a short time together. He was already Chairman of the BRB when he submitted in 1962 the final—the fifteenth—Annual Report of the British Transport Commission.

For fifteen years the British Transport Commission had controlled one of the largest single industrial organizations in the world, employing 700,000 people, covering rail, road, canals, ports, shipping, hotels, catering, and travel agencies. The cards had been heavily stacked against it from the beginning. Yet the London Passenger Transport Board had flourished, and the Docks Board turned a loss of £3¼ million in 1947 to a working surplus in 1961 of over £4 million. And railway decline was not peculiar to Britain. Railways all over the world were declining before the onslaught of the motor vehicle. The obsequies of the British Transport Commission were short, and while the Minister of Transport was somewhat uneasily surveying his new brood investigations were going on, material was being collected, statistics were being compiled for the proposals for railway reform which was Dr Beeching's chief assignment.

The Beeching Report was published in 1963 and came as a considerable shock to the railways themselves and to a public who, although grumbling at the railways and deserting them for other forms of transport, yet liked to know they were there. The Report was remarkable for an unsentimental assessment of the situation, for an economic use of words as finely cut as the railway system it envisaged. It was true, as his critics said, that Beeching avoided social issues. But he argued that an efficient railway system is itself a social service. He denied that he was simply cutting off unremunerative lines: he was looking further, he said, as the title of his Report implied, to a *re-shaping* of British railways which would concentrate on lines whose potential was good while giving up those which, of their nature, were uneconomic. Whether or not the hair was worth splitting, the result was that, while keeping lines where reorganization and re-equipment could provide a remunerative service, Beeching without sentiment recommended a drastic lopping off of lines

1 A slightly different arrangement from that proposed in the White Paper.

and closing of stations where the long-term potential was low. "The thought underlying the whole Report", he said, "is that the railways should be used to meet that part of the total transport requirement of the country for which they offer the best available means, and that they should cease to do things for which they are ill suited".[1]

The railways' "specialised and exclusive route system" was highly expensive to maintain. While light traffic flows or partly loaded trains were uneconomic, traffic carried in dense flows by well-loaded through trains could yield a profit. "The proposals for reshaping the railways are all directed towards giving them a route system, a pattern of traffics, and a mode of operation, such as to make the field which they cover one in which their merits predominate and in which they can be competitive." There were many routes on which revenue did not pay for the maintenance of the track and the operation of the signalling system, quite apart from the cost of running trains, depots, yards, and stations. There were also many stations—more than half the total number—where costs were greater than the receipts from traffic which they originated. Stopping passenger trains were among the poorest payers. They did not cover their own movement costs, and were one of the reasons for maintaining small and uneconomic stations. Suburban services feeding other centres of population were serious loss-makers. So was high peak traffic at holiday periods. All these it was proposed to cut. On the other hand, fast and semi-fast inter-city transport and suburban services feeding London would be developed. The former were among the best potential profit-makers with their possibilities of high speeds and high loading. The latter, although coming close to covering expenses, gave no margin for increases in capacity, and their development and expansion would need to be considered. In all, the cuts proposed amounted to 2363 stations and halts to be closed, including 435 under consideration before the Report appeared, the withdrawal of services from about 5000 route miles, the "damping down" of seasonal peak traffic, largely holiday traffic, and the reduction of railway staff by over 16,000; the last was in addition to a reduction of some 174,000, or nearly 30 per cent, between 1948 and 1962.

The reasoning behind this may have been sound. Indeed, the British Transport Commission had itself closed over a thousand small stations between 1950 and 1962.[2] And in assessing the Beeching cuts it was commonly overlooked that in 1954 the BTC in its memorandum on *Modernisation Re-equipment* had recommended a "marked reduction"

---

[1] *The Reshaping of British Railways*, Part I: Report, 1963, p. 57.
[2] Annual Report for the year ended December 31, 1962, of the Central Transport Consultative Committee for Great Britain, p. 7.

in stopping and branch-line services "which are little used by the public and which, on any dispassionate review of the situation, should be largely handed over to road transport".[1] But the Beeching axe had fallen heavily. When the proposed cuts were published it was found that there was to be no railway north of Inverness, that Scotland as a whole was badly denuded; that Wales, for all practical purposes, was to be denied rail transport; that the South-west would be crippled and quite unable to take her seasonal holiday traffic; that a town like Skegness, a holiday resort which had 350,000 visitors, of whom a third came in the thirteen summer weeks, was to be without a railway although the road approaches to the town were already overcrowded and inadequate. If he stopped a train he would be fined £5, remarked T. W. Jones in the House of Commons, but Dr Beeching proposed to stop a third of the railway system and he got a cheque for £24,000.[2]

From all over the country, from people of all kinds of age and occupation, objections poured in. Some protests were sentimental, many argued from an amenity point of view. The line north of Inverness, for example, served both a local population and visitors, for roads were bad and difficult to improve. Besides—and this argument held good for many routes —was the population to be bludgeoned into acquiring more cars than it owned already? Perhaps the most cogent argument concerned the roads. With traffic congestion as severe as it already was in the sixties what would be the future if rail services were cut? More congestion on existing roads, more traffic cluttering up towns, more bypasses, more cuts into more green belt areas or open country. Why not use the permanent way which was there already and needed only a little intelligent modernization to attract more passengers and make it pay? Colourful observation cars, comfort, service, sleeping-cars and restaurants with charges kept low were the answer. Sometimes the argument against Beeching did not even assume that the railways could, or should, be made to pay, but regarded them as a public service which should be kept in existence by subsidy.

More palatable were Beeching's proposals for improving the competitive capabilities of British Railways as freight-carriers. Arguing that freight traffic, like passenger, included both good and bad flows or unsuitably handled flows, he set out to eliminate the last two. The greater part of freight was handled by the staging forward of individual wagons from yard to yard instead of by through-train movement. This was costly, it caused transit times to vary, it led to a low utilization of wagons, and to the provision of a large and costly wagon fleet; wagon-load, siding-to-siding traffic moving in trainload quantities was required instead. Freight sundries traffic was a bad loss-maker; being handled between over 900 stations and depots, it resulted in very poor wagon-loading and a high level of costly transhipment of the freight while in transit. The railways handled about 45 per cent of this kind of traffic over the country without discrimination. "If they are to stay in the business", wrote Beeching, "British Railways must concentrate more upon the inter-city flows and reduce the number of depots handling this form of traffic to not more than a hundred." He estimated that the railways could carry an additional 8 million tons of traffic in train-load quantities, and a further 30 million tons which was favourable to rail by virtue of consignment sizes, length of haul, and terminal conditions. He also suggested a new kind of service for handling a further 16 million tons of freight—a Liner Freight Service—for the combined road and rail movement of containerized merchandise. This would entail the dovetailing of road and rail services, with road transport waiting at sidings or railway yards where cranes or other mechanical loaders would handle specially made containers of common size between the trains and lorries. Speed would be the essence of the operation; it would hasten delivery, give the trains a rapid turn-round, reduce costs, increase the quantity of freight handled, and be of special help to consignments too small in themselves to justify through-train operation.

Coal traffic had long been closely related to the railways, and Beeching reported that this just about paid its way, although many improvements could be made, particularly in accelerating the movement to block-train transit. About two-thirds of the coal handled still moved by the wagon-rather than the train-load, there were insufficient loading facilities at the pits and at the ports, and a multiplicity of small receiving terminals everywhere. Block-train transit and an improvement of facilities generally were obvious methods of improvement which should be accelerated or begun.

The House of Commons approved the Beeching Report on April 30, 1963,[1] and Transport Users' Consultative Committees got to work to lodge objections to railway closures. In some cases they were successful, the Inverness–Thurso line, for example, being reprieved. But where there were none to speak for them, or where the objections were overruled, little stations were shut, branch lines closed, some trains taken off, familiar timetables altered, railway information and ticket offices closed, economies enforced at stations. Some of these measures caused definite hardship, others inconvenience, others were merely irritating. But there were

1 The debate lasted two days. See Hansard, fifth series, vol. 676, cc. 722–1028.

improvements. Some inter-city services, like those between London and Newcastle, London and Cardiff, London and Liverpool, were speeded up. There was some improvement in the carriage of freight, but the introduction of liner trains met with passionate opposition from the railwaymen, who feared an accelerating redundancy rate and the competition of road hauliers, whom they refused to allow into railway goods yards to collect freight.

When the Labour Government took office in October 1964 the Beeching Plan was beginning to operate and the first two Annual Reports of the British Railways Board (for 1963 and 1964) showed a financial improvement. Four months later Beeching's second Report, dealing with the main railway trunk routes, was published.[1] The Report made no specific closure recommendations, but estimated that of Britain's 7500 miles of trunk railway only about 3000 should be selected for future development.

But a week before this Report appeared the Labour Government had changed once more the organization of British transport, and a new traffic overlord appeared in the person of Lord Hinton, who was to be Special Adviser on Transport and Planning (with a salary of £7000 a year), assisted by a Transport Advisory Council. His brief was to cover all forms of transport—road, rail, air, waterways, and ports. It was allowed to be known that Dr Beeching was planning his return to ICI— it had emerged, after a good deal of confidential discussion, said the Ministry of Transport in explanation, that Dr Beeching would not be able to do the job in the way the Government wanted it done, and they had therefore called for a further report from Lord Hinton. Further study, as Dr Beeching pointed out in a final and dignified statement, is often a device for avoiding unpleasant decisions. But, pleasant or unpleasant, having for nearly twenty years played the whole gamut of change upon the nationalization theme, the Government had now to make up its mind if it were not to become a laughing-stock and British Railways a permanently wasting asset.

By this time British transport as a whole was suffering not only from the various forms its organization had assumed but from the fact that in all their schemes no Government had yet been able to integrate all kinds of transport—airways, although nationalized, had never been considered a part of the whole; private motoring was in a category of its own. Moreover, the three forms of transport—rail, air, and road—were all in effect subsidized in one way or another to compete against each other at the

[1] *The Development of the Major Railway Trunk Routes*, February 16, 1965.

expense of the taxpayer.[1] None of the legislation had dealt with this aspect of the situation. Having, in the form of Dr Beeching, concentrated on the railways, the Government was now, in the person of Lord Hinton, taking a look at the whole. The move was encouraging, largely because of the inclusion of road and air in the brief of the Special Adviser and the expectation that the growth of private motoring would be considered as part of the problem. The new plan for "transport co-ordination" was promised by January 1966. The words had a familiar ring. Did anyone turn the pages of Hansard? He would need to go back twenty years to read how the Minister of Transport, Alfred Barnes, with sincerity and idealism, introduced the Nationalization of Transport Bill to provide "an efficient, adequate, economical, and properly integrated system of public inland transport and port facilities" that would give Britain "the most efficient, comfortable, speedy and cheap system of transport in the world."[2] If the words left a bitter taste in the mouth there was at least some credit in having the courage to start again.

But there was little opportunity for comparisons. A new Chairman of British Railways took over from Dr Beeching, a new Minister of Transport was appointed at the end of 1965, and a new Special Adviser was announced With a new adviser the new Minister was starting all over again on a transport plan at the beginning of 1966—just at the time the Hinton plan for "transport co-ordination" should have been ready. The new Chairman tackled the problem of the railway track, whose cost, he said, currently around £130 million a year, was roughly the same as the total deficit. He suggested a new Transport Highway Authority which would be responsible for allocating capital from public funds for the provision of highways for each form of transport—railway track, road, canal, and air—and for maintaining and servicing those highways. With a highway authority under the umbrella of a national transport policy, he averred, much progress would be made towards a rational solution of Britain's transport problem.[3] Six months later the Minister's new transport plan was published.[4] It did not appear to offer any radical solution to the transport problem, although it proposed subsidies for railways and canals, and spoke of "integrated planning" and detailed research. But the credit due to fresh starts was a diminishing asset, and neither Minister nor Chairman could generate much enthusiasm: the cheering was reserved for a demonstrably effective policy.

[1] *The Times*, leading article, February 9, 1965.   [2] *Supra*, p. 72.
[3] Mr Stanley Raymond, speaking to the National Liberal Forum in London, January 4, 1966, reported in *The Times*, January 5, 1966.
[4] *Transport Policy*, Cmnd. 3057.

Britain's airways services are operated in the main by British Overseas Airways Corporation and by British European Airways, although the Civil Aviation Licensing Act of 1960 provides for the Air Transport Licensing Board to grant licences, subject to a right of appeal to the Minister, to private companies to operate specified services. The largest of the private operators are British United Airways and British Eagle Airways.

The British Overseas Airways Corporation was established by Act of Parliament in 1939 as successor to Imperial Airways, Ltd. After the War a Government White Paper on British Air Services set the framework within which BOAC has operated,[1] and by the Civil Aviation Act of 1946 it was made responsible for air services on routes between the United Kingdom and other Commonwealth countries, the U.S.A., and the Far East, and given a monopoly of British scheduled services on these routes. The Corporation was required to fly British aircraft, which implied, at first, aircraft developed from the existing military types.

In 1951 the Corporation was in a good position, with monopoly routes to the Commonwealth and favourable partnerships in routes linking Commonwealth countries. But operating costs were very high, mainly as a result of the older types of aircraft which were being flown, and by that time BOAC had received £32 million in grants from the Exchequer. It had been recognized that, if the Corporation was to fulfil its function of providing services in the public interest, some measure of State aid might be necessary to support essential but unremunerative services, but the price being paid was clearly very high. However in 1952 a new aircraft, Comet I, enabled BOAC to pay its way—incidentally demonstrating the importance of new types of aircraft in attracting custom. Then, in 1953 and 1954, a series of air disasters discredited the Comet; it had to be abandoned, and the Corporation was compelled to buy American aircraft off the shelf at high prices to maintain its services. Not only was this expensive, but the types of aeroplane were not particularly attractive, and BOAC's share in the expansion of world air traffic dropped sharply. Nevertheless, the years 1952–56 showed a profit, and hopes were pinned on the new Britannia aircraft which were in preparation. Unfortunately, the delivery of Britannias was delayed by two and a half years through technical difficulties, particularly concerning icing and the electrical system, and when the Britannia 312 was introduced on the North Atlantic service at the end of 1957 it was only a year ahead of the American long-range pure jets, which soon drew traffic and orders for aircraft away from the slower turboprop Britannias.

[1] Cmd. 6712, 1945.

6+

Between 1956 and 1962 BOAC introduced five different types of aircraft, each costing from about £1 million to £2 million. The Corporation was acting on the assumption that the useful life of a new aircraft would be seven years and that if disposed of then it would realize 25 per cent of its original cost. This proved unrealistically optimistic. At the same time the expense of introducing a new type of machine was very heavy in terms of pre-operational and training cost, of trial runs and the distribution of spare parts to different ports of call.

Britain's position was made more precarious by the fact that colonies were becoming independent and, like smaller countries generally, were establishing their own airlines as a matter of prestige. Also several subsidiary and associated companies in which BOAC had interested itself for 'feeder' purposes, such as British West India Airways and Bahamas Airways and Middle East Airways, were showing a loss, British interests to the extent of about £15·3 million being written off. At the same time air traffic as a whole expanded rather less than had been expected. The year 1961–62 was the worst year financially that BOAC had ever had; by March 31, 1963, its accumulated deficit amounted to £80 million, and the Government authorized a confidential Inquiry into its affairs by a professional consultant. Part of this was published in November as a White Paper.[1]

The White Paper was critical. Nearly half the accumulated deficit of BOAC was attributable to losses on aircraft resulting from a shorter life in service than had been allowed for, or a loss on disposal. A small proportion of this was due to losses on the Tudor, Hermes, and Comet I, which had all entered service before 1953; the major portion was due to the D.C.M.C., Britannias 102 and 312, and the Comet IV, all of which had entered service since 1956 and all of which had incurred very heavy amortization charges. Yet the Corporation had made no change in the rate of amortization of aircraft until the Accounts for 1961–62 were presented. The policy underlying the investment in associated and subsidiary companies was criticized, engineering and maintenance costs were considered "excessive", financial control was found to be generally weak. Above all, the White Paper was critical of the Corporation as being "unduly optimistic" concerning its rate of expansion. Praise was reserved only for its advertising and publicity services, which were said to be "at about the right level and well directed".

The year 1963–64 was better all round for BOAC: even while the

---

[1] *The Financial Problems of the British Overseas Airways Corporation*, November 20, 1963, Ministry of Aviation, H.M.S.O. Mr John Corbett was the consultant engaged.

White Paper was being studied its position was improving. Traffic increased, the number of passengers carried increased, profit increased. For the first time revenue exceeded £100 million and was up by 12 per cent on the previous year. What was more, expenditure was down by 3·5 per cent, so that there was an operating surplus of £8,651,000, the highest ever recorded. A staff of over 20,000, of whom aircraft officers accounted for 1500, flew well over a million people a total distance of more than 3 million miles, and there were no major labour disputes. But the White Paper was published before the annual financial statement of the Corporation was out, and the Chairman, the Managing Director, and later the Secretary of BOAC resigned.

By that time nothing could alleviate public concern but a full-scale Inquiry, and the Select Committee on the Nationalized Industries turned its attention to British Airways. Its Report was published in June 1964, by which time the public knew of BOAC's better record for the financial year. It covered wider ground than the White Paper, but what it said was in some ways even more disquieting.

In particular it told, as far as it could be unravelled, the story of the V.C.10's. In 1956 BOAC was considering new aircraft to replace its fleets of Comets and Britannias on its Eastern and Southern routes. The Boeing 707 was not yet in service, but, in any case, it was then believed that the shorter runways and different airport conditions in these countries would require aircraft of a somewhat different pattern. Discussions on a suitable type began with Vickers. But by the autumn of 1956 the Minister had decided that what was, in effect, a Comet V should be used for both the Atlantic and the Eastern and African routes, and that in order to preserve "overall balance and welfare in the aircraft manufacturing industry" the financing of a new British aircraft would be agreed only if it were bought from de Havilland's. He did, however, allow that the specification must be satisfactory, and BOAC were not required to order a specific number of aircraft. Here, however, de Havilland intervened and refused to proceed unless a minimum number of fifty aircraft were ordered. The Government thereupon released the Corporation from its obligation, and they proceeded with their discussions with Vickers. The V.C.10 specification appeared satisfactory, but, because it was believed the Government would not contribute to its production, Vickers required a large order to make the project economic and spoke of a break-even number of forty-five aircraft.

The V.C.10's would be in addition to the planes used on the Atlantic service, where, in order to hold the competitive position, the Government had agreed to the buying of fifteen Boeing 707 jets. Vickers's figure of forty-five V.C.10's was therefore high, and in negotiation BOAC finally arranged to buy thirty-five, with an option of twenty more, delivery to be in the sixties. They were committing themselves to a large number of aircraft a long way ahead, but they were pleased with the specification, which, they said, "fulfils technically and operationally all the requirements of the Corporation on these routes". Nevertheless, before the agreement was actually signed in January 1958, modifications were being made in the V.C.10, partly because runways everywhere were being lengthened and the initial considerations which governed the design of the aircraft no longer held good, and partly because, by becoming bigger and more powerful, they would be more competitive with the Boeing 707's, which were by this time in operation. BOAC's own engineering department expressed doubts as to the performance of the V.C.10, in spite of modifications, but the Corporation itself was still confident, and in January 1958, overruling its own engineering department, BOAC signed the order for thirty-five V.C.10's: there is little doubt that Vickers thought that the optional additional twenty would, in fact, be required.

As production proceeded costs rose, and in January 1960 Vickers announced that production would be jeopardized unless ten more V.C.10's were ordered immediately, as part of this option. They would be of rather different specification and were called Super V.C.10's. At this point Government policy again became operative. Vickers were merging with other aircraft companies to form the British Aircraft Corporation, and the Minister, as a measure of support to the Corporation, wanted the order to go through. It was, in fact, placed in June 1960, for delivery after 1968, and although the design of the super V.C.10 appeared to suit all parties there is little doubt that pressure had been put upon BOAC.

In the event an order for only twelve standard but for thirty super V.C.10's went through, their cost was high, the Corporation was saddled with orders in excess of the number of planes it really required, and its financial position was affected accordingly. BOAC cannot altogether be blamed for continuing an expansionist policy when growth did, in fact, begin to slacken, a mistake not confined to Britain; and expansion was inherent in the decision to buy British jets—for an optimum number, as Vickers pointed out, is certain to be fairly high. But overoptimism on the part of BOAC is only one of many considerations involved; there is also the question of the relationship of the Corporation, the Minister, and the aircraft industry, involving issues of how far the national interest in British production could, or should, override any other consideration such as cost, performance, or speed of delivery. Bound up with this are two issues fundamental to the whole concept of nationalization: the obligation of a nationalized industry to act as a commercial concern—and some industries had already been told clearly what their profit targets should be—and the working relationship between a Minister and the Chairman of a nationalized undertaking, particularly the part which political considerations should play in policy decisions.[1]

On the political side changing Ministers will always make for difficulty. In the case of BOAC difficulties had been exacerbated by the fact that over the twenty-five years since it came into being it had had as many as nine different Chairmen, twelve Deputy Chairmen, and seven Chief Executives, while for fifteen years the majority of the Board had been part-time. It had therefore been lacking in the firm and continuous leadership which was the one thing that might have enabled it to see its position clearly and as a whole. Perhaps as a result of this lack of continuity on both sides the responsibility for choosing new aircraft had never been defined, and there had never been any definite statement of the Corporation's commercial role or obligation. It was an extraordinary position, for which successive Ministers must share the blame with the Corporation, that not until January 1, 1964, when the Minister of Aviation wrote to Sir Giles Guthrie, the new Chairman of BOAC, was it laid down that the "choice of aircraft is a matter for the Corporation's judgement" and made clear that the Corporation was a commercial undertaking expected to function as such subject to commercial standards of profit and loss. It is the "fundamental responsibility of the Corporations", the Minister then wrote, "to act in accordance with their commercial judgement. If the national interest should appear, whether to the Corporations or to the Government, to require some departure from the strict commercial interests of the Corporation, this should be done only with the express agreement or at the express request of the Minister."[2]

The Government's ruling came to an organization saddled with debts from the past for which it was only partly to blame. The new Chairman made plans for the future concerning routing for the period up to 1967–1968 and concerning the aircraft needed in the near future. The conclusion reached was that BOAC's route structure was sound on the whole but that it must concentrate ruthlessly upon routes which had

---

[1] *Supra*, pp. 126, 121–122.

[2] The letter is reproduced in *British Overseas Airways Corporation Annual Report and Accounts*, 1963–64, Appendix 1, p. 53.

an inherent commercial advantage, like those for which there was a constant home demand or which fed Commonwealth countries or other centres where inter-exchange with Britain was constant. At the same time services would be speeded up and costly stopovers avoided where possible. This would entail, for example, more through services to the Near East and the concentration of services through Europe upon Rome, Frankfurt, and Zürich. The route system having been decided upon, it was necessary to consider the number of aircraft needed to operate it successfully. In 1964 BOAC was in process of taking delivery of the twelve standard V.C.10's. With the twenty Boeings already in use it reckoned that only seven more planes would be required, and it preferred to take them in Boeings. In May 1964, consequently, it sought to cancel its order for all thirty super V.C.10's, at the same time asking for authority to order eight Boeing 707—320 C's, which could be employed either as passenger aircraft, as passenger-freighters, or as all-cargo planes: the expected total of sixty-two would be reduced to forty.

The Government accepted the revised route-structure, but would not agree to such heavy cancellation involving compensation which they would be called upon to pay. The Minister accordingly asked the Corporation to take delivery of seven super V.C.10's for operation up to 1968 and to maintain its order for a further ten. The Ministry arranged that the Royal Air Force should take three super V.C.10's, thus covering the original option on twenty aircraft, and reserved its decision on the ten that remained. At the same time it gave a guarantee that the Government would "take the necessary action to re-organise the capital and financial structure of the Corporation so as to enable it to operate as a fully commercial undertaking with the fleet of aircraft now envisaged".[1]

Whether BOAC had over-ordered or who was to blame was not made clear. But six months later a new Government was considering the relation between the nationalized airways and the private companies operating under the Civil Aviation Licensing Act, and the Minister of Aviation in the Labour Government made a statement in the House of Commons on February 17, 1965. Holiday air traffic had been built up on the basis of inclusive-tour services operated largely by private aircraft carriers chartered by the Air Transport Licensing Board on the basis of an agreed European policy of licensing reputable operators in each other's country. It was not intended to restrict this development in any way. On scheduled international routes, however, the Minister was "not

---

[1] *Report of the British Overseas Airways Corporation for 1963*, pp. 48–50. Minister of Aviation, July 20, 1964 (Hansard, fifth series, vol. 699, cc. 39–49).

convinced that the national interest is, in general, served by more than one British carrier operating on the same route". Moreover, no other European country had attempted this, and no other country had granted the necessary traffic rights to more than one British line. While not, however, countenancing any duplication of international services, the British Government would consider supporting any new service which might be proposed.[1]

A fortnight later came the announcement that wiped the slate clean and gave BOAC its full charter for starting afresh: its £80 million accumulated deficit was to be wiped off and £30 million provided for further contingencies. By the middle of 1965, with V.C.10's coming into operation, BOAC claimed, "We have had our best year ever".

During the War the scheduled British civil air services within the United Kingdom and Eire were operated on behalf of the Government by the railway-controlled group of companies known as the Associated Airways Joint Committee. In 1946 the Civil Aviation Act established British European Airways Corporation "with a view to providing civil air services in various parts of the world, and in particular, in Europe (including the British Islands)". In August BEA officially took over British airlines in Europe and at home.

BEA has had twenty years of successful operation. Between 1949 and 1964 traffic increased thirteenfold, average fares were reduced by 5 per cent, and unit costs of production were almost halved. In 1963–64 it made a profit of over £3 million after taking account of losses on social services operated in the Scottish Highlands and Islands; it produced more capacity, carried more traffic than ever before, and passengers topped the 5 million mark. Staff totalled over 17,000, of whom 1627 were engaged on flight operations generally, and 930 were pilots. Wages had generally been adjusted within the negotiating machinery, the National Joint Council for Civil Air Transport bringing together employers and representatives of unions connected with air transport. It did not, like the parent organization, have to experiment with new types of aircraft, its flights were shorter, the area it covered was more homogeneous, fewer extraneous factors needed to be taken into account in planning its services. For all these reasons it was less vulnerable than BOAC; and it had, in addition, the great advantage of continuity, of understanding bred of continuous association, in having the same

---

[1] Hansard, fifth series, vol. 706, cc. 1186–89. And see *infra*, p. 156, for the part of the statement that concerned BEA.

Chairman, Lord Douglas of Kirtleside, for fifteen years until his retirement in 1964.

In only one direction was there cause for apprehension: in the growing competition from the airlines licensed by the ATLB, particularly from British Eagle and British United Airways. In his statement on civil-aviation policy in the House of Commons on February 17, 1965, the Minister of Aviation announced that, while allowing the independent operators to continue their existing services, the Government was not prepared to allow them unrestricted rights[1]; in other words, there would be a severe restriction, if not complete curtailment, of further flights. Recognizing the threat to passenger amenity that lay in this move towards complete monopoly, the Minister announced the appointment to the Board of BEA of a member charged with special attention to the interests of the passenger. But the relationship between the Government and the aircraft industry, further exemplified by the affair of TSR2, remained unsatisfactory, and the Report of the Plowden Committee gave little comfort.[2]

In a different category from other State services or industries is the three-hundred-year-old General Post Office. Over 25,000 post-offices, a staff of over 380,000, provide general services which put the Post Office in the position of Universal Aunt rather than of public corporation. In friendly post-offices all over the country postage stamps and insurance stamps can be bought, parcels or letters weighed, customs declarations made; money can be sent to any part of the world, remittances from anywhere can be cashed; telegrams and cables can be sent, telephone calls made; seats, tables, pen and ink are available for post-office business or private letters. Nearly 4 million people collect family allowances from the post-office, nearly 6 million their retirement pensions. The Post Office Savings Bank, over a hundred years old, holds 23 million live accounts, £1760 million of money, mostly in small savings belonging to people who require a constant deposit and demand service.

Over 100,000 pillar-boxes stand about the country to take mail, over 110,000 postmen handle 30 million letters, circulars and printed papers, and some 650,000 parcels a day—11,000 million items of correspondence, 230 million parcels a year. Twenty million households and thousands of business firms receive by first post the bulk of letters posted the day before. The public sends or receives 31 million telegrams a year, over

---

[1] Hansard, fifth series, vol. 706, c. 1188.
[2] *Report of the Committee of Inquiry into the Aircraft Industry* December 1965 (Cmnd. 2853).

25 million Telex calls; from 10 million telephones it makes over 6000 million telephone calls. It spends annually over £400 million on its postal, telephone, and telegraph services, but more than twelve times that amount passes over the post-office counter, involving the handling of more than £5000 million year by year.

For this efficient service, as well as broadcasting, television, radio stations, cable ships, links of all kinds all over the world and beyond into space, the Postmaster General is responsible. Not only is he responsible but, friendly or not, he is expected to make an overall profit, the Post Office being required by the Committee on the Nationalized Industries to reach a profit target of 8 per cent overall on net assets for the five years beginning 1963–64. Broadcasting and television are subject to their own particular systems of accounting, while the services for which the Postmaster General is reponsible are divided into telecommunications and postal services.

The telecommunications service is alert and vigorous, the title of the White Paper issued in November, 1963—*The Inland Telephone Service in an Expanding Economy*[1]—indicating its awareness of its responsibilities. In the five years from 1958–59 to 1962–63 investment in the inland telephone service was £490 million. Between 1963–64 and 1967–68 it will amount to nearly £900 million, the aim being to increase the number of telephones by 2 million, to deal with an additional 2000 million telephone calls a year, to eliminate manual exchanges, to complete subscriber trunk dialling, to familiarize such new services as telephones in cars. This expansion takes account of increasing business activity, the rise in real consumption, which produces a constantly growing demand for the telephone, the increase in population, the building of more houses and flats, earlier marriage, and the attitude of the young to the telephone.[2] Technically it relies increasingly upon the use of computers; the telecommunications service, which includes telephones, telegrams, and Telex calls at home and overseas, spent £150·9 million in 1963–64, and £173·7 million in 1964–65 on fixed assets, including computers. There are complaints over wrong numbers, scrambled lines, operators who fail to answer, public telephones which fail to function: but the economic life of the country, and to an increasing extent its social life generally, is based pretty firmly upon confidence in telephonic communication.

The profit on telecommunications of £38·5 million in 1963–64 and of £39·7 million in 1964–65 has to be shown against a loss on the postal

---

[1] Cmnd. 2211.
[2] *The Inland Telephone Service in an Expanding Economy*, November 1963, Cmnd. 2211; *Post Office Report and Accounts*, 1963–64, 1964–65.

6*

services in 1963–64 of £7·8 million and a loss in 1964–65 of £19·6 million. The Post Office has a greater variety of services to deal with than tele-communications. Although it receives direct payment from the public for postal services and such things as remittance of money, for receiving savings deposits, selling Development or Premium Bonds, for paying out pensions and allowances over the post-office counter there is no direct payment: the service is given by post-office clerks whose wages and salaries are charged to Post Office account. Moreover, its very age subjects the Post Office to disabilities in the form of old buildings and uneconomic methods which are costly to operate and expensive to replace. The £12·9 million which it spent on fixed assets in 1963–64, the £13·6 million in 1964–65, was used mostly in overdue improvements to old buildings, in constructing new, in modernizing techniques, in providing better conditions for staff, in increasing mechanization in the handling, sorting, and delivery of mail.[1] But it was not enough.

Until March 1960 all Post Office receipts were paid into the Exchequer, and money needed by the Post Office was issued by the Exchequer. It was then proposed by the Committee on the Nationalized Industries to give the Post Office greater commercial freedom without taking it from the control of the Postmaster General. He would still be responsible for it to Parliament, but it would operate financially as a self-contained business. The reason for this was not so much to assist the Post Office as to prevent it from operating upon anything but a profit-and-loss basis. "The Post Office has many social obligations," said the Committee, but "the existence of these obligations does not mean that the Post Office should be run primarily as a vast social service without regard to the economic facts of life." The spur of commercial standards was necessary for gauging efficiency. Accordingly, the Post Office Act of 1961 established the Post Office as a nationalized industry required to lay its accounts before Parliament, responsible ultimately to Parliament, but organized rather differently from the others. There was public concern at the failure of the Post Office to balance its accounts. But there was, on the whole, an appreciation of the fact that an efficient postal service had to be paid for and that "balancing its accounts" included substantial increases in the wages of post-office workers. These had never been high, the Post Office had never been in a position to be generous with increases, and postal workers had been too loyal to disrupt the economy with strikes. When they finally staged first a Go Slow and then a one-day strike in July 1964 (the first strike of postmen for over seventy years), the public was inconvenienced, amazed, and not a little perturbed

1 *Post Office Report and Accounts*, 1963–64, 1964–65.

at the interruption of a service so readily taken for granted for so long. But the men won their increase, partly through excellent trade-union leadership, and won, moreover, the right to advance with other sections of the economy. The public had to pay for wage increases and for capital development, all inland postal charges being increased in 1965.[1] But a service so rapidly expanding could not be kept efficient by patchwork methods; and efficiency in communication was necessary to an efficient economy. So first a firm of industrial efficiency experts was appointed to advise on the raising of productivity in the Post Office, and then, in August 1966, the Postmaster General announced the intention of converting the Post Office from a Department of State to a Public Corporation whose members would be appointed by and responsible to the Minister, like any other nationalized concern. The Select Committee on the Nationalized Industries was again examining its position.

The British Broadcasting Corporation, with the status and duties of a public corporation, owing ultimate responsibility to the Government yet free to make its own programmes, to conduct its own administrative affairs, and to handle day-to-day business, is in a position not unlike that of the nationalized industries, even to the requirement in its Charter of submitting an Annual Report and Statement of Accounts to the Postmaster General. Unlike the nationalized industries, it was incorporated by Royal Charter and not by Act of Parliament; unlike most of them, it has to meet competition from a variety of other sources, one of which is sanctioned by Act of Parliament.

The British Broadcasting Corporation was incorporated by Royal Charter in 1927, taking the place of the British Broadcasting Company, which had been inaugurated in 1922 to provide the first public service of broadcasting. It is now responsible for both sound broadcasting and television. The Independent Television Authority was incorporated by Act of Parliament in 1954 and presents only television services. Both BBC and ITA require a licence from the Postmaster General for the right to broadcast, but while the BBC is financed by the licences required for both sound and viewing, the ITA at present depends for income upon the advertisers who use its services, being paid through the medium of programme contractors who farm out television time. Although there was nothing in its incorporation to imply this dependence upon advertisement revenue, it was clear from the beginning that advertisements would be the most likely source of income for the ITA, and the prospect aroused a storm in the country and much heated argument in

[1] *Post Office Prospects*, 1965–66, March 25, 1965, Cmnd. 2623.

Parliament. Advertisers, it was maintained, would be running the service, programmes would be secondary to advertisement, their culture value would be reduced to the lowest common factor of taste and intelligence, a vested interest would achieve a dangerous power over an organ of opinion. The supporters of ITA rested their case largely on the need to break the monopoly of the BBC and denied the power of the advertiser either over the programmes of an Independent Television Authority or over the minds of its audience: that the advertisers disagreed on the second score became clear by their continued use of the medium for advertisement. The Act as it passed into law tried to safeguard the content of programmes by laying down that a "proper balance" should be maintained in their subject-matter and a "high general standard of quality" in their presentation, "that the tone and style of the programmes" should be "predominantly British", and "that a proper proportion of the films and other recorded matter" should be of British origin. It also laid down that events of national importance and interest should be shown by both services and that, in general, the Postmaster General could instruct to broadcast, or to refrain from broadcasting, if he thought necessary. The ultimate veto rested, in any case, with the Postmaster General through his right of refusing a licence. On the advertisement part of its programmes the Independent Television Authority was instructed that advertisements must begin and end clearly, that they must be clearly identifiable as such, and that they might be shown only in clear programme breaks.

The power of broadcasting in general was recognized from the beginning, and a series of Committees have examined its potential and its actual performance. The Sykes Committee of 1923 conceived of broadcasting as a public service for instruction and entertainment; the Crawford Committee of 1926, discussing the educational aspects of the medium, decided that programmes should not be judged by the size of the audience they attracted; the Preamble to the Charter of the BBC refers to the value of its services "as a means of disseminating information, education and entertainment". The Beveridge Committee, reporting in 1951, stressed that it was the agreed policy of successive Governments that the Corporation should be independent of the Government in the day-to-day conduct of its business, including both its programmes and its administration. The Pilkington Committee, reporting in 1962, recommended the renewal of the Charter for a further twelve years from July 1964, and laid down that there should be "unremitting observance of the fundamental principle of the independence of the broadcasting authorities from Government intervention in the day-to-day manage-

ment of their affairs, including programme content", but emphasized
that the Government should remain ultimately responsible for the social
consequences of broadcasting.[1] According to the recommendations of
the Pilkington Committee a new Royal Charter was granted on July 30,
1964, to run until July 29, 1976, covering not only the existing BBC network but a second television service (subsequently opened as BBC-2),
the introduction of colour television, and an extension of sound broadcasting hours. The new Charter made no difference to the constitutional
position of the BBC and endorsed its traditional independence. The only
variants were an enlargement of its borrowing powers, and an extension
to Welsh and Scottish television of the freedom over programmes they
already enjoyed in sound broadcasting.

In 1927 over $2\frac{1}{4}$ million licences for sound were issued; in 1965 over
$2\frac{3}{4}$ million for sound and $13\frac{1}{4}$ million for sound and television combined. The broadcast receiving licence of £1, the combined broadcast
and television licence of £4, each covering a year, provided the cheapest
entertainment in Europe and good value by any standard. Like every
other organization, however, the BBC had to face increasing costs on
every hand—in particular those incurred by the opening of the second
television channel in 1964. Its staff of nearly 20,000 is represented by a
variety of trade unions, who together have kept up the level of salaries.
A deficit in its accounts of £2,680,000 in 1962–63 rose to £3,237,000 in
1963–64, but the latter was offset by income tax recovered by the Corporation in the Court of Appeal, and finally stood at £2,223,000. On an
expenditure of £16·78 million on sound programmes in 1963–64 there
was a net loss of £391,000; on an expenditure of £34·8 million on television a net loss of £622,000. The Corporation warned the public that
the effect of wage, salary, and operating increases would make a higher
licence fee necessary, and this, in fact, became operable from August
1965, when the combined sound and viewing licence was raised to £5 a
year and the radio licence to £1 5s.[2]

[1] *Report of the Committee on Broadcasting*, 1960, Cmnd. 1753, p. 287.
[2] See *infra*, pp. 291–293, for a discussion of broadcasting in its social setting.

CHAPTER XII

The Nationalized Undertakings: Power

"The productivity of labour is closely linked with the power at its disposal and increasing quantities will be needed to support the growth of the economy and the rise in living standards. The pattern of fuel supplies depends primarily on the requirements of the consumers. The size and nature, however, of the fuel-producing industries are such that Government is inevitably involved. It is a function of Government to ensure that national considerations . . . are reflected in the situation."

Fuel Policy, October 1965, Cmnd. 2798

POWER SUPPLIES are co-ordinated by the Ministry of Power, which, as the Ministry of Fuel and Power, was created at the beginning of the War in 1939. The Ministry of Fuel and Power Act, passed by the the Coalition Government in April 1945, provided for the continued existence of the Ministry, the Act placing upon the Minister the duty of "securing the effective and co-ordinated development of coal, petroleum and other . . . services of fuel and power in Great Britain . . . and of promoting economy and efficiency in the supply, distribution, use and consumption of fuel and power, whether produced in Great Britain or not". In 1956 the Ministry became simply the Ministry of Power. In January 1965 an Energy Advisory Council was set up to advise the Minister. The conventional energy industries together—coal, electricity, gas, and oil—employ about a million men, 4 per cent of the working population; their capital investment in 1965 was about £1000 million; they have an annual turnover of about £3000 million; the value of their net output is about 5 per cent of the national product.[1]

Coal, electricity, and gas are nationalized.[2] Oil is imported, mainly

[1] *Fuel Policy*, October 1965, Cmnd. 2798, p. 1.   [2] *Supra*, pp. 70–72, 73–74.

from the Middle East, by big private companies; there are vast resources in many parts of the world and no fear at present of supplies giving out. Much of the import is of refined oil, but the Government is encouraging the growth of British refineries, which, using unrefined imported oil, would both lessen the cost and reduce dependence upon foreign sources of supply. Water-power, as a generating agent, has become important only in Scotland, where it is incorporated in the nationalized Hydro-electric Board. Nuclear power and natural gas have in the last few years come into the picture as alternative sources of power—nuclear power only as a primary agent, but natural gas in a form not unlike the present product of coal or coke gasification. The competition they offer to the conventional forms of power is still of the future—though of a rapidly approaching future. Since the War the main upstart has been oil, whose challenge to the established forms of power has been decided and considerable. For many uses there is no effective substitute for oil—for road and air transport and as a refinery fuel—but in other uses, particularly in power stations, oil has grown at the expense of coal, while in domestic heating appliances it has grown at the expense of all three traditional forms of heating.

The four conventional sources of power—coal, electricity, gas, and oil—are competitive yet interdependent. They have their own individual problems of production, yet are influenced by common economic conditions, social patterns, and ways of life. Coal, electricity, and gas were in various stages of depression and disorganization when nationalized, but all three have been characterized by effective reorganization, vigorous development, and expansion. The difference between the three is that, while there is at present a seemingly unending demand in front of the gas and electricity supplies, the market for coal has already contracted.

The National Coal Board was constituted by the Minister of Fuel and Power under the Coal Industry Nationalization Act of July 15, 1946. Vesting Day, when the coalmines were formally handed over to the NCB, was January 1, 1947, when the flag of the Board was run up over their headquarters in London. The Board, in turn, created Divisional Boards, at first eight, later nine, which were subdivided into forty-eight Areas. Though not all the men from the coalfields whom the Board wanted were able or willing to accept appointment, most of the members of the Area Boards came from within the industry. This was less true of the Divisional Boards, where it was necessary, for the chairmen at least, to be men of wide administrative experience; but at pit-level the 800-odd colliery companies and their directors remained in being, and each colliery manager remained in charge of his pit, although he looked to the new authority for his instructions. The Coal Act of 1938 had nationalized coal deposits which were administered by a Commission who granted leases in such a way as to promote "the interests, efficiency and better organisation of the coal-mining industry", and all the assets of the Commission now passed to the National Coal Board.

British coalmines in their period of maximum productivity before the First World War were producing something like 287 million tons of coal a year, of which 94 million tons were exported or shipped as bunkers. During the First World War overseas markets were lost and coalfields overseas increased their own production. When the War was over currency difficulties and the impoverishment of coal-importing countries prevented a rise in the export of British coal, and strong competition developed from Germany and later from Poland. General trade depression further prevented a rise in the export of coal from Britain, and by the early thirties output had shrunk to little more than 200 million tons, exports to 50 million tons. Prices dropped, wages, which had never been high, were cut, unemployment mounted, and technical progress was arrested. Between 1913 and 1938 British output per man shift increased by 13 per cent, compared with America's 40 per cent and Germany's and Poland's 60 per cent each. Upon the outbreak of the Second World War the industry was in the position described by the Reid Report.[1] At the end of it, like everything else, it was run down, short of labour, short of capital, and coal had to be imported to meet urgent requirements. When the National Coal Board took over it inherited an industry with a bad record of labour relations, badly organized, insufficiently mechanized, and with all the marks of destitution. Its big asset was the workers' faith in nationalization.

Although the Government was at this time encouraging conversion to oil to eke out coal, oil was still a makeshift, there was no feeling that the fundamental position could change, and the National Coal Board swung into its task with the assumption that "coal was still unchallenged as the fuel upon which the country's economy depended". Results, after making every allowance for the general effects of the War, were at first disappointing. In 1947, 184·7 million tons of deep-mined saleable coal were produced. There was a steady rise to 212·2 million in 1952, a fall to 207·8 million in 1955. This was a year of one major strike, many lesser disputes, and a fall in manpower, when home demand had to be met by a reduction in coal exports and by massive imports.[2] Both the Board's finances and the country's balance of payments were serious-

---

[1] *Supra*, p. 70.　　　[2] Of 11 million tons.

ly affected. The next year production was even lower, but only 5 million tons were imported, and productivity was rising again at the end of the year. There had been fewer strikes and disputes, and manpower rose. The Board made a profit that year of £12·8 million and planned big increases in production.[1] "The industry entered 1957 in better shape than at any time since the war," it announced.

Nevertheless, the decline continued. And now it was not only a decline in production but a falling off in consumption which was the trouble. Between the end of 1956 and the end of 1959 the total consumption of British coal fell by 33 million tons. Abroad Britain had to face the competition of other coal-producing countries, of oil, natural gas, and other competing fuels. At home the reasons were partly the transient recession of 1957–58, when the heavy coal-consuming industries were worse hit than light industries, partly the mild winter of 1959, when the inland consumption of coal fell by 9 million tons in the first half of the year. But there were more stable causes at work. The Clean Air Act of 1956[2] contributed to the decline of domestic demand. Coal-using industries were learning fuel efficiency, and, above all, were turning to other sources of supply: while the inland consumption of coal fell by 10 million tons in 1958 that of oil increased by 6·5 million tons of coal equivalent.

The industrial coal-consumers—railways, coke-ovens, gas, electricity —are between them responsible for more than half the inland consumption of coal. Railways have been using less coal each year since the War through greater efficiency in combustion and a general loss of traffic as well as through electrification and a conversion to diesels: they used 14 million tons in 1948, 10 million tons in 1958, 6 million tons in 1965. The use of coal in coke-ovens has declined relatively as increasing efficiency entails less coke to produce one ton of pig iron, although the overall demand for coal by coke-ovens is still growing.

The demand of the Gas Industry for coal is complicated by the high cost of the special coals needed and the accumulation of the by-product, coke. The Gas Industry is searching for, and is preparing to use, other agents such as oil and liquid methane,[3] but total coal gasification processes are being tried. Electric power stations are the biggest users of coal. Here also oil can take the place of coal, and a number of stations had been converted to oil-firing when it seemed that coal could not meet the rising demand. But the Coal Board assured the Electricity Authority that coal would be available, and new power stations have been authorized near the coalfields in the Midlands, Northumberland, Lancashire, and elsewhere. The estimated cost of operating nuclear power stations

[1] *Investing in Coal*, April 1956. [2] *Infra*, p. 166. [3] *Infra*, pp. 176–178.

makes it unlikely that they will compete with coal until the nineteen-seventies or nineteen-eighties.[1]

Until 1956 the domestic demand for coal remained fairly steady. Until the middle of 1958 it was subject to war-time controls, and this in itself tarnished its image in the public eye. As other types of fuel began to appear the disadvantages of coal became more apparent—it was dirty and cumbersome to handle, there was difficulty in obtaining the type of coal wanted when it was wanted; its actual delivery was a dirty operation and entailed waiting at home until the coalman called; a coal-fire meant ashes to clear from the grate, dust to clean from room and furniture; it was subject to periods of frustrating shortage; the moves for clean-air zones were bad advertisements generally, and the Clean Air Act of 1956, based largely on the Report of the Committee on Air Pollution,[2] was a direct disincentive to the use of coal. The Act prohibited the emission of dark smoke from chimneys, required new furnaces, so far as practicable, to be smokeless and to be fitted with grit- and dust-arresters, and provided for the establishment of smoke-control areas by local authorities in which the burning of bituminous coal in open grates was prohibited. It was intended that by 1970 bituminous coal should no longer be used in private dwellings in 'black areas' where air pollution was dense and that 19 million tons of coal would be involved. The process was slow but nevertheless unsettling and restrictive.

The Coal Board rose splendidly to the challenge. It accepted the fact that it must secure a reduction in output, and in its *Revised Plan for Coal* of 1959 assumed a demand of some 200 or 215 million tons a year. It then planned to secure this lower output without the loss of valuable reserves of coal or heavy redundancy of workers. It spread its cuts widely, refraining from a large-scale closure of collieries, and although the labour force was reduced by over 47,000 in 1959 alone, by careful control of recruitment and by intelligent redeployment few of the men were left without alternative employment at the end of the year. Renewed attention to mechanization and efficiency made the most of those that remained, and productivity reached a record level in 1959 of 1·3 tons a man shift.

In 1960 mergers and closures of pits continued, but the degree of unemployment was small, and in 1961 the Board could boast that the industry had weathered a fall in demand unexampled since the early nineteen-thirties with its productive capacity unimpaired, its efficiency

[1] *Infra*, p. 175.   [2] Cmnd. 9322.

increased, and without serious hardship to its workpeople and their families. In 1961 and 1962 mechanization, particularly power-loading, was extended, and productivity rose still further.

By that time three-quarters of the coal produced by the Board was being mechanically cut and loaded, and an all-round willingness to experiment, to try out new machinery, to concentrate colliery workings, to change over to new and reconstructed collieries, was paying high dividends. Productivity was up by a further 6 per cent in 1963, a further 4 per cent in 1964. In 1965, in a fully automatic pit at Bevercotes, Nottinghamshire, the first colliery in the world to have full mechanical control from the coalface to the surface, productivity was still higher. No miners were actually working at the coalface at Bevercotes, mechanically mined coal being mechanically fed into non-stop, automatically unloading wagons which delivered their loads direct to the West Burton power station. Something like 1·5 million tons of coal a year were expected to be produced by 700 men at Bevercotes—a quarter of the number required in a normal, partially mechanized pit. Increased productivity enabled the Board to absorb an increase in costs without raising prices. It made a small profit, but, except for the Scottish and Lancashire Divisions, there was no increase in the price of coal for three and a half years—a period when the index of retail prices had risen by 12 per cent. Partly as a consequence exports for the twelve months ended March 1964 stood at 7·9 million tons, 66 per cent higher than in 1962.

At home the Board's production policy had been accompanied by a vigorous marketing campaign. Competition from other fuels remained keen on the domestic front, and the Board worked hard not only at popularizing coal in the public mind but in making known various smokeless varieties. Coke had never been popular, but several new types of fuel marketed by the Board—Coalite, Cleanglow, Glow, Warmco, Homefire—began to find a market; so did a type of pre-packed solid fuel suitable for flat-dwellers. Other forms of coal for central heating and water-heating, like Phurnacite and the newer Sunbrite, were also publicized. Nation-wide newspaper coverage pressed the advantages and cheapness of coal in all these forms, a Coal Utilization Council advised the householder, Housewarming Centres displayed various types of coal heaters for all household purposes. In 1960, 90 per cent of households in Britain were using solid fuel in one form or another to heat their living-rooms in winter, over 50 per cent for heating their main water-supply. In 1963 over 200,000 new central-heating systems with solid fuel were installed, more than of any other type. For some time only specially selected coals could be used for the new purposes, but the Coal Board, by developing new processes, was able to extend the usefulness of lower-grade coal.

On the domestic front coal is at a disadvantage compared with electricity and gas in having no natural advertising centre. Each important town has its Gas and Electricity showrooms where accounts are paid, complaints noted, maintenance requests attended to. These showrooms are a natural focus for various developments in the industry, and in the hands of skilful publicists become the industry's shop-window. Coal, on the other hand, is marketed through numerous small agents, and the householder need never know the source of his supply. The industry has become aware of this shortcoming, and in the spring of 1966 Lord Robens announced plans for coal showrooms that would become focal points for display and sales. To industry, meanwhile, the Coal Board offered free of charge the services of a Technical Advisory Service and of a National Industrial Fuel Efficiency Service. But although electricity power stations took more coal in the year ended March 1964, the railways, partly because of their own retrenchment, took less, and total sales of coal to industry were down by 2·1 million tons.

If the Coal Industry is to take full advantage of the mechanization now possible it must produce not less than the 200 million tons of coal a year assumed in the *Revised Plan for Coal*. Any significant reduction in output below 200 millions would push up costs per ton. An increase in output by ten to twenty tons a year, on the other hand, would provide opportunity to produce marginal tonnage and so lower cost.

The Coal Board was bitterly disappointed, consequently, when the Government estimated that only 170 or 180 million tons of coal a year would be required in the nineteen-seventies,[1] and Robens remarked that the Government might as well have a schoolboy to do his job if he was not to be allowed to sell more coal than that! But to set against the disappointment was the news that the Government would wipe off £400 million from the Coal Board's accumulated capital debt of £1000 million, so saving it something like £44 million a year in interest charges. The Minister of Power also promised, subject to review, the continuation of the heavy duty on oil and the virtual ban on coal imports. The speedy disappearance of uneconomic collieries was meantime expected, the Government promising help in siting new industry as alternative employment, in paying removal, travelling, and other expenses, in providing new houses and doing all that was possible to help those whose place of employment or whose actual work would be affected by closures.

[1] *Fuel Policy*, October 1965, Cmnd. 2798.

The cost of the change-over, promised the Government, as well as its benefits, would be spread over the community as a whole.[1]

Lord Robens, for his part, announced in December 1965 an administrative reshaping of the Coal Industry. The original arrangement, allowing for divisions, areas, groups of collieries, and individual mines under the National Coal Board, would be replaced by a three-tier system of National Coal Board, areas, and collieries that would cut administrative costs, it was estimated, by some £15 million and reduce staff by about 14,000 over five years.

No-one needed to improve his standard of living more than the miner, and the Coal Board accepted this as part of its obligation. "One of the Board's first objectives was to change the spirit of the industry and dispel old bitternesses and old grievances. They had to earn the confidence of the mineworkers and attract men to the industry, and they had to act quickly if the opportunity was not to be lost. At about the time the Board took over the industry they announced that the five-day week would probably be introduced in May. Later they raised the minimum weekly wage and increased the pay of the lower-paid workers. They made other concessions to remove pin-pricking grievances. For example, they relieved mineworkers of the need to pay for pithead baths, bringing British practice into line with practice elsewhere. How far these measures, which were desirable in themselves, led to the increase in manpower and production must be a matter of speculation."[2] The Board had to accept both the essential nature of the miner's work and his propensity to strike: there are more small strikes in the mining industry than in any other, largely because of the dispersed nature of the work, the problems peculiar to one pit or one coalface, the tradition of argument, the solidarity which binds together men who spend their working day below ground sharing a common danger, the exacerbation caused by closing down the less efficient pits. But the miner appreciates the mechanization which lightens his work, the measures which make it safer, and the general amenity which goes with it. Pithead baths, canteens, rest-rooms, recreational and sports facilities are taken for granted. Though the seven-hour day has not been agreed, a proposal for additional rest days instead was accepted. Rehousing schemes have given the miner a home as modern as those in any prosperous town in the land;

[1] *The Coal Industry Act*, 1965; House of Commons, July 1, 1965 (Hansard, fifth series, vol. 715, cc. 838–842); November 25, 1965 (Hansard, fifth series, vol. 721, cc. 779 ff.); *Fuel Policy*.

[2] *Report of the National Coal Board* for the year ended December 31, 1947, p. 121.

he takes his holiday with pay. He has his car, enjoys hobbies probably more varied than most other workers', for his work breeds independence; whippets have come back to the North, sport is still something to be played as well as watched. In comparative prosperity the miner still remains an individual—enough of an individual to make him critical of the development of the Coal Board, keen to urge his rights, anxious to welcome mechanization and any aid to the work below ground, which, although infinitely safer, infinitely healthier, infinitely less arduous than in the old days, is yet dangerous and exhausting to an extent unrealized by many other workers. Yet perhaps it is this very individualism which keeps him from direct participation in the day-to-day work of the Coal Board. There is still something of "them" and "us" in his attitude. Lord Robens, who became Chairman of the Coal Board in 1961, had been an official of the Union of Distributive and Allied Workers, and Minister of Labour in 1951. If he could break down this attitude and bring the workers into full participation in the coming automation of the industry he would have consolidated the already very considerable achievements of the National Coal Board. Starting with the odds pretty high against it, the Board has moulded the industry to the required size, improved it technically, and yet maintained a good labour record. If, as the world thinks, and America and Russia have announced, the world's energy requirements will look to more coal in ten or twenty years' time, the United Kingdom must do as the U.S.A. and U.S.S.R. have done and plan for a big increase: "The coal will not be there in the 1970's if the capacity needed to get it is abandoned in the 1960's."[1] The National Coal Board has every intention of ensuring that it is there. At the same time the Minister of Power, with the help of his Energy Advisory Council, has to consider not only the established alternative forms of power but newly discovered natural gas, as well as the potentialities of that still slumbering giant—nuclear power.[2]

Electricity and gas are rivals on the domestic front, but in no other respect are they comparable, there being a wide range of uses from industry to shops where gas cannot compete with electricity. Twenty-nine per cent of the primary fuel used in 1964 went to power stations, 9 per cent to gasworks; the investment requirements of the Electricity Industry amounted to £700 million in 1965, five times as great as the Gas Industry's; its annual turnover, around £1000 million, is twice as large.[3]

---

[1] E. F. Schumacher, Economic Adviser to the NCB, in *The Financial Times Annual Review*, July 6, 1964.
[2] *Infra*, pp. 173–175.   [3] *Fuel Policy*, p. 27.

The Electricity Act, 1947, provided for the establishment of a British Electricity Authority responsible to the Minister of Fuel and Power and fourteen Area Electricity Boards to own and operate the industry, the existing North of Scotland Hydro-electric Board retaining separate responsibility. The 1947 Act left a South-east Scotland and a South-west Scotland Division under the authority of the British Electricity Authority, but in 1955 these were taken away to form a South of Scotland Electricity Board, and the British Electricity Authority became the Central Electricity Authority.[1] The Electricity Act, 1957, dissolved the Central Electricity Authority and established two new bodies—the Central Electricity Generating Board, to be responsible for generating power and transmitting it to the regions, and the Electricity Council, responsible for general policy and programmes and for advising the Minister. The Area Electricity Boards remained responsible for distribution and sales to consumers. It was a workmanlike division into technical and administrative functions which gave greater freedom to the power engineers. At the time of nationalization Lord Citrine, formerly associated with the engineering, shipbuilding, and electrical trade unions and Secretary of the Trades Union Congress, left the Coal Board to become first Chairman of the British Electricity Authority, and Thomas Johnston, who had been responsible for establishing the North of Scotland Hydro-electrical Board in 1943,[2] remained Chairman of the Board after nationalization.

After the early years devoted to organization and to climbing up out of the war-time depression, sales of electricity began to rise. Between 1947–48 and 1957–58 total sales of the British Electricity Authority increased from 32·7 thousand million units to 72·6 thousand million units, a rise of nearly 123 per cent. Seven years later 17 million consumers in England and Wales consumed over 130 thousand million units, when industrial users took over 58 thousand million units, domestic users over 47 thousand million, and commercial users over 17 thousand million.[3]

The main industrial users are the chemical, iron and steel, and general engineering industries, whose requirements are still growing and will continue to grow if the economy remains expansive. The domestic market was expanded quite early at the expense of both coal and gas; not only was the coal industry more depressed than the electric, but both coal and

---

[1] Under the Electricity Re-organization (Scotland) Act of 1954.

[2] *Supra*, p. 73.

[3] Annual Reports of the British Electricity Authority, the Central Electricity Authority, and the Electricity Council.

gas had a more difficult task to make their products attractive to consumers. The publicity of the Electricity Area Boards, the layout of their showrooms, their attention to customers, has, moreover, always been good, and with the initial advantages of simplicity in use and cleanliness they took advantage of the growing consumer expenditure on goods and services which expressed itself in the demand for household durables powered by electricity. The Electricity Council noted in 1964 that a higher rate of increase in consumers' expenditure on goods and services in one year results in a higher rate of increase in the consumption of electricity, both domestic and commercial, the next. With hot-water and central-heating systems electricity at first made little more headway than coal against oil, which for some time after the War carried all before it. And then, as the Electrical Industry pushed into the central-heating market with such offers as off-peak stored electrical power, so coal was making a come-back on the domestic front and gas was becoming highly attractive over a range of household articles, and the four sources of power remained competitive. For most lighting purposes, however (commercial, public, or domestic), electricity has no rival; very few oil-lamps are now turned up, in even the remotest villages, and the last gas lights are flickering out of streets and homes.

The rapid growth in consumption was possible only with large-scale capital development, and increasingly ambitious programmes were undertaken, whose cost rose from £322 million in 1961-62 to £587 million in 1964-65. Expenditure on research remained comparatively low, but expanded from £2 million in 1959-60 to £8 million in 1964-65.[1] The severe winter of 1962-63 subjected the industry to a gruelling test when for short periods the margin of capacity was insufficient and consumers were without power. The inconvenience was less than might have been expected, electricians and maintenance men continuing to work in Arctic conditions, but the industry nevertheless determined to increase its capacity, and by the end of the sixties hoped to have a 14 instead of a 7 per cent safety margin of reserve. It was somewhat worried over the size of generating plant using traditional power which this entailed. Plants of 200,000-600,000-kilowatt generating capacity were common, and there were two 1 million kilowatt stations which consumed 20,000 tons of coal each day. Sites for such giants are difficult to find, their fuel-feeding must be unbroken, and the provision of water for cooling is often a difficulty, though experiments with 'dry' cooling towers are being made.

The bulk of the fuel used for electrical generation is still coal. Power stations take nearly 70 million tons of coal a year, and by 1970 may be

[1] Annual Reports of the Electricity Council.

taking nearer 90 million. Though oil and nuclear power were rivals—and the latter a lustily growing rival—coal in 1964 still provided 82 per cent of the power for electricity, while oil provided 12 per cent, nuclear energy 4 per cent, and hydraulic power 2 per cent.[1]

In the north of Scotland, meanwhile, the Scottish Hydro-electric Board had by the end of 1958 completed the development of about a quarter of the estimated usable water-power resources of the Highlands. There were then in operation thirty-five hydro-electric power stations with a total capacity of 813,000 kilowatts, and supplies of electricity were available to more than 90 per cent of the premises in the Board's area.

Atomic or nuclear energy stands apart from the others in being still something of an unknown, its costs not fully ascertained, its possibilities barely realized. That it represents a tremendous advance in the power potential of the whole world is indisputed. The United Kingdom industry—if what is still something of a gigantic research project can be so called—has been nationalized almost from its beginnings. During the War work on atomic energy was entrusted to a special directorate under the Department of Scientific and Industrial Research. At the end of the War the Government decided that only a State-sponsored organization could provide the resources necessary to it, and by the Atomic Energy Act of 1946 nuclear research and development proceeded under the auspices of the Ministry of Supply. In January 1954 general responsibility was transferred to the Lord President of the Council, while a United Kingdom Atomic Energy Authority was given independence subject to an expenditure control. The following year the Atomic Energy Authority issued *A Programme for Nuclear Power*,[2] envisaging the installation of some 1500–2000 MW of nuclear capacity in twelve nuclear power stations by 1965; in March 1957, in face of a shortage of coal and difficulties with oil, it accelerated this programme[3]; in October of the same year, because of restrictions on capital expenditure, it modified it; in 1960 it reassessed the situation.[4]

At that time five nuclear power stations were being built, specifications for two more were approved, and the prototype of the Advanced Gas-cooled Reactor at Windscale was nearing completion. The Authority, in assessing the future role of atomic energy and the rate at which nuclear power stations should be built, had to consider the improvements

[1] *Fuel Policy*; Annual Reports of the Electricity Council.   [2] Cmd. 9389.
[3] *Capital Investment in the Coal, Gas and Electricity Industries*, April 1957, *Appendix* (Cmnd. 132).
[4] *The Nuclear Power Programme* (Cmnd. 1083).

at that time in the coal and oil prospects and a reduction in costs effected by the conventional stations. On the other hand it had to weigh the undesirability of a too great dependence upon imported oil, the eventual prospect of a demand for power greater than coal could supply,[1] and its belief that the operating costs of nuclear power stations would continue to decline. It came to the conclusion that orders for nuclear power stations should be placed at the rate of one a year and that at any time five or six stations should be in various stages of development both in order to provide power and to maintain a satisfactory rate of development in nuclear technology.[2]

In April 1964 *The Second Nuclear Power Programme*[3] was published. Nine commercial stations were by that time completed or in process under the first programme, the ninth being due for completion in 1969,[4] and prototype or experimental stations at Windscale, in Cumberland, and Dounreay, in Caithness, were also contributing to the 5000 MW of nuclear generating capacity which it was estimated would have been fed to commercial stations in the fifteen years between 1955 and 1969. The second programme aimed to produce the same amount in only six years, and hoped for one new atomic power station each year between 1970 and 1975, with a possible further station in Scotland.

In October 1959 responsibility for nuclear energy was transferred to the Lord Privy Seal and his newly created office of Minister for Science; in January 1965 yet another administrative change was made and a Ministry of Technology was established which took charge of nuclear development. Later in that year the Ministry of Power reviewed its fuel policy, including the nuclear-power programme, for 1970–75. Like *The Second Nuclear Power Programme*, it assumed an average over the six years 1970–75 of one new nuclear power station a year, starting with the Dungeness 'B' station,[5] and it assumed their output, like that of Dungeness 'B', would be based upon the advanced gas-cooled reactor on the model of the Windscale prototype. Going beyond *The Second Nuclear Power Programme*, the estimates of October 1965 thought that a total of some 8000 MW of nuclear generating capacity might be in commission under the second nuclear power programme by 1975.[6]

Nuclear power stations, as at present envisaged, can supply basic

---

[1] The Coal Industry would deny this.
[2] *The Nuclear Power Programme.*   [3] Cmnd. 2335.
[4] Berkeley, Bradwell, Hunterston, Hinkley Point, Trawsfynydd, Calder Hall, Chapelcross, Dungeness, Wylfa.
[5] Sanctioned May 25, 1965—the second station at Dungeness.
[6] *Fuel Policy*, October 1965, Cmnd. 2798.

power for the generation of electricity, and thus take the place of coal or oil, the so-called 'conventional' forms of power, but they are not themselves direct suppliers of energy. Their advantage is in being large, with great capacity, low running costs, and simple methods of supply. The uranium or thorium needed to produce the fuel for nuclear stations is imported, but it costs less per ton of coal equivalent than oil, and is widely scattered over the world so that sources of supply are usefully divergent. Moreover, a nuclear power station, once fuelled, does not need frequent refuelling. Their disadvantages lie in heavy capital cost, though this has proved less than originally expected, and in their very size, which can seem to entail putting too many eggs in one basket. There is, moreover, still some dispute as to the best form a nuclear power station should take. Until this is decided by experts Governments are not willing to sink millions of pounds of capital. At something around £100 million for one atomic power station nuclear energy is not yet fully competitive with conventional power, and Britain has, in fact, found its running costs less cheap than she expected[1]—though they are being considerably reduced at the newest stations. With coal and oil becoming easier, and the expanding requirements of the country still fed primarily by traditional forms of power, nuclear energy cannot hope to play a major part in British industrial development until the mid-seventies or -eighties.

The United Kingdom is, nevertheless, leading the world with the number and size of her atomic power stations as well as in her forward programme. Progress can be measured in the 0·2 million tons of coal equivalent fed by nuclear reactors to electric generating stations in Britain in 1957, 2·5 million in 1963, and 3·2 million in 1964.[2] By March 31, 1965, nuclear reactors in the United Kingdom had fed a total of some 26,000 million units to the grid—substantially more than the total for the whole free world outside Britain.[3]

Gas, the third of the fuel industries to pass into national ownership, differed from the other three in the degree of decentralization explicit in the Act. Emphasis is on the twelve Area Boards responsible to the Minister and given, therefore, the necessary powers. The Gas Council, covering the whole of Great Britain, represents the industry as a whole, assists the Area Boards, advises the Minister, and is responsible for matters that cannot be confined to any one area. It is composed of a Chairman,

---

[1] See Appendix B III(*b*).   [2] See Appendix B III(*a*).
[3] *Report of United Kingdom Atomic Energy Authority*, 1964–65, p. 1.

Deputy Chairman, and the Chairmen of the twelve Area Boards, all appointments being made by the Minister.

The first ten years after nationalization were difficult. Apart from the weaknesses of the economy generally, the public image of gas was of a dirty, smelly, occasionally leaking means of lighting, heating, and cooking that could come into operation only with the help of a box of matches. Even the gas fire in the office rest-room, the gas-ring for the office tea, became more rare as new office blocks went up complete with central heating and electric switches. The wider uses of gas as a central-heating or refrigerating agent or as a main hot-water heater were hardly considered. Moreover, nearly half of the 1050 separate works producing gas which the Gas Council inherited had been constructed before 1930, and nearly all were in need of major reconstruction if they were not to be shut down completely. Actually about one-third were shut down and new plant built.

As the economy expanded and the industrial market for gas grew the Council laid many thousands of miles of mains, and between 1949-50 and 1958-59 the quantity of gas sold increased by 12 per cent, mainly to industrial users. By this time consumer spending was increasing, and a very good gas publicity service, together with a rooted public preference for gas as a medium of cooking, boosted domestic sales generally. Total consumption grew from nearly 2600 million therms in 1957-58 to over 2900 million therms in 1963-64, and it was the domestic consumer, above all, who took more gas. Sales of cookers were up in 1963-64 over the previous year by 11 per cent, of space-heaters by 38 per cent, of central-heating appliances by 39 per cent, of water-heaters by 7 per cent, of refrigerators by 4 per cent. The excellent showrooms of the Area Gas Boards, good newspaper and other publicity, the improved appearance of gas appliances, as well as their better performance and devices for automatic lighting, did much to boost sales.

Gas was doing well on its own account. Helped by the Lurgi process of gasifying coal by steam and oxygen which had resulted from post-War research, it relied on coal for the bulk of its output, even oil having grown to no more than the equivalent of 1·3 million tons in 1963-64 against coal's 21·8 million tons. But at the end of the fifties a search which had been proceeding in various parts of the world bore fruit with the discovery of natural gas in the Sahara. Natural gas has the advantage over other primary fuels in requiring very little processing. Like manufactured gas, it can be piped direct to the point of use, it is normally sulphur-free, and it can be burnt completely with simple apparatus and without a residue. One immediate disadvantage is that it is much richer than man-made gas and gives a far fiercer heat. Unless Britain is to convert her existing cookers and heaters she needs, therefore, to combine natural gas with manufactured gas. Also, it is more difficult to transport natural gas than oil or coal. Canada and the United States, where natural gas has been in use for some time to the extent of about 16 per cent of energy requirements in Canada and about one-third in the United States, have developed transportation methods which consist, broadly speaking, of condensing the gas to a liquid and transporting it under pressure and refrigeration, both by pipeline and tanker.

In this form Britain began the import of cargoes of liquefied gas from the Sahara in two ships specially built for the purpose. Further import was being considered when the situation was revolutionized in 1959 by the discovery of natural gas in the North Sea off Groningen. Britain's surveyors were quick to follow. The area whose mineral rights, by international agreement, would fall to Britain was divided up and leased to prospectors who began the difficult, expensive, skilled, dangerous and often unrewarding work of drilling for gas about $1\frac{1}{2}$ miles under the ocean bed. They worked from surface rigs or derricks set up on giant legs which reached to the ocean floor. The Gas Council itself sent in a rig; B.P., Shell, Burmah Oil, and four other companies were at work by the middle of 1966.

First to strike was B.P.—in September 1965. The Gas Council followed in May 1966. Lesser strikes were made by two other companies. A disaster to *Sea Gem*, the B.P. rig, in December 1965 caused it to sink, and ten of the crew of twenty-three were lost. But the work continued. Although its full extent and importance had not yet been measured the search was still going on for fresh areas of supply, for new means of transporting the natural gas, and for methods of underground storage. It was a hard blow for the Coal Industry to take. And there was irony in the fact that, as well as natural gas, fresh deposits of coal were located off the Durham coast.

But in the Gas Industry optimism prevailed. By the spring of 1966 the Chairman of the Gas Council was saying that most, if not all, of Britain's gas supplies might come from natural gas within the following ten or fifteen years. By the summer he was speaking of the strikes of natural gas as the most important development in Britain since the Industrial Revolution. He assumed that town gas would be replaced by natural gas in the near future and that the Council would make the conversions in appliance necessary to use the richer natural gas undiluted. He thought that Britain would be able to count upon 4000 million cubic feet of natural gas daily from the North Sea gasfields for as long as thirty-five years. That would be four times as much gas as was used in Britain in 1966.[1]

Coal, Electricity, and Gas each agreed profit targets with the Government.[2] That for Coal was somewhat speculative, but the industry appears to be achieving it. Electricity and Gas, however, each had a clear target. For the Electricity concern the gross return on average net capital employed was to be about $12\frac{1}{2}$ per cent; returns were, in fact, 9·5 per cent for 1960–61; 10·5 per cent for 1961–62; 10·7 per cent for 1962–63; and 11·8 per cent. for 1963–64. The Gas Council agreed to an average gross return on average net assets of 10·2 per cent; in 1962–63 it achieved 9·3 per cent; in 1963–64, 10·1 per cent. With atomic energy and natural gas reinforcing the older sources of power, and the coal industry holding steady for whatever may be asked of it, the power potential of the United Kingdom is one of the most cheering aspects of her economy.

[1] Sir Henry Jones, May 5, 1966, and June 21, 1966, reported in *The Times*, May 6 and June 22, 1966.
[2] *Supra*, p. 126.

CHAPTER XIII

Land, Sea, and Forest

"Agriculture is the bread of the nation; we are hung upon it by the teeth; it is a mighty nursery of strength."

James Harrington, *The Commonwealth of Oceana, 1656*

". . . a healthy and efficient domestic food production is something no nation, however strong its industrial and financial position, can afford to be without."

The Times, Supplement on Agriculture, July 6, 1965

COMPARED WITH industry, the development of British agriculture over the past two decades has been serene, and on the 50 million acres of her agricultural land the United Kingdom has maintained a productivity which compares favourably with most of Europe. Just over one-third of this land is rough grazing; the rest is divided into about half a million holdings, of which some 300,000 constitute the major part by acreage, the rest being so small that they provide only a part-time livelihood for their occupants. About 50 per cent of all farmers are owner-occupiers.

Of the 32 million acres or so under crops and grass, 14 million acres are pasture and over 18 million are arable, of the latter over 11 million being under tillage and 7 million under temporary grass. With annual production to the value of about £1800 million, and directly employing some 900,000 people, or $3\frac{1}{2}$ per cent of the working population, agriculture is one of Britain's largest industries. The percentage of the British population working in agriculture is, however, very low compared with the rest of the world: in no other country is the percentage below 10.[1]

[1] *The National Plan*, Part II, p. 7; Gavin McCrone, *The Economics of Subsidising Agriculture*, pp. 23, 24.

British agriculture had entered the War in a depressed condition, yet under the stimulus of providing more food with less resources, and with considerable Government aid, it did well during the War and continued to prosper after it, providing about half of the country's total food needs, compared with a third before the War. The official policy of encouraging the home production of food took the form of various kinds of assistance to the farmer, and not only resulted in increased production but influenced the whole pattern of British food production.

Perhaps the most extensive agricultural aids are the price guarantees, based upon the Agriculture Act of 1947, which cover about three-quarters of agricultural output. There may be a guaranteed price-level, as with milk and sugar beet, or the Government may make certain deficiency payments which involve making up the difference between an agreed price and an actual price. If cheap imports bring down the price of a product (and the duties on imported agricultural produce are mainly low) the Government will pay the difference to the British producer up to the price agreed at the annual review of prices and guarantees. The producer and the consumer will therefore gain, the taxpayer loses; the greater the gain on cheap imports the more the loss on deficiency payments. It is borrowing from Peter to pay Paul, but it preserves the farmer's standard of life and gives the British consumer cheaper food than in most parts of Europe: the farmers' fear that they might lose their privileged position contributed to the British opposition to entry to the Common Market.

The Exchequer also gives various kinds of production grant, like the fertilizer subsidy, which lowers cost of production to the farmer; it gives specific development or improvement grants, like those covered by the Farm Improvement Scheme or the Hill Farming, Livestock Rearing Scheme; it gives ploughing grants to encourage arable farming on marginal land; winter-keep and grassland renovation grants as an aid to cattle and sheep farming; it offers research and advice services, grants to machinery syndicates to provide machines for grouped farms; it also gives certain rating exemptions, which are not easy to measure and are of limited importance. It allows producers to set up Boards, like the Milk Marketing Board and the Potato Marketing Board, which operate as central marketing bodies and price-fixing authorities, have extensive powers over production and sales, and can control entry into the industry. Roughly half of farm sales are being marketed through such national organizations.

The cost of all this to the Exchequer has been heavy. Total aid to agriculture amounted, on an average, to £260 million a year between 1956–57 and 1960–61; in 1961–62 it was £343 million, in 1962–63 £310 million, and thereafter dropped to an annual figure of around £294 million. Of the 1962–63 figure farming grants and subsidies took £109 million, the implementation of price guarantees £190 million.[1] The results of this expenditure have been satisfactory, total output growing by 13·5 per cent between 1960 and 1964, an annual average percentage increase of 3·2. *The National Plan* looks to an accelerated growth of 3·6 per cent per annum between 1964 and 1970.[2]

The total cereal acreage rose from 3 million acres before the War to 7½ million acres in 1957 and 8 million in 1963. Barley was the biggest of the corn crops both in acreage and product, having overtaken both wheat and oats in a spectacular way. Potatoes remained fairly steady in acreage, but yield was substantially up: the Government would like to increase the acreage. Sugar beet was up on both counts: the Government would like to increase beet of high sugar content, though not the acreage. The 12 million head of cattle in 1963, the 30 million sheep and lambs, were increasing as the decade advanced; there were 7 million pigs in 1963, breeding at such a high level that the annual marketing of about 12½ million was expected; the poultry population numbered over 112 million.[3]

The United Kingdom produced in 1961 about 2500 million gallons of milk, compared with a pre-War average of 1500 million; 1126 million dozen eggs, compared with 545 million dozen before the War; 900,000 tons of beef and veal compared with 578,000; 250,000 tons of mutton and lamb compared with 191,000; 740,000 tons of pig meat compared with 435,000; and 360,000 tons of poultry meat compared with 89,000 tons before the War.[4]

Mechanization had become increasingly necessary after the War as farm workers left the land to take up work in expanding industry; from a total of 1·2 million full-time workers they had declined to the 900,000 of 1965. In all branches of agriculture, but particularly on the large, grain-growing farms, mechanical vehicles and tractors of all kinds had superseded the horse and manual labour: until 1954 the official returns still showed a small, though decreasing, number of horse-drawn ploughs, but subsequently horses were not mentioned. After 1962 the

---

[1] *Annual Review and Determination of Guarantees.*
[2] Vol. II, p. 8, Table 1. For *Plan* see *supra*, pp. 115–117.
[3] *Agricultural Statistics 1961–62* (Ministry of Agriculture, Fisheries and Food); *Annual Review and Determination of Guarantees*, 1964.
[4] *Ibid.*

7+

rate of expansion of mechanization was slowing down, yet agricultural investment was still rising, the £155 million of 1961 growing to an estimated £170 million by 1966.[1]

Internationally the reward is shown in an index number for total agricultural production of 129 in 1962–63, which compares favourably with the average for Western Europe of 123. No country had a higher rating, and only Austria was our equal. A *per capita* estimate gave us, at 123, the lead over all countries but Austria with 125. Growth rates from 1952–53 were 30 per cent for Western Europe as a whole; Austria made the best individual showing with a 42 per cent growth, France had a 40 per cent, the United Kingdom a 33 per cent, Denmark and Germany each a 26 per cent growth rate over the ten years.[2]

Seen from the domestic angle, the capital–labour relationship established in agriculture has given an increasing productivity per man year, which grew at the rate of about 5·5 per cent per annum between 1956 and 1961 and 6·3 per cent per annum between 1960 and 1964. An average annual percentage increase of 6·6 is expected between 1964 and 1970. Meanwhile total agricultural output grew, taking 1960 as 100, to 113·5 in 1964, and is expected to reach 140·5 in 1970.[3]

	1960	1964	1970	1960–64	1964–70
AGRICULTURAL OUTPUT, MANPOWER, AND OUTPUT PER HEAD					
				Annual average percentage increase	
Output	100	113·5	140·5	3·2	3·6
Manpower	100	89·5	75·5	−2·8	−2·8
Output per head	100	127·0	186·0	6·3	6·6

Scotland benefits from the same subsidies as England and Wales, but much of her farmland is difficult to work and yields a poor return, particularly in the Highlands and in the Scottish Islands. Any bad winter, like that of 1962–63, will exaggerate normal difficulties, farmers in isolated districts having trouble even in getting feed to their animals. In January 1963 emergency food drops were made by Service helicopters and 150

[1] *Growth to 1966*, National Economic Development Council, Table 34, p. 63.
[2] Based on an average of the years 1952–53 to 1956–57=100. *The State of Food and Agriculture*, 1964, Annexe Tables 1A and 1B, pp. 195, 197 (Food and Agriculture Organisation of the United Nations).
[3] *The National Plan*, vol. II, p. 8, Table 1.

tons of supplies delivered, mainly feeding-stuffs for sheep and cattle. Public funds then met the £18,000 cost of the air transport. But, apart from seasonal worries, the Highlands and Islands have their own special problems bound up with geography, history, and transport which have resulted in underdevelopment and depopulation. Nearly half of the whole area of Scotland—some 9 million acres of land—consists of crofting counties. Here, although there are only 275,000 inhabitants, there is a land shortage due to the existence of big private estates and the difficult nature of the country. The problem is both to help the small crofter to work his land more remuneratively and more extensively and at the same time to encourage local crafts, to start new viable enterprises, that will stimulate the district, provide an addition to crofting, keep young men in the area and provide a part-time occupation for the older ones. The tourist industry is a help, and with the growth of winter sports provides an all-the-year-round income; the Government's atomic power station at Dounreay has given work to many crofters' sons and has helped to provide attractive new housing estates, a new school, and other facilities at nearby Thurso. The Conservative Government in 1963 offered loans of up to £50,000 a year for three years for the starting of small enterprises, and the new Labour Government of 1964, four months after it took office, produced its own scheme in the form of a Bill for a Highlands and Islands Development Board which would work through a new Highlands and Islands Consultative Council. Besides increasing the aid given to farmers and extending it by, for example, including grass conserved as hay or silage as an eligible crop grant, and making loans for soil improvement, it gave certain powers to the Board to acquire land compulsorily if necessary.[1]

In much of Scotland the standard of living is low by present standards, but many blessings lost by the more prosperous South still remain. In the long run Scotland—right out to the Highlands and Islands —will find itself filling up, and the 'amenities' will be arriving, though perhaps not in the way it would wish, as the population bulge from the South is forced back into the North of England and over the border. The work a Development Board can do immediately will not only help the population now but, if care is taken, will protect it from much that has gone wrong in the South.

Her considerable agricultural progress cannot conceal the fact that Britain is near the top of the European table in the extent of her

---

[1] The Highlands and Islands Development (Scotland) Act, 1965.

subsidization of agriculture. Taking European price-support levels as a percentage of output at national prices, Britain gets a rating of 24, with only Switzerland (30) and Finland (42) above her. Denmark, Austria, Belgium, the Netherlands, Ireland, are all between 3 and 5 per cent. France is 15, Italy 14, West Germany 18, Sweden 21 per cent.[1]

Nor can overall progress hide the fact that there are many farmers, particularly those with farms too small by modern standards yet above the smallholder limit, who, "however hard they work, and however well they manage their businesses, just cannot hope to get a decent living from their farms at prices which the taxpayer and the consumer can afford".[2] "The problem of the small farm", said the Minister of Agriculture, speaking in the House of Commons in August 1965, "has never been comprehensively tackled in this country before. We have far too many farmers trying to win a reasonable living from insufficient land."[3] Proposals in a White Paper published at that time offered grants for private amalgamation schemes, for the buying by the Government on a voluntary basis of land for future amalgamation schemes, and compensation for those who wished to leave such farms.[4] In hills and upland country, where the small farmers' problem was particularly acute, a series of rural development boards was proposed "to plan the integrated development of agriculture and forestry together with related uses such as recreation and tourism."[5] While the Tories alleged that the proposed sale of land to the State amounted to "creeping nationalisation" the Labour Government brought in a Bill embodying the proposals of the White Paper which passed its second reading on May 6, 1966.[6]

There are many factors to take into account in considering the extent and size of the British agricultural subsidies. Justification is seen in increased mechanization, a high land utilization, an increasing productivity per man year, and in the comparatively cheap food which benefits industry as a whole as well as the consumer. But might not competition with imported food provide an equal stimulus to efficiency and, while being more painful, be less enervating? Certainly the case for feather-bedding an industry which would not be viable without high subsidy depends upon other than economic factors. Economically it is difficult to justify. Would we not be better off importing the food which other

---

[1] Gavin McCrone: *The Economics of Subsidising Agriculture*, p. 51, Table 2.
[2] *The Development of Agriculture*, August 1965, Cmnd. 2738.
[3] August 4, 1965 (Hansard, fifth series, vol. 717, c. 1697).
[4] *The Development of Agriculture*, Cmnd. 2738.
[5] Minister of Agriculture, House of Commons, August 4, 1965 (Hansard, fifth series, vol. 717, c. 1698).
[6] Hansard, fifth series, vol. 727, cc. 2020–2114.

countries produce with lower subsidy and selling in return our manufactured goods? But would the imported food be cheaper than our own
subsidized products? If not, it would cause a price rise and a reduction
in the quantity of goods we exported in exchange. Such balance-of-payments considerations would be weighed in considering any sector of
industry. But agriculture must always be a special case because it affects
our way of life to a different and wider extent. Against the cost of the
subsidy we have to weigh our need to be self-sufficient in time of war;
our desire for farm products which are fresher than those which come
from overseas; our need to retain open farmland as a social amenity; a
general feeling that a country divorced from contact with the soil has
lost something basically desirable. We have to ask whether the farmers'
occupation and the farmers' acres add to the amenity of life in Britain:
it would be difficult to argue that they do not. And in all our talk of
subsidizing agriculture it should be remembered that several industries
enjoy tariffs of 30 per cent—for example, the motor-car industry—and
this probably exceeds the level of protection given to agriculture by
subsidies and other means.[1] With the taxation that pays for the subsidy
falling most heavily on the high-income groups and amounting, in effect,
to a cheap food bonus for the less well-off sections of the community,
the agricultural subsidy is of general benefit to the country as a whole as
well as an indirect help to industry generally.

Apart from the land, Britain has a source of food in the seas around
her coasts and in the more distant oceans, from the Barents Sea across
the North Atlantic to Greenland, and her people eat more fish than the
inhabitants of any other country in Western Europe. Deep-sea trawlers
to the number of 635, of whom 200 fish in distant waters and 435 in the
high seas round the British Isles and the Faroes, bring in their catch,
often frozen to withstand the time-lag between their life in the ocean and
their appearance on the fishmonger's slab. Some 2000 smaller vessels
comprise the inshore and herring fleets. The total catch in 1964 was to
the value of £57 million at first-hand sale. The Government subsidizes
the industry to the extent of £4 million annually, with a further £1 million towards the cost of vessels. There is no longer need to keep the fisherman and his boat as an aid to defence, but to raise the standard of living
of the fisherman while keeping the price of fish reasonably low is
accepted Government policy.

While the Government and the farmers under the stimulus of two
world wars and a rapidly growing population had evolved a working

[1] McCrone, *op. cit.*, pp. 18–19.

partnership that revitalized British agriculture, forestry policy had been no less radically transformed.

In 1914 there were not more than 3,000,000 acres of woodland in Great Britain, the quality of much of the timber was very poor indeed, and for the bulk of her supply Britain depended on imports. The First World War exposed the danger of the situation. The increasing success of the German U-boats compelled her to restrict timber imports to the minimum and expand home production at almost any cost. By the end of the War some 450,000 acres had been stripped, but it is to the Government's great credit that even at the height of the crisis it began to plan for the future. A Forestry Subcommittee of the Reconstruction Committee of the Cabinet was appointed by the Minister of Agriculture in 1916, and from it emerged in 1918 the Acland Report[1] which was the basis of the Forestry Act of 1919. By this Act the State for the first time formally assumed responsibility for forestry policy. Its agent was to be a Forestry Commission, receiving annual grants from the Treasury; the Commission's function was to build up a national reserve of State-owned forests and to encourage and assist private estates. But these admirable intentions could not withstand the cold wind of economic crisis. When economies were demanded the Forestry Commission was one of the first to suffer, and long-term planning became increasingly difficult. As the memory of war receded it was less easy to appreciate the need for strategic reserves, and by 1939 the Forestry Commission had planted only some 361,000 acres. Nor had the Commission been as successful as had been hoped in stimulating landowners to develop their own woodlands. It had helped by grants in the planting of nearly 126,000 acres, but little impact had been made on the general standard of woodland maintenance. The country entered the Second World War with even more critical timber prospects than in 1914. But the lessons of the First World War had been learnt, and by better planning more timber was produced from much leaner forest resources. Before the War more than 95 per cent of total consumption was supplied from abroad; during the war some 60 per cent of the 30 million tons required came from home woods. Though felling was strictly controlled many promising stands had to be taken before they had reached maturity, and the prospects of private forestry became even more gloomy. It was against this background that the Forestry Commission produced in 1943—even before the War had finished—its Post-War Policy Report which formed the basis of the Forestry Act of 1945.

[1] *Final Report of the Forestry Sub-Committee of the Committee on Reconstruction, 1917–18* (Cd. 8881).

The main factor influencing the new plan was the danger that two wars has emphasized of relying almost exclusively on imports of timber; an ambitious programme was now adopted to build up a strong strategic reserve. The total woodland area was to be increased over fifty years from some 3 million to 5 million acres, of which rather more than 3 million acres would be managed by the Forestry Commission, and rather less than 2 million would be private woodlands. Though the overriding factor in framing the programmes was strategic, it was considered that the return on the capital invested would be not unsatisfactory, and there were social advantages also to be gained in providing rural employment in areas that were threatened with depopulation. The Act of 1945 was concerned with the broad outlines of policy; a further Act in 1947 defined the measures proposed for the assistance of private forestry. Of these the most important was the Dedication Scheme, by which an owner binds himself and his successors in title not to use the lands he has dedicated for any other purpose than growing timber: he also has to ensure skilled supervision. In return he receives a Planting Grant for every acre satisfactorily planted or restocked after dedication, and an annual Management grant, the scales of payment for both being subject to periodic review. Alternatively he may elect to receive 25 per cent of the approved net annual expenditure on the woodlands dedicated until they become self-supporting. Owners who cannot or do not wish to undertake the long-term binding arrangements of the Dedication Scheme are eligible for Planting Grants, but no Management Grant is paid.

The policy crystallized in the Forestry Acts of 1945 and 1947 marks a tremendous advance on the Act of 1919, and the actual progress made since the Second War eclipses the achievements of the inter-war period. The assistance given to private owners proved more successful than had been anticipated, the total area dedicated by September 1963 being over 760,000 acres and planting grants covering more than 100,000 acres more. Not everything, however, went according to plan, and the rate of Forestry Commission afforestation fell considerably short of expectation. Between 1947 and 1951 the short-fall in planting was over 72,000 acres; from 1952 to 1958 only 440,000 acres were planted of an 860,000 acre target. The main difficulty was the acquisition of land. To avoid undue competition with agriculture a limit had since 1919 been set to the price per acre that the Forestry Commission could pay. This meant in practice that lowland woodlands, primarily suited to hardwoods, were left in the main to the private sector, while the Commission concentrated on the less productive uplands and the planting of conifers. Here the main competition came from hill farming, which was heavily subsidized, and sentiment tended to obscure the comparative economics of the two forms of use.

The failure to maintain the intended rate of expansion was, however, less serious than pessimists thought, for issues that seemed clear enough when the War ended were becoming considerably more clouded. The concept of the strategic reserve for example, looked considerably less realistic than when shipping space had been an essential condition of survival. By the fifties it was clear that in the kind of war that could be expected, shipping economies would be irrelevant; the question was rather one of the balance of payments. Here the economic factor dominated, but the economics of forestry are notoriously complex. Timber is a long-term investment since trees are unproductive for at least fifteen years, and most plantations do not show a profit for forty years. To calculate the movement of prices, costs, supply and demand over such a long period requires a fortune-teller rather than an economist. The sharp rise in labour costs from an index number of 100 in 1938 to nearly 600 in 1961 upset calculations. The future of world supplies will depend partly on the rate of economic growth in such underdeveloped areas as Africa and parts of South America—another factor in the equation which is difficult to determine.

It is not surprising that in 1958 a slowing down of the planting rate was accepted and more emphasis placed on the social as well as the economic aspects of forestry. Plantations in the Scottish Highlands and in the central uplands of Wales may not yield a rate of interest comparable with industrial investment, but they help arrest the depopulation of areas where people still want to live if they can make a living. A population increasingly confined to towns will eventually sicken. Nor should the development of National Forest Parks be underestimated. The Forest of Dean has a future in serving the interests of holidaymakers as well as a past of providing oaks for the Navy and coppice for iron foundries. Regimented rows of young conifers on the hills are not to most people's tastes, but the grown forest, tactfully thinned, adds considerably to the pleasures of our landscape.

CHAPTER XIV

The Health Service in Operation

"... a constant endeavour to fence against the infirmities of ill-health."

Laurence Stern, Tristram Shandy, 1759

"Finance is always likely to be a key factor in the development of the National Health Service."

Report of the Ministry of Health, 1965

WHEN THE Labour Government was defeated in 1951 it left to its successors a National Health Service full of such lusty energy that even its sponsors were amazed and not a little bewildered. Its own inherent growth was magnified by the general expansion of the economy and by the price rise which affected it in every direction, through every element of cost, from the wages of the clerk who filed a prescription to the salary of the most eminent surgeon, from the box of matches that lit a fire in the nurses' sitting-room to the oxygen that saved a man's life. The Labour Government had imposed a half-charge upon dentures and certain payments upon spectacles above the original schedule, but the administrators of the Service were in an Alice-in-Wonderland position: run as hard as they might they were always overtaken by costs. When R. A. Butler, the Chancellor of the Exchequer in the Conservative Government, made a statement to the House of Commons on January 29, 1952, concerning the gravity of the economic situation generally[1] he also foreshadowed further Health Service charges. These were proposed by Harry Crookshank, the new Minister of Health, two months later. He asked for a charge of 1s. on each prescription presented, a charge of £1 towards the cost of each session of dental treatment, of £3

---

[1] *Supra,* p. 85.

towards surgical boots, of £1 towards abdominal supports, of 5s. to 10s. towards elastic hosiery, of £2 10s. towards wigs. There were various exemptions. War pensioners with accepted disabilities would not pay for boots, children and expectant and nursing mothers would not pay for dental treatment, those in receipt of National Assistance and their families would be exempted from all payment, including the prescription charges, for which they could claim rebate on the basis of a receipt from the chemist.

The second reading of this Bill was carried on March 27, 1952, but it was trying to hold water in a sieve. The rising tide of prices had engulfed the doctors too, and while the House was approving charges which would lower the Exchequer bill for England and Wales by some £20 million Mr Justice Danckwerts was awarding increases in salary to the doctors which raised it by £40 million. "Something has gone wrong with the sense of values in this country", exclaimed Bevan, "when we can confer £40,000,000 upon one branch of the medical profession and at the same time propose to impose charges on old age pensioners."[1]

It was not as simple as that. The Spens Committee had recommended what amounted to an average income for general practitioners of £1111 at 1939 prices,[2] and when rates were worked out in detail before the Service started this was adjusted by roughly 20 per cent to allow for the increase in prices since 1939. By 1951 this was considered by the profession to be inadequate, and in the summer negotiation gave way to an ultimatum that unless the Government would accept arbitration there would be a mass resignation of all G.P.'s from the Health Service.

In December the Government appointed Mr Justice Danckwerts to adjudicate. His conclusion, delivered in March 1952, was that the advances on the Spens figures had not fully allowed for rising costs, that there should have been for 1948 an 85 per cent increase on the 1939 estimate, and a 100 per cent increase thereafter.[3]

The doctors' backdated higher salaries helped to swell the Health Service bill which for the United Kingdom was £518 million in 1952–53. For England and Wales the bill was £486 million, of which £384 million fell to the Exchequer. The £76 million which went to the doctors as a result of the Danckwerts award far more than outweighed the £20 million from the new charges, which, with one or two other small charges, was all that came in from the patients.[4]

---

[1] Hansard, fifth series, vol. 498, c. 878.   [2] *Supra*, p. 58.

[3] See Appendix, A V(*a*).

[4] The new charges brought in for England and Wales: £5½ million in respect of dental treatment and dentures; £4 million in respect of spectacles; £4¾ million in respect of drugs and appliances.

In April 1953 the whole question of Health Service expenditure was handed over to a Committee presided over by Mr C. W. Guillebaud. But the Guillebaud Committee, reporting three years later, found no opportunity for making recommendations which would reduce in substantial degree the annual cost of the Service; it found no grounds for a charge of widespread extravagance, and it recommended no major change in the general administrative structure. The increasing cost of the National Health Service was largely—to the extent of 70 per cent—due to the inflationary trend in the economy, which included higher prices and wages all round.[1] By the time the Committee had reported it had risen in England and Wales to £585 million,[2] and in 1958, ten years after the inception of the Service, it stood at £671 million, of which the Exchequer bore £486 million.[3] By that time the total United Kingdom Health Service bill was £710 million, of which the Exchequer bore £562 million.

But it was as important to assess the achievements as to evaluate the cost of the National Health Service. In return for this expenditure the Ministry of Health's Report for England and Wales at the end of the first ten years showed an impressive all-round development. The numbers of in-patients treated in hospitals had increased by a million, or 30 per cent. Waiting-lists has been reduced by about 90,000 from the peak figure of 1950, and urgent and necessary cases were in most districts being admitted immediately. Expenditure on new hospital building and improvements was rising, from £10½ million in 1954–55 to £20·8 million in 1958–59. The number of general practitioners in the Health Service rose steadily—there were 16,750 in January 1950, 19,599 at July 1, 1958, and there was a better all-round distribution of consultants and specialists throughout the country. The number of full-time nurses grew from 126,000 in 1949 to 153,000 in 1958; part-time nurses from 23,000 to 41,000 over the same period. A total of over 2250 million prescriptions had been dispensed between 1948 and 1958, a record being reached with the 229 million of 1956. The figures for Scotland and Northern Ireland showed all-round comparable increases.

Once it was accepted that the whole tone was expansion—of population, of patients, of doctors and specialists, of nurses and almoners, of beds and supplies, of training and research, of confinements, of road accidents, of accidents in the home, of industrial accidents, of new drugs and surgical advances, of cures and rehabilitation—it was easier

---

[1] *Report of the Committee of Enquiry into the Cost of the National Health Service*, 1956, Cmd. 9663.

[2] For the year 1956–57.

[3] For the year 1958–59. For the year 1957–58 it had been £626 million and £480 million respectively.

to accept the expansion of costs, but not always easy to meet them. In December 1956 the prescription charge was increased to 1*s.* for each item dispensed. National Health contributions were raised in 1957 and again in 1958. But the doctors, feeling once more that they were left behind by the general rise in the cost of living, were already demanding an upward revision of the Danckwerts figure. The Government, attempting to check inflation all round, rejected their main demand, but made small general increases and set up a Royal Commission under Sir Harry Pilkington, an industrialist, to examine the whole question of doctors' and dentists' remuneration. The medical profession felt that the assurances implicit in the Spens and Danckwerts findings were being jettisoned, and in a series of impassioned meetings again seriously considered withdrawal from the National Health Service, being placated only by a public statement issued by the Pilkington Commission.

The Pilkington Commission took three years over its labours and reported early in 1960.[1] The pool was to remain, but certain primary calls upon it, including group-practice loans and extra-panel earnings, were to be excluded, so that the doctor could call upon a higher total for capitation distribution. A series of merit awards, comparable to those given to consultants,[2] was also suggested. Average net income should be increased by about 14 per cent, and a review body of six outstanding persons and a chairman should keep the subject under permanent review and prevent the recurring crises that had bedevilled the relationship of the medical profession and the Government. A working party, settling the details of the Pilkington award, raised the capitation fee to 19*s.* 6*d.* with a loading of 14*s.* extended to cover 200 more patients in the middle grouping.[3]

The Pilkington Commission considered also the payment of dentists, and of doctors and dentists in the hospital service. After the initial rise the salaries of dentists working outside the hospitals had failed to keep up with the cost of living, but new techniques which speeded up their work were again redressing the balance, and the Commission concluded that most dentists were earning the average of £2500 considered appropriate. Nevertheless, a standing Dental Rates Study Group should keep chairside times for each operation under review.

Doctors and dentists in the hospital service were, like the general practitioners, to receive increases; all would be backdated. The Government accepted the findings, and for the year 1960–61 a sum of over £40

[1] *Royal Commission on Doctors' and Dentists' Remuneration, 1957–60,* Cmnd. 939, February 1960.
[2] *Supra,* p. 62, and Appendix A V(*b*).
[3] 401–1600 patients for a single doctor, 500–1700 for partnerships.

million was earmarked in Great Britain for these payments. Thereafter the increase would add an estimated £12 million annually to the Health Service bill.

But in an inflationary situation there can be no stability, and the Pilkington awards were soon out of date. The doctors' Review Body, under the chairmanship of Lord Kindersley, early in 1963 gave G.P.'s a 14 per cent increase on the understanding that it would last for three years or more, but by the beginning of 1964 doctors were claiming that they had not received it and were questioning the whole concept of assessment. The population was growing and becoming more doctor-conscious, while the number of doctors was now failing to keep up. Yet the pool was still determined by the number of doctors and not by the number of patients, and while the capitation fee paid them for more patients it did not pay them for more work on each patient. "With an average list and even a conservative estimate of the number of services given per annum, the gross payment per service averages the paltry sum of about 6s. The long training of a professional man should receive better financial recognition."[1] To find doctors petitioning Parliament in January 1964 to look into their "oppressive terms of service" was remarkable—but not more so than the fact that a General Practitioners' Association had been founded the previous October to organize their dissatisfaction. More than 6000 general practitioners signed the petition which described family doctors' terms of service as "inequitable and oppressive" and asked that their terms of service be reviewed.

But while the general practitioner was being forced into the arena where wage agreements are made his whole relationship to his profession and to society at large was changing. He had been highly suspicious of the National Health Service Act in its early stages. But the very fact that medicine is such a highly personal profession had in itself gone a long way towards ensuring its success. The doctor suffers no metamorphosis as he ceases to dispatch bills to his patients: on the contrary, the absence of direct payment often helps the doctor-patient relationship. Nor have doctors suffered direction from the top, except in such matters as having to obtain approval from the Medical Practices Committee before starting a practice or filling a vacancy. But the power of the MPC is purely negative, and while it can refuse permission because it feels an area is over-doctored it can do no more than persuade, by means of initial practice allowances, into an under-doctored area. Nor has there been complaint over the disciplinary action of the Medical Tribunal. In 1960, 1961, and 1962 only one medical practitioner was removed

[1] See report in *The Times*, February 24, 1964.

from the list. In the whole of 1962 only just over a thousand cases concerning doctors, dentists, pharmacists, and opticians from the whole of England and Wales were reported to the Tribunal. About 90 per cent of the cases concerning doctors were initiated by patients usually alleging that a doctor had failed to visit or to provide proper treatment. About half were dismissed without a hearing as "frivolous or vexatious", but cases like that of the doctor who, for the second time, was found absenting himself from his practice without making adequate arrangements for a deputy were dealt with by fine. The main subject of complaint concerning dentists referred to the fit and efficiency of false teeth, though one dentist was found guilty of regularly extracting all teeth and providing full dentures. He was punished by the withholding of £600 from his fees.

The fears which began to grow towards the end of the fifties were of a different nature. An enormous increase of specialist skills and techniques has helped to concentrate attention on the hospitals, and the general practitioner must inevitably pass on to the specialist a patient whose case might benefit from such treatment. The family doctor is still left with a large number of ills to deal with, and his work is made more difficult by the proliferation of drugs, by an increasing resort to the doctor, by a relationship which in many cases is casual and assumes that the doctor is on call for any minor mishap. Too often he works in isolation, too often he is regarded as a sorting-house on the way to the specialist, too often he retains virtually a twenty-four-hour-a-day responsibility in contrast to the general five-day week of the bulk of the population. It was a situation summed up by a member of the British Medical Association in 1962 when he described the family doctor as the Cinderella of modern medicine. He was being asked to do a twentieth-century job in a nineteenth-century framework. All over the world money was poured into hospital services, but the general practitioner was left to shift for himself—to find capital, premises, and staff and to organize his own affairs to the best of his ability and resources.[1]

The difficulty is not one which arises necessarily from the National Health Service—and the various committees which have examined the subject agree on this point—it is inherent in the rapid advance of medicine, which has resulted in diagnostic aids and methods of treatment beyond the scope of private practice and a degree of specialization not possible in a general practitioner, the very essence of whose training must be breadth and versatility. Yet the eminent consultant physician is as necessary to medicine as the eminent specialist, the family doctor

[1] Dr Bruce Cardew at an international medical conference in London, October 22, 1962, reported by *The Times*, October 23, 1962.

as the hospital consultant; it would be a poor exchange to sacrifice the general practitioner to the hospital technician: "Are we safer in the hands of a doctor who cannot know everything but who cares for his patient, or in the hands of a technician who knows everything except the patient?"[1] The dilemma need not arise. We are safer in the hands of men united professionally by a synthesis of effort, by a closer relationship between family doctor and hospital. It is just this which the health centres had hoped to provide. But, though Bevan referred to them as "a very vital provision in the Bill",[2] yet for various reasons—lack of money and manpower, the individualism of the doctor, perhaps an all-round preference for the familiar doctor's surgery—only twenty-one health centres had been established in England and Wales and four in Scotland by the end of 1964. The alternatives of partnership and group practice were, however, spreading widely, helped, since 1953, by the setting aside of £100,000 annually for a group-practice loan fund from which doctors might borrow for building and improvements: but, in so far as the doctor adopts a system of group medicine to give him greater freedom and better equipment, his patients tend to suffer the loss of that very personal relationship which has been deplored.

If health centres are not developing, then the doctor should have direct access to the pathology, radiology, and other diagnostic units of the hospital; there should be a number of general-practitioner beds where the doctor should be able to care for his own patients; consultation between the G.P. and the consultant should be accepted; his contacts with hospital and ward staff should be taken for granted; and he should be able, if he wished, to return to the hospital for a certain amount of part-time educative work—a service which would be as welcome to the understaffed hospital as useful to the practitioner. At the same time, doctors' lists should be kept under review, more should be done by the Medical Practices Committee to improve the distribution of doctors, and their salaries should be periodically revised by some device less clumsy than the pool. Meanwhile the doctors' reaction to their remuneration and conditions of work was indicated first by the slowing down in the growth-rate of full-time general practitioners and by the decreasing number of applicants for any advertised vacancy, and then by an actual decline in their numbers. The number of general practitioners, which between 1952 and 1958 had grown from 17,204 to 19,599, an average annual increase of about 400, grew in the following five years

---

[1] Mr Ian Fraser, in Presidential Address to the British Medical Association, Belfast, July 23, 1962.
[2] *Supra*, p. 59.

to only 20,335—an annual average increase of about 147. At the end of 1965 there were just over 20,000 full-time general practitioners in England and Wales.[1] In Scotland meanwhile, a similar situation had reduced their numbers from 2666 in July 1963 to 2611 at the end of 1965.[2]

While it was accepted that the cost of the Health Service could not fall while people needed treatment and all-round prices continued to rise, yet the increase in the cost of drugs and medicines was disturbing. Before the Health Service the quantities of drugs prescribed and dispensed had a direct relationship to the wages and salaries of the majority of the recipients. Under the Health Service the limiting factor was the doctor's willingness to prescribe. Since the War more drugs than before have been in use and there is an increasing reliance on the more expensive ones, particularly the antibiotics, barbiturates, tranquillizers, and similar drugs. At the same time the growing number of advertisements of all kinds for drugs and pharmaceutical products have produced a more introspectively medicine-conscious nation. One result of this is that the drug industry has become one of the best growth investments in the world. High profits enable most companies to carry out their own research, each competing with the other, both in producing new 'ethical' drugs which are sold only on doctors' prescription and in making variants of the normal pharmaceuticals which are obtainable over the counter. This is valuable. But 400 or so drug firms competing so closely with one another that there is often only the smallest divergence between one product and another bespeaks a certain extravagance, particularly since each manufacturer deluges the medical profession with expensive advertisements (ethical drugs are not allowed to be advertised to the public) to the weight of some hundredweights and the cost of some £15 in postage annually for each of Britain's 23,000 doctors. The doctor, generally disliking the advertisements and resenting the high-pressure salesmen who are sometimes sent as well, yet frequently prescribes the proprietary article because the firm's name gives him a guarantee that the product has been tested. Even this guarantee is not always sound, however. Some drugs require years of use before their full effects are seen, and this is longer than a commercial company can afford to give. The side-effects of cortisone and thalidomide were observed only after a period of years.

The large number of prescriptions dispensed in the first years of the

[1] The Minister of Health, House of Commons, November 22, 1965 (Hansard, fifth series, vol. 720, c. 7).
[2] The Secretary of State for Scotland, House of Commons, November 22, 1965 (*ibid.*, vol. 720, cc. 15–16).

Health Service continued with little abatement, and there were well over 200 million annually in England and Wales right into the sixties, with a slight falling off to 197 million in 1962 after a further raising of the prescription charge in March 1961 to 2s. for each item. Scotland reached a peak of over 22 million in 1959–60. In Northern Ireland there was a steady rise from 4 million to 5 million between 1954 and 1961. The cost in England and Wales alone was something like £85 million in 1962, when two-thirds of the drugs dispensed—nine-tenths of the total net ingredient cost—was in respect of proprietary preparations, and the average total cost per prescription in the National Health Service was a little more than 8s. 8d.

The prescription charge was paid over the counter, and the chemist kept it as part of his total remuneration. This total is worked out on the basis of each item dispensed, the calculation consisting of the net or wholesale cost of the ingredient or appliance, an allowance of 25 per cent on this cost for overheads and profit, a dispensing fee, and a payment of about 1½d. for providing a bottle or container. Prescriptions surrendered by the chemists are priced under the direction of Joint Committees working through local offices; but since the millions of prescriptions turned in have made individual pricing impossible, an averaging system has been adopted. Chemists are paid by the Local Executive Committee. In March 1950 a prescribing investigation unit was set up at the Ministry of Health to examine the prescriptions of doctors believed to be prescribing excessively or extravagantly, doctors were exhorted to prescribe standard rather than proprietary preparations, and a Committee, appointed in 1954 to examine the problem, circulated lists of publicly advertised proprietary drugs which it felt ought not to be prescribed on grounds of cost. The pharmaceutical manufacturers themselves also put in operation a voluntary price-regulation scheme relating to drugs prescribed under the National Health Service, but its success was limited, and the proportion of the National Health Service bill attributable to drugs remained steady at about 10 per cent. The Association of the British Pharmaceutical Industry pointed out early in 1964 that the cost of medicine per head of the population worked out at one penny a day, compared with 2s. 3d. spent on smoking, 1s. 2d. on drinking, and 5s. 4d. on food.[1] And, as *The Times* in a leading article pointed out, it is absurd to plan for an expanded Health Service on the one hand and, on the other, to expect the drug bill to dwindle.[2] Moreover, negotiation with the manufacturers of certain widely used patented drugs resulted in substantial

[1] See leaflet published January 20, 1964.   [2] December 13, 1963.

reductions in their cost; in 1961–62 over £1 million in ingredient cost was saved.[1]

But there is still scope for disquiet on the whole question of drug-testing and drug research and the relative merits of proprietary and other drugs. In August 1962, after widespread dismay at the effects on foetal abnormalities of the drug thalidomide given as a sedative during early pregnancy, a joint subcommittee of the Standing Medical Advisory Committees for England and Wales and for Scotland on the Safety of Drugs was set up. In an Interim Report in November and a Final Report in March 1963 it advised that the responsibility for experimental laboratory testing of new drugs before they are used in clinical trials should remain with the individual pharmaceutical manufacturer; that it was neither desirable nor practicable that at this stage the responsibility for testing drugs should be transferred to a central authority; but that there should be an expert body appointed by the Minister of Health and the Secretary of State for Scotland to review the evidence and offer advice on the toxicity of new drugs.[2] The Minister and the Secretary of State accepted the advice, and, in association with the Minister of Health for Northern Ireland, appointed a Committee on Safety of Drugs under the Chairmanship of Sir Derrick Dunlop, which began its work on January 1, 1964. The Association of the British Pharmaceutical Industry and the Proprietary Association of Great Britain undertook not to submit a new drug for clinical trial or to market a new drug after that date against the advice of the Committee.

Yet, in spite of the willingness of the drug firms to co-operate, there still remains the anomaly that laboratory and other research work should depend so largely upon the profits of competing pharmaceutical firms and that the price of a drug should be weighted with high advertisement cost as well as the cost of intensive research done at breakneck speed in order to forestall a rival. It is right that the cost of further research should to some extent be borne by the profit from a drug already on the market, but it is unethical that profit should play a large part in determining the need for a new drug or in determining the speed with which it is marketed.

The hospitals, meantime, had been adjusting themselves to regional grouping and to the machinery of regional boards and management committees. They had to face criticism on grounds of extravagance and niggardliness, of bureaucracy and of irresponsibility, of closing small

[1] *Ministry of Health Report* for the year ended December 31, 1962, p. 4.
[2] 1962 and 1963, H.M.S.O.

local hospitals and failing to provide major diagnostic and surgical centres. But whatever they did required money. Making the best of their resources, they had made good some of the deficiency they inherited by urgent addition to existing hospitals rather than by building new, by the modernization of old wards and the decoration of old waiting-rooms. Together with rising wages and salaries, with increasingly high bills to meet in every direction, the hospital commitment for all purposes had grown to some £500 million by 1961–62 and was about 52 per cent of the whole National Health bill for England and Wales. In Scotland hospital expenditure was nearly £61 million, 63 per cent of the whole.

But there came a time when old walls and ceilings could no longer be patched, when repairs were finally yielding to decay, when new equipment, more operating theatres, more wards, better kitchens—all sensibly located and related to each other—were necessary. Although fully aware of their rising expense sheets, the hospitals were equally aware of their needs, and had been at work on a long-term plan for building and re-equipment. In January 1962 their regional boards and management committees published *A Hospital Plan for England and Wales*[1] and *A Hospital Plan for Scotland*.[2]

The plan for England and Wales envisaged work on ninety new and 134 substantially remodelled hospitals to be begun by 1970–71 as well as 356 other schemes of major additions and improvements to existing hospitals. The capital expenditure was estimated at £200 million between 1961–62 and 1965–66 and at £300 million between 1966–67 and 1970–71. The Scottish plan estimated a capital expenditure of £70 million over the same ten years, including the building of ten new hospitals.

The schemes were big not only in the amount of money to be spent but in what they envisaged. Yet although they planned for some 400 district general hospitals covering the country giving ordinary general service, and gave an important place to teaching hospitals, they also spoke of closing still more of the small cottage hospitals or geriatric homes. Criticism came from several sides. On the one hand the closing of small hospitals with inadequate compensation in local services was regarded with concern, particularly since the railway closures entailed in the Beeching Plan would increase the geographical barrier between a patient and his nearest hospital. On the other hand, the plan was criticized for the lack of any really comprehensive centre. There should be in Britain "hospitals covering the whole of medicine with all specialities and all services aggregated to the most advanced degree and with comprehensive facilities for . . . the most advanced research". Such

1 Cmnd. 1604.   2 Cmnd. 1602.

hospitals, "challenging comparison with any in the world and in situations where populations and communications indicated the need for them", should "be the very foundation of the replanned national service unless we were to be content with something less than first-class. Without them, British medicine might fail to reach its full potential".[1] The vision was splendid. But nearer to reality was the speaker at the annual conference of the Institute of Hospital Administrators at Cardiff in May 1962 who asked, "Will the harsh realities of the national economy falsify the promised vision?"[2]

Whether it considers the hospital programme in terms of vision or of economics, the public is bound to ask what return it is getting for its increased expenditure. More patients are being treated in better wards than before the days of the National Health Service; the number of patients in England and Wales treated in a year grew from 3 million in 1949 to 4 million in 1960 to 4·7 million in 1964; attendances in out-patients' departments grew from 26 million to 29 million to 31 million, of casualty patients from 10 million to 12·5 million to 13·4 million in the same period.[3] Improved techniques of medicine and nursing reduced a patient's stay in hospital, devices that enabled a nurse in a control room to note the temperature and blood-pressure of patients in her care made for efficiency.

While it is not always easy for a layman to estimate the advantages that accrue, the large hospital goes on its way, an entity in itself, supplying a complete range of medical and surgical appliances and equipment, drugs and medicines as well as the services of the doctors, nurses, anaesthetists, dentists, radiologists, physiotherapists, orderlies and porters, kitchen staff and cleaners, gardeners and almoners, and all the rest who run it. It is laundry and hotel, washing its own linen, cooking its own food, often supplying its own vegetables, often generating electricity for emergency supplies. With 424 hospital authorities in England and Wales and in Scotland the administrative side of the hospital service has increased vastly since 1948. Hospital management within the National Health Service is still a new career, but with its own training schemes and its own satisfactions it is of growing importance.

At the apex of the medical pyramid, ultimately responsible for all the medical work that goes on within the hospital, are the hospital consultants. Doctors of consultant rank "are recognised—and are the only

[1] D. T. Rowland Hill, speaking to the British Medical Association in Edinburgh, October 1, 1962, reported in *The Times*, October 2, 1962.

[2] Arthur Keates, quoted by Llewelyn Williams, House of Commons, June 4, 1962 (Hansard, fifth series, vol. 661, c. 74).

[3] Annual Reports of the Ministry of Health.

doctors so recognised in the Hospital Service—as being qualified by professional experience and training to take full personal responsibility for the complete medical care of all patients within their particular specialities".[1] Since the inception of the Health Service more consultants than before have made full-time careers in the hospitals, though some also conduct practices outside. By 1965 there were over 10,000 in Great Britain working wholly or partly in the hospitals.

All grades within the hospital service, like the general practitioners outside and the whole working population, had been swept along on the tide of inflation. Pilkington included the hospital doctors and dentists in his report and recommended all-round increases of salary, particularly for the lower grades and for consultants whose monetary reward lagged behind that of other professions, in spite of the distinction awards recommended by the Spens Committee.[2]

The nursing staffs of hospitals, who were not included in the Pilkington Report, were not so fortunate. The numbers of registered whole-time nurses had grown to 170,000 in 1963, part-time to 58,000, but their pay lagged sadly. The increase in numbers was made up by a very determined recruitment in Ireland and the Commonwealth, and the large numbers of part-time workers indicated the stress of demand. But supply still fell short of need; there were more nurses, but very much more work, particularly in geriatric and maternity centres. Two organizations represented the nurses—the National Council of Nurses, founded in 1904, which was a federation of nursing associations and hospital leagues with a membership of about 68,000, and the Royal College of Nursing, which was founded in 1916 and numbered some 45,000. In June 1962 they amalgamated under the title of the Royal College of Nursing and National Council of Nurses of the United Kingdom. Commenting on this move, the President of the Royal College of Nursing said that nothing less than a revaluation of the Service would be acceptable to them.

Neither of the nurses' organizations had been concerned with wage-fixing. This had been the province of a Whitley Council, where representatives of the nurses negotiated with representatives of the management. For the previous two years, and this is undoubtedly what the President had in mind, the nurses had been negotiating a pay increase, but without success. They had rejected an offer of 2½ per cent and referred the matter to the arbitration of a higher body—the Industrial

---

[1] *Report of the Joint Working Party on the Medical Staffing Structure in the Hospital Service* (H.M.S.O., 1961), p. 9. The Chairman was Sir Robert Platt.
[2] *Supra*, p. 62, and Appendix A V(*b*).

Court. Bearing in mind the Government's efforts to stem inflation by means of a pay pause, the Industrial Court in June 1962 repeated the offer of 2½ per cent, with the promise of a balance of up to 7½ per cent at some unspecified time. The nurses were restrained, but made it clear that they would fight the award; the pill was particularly bitter to swallow since almoners and psychiatric workers were given a 13 per cent immediate increase, and in the same months the Civil Service Arbitration Tribunal awarded 4 per cent to nearly half a million civil servants. There were demonstrations by the nurses and much popular support on their behalf; in one hospital the Minister of Health made a hurried exit by the back door while nurses lobbied the front. But there was no suggestion of striking, going slow, or of any action that would interfere with the quality of their nursing.

During 1963 discussion with the Industrial Court continued; the salary scales, with board and lodging charges, which were announced were unsatisfactory to the nurses, and negotiations went on. Increases in training allowances finally took effect from March 1, 1965, and more favourable salary scales from July 1, 1965.

The third leg of the National Health tripod is supplied by the local authorities and supported in large part by the Medical Officers of Health. In 1948 the localities lost control of the hospitals, though the ambulance service remains with them; they retain responsibility for environmental health, for preventive measures like inoculation and vaccination, general diagnostic measures like chest X-rays, maternity and child-welfare services, homes and houses for the old, and an ever-widening programme of community care.

Community care was practised long before the National Health Service or even local-government services came into existence. For a time it was in danger of being stifled by an all-round professionalism which preferred to treat patients in the most efficient place, which was the clinic or hospital, rather than in more makeshift fashion in their own homes. But pressure on hospitals and the growing number of people who need assistance but not medical attention, has emphasized the importance of home care, and of care in institutions which are not hospitals. The services which have grown up round this concept constitute the Community Care which is now central to the health and welfare work of the local authorities.

Health and Welfare: The Development of Community Care was published in April 1963. It outlined the long-term plans of 146 local health and welfare authorities in England and Wales and made also a modest appraisal of work not highly publicized yet of great importance. By the financial yardstick it had grown by 50 per cent over the previous five years, and capital expenditure had quadrupled. For the period 1962–63 to 1971–72 an expansion of from £111 million to £163 million was expected. In terms of staff this meant an increase of from 81,000 to 119,000, ranging from Medical Officers of Health to ambulance staff, from trained social workers to home helps.

The work these people do covers a wide field. Maternity services provide ante-natal and post-natal instruction and care both at home and in clinics; the services of midwives are provided for babies born at home. Home nurses, health visitors, and home helps are available for mothers with young children, for the old and for the handicapped. "Meals on wheels" provide for the old and the ill who are without help. The physically handicapped are provided with hostel accommodation and residential care when necessary, but as far as possible are given rehabilitation courses and training for employment in special day centres where they also have the benefit of company and social life. There are deaf centres, centres for the blind, centres which teach wood-work, flower-making, the making of toys and decorations for Christmas and other festivals. Sometimes a home can be suitably adapted and equipped to enable a physically handicapped person to make a living from some worth-while work in his own home. For the mentally disordered the local authorities similarly give training at special schools where they are taught to develop their potentialities and to live more or less independent lives. The old are provided for, where necessary, in residential homes which are becoming increasingly geared to personal needs: many authorities are building individual flatlets where old people can keep their own possessions around them but where there is always a nurse on call in emergency. But as far as possible the old are encouraged to stay in their homes in the community, and the home help, home nurse, and 'meals on wheels' services do a great deal of house-to-house visiting of the elderly. Local-authority services have received less publicity than either hospital or general-practitioner work. Yet they are concrete, effective, and expanding. They also illustrate the close connection between health and welfare and between the voluntary and the professional worker: the kind of connection that health centres could be expected to sponsor.

Apart from financial considerations, the chief arguments urged against the National Health Service add up to the case which can be made against every large organization. They concern size, uniformity, standardization, regulation, inflexibility, form-filling, delay, lack of personal contact, and the danger of getting bogged down in a morass of committees.[1] The five-tier hospital system[2] is, perhaps, most likely to suffer in this way. Yet it is also the section of the Health Service which gains most from central directive and least lends itself to 'individuality'. Good beds, good amenities, modern buildings, clean and bright wards with provision for privacy are not necessarily the outcome of autonomy; they result from efficient organization on whatever scale. But the scope to use new techniques and treatments, new drugs and new skills, is most likely to be found in a large hospital with the resources of a State medical service behind it. Imponderables like the character of a physician, his skill and the confidence he inspires in the patient, the character of the matron, her relation to her staff, the kindness and efficiency of the nurses who provide daily care, have no necessary connection with the wider hospital organization—except that a well-paid and respected nursing service is more likely to be obtained in a large unit than a small.

So far as dispensary services are concerned size appears to have had no detrimental effect. The ascertainment of individual chemists' payments for drugs dispensed under the Health Service is an enormous task, entailing millions of prescriptions a year, but it does not prevent the speedy supply of the medicine to the patient or the payment of the chemist. As to the family doctor, it is the increase in population, the widening of knowledge, the diversity of techniques, the sheer weight of people and information that one man has to bear which is a greater danger to personal relationships than the organization of the National Health Service.

Not that the problem of organization within the Health Service can be anything but complex. Direction from the top—whether from the Minister or from the Regional Hospital Board—will always be resented; initiative at the periphery—whether by the hospital itself or by a group of doctors—will always be taken as revolutionary. An enterprise of the size of the National Health Service can succeed only if, like Hobbes's Leviathan, it goes one way. Leviathan is notoriously less agile than the smaller creatures of sea and land, and a nationalized health service is less easy to divert than a series of local Boards of Health. But it is precisely because we want to universalize the best that we have abandoned the small units in favour of the large. It is a major task of govern-

---

[1] See, *e.g.*, John and Sylvia Jewkes, *The Genesis of the British National Health Service*, pp. 27 ff.

[2] The House Committee, the Hospital Management Committee, the Regional Hospital Board, the Ministry of Health, the Treasury.

ment in every modern state to learn how to marry size and flexibility, co-ordination with initiative, direction from the centre with freedom at the periphery. If there is not enough movement at the periphery the unit will become static. If there is not strong enough direction at the centre the unit will be equally incapable of movement, because its energies will be vitiated in too many directions. The dilemma might more easily be resolved if the Minister of Health were given a place in the Cabinet. He would then not be tempted to regard his office as a step towards a higher one, and the gesture would serve as the public recognition of the importance of the health of the nation.

Even so, it would not always be easy to determine the scope of the Ministry of Health. The Mental Health Act of 1959, which replaced the Lunacy Acts and Mental Treatment Acts of 1890–1930 and the Mental Deficiency Acts of 1913–38, fell naturally under the jurisdiction of the Health Minister: the changes in name were significant of the changing attitudes of society to the mentally ill. The new Act, which was in full operation by the end of 1960, gave effect to the recommendations of the Royal Commission on the Law relating to Mental Illness and Mental Deficiency. It made possible a comprehensive mental-health service, fully integrated with the National Health Service, and provided treatment for those who needed it with no more formality than was required for other kinds of illness.

Allied to the preventive side of the Health Service, yet sponsored by the Minister of Labour, was the Bill to safeguard the health, by controlling the working conditions, of some eight million workers in offices, shops, and railway premises. About 400,000 offices covering four million employees, more than 650,000 shops covering over three million people, and about 30,000 railway premises involving over 400,000 were concerned. Cleanliness, temperature, fresh-air circulation, lighting, space, sanitary convenience, washing facilities, drinking-water, first-aid, fire precautions, the fencing of exposed machinery, were covered by the Act, which came into force on January 1, 1962.[1] The measure was significant, not only for the people directly concerned, but because it emphasized once more the relationship between environment and health and because, by including in its scope premises in which meals or refreshments are sold to the public for immediate consumption, it stressed the necessity of absolute cleanliness in the preparation of all food sold. A year after the passage of the Offices Act a new Factories Act consolidated the factory Acts of 1937–59 relating to the safety, health, and welfare of employed persons.[2]

[1] The Offices Act, 1960.   [2] The Factories Act, 1961.

If the Offices and Factories Acts might have lain within the jurisdiction of the Minister of Health, the School Health Service, which remained in his care, was one which some observers thought he might modify or abandon. School medical examinations were of great importance in the days before the National Health Service; twenty years later, with 99 children out of every 100 examined at school physically fit, and with every child having its own family doctor, it should be possible to release some of the doctors and nurses working in the service.[1] Such argument bears the stamp of efficiency, yet the opportunities provided by a school medical service for observing as a matter of routine all the young, at least once or twice in their school lives, are too valuable to be lightly discarded.

With expansion on every front, with prices everywhere rising, the cost of the National Health Service in England and Wales soared to £860 million in 1960–61, to £962 million in 1962–63, to £1028 million in 1963–64: it was the equivalent of about £14 for each of the population for the year, about one-ninth of total public expenditure by the Central Government and local authorities, and about 4 per cent of the national income. When it rose to £1122 million in 1964–65 about two-thirds of the increase over the previous financial year was due to increased prices and higher remuneration—not to increased service. In Scotland the Health Services bill stood at £130 million for 1964–65, having grown from £93 million in 1960–61.[2]

Contributions had been raised over the years. By 1964 a man over eighteen years of age was paying 3s. 4d. a week as National Health contribution (of which his employer paid 7½d.)[3]; he was liable for 2s. for each item a doctor prescribed for him; he paid £1 towards any dental treatment he received, £4 or more towards the cost of a denture, £2 or more, according to his choice of frame, for spectacles. Yet this was but a drop in the ocean compared with the total cost. Of the £1028 million for 1963–64 total National Health Service contributions amounted to only £146 million, total patients' charges to £68 million, and the Exchequer contribution was £690 million.

It was in this situation that the Labour Government abolished prescription charges from February 1, 1965, largely on the grounds that their payment caused hardship to some people. Critics of the move

[1] See, *e.g.*, Brian Didsbury "The School Health Service and the Family Doctor", in *The Lancet*, January 11, 1964, pp. 101–104.

[2] Reports of the Ministry of Health and of the Scottish Home and Health Department.

[3] A woman paid 2s. 8d., a boy or girl 2s.

pointed out that the charge was refundable to those receiving National Assistance and that free prescriptions would fill the doctors' surgeries with many who had no need to be there and would charge to National Health the contents of many normal household medicine cabinets. In seven months from the waiving of the charge chemists in England and Wales dispensed 23 million more National Health prescriptions than in the corresponding months of 1964, an increase of about 19 per cent. The cost was £13 million, or 22 per cent, higher.[1] By the end of the year the increase had flattened out somewhat and for the whole of 1965 stood at 16·7 per cent in numbers, 19·3 per cent in value—an actual amount of some £16 million. It was asked whether this demonstrated a previous demand veiled by the charge, but it was equally likely that the critics were right. In either case £16 million was a large sum to add to National Health expenditure.

But an even larger was impending. The cost of general medical services in England and Wales was 7¼ per cent of the whole in 1963–64, when it stood at £81 million. It was over £82 million in 1964–65. Yet the general practitioner was not satisfied. He wanted to find some better way of assessing his salary than the central pool, some more adequate way of calculating the expense of surgeries, staff, and equipment. He wanted some recognition for the work of a wife or other member of the family, more opportunity to make arrangements for absence, some recompense for night visiting.

At the beginning of 1965 the independent Review Body on Doctors' and Dentists' Remuneration was considering a proposal from the medical profession for an increase of about 30 per cent in the remuneration of family doctors. The Review Body suggested instead 10 per cent, together with help in the payment of rent and rates of surgeries and other expenses. The medical profession exploded in anger, and in March submitted to the Minister of Health a "Charter for the Family Doctor Service" which demanded, among other things, the abolition of the pool.

The next twelve months were spent in intensive discussion, in the course of which a substantial majority of G.P.'s handed to the British Medical Guild to hold signed, but undated, cards signifying their resignation from the National Health Service. This threat of resignation remained until the end of negotiations. By the end of March 1966 the Review Body had hammered out a report which was published on May 4.[2] It agreed to the abolition of the pool, and a capitation fee which

[1] The Minister of Health, House of Commons, November 22, 1965 (Hansard, fifth series, vol. 720, c. 12).

[2] *Review Body on Doctors' and Dentists' Remuneration:* Seventh Report, Cmnd. 2992.

involved a higher rate for patients over sixty-five years of age, direct payment for ancillary help, a basic practice allowance which would cover the services of a wife or similar help, higher payments for night visiting, and supplementary payments for rent, rates, and other expenses. The proposals would amount in all to an increase in salary of some 32 per cent.

Dentists and hospital medical staffs were also covered by the Review Body's Report. Dentists were to have increases amounting to about 10 per cent, consultants and senior hospital doctors to about 10 per cent, but the junior hospital doctors an increase of some 35 per cent.

The Prime Minister announced in the House of Commons on May 5 that the Government was prepared to accept the recommendations concerning dentists and hospital medical staffs outright, but in view of the very large increases suggested for general practitioners proposed that they be implemented in two stages—about 15 per cent immediately, retrospective to April 1, 1966, and a second stage from April, 1, 1967. A special meeting of doctors at BMA House, London, on June 21, 1966, decided to accept the award, thus phased, which would give them, in all, an average of an extra £1000 a year. They asked the BMA to withdraw the resignation cards held by the British Medical Guild.

A postscript to the affair was the rejection in the same month, after twelve months' negotiation, of the claim for an extra 12s. a week by 70,000 hospital porters, cleaners, ward orderlies, stokers, laundry workers, kitchen staff, and others. We are as much entitled, they said, to a square deal of pay as the doctors.

Figures need interpretation. In a healthy nation the National Health bill would be small. In a niggardly nation it would also be small. In a hypochondriac society the bill would be large; it would also be large in a society stricken by plague. There is danger, on the one hand, of a cry for economy damping down necessary expenditure on health, but, on the other, there is a danger of regarding every increase in expenditure as a good thing, without regard to what it is spent on—of considering that the bigger the National Health bill, the better the national health. One thing is certain; if the only criterion recognized is to be the size needed to meet the demand, then the bill will grow so long as the population expands and the incidence of disease, birth, and old age continues on anything like its present scale. The question then becomes whether the Exchequer pays the whole bill or whether part is paid by National Health 'insurance'; which only means whether part shall be paid by the nation through income tax and other taxation and part through National Health contributions, or whether the whole apparatus of National Health stamps be abolished and the whole cost of the National Health Service be met through taxation. In an affluent society with differences in income becoming less pronounced there is much to be said for the nation taking the whole burden squarely upon its shoulders, as it does street-cleansing, water supply, defence, and education. Self-help, meantime, continues through the additional voluntary insurance taken up by a growing number of people which entitles them to refunds for specialist attention or for single hospital rooms if they seek private advice or desire privacy in illness. This is a situation which might be regretted in a nation where great inequalities of wealth existed; but with a wage and salary level rising and fewer great inequalities of wealth, there seems no reason why freedom of choice should not exist between different kinds of expenditure; privacy in illness is ranked by some people higher than a motor-car or a television set.

Until 1949 the National Health Service remained completely free to anyone who stepped on to the shores of the United Kingdom. In that year the law was amended to give the Minister of Health authority to require aliens to pay for medical care, but so far neither Labour nor Conservative Ministers of Health have made use of the right. Compared with total cost, the charges on account of aliens are small; the United Kingdom hopes for reciprocal agreements with other countries—by 1964 these had been given completely by Norway, Sweden, and Yugo-slavia, and to a limited degree by Belgium, Denmark, the Federal Republic of Germany, France, Luxembourg, the Netherlands, and Switzerland; the example and goodwill engendered is a force for good in international relations. Most people who stay in Britain long enough for extended medical treatment give something in some form to British life; and, as Aneurin Bevan once said, anyone who steps on these shores is likely very soon to make an indirect contribution to the Exchequer.

A rather different line of inquiry has been pursued by some observers who are concerned to discover who are the real beneficiaries under the National Health Service Act and whether one class has benefited more than another. The conclusions of both an American and a British observer are the same. The American pointed out that the "social distribution of the British medical services before the Appointed Day was biased very much in favour of the lower classes. . . . It was the middle class which bore the principal burden of neglect. It received no concessions at all in the finance of its medical requirements and it was forced, by indirect means, to subsidize the medical coverage of the rest of the population."[1] Now, being treated on equal terms, it reaps the benefit of the public service. The Englishman was even more emphatic: "the major beneficiaries of the post-war changes in the social services," said B. Abel-Smith, "have been the middle classes".[2] Such discussion becomes unreal in face of rising wages and a changing class structure. What does emerge is that by yesterday's yardstick very few people would be receiving free medical benefit today; which prompts the question whether the Health Service would have started at all if the present trend to affluence had begun earlier.

But fundamental to the success of the Health Service—more so than to any other nationalized concern—is the character of the people whose work lies at its core. As medical practitioners have been brought into the economic arena, as they become 'political' creatures and lose the prophylactic qualities of apartheid, the profession is more likely to attract recruits who are not primarily humanists. The enthronement of Mammon is one of the characteristics of the Affluent Society. It is the obverse of the humanitarianism that abhorred poverty, but, as frequently happens in similar cases, the fight against poverty has been carried too far by its own momentum and by the values it has bred. By fighting so long for a higher share of worldly goods for the under-privileged, society as a whole has come to regard worldly goods as the only yardstick of the good life, and it is inevitable that some recruits to the doctor's profession will measure it in this way and not in terms of personal service. It is true that the Affluent Society and the National Health Service together have largely removed the opportunities for "Robin Hood" activities, as one practitioner called them. But in a profession which deals with human suffering the ministrations of the doctor are not confined to those which are measured in terms of money.

With attention focused upon the cost of the National Health Service, upon the salaries of doctors and nurses, upon the amount of money earmarked for hospitals and local authorities, upon the cost to the Exchequer and the amount paid in insurance stamps and charges, the actual picture of medical development becomes, in the public eye at least, a little blurred. Does a greater intake of patients to hospitals mean a better hospital service? Is a patient sent home a week after an opera-

[1] H. Eckstein, *The English Health Service*, p. 9.
[2] "Whose Welfare State", in *Conviction* (1958), p. 57 and *passim*.

tion more efficiently treated than one who remains in for two weeks? What is the real story told by hospital waiting-lists? Is the closed-circuit television system for watching patients more efficient than walking the wards? Is push-button temperature-taking and blood-pressure registration more efficient than the personal bustle of the nurse at the bedside? Amazing new techniques and skills cure illness and prolong life, yet the common cold is elusive, and the penalty of knowledge of the major medical revolutions is sometimes ignorance of the smaller ills of mankind. At the *Medical World* conference in London in the autumn of 1962 a general practitioner reported that young doctors attached to his practice "knew nothing about the common diseases of the British people and had never even seen a case of bronchitis or influenza. One, asked to diagnose a patient, went through a list of illnesses mentioning practically everything except the one thing the patient had, which was influenza."

In the same way, in a rapidly growing population, new problems relevant to health are developing the whole time, yet society is either unaware of them or too fully engaged elsewhere to understand their significance. The problem of feeding a concentrated population, for example, presents many difficulties. More food must be produced at home or imported, retail shops must carry larger supplies, not only higher production but longer keeping qualities are asked for; to increase turnover and speed pre-packaging is introduced; to attract customers eye-appeal becomes important. All this has resulted in preservatives, chemical fertilizers, artificial colouring, 'tenderizing' processes, synthetic flavourings, as well as methods of animal-breeding and egg production which produce a product whose value to the consumer has not been fully assessed. A Food Hygiene Advisory Council exists to keep such matters under review, Consumers' Councils and journals make their own assessments. A Committee tightened up the regulations governing the labelling of foods and the disclosure of their constituents. But professional analysts have difficulty in keeping up the testing which should be the absolute pre-sale requisite, and bad mistakes occur. Red powder to colour meat, for example, was banned only after it had been in use for some time. 'Tenderizing' tests were concluded only after the process had been in operation—though here it was decided that the method might be continued so long as the product was labelled accordingly.

Many processes are the subject of keen disagreement. What is the effect of artificial fertilizers on health? Does fluoride in water, which improves teeth, do harm in other respects? How harmful is tobacco-

CHAPTER XV

Space and Population

"Quousque tandem?"
Cicero, *First Catilinarian*

IT WAS paradoxical that once the economy had weathered the immediate post-War difficulties its main troubles concerned expansion in one form or another. This was true of population growth.

As late as 1941 it had appeared that the trend of population was downwards. Before 1930 the birth-rate had been falling for several decades; it remained more or less constant from 1930 to 1938, and fell again after the outbreak of war. In 1942 there began a marked rise. Nevertheless, when Herbert Morrison for the Coalition Government appointed a Royal Commission on Population in March 1944 it was still with fears of a fall in mind, based partly upon the experience of the 1914–18 war, when a short rise in 1919–20 had been followed by a downward trend.

The Commission inaugurated exhaustive inquiries, and reported five years later, in June 1949. It envisaged a slowly growing, then a falling population, with the number of people of working age stationary, of young adults falling, and of those over sixty-five growing. This was in spite of the fact that the rising birth-rate continued after 1942 and that in 1947 it was the highest since 1920. In mid-1947 a fall had begun, but the birth-rate for 1948 was still 25 per cent higher than the average of the years 1935–38, and the first Census after the War, in 1951, falsified the Commission's findings with its figures of 49 million for Great Britain and 50 million for the United Kingdom, against 45 million and 46 million in 1931. The Census of 1961 reported nearly 53 million persons in the United Kingdom. There were an estimated 54 million in the middle of 1964, with the expectation of more than 74½ million by the turn of the century.[1]

A falling population was no longer a trouble. On the contrary, with far less space at her disposal than the Victorians had when the Industrial

---

[1] Projection given in *Abstract of Statistics*, December 1965, Table 12.

8+

Revolution burst upon them, Britain's population explosion could, from the purely physical angle of space per person, become far more serious. And throughout the world the problem was basically the same —how to provide space and sustenance for an expanding population. A statement on the subject presented to the United Nations in 1960 by thirty-nine Nobel Prize winners and other distinguished men and women foresaw a pressure upon resources by a growing world population which would produce "a Dark Age of human misery, famine, under-education and unrest which could generate growing panic, exploding into wars fought to appropriate the dwindling means of survival".[1] Two years later a distinguished scientist could foresee "a major and frightening increase" in world population during the next thirty or forty years which birth-control was unlikely to affect materially and which our resources would be insufficient to nourish.[2]

In the West the reasons for larger families are partly economic— higher incomes, an extension of social services—partly women's reaction from being 'professional'; partly labour-saving in the home and 'easy-cook' food in the supermarket; with Roman Catholics it is the teaching of their Church. But partly the rising birth-rate is a swing of the pendulum, a reaction from the pre-War family of one or two children and a return to the larger family of earlier days; and in part it is simply due to the fact that many people like children and enjoy large families and that an increased prosperity enables them to afford this pleasure. In few cases in Britain is it ignorance, laziness, or prejudice that keeps people from family-planning. Pressure of numbers will have to become far more uncomfortable, or there will have to be some violent reversal of existing conditions, before the attitude changes materially.

At the same time the number of illegitimate births causes concern, being associated with a wider promiscuity from an earlier age than has formerly been known in Britain. While sex education in schools helps to counter the promiscuity due to ignorance, the parade of sex in every medium of public opinion goes to the other extreme of loosening standards; but basically it is the temper of society itself that is responsible. Some medical men favour an easing of the abortion laws to allow the termination of unwanted pregnancies, and on July 22, 1966, the second reading was given to a Bill to legalize the medical termination of pregnancy in certain circumstances. The circumstances included danger to the health, physical or mental, of the pregnant woman; the risk that

[1] Quoted in letter to *The Times*, December 23, 1963.
[2] Sir George Allen, Secretary of the British Association for the Advancement of Science, reported in *The Times*, March 8, 1962.

the child would be physically or mentally abnormal; the possibility that the pregnant woman's capacity as a mother would be severely overstrained by the care of another child. Each of these reasons for terminating pregnancy could be seriously disputed. The fourth set of reasons for allowing abortion covered the cases of pregnancy in a girl under sixteen years of age and pregnancy as a result of rape.

World-wide instruction in birth-control is one of the consequences of the population explosion. In Britain a National Birth Control Clinic was opened in 1930, which in 1938 became the Family Planning Association. By 1962 the FPA was running some 360 birth-control clinics, but it seemed that fewer people sought their advice than consulted their family doctors; a Marriage Survey made by the Population Investigation Committee in 1962 believed that more than two-thirds of the couples who married in 1950–60 used birth-control of some kind. In 1963 it was suggested in a Report on the work of the FPA that family-planning might become a statutory duty of the National Health Service, which might provide free advice on contraception and "possibly", as the Report put it, make the same arrangements for charges for contraceptives as for other prescriptions.[1] Birth- control, although publicly discussed and widely approved in Britain, has not yet, however, moved into the realm of national policy. By 1965 the most controversial aspect of the situation concerned the use of an oral contraceptive. Some medical opinion would wait for further tests before the pill was considered entirely free from adverse side-effects. But the Dunlop Committee[2] announced in November that, after reviewing the available evidence, it did not feel justified in objecting to the marketing of oral contraceptives.[3]

Other questions concern the age-composition of the population, its distribution, and the varying ways in which its members earn their living, contribute to the common pool, and take their leisure. It has for some time been noted that the rising standard of living and the advance of medicine have enabled people to live longer, have contributed to the birth of more healthy babies, and have consequently caused a decline of the mid-age, working section of the population relatively to the young and the old. Of the United Kingdom's 52·71 million inhabitants in 1961 the young, those aged under fifteen, had grown from 11·18 million in 1931 to 12·34 million. The old, taking these in accordance with present-

---

[1] October 25, 1963, under the chairmanship of Professor Lafitte.
[2] *Supra*, p. 198.
[3] Minister of Health, House of Commons, November 29, 1965 (Hansard, fifth series, vol. 721, c. 983).

day standards of fitness as those aged seventy-five and over, grew from 0·96 million in 1931 to 2·22 million in 1961. Mid-age groups grew from 34 million in 1931 to over 38 million in 1961. Of a total increase of 6·7 million the young accounted for 1·16 million, the old for 1·26 million, while the mid-age groups accounted for about 4·26 million. Very roughly the young had increased by 10 per cent, the old by 130 per cent, and the mid-age groups by 12·5 per cent. But this meant merely that while every group of 100 people in 1931 supported 36 old and young people, in 1961 every group of 100 supported 38 of the young and old.[1]

As the economy expanded the need for labour was so great that immigration, particularly from countries within the Commonwealth, was encouraged, and men and women came to work in Britain from all over the world. From Canada, Australia, and New Zealand some 50,000 people annually were coming to the Mother Country by the fifties; by no means all were settlers, but a high proportion worked at permanent or temporary jobs. The Irish had always come. By the early fifties some 60,000–70,000 were swelling the British labour force each year; again, not all were settlers, there was much temporary work, much crossing and recrossing of the Irish Sea, and statistics were not easy to keep. There were also people from Cyprus and Hong Kong driven to seek a higher standard of life in Britain. From outside the Commonwealth there were Central and Western Europeans, including Greeks, Poles, Hungarians, Italians, Spaniards. Entry was more difficult for an alien, who was allowed to stay only if he made a case first for admission and then for permanent residence, but by the middle of the century about 360,000 aliens of all nationalities were settled permanently in Britain.

Until 1962 every Commonwealth citizen was entitled to enter the country at will, and from 1953 onwards the coloured immigrants began to arrive—from Africa, from India and Pakistan, from Ceylon and the West Indies. They took jobs in factories, on building sites, in the transport services, as hospital orderlies, in canteens and restaurants. Many trained as nurses, others came to study and afterwards worked as doctors, teachers, and scientists. Immigration, scarcely noticed as a phenomenon until the mid-century, was attracting attention by 1953, and in 1955 the Government attempted to keep statistics of the intake—particularly of the newer, coloured entry. In that year about 43,000 people entered from the West Indies, India, Pakistan, Cyprus, and to a lesser extent from Hong Kong, Aden, and Africa. The numbers for a while appeared

[1] Based upon *Annual Abstract of Statistics*, Population Tables.

to keep steady, they declined in 1958 and 1959,[1] but in 1960 rose to some 58,000, and in 1961 amounted to about 136,000 for the year, of whom 60,000 came from the West Indies and about 20,000 each from India and Pakistan. The 1962 figure was estimated at some 150,000 for the year, about half the natural increase of the population, but it was likely to have been far higher: neither the statistics of annual immigration nor those showing the rate of natural increase of the immigrants were reliable. At the end of 1964 an estimate of a million coloured immigrants since the War was not generally considered too high.[2]

The economy could hardly have functioned without them. From street-cleansing through transport and catering, from building and factory work right through the hospital and medical services, the immigrants took their places in an expanding society. There was little resentment. The economy was at stretch, and they were encroaching upon no man's job. It was rather a matter for pride that the emaciated stranger, shivering under an English sky, should become, under English influence, a well-turned-out and self-respecting worker with a merry smile and a fund of good humour. The trouble was social rather than economic, for many of the immigrants were from a country, or were themselves of a class, whose standards of building and hygiene were lower than in Britain and whose social outlook and habits were far different. The coloured workers from the West Indies, from India and Pakistan, were the most conspicuous in this way. Some were infected with tuberculosis when they arrived; many contracted venereal disease. The acute housing shortage in Britain exacerbated the problem. Immigrant pressure on accommodation, the degree of overcrowding which they tolerated as one immigrant family joined another, their high fertility rate, different customs, the lower standards of cleanliness of many, their demands upon the already overweighted health and education services, gave rise to feelings ranging from antagonism and resentment to a general realization that it was no use welcoming immigrants to help the economy in one way if they were depressing it in another. Moreover, the numbers were increasing far too rapidly; what began by being a help to the economy could soon be a drain upon it.

[1] Partly because of measures by India and Pakistan to restrain their emigrants, partly because of the recession in Britain.

[2] *Immigration from the Commonwealth*, August 1965 (Cmnd. 2739); speeches by the Home Secretary, R. A. Butler, House of Commons, November 16, 1961 (Hansard, fifth series, vol. 649, cc. 687 ff.), and by the Home Secretary, Sir Frank Soskice, House of Commons, May 3, 1965 (*ibid.*, vol. 711, c. 926). Soskice estimated 800,000–1,000,000 coloured citizens or citizens from such countries as Malta and Cyprus.

The Commonwealth Immigrants' Act of April 1962 gave rise to a great deal of bitter feeling, since for the first time it controlled the immigration into the United Kingdom of Commonwealth citizens. Under the Act entry was limited to those, with their wives and children, who held employment vouchers issued by the Ministry of Labour; to those who could support themselves and their dependents without working for the duration of their stay—a clause which covered visitors and tourists—and to students and others in a similar capacity. Immigration officers, on the advice of Medical Officers of Health, could refuse entry on medical grounds alone. Two and a half years later the Labour Home Secretary was taking steps to prevent the evasion of the Act and estimating that something like 10,000 immigrants had gained admission to the country illegally in the previous two years.[1]

By this time feeling was running high in several parts of the country, and, whatever their point of view, few people would deny that the country had a serious problem upon its hands. The position was the more difficult since the coloured immigrants were not distributed over the whole country but were concentrated upon certain areas, notably parts of London, Birmingham, Bradford, Liverpool, and South Wales. Here even the virtues of spontaneous gaiety, the love of parties, the uninhibited social occasion, made trouble in terraced houses and flats. There was also a quite understandable fear by the home population that clubs and public-houses they had enjoyed for years would be swamped, and their nature changed, by persons of different habits and outlook. A clergyman who ran a large and successful community scheme at Sparkbrook, Birmingham, an area heavily settled by immigrants, said at a conference in London on race relations convened by Christian Action that the standards commonly imported by immigrants were not high enough for a thickly populated community. "Where Irish immigrants were rowdy and aggressive, or Pakistanis made bonfires of old mattresses and chicken, neighbours who suffered should receive statutory help. If a friendly approach to the immigrants concerned failed, they should be deported." The situation would be eased, he urged, if immigrants were not admitted to Britain unless they had undergone cultural preparation in their home countries and if they were dispersed around Britain on arrival.[2]

Beyond this were three very real problems. Housing was short, and many English families had been on Council housing lists for years. No

---

[1] House of Commons, February 4, 1965 (Hansard, fifth series, vol. 644, cc. 1284–85).
[2] *The Times*, February 9, 1965.

amount of hardship could justify, in these people's eyes, a higher priority being given to an immigrant family. Yet sometimes the job he took, or distress in his family, would justify some special concession to the immigrant. Whatever was done—whether it was doubling up on existing accommodation or moving him into new—the immigrants could only make a difficult position worse.

It was the same with schooling. Schools take all children, regardless of race, colour, or creed. Yet if a high proportion of children cannot speak English, or have an imperfect knowledge of the language, or have such a background that their development is slow, the other children in the school are penalized. Bradford, with more than 1500 immigrant children in its schools, proposed that not more than 25 per cent in a primary school, or less in a secondary school, should be immigrant children and that they should be spread over all the schools in the city in order to break down the concentrations on one or two. They suggested that there should be not more than 30 per cent in a class if they were able to speak English, but not more than 15 per cent if they could not speak the language.

Health is another disturbing problem, and particularly the question of tuberculosis. This is a disease which a century's hard work has virtually eradicated from Britain. Now it is found that many immigrants arrive with the disease and often in a highly infectious condition. Airport and seaport controls are lax, the 1962 Act was weakly and loosely worded concerning medical grounds for refusing entry, and doctors in 1965 reported a still disturbingly high number of immigrant patients with tuberculosis. The Government spoke of stricter measures at ports, with X-ray apparatus available to detect the disease, but port authorities found it not practicable to subject every entrant to the test, and the Government fell back upon a letter to general practitioners asking them to look out for any immigrants among their patients who might be in need of an X-ray examination.

On March 9, 1965, the Prime Minister made a statement in the House of Commons. The Government was urgently reviewing the problem of immigration. The 1962 Act was not working as intended—false passports, false statements, impersonation, and other fraudulent devices were nullifying its intentions. A fresh examination was required, and a high-level mission was being sent to consider the whole problem with Commonwealth Governments. Meanwhile the Government insisted that, once they were here, all immigrants should be treated for all purposes as citizens of the United Kingdom; there should be no discrimination on any grounds whatsoever. To this end a Race Relations Bill was presented to the House a month later "to prohibit discrimination on racial grounds in places of public resort; to prevent the enforcement or imposition on racial grounds of restrictions on the transfer of tenancies; to penalise incitement to racial hatred". The fact that such a Bill was necessary was a commentary on the worsening of the relationships in some quarters between coloured immigrants and natives; whether it was a wise move is open to doubt. The Bill was carried by only 9 votes on May 3, 1965, but so mixed were people's motives, so confused was the issue, so much of a boomerang the measure itself, that it cannot necessarily be concluded that those who opposed it were less sympathetic to the coloured immigrant than those who supported it. The immigration question is bound up with a colour problem partly because the coloured immigrant is the most conspicuous, partly because his customs are, on the whole, least like those of the country he has come to. But legislation against racial discrimination, campaigns against racial intolerance, talk of "increasing signs of colour prejudice at all levels of British society", do far less good than the straightforward tackling of the problem by the Birmingham parson.

Basically the problem is economic and applies to immigrants of all nationalities; its solution may well be soon forced upon us. Immigration was welcomed when Britain was short of labour. But with employment tax and increased automation Britain is likely, in the long run, to have a labour surplus, whatever the immediate position. Already there is talk of 'redundancy', 'retraining', reduction of working hours. In an overcrowded economy only the most carefully controlled immigration makes sense: it is no more kind to the immigrant than to the native to build up an unemployment problem as well as a housing, an educational, and a social problem. With this aspect of the situation in mind, the Government, from August 2, 1965, cut the number of work vouchers for immigrants into Britain from the whole Commonwealth to an annual rate of 8500 which halved the rate at which vouchers had been taken up in the first half of the year. Of the vouchers issued about 2500 would go to workers with jobs to go to, the remainder to qualified professional workers, including doctors and nurses, scientists, and teachers. There would also be stricter control of the entry of dependents, except wives and children, and the repatriation of any who entered illegally. On health a double check was to be introduced, both at home and at the port of entry; overcrowding, housing, and educational problems were to be re-examined.[1]

The difficulty of suiting action to intent was demonstrated by the increasing difficulties of schools in immigrant areas and by the increas-

[1] *Immigration from the Commonwealth*, Cmnd. 2739.

ing gravity of medical opinion. Reports spoke of the growth of cases of leprosy in Britain from 70 in 1945 to over 600 in 1952, when it became a notifiable disease; of cases of hook-worm, a highly infectious disease, in immigrants; and of the danger of the spread of other tropical diseases.[1] "Whatever may be the pros and cons of the Government immigration policy," wrote *The Times*, "it is utterly inadequate from the point of view of the protection of the health of the community. Doctors recognise neither race, colour nor religion. Neither does disease. To the doctor a patient with leprosy, tuberculosis, smallpox or syphilis is a menace to his fellow-citizens, irrespective of whether his skin be white, black or yellow."[2]

London and the South-east were still the most crowded parts of the Kingdom in 1964, with over 11 million people, 23 per cent of the population of England and Wales, in an area of 4000 square miles, 7 per cent of its area. The whole of Wales, on the other hand, in an area twice as large, contained only 2·7 million people, or 5·6 per cent of the population of England and Wales. Greater London still made the largest conurbation, containing 8·2 million persons in 1964, more than three times the population of Wales, in an area of 722 square miles. The West Midlands and South-east Lancashire were a long way behind, with 2·4 million each. Of single cities Birmingham and Glasgow remained the largest, with a population of just over a million each. At the other end of the scale 7000 square miles in the North of England, including Tyneside, were occupied by 3·3 million people, another 7000 square miles in the Eastern counties by 3·9 million people, and over 9000 square miles in the South-west by 3·5 million people.

The populations of the big cities have, generally speaking, continued to move from the centre of towns to the periphery and beyond in search of more space, cheaper houses, and better living conditions generally. Large-scale suburban 'sprawl' has consequently become a feature of city development, one town frequently merging into another, independent towns becoming suburbs, outlying villages turning into towns linked to the parent city by rail and road. After the War the Labour Government tried to stem this kind of development by planning new towns where factories or other places of work would exist in the same unit as houses and public buildings. The New Towns Act of 1946 empowered the Minister of Housing to construct new towns to take the over-spill from London and other big cities; the Town Development Act

---

[1] Dr R. G. Cochrane, Secretary of the Leprosy Study Centre, speaking to the General Assembly of the World Medical Association in London in September 1965.
[2] December 9, 1965.

8*

of 1952 was to help the expansion of any small town willing to take population from overcrowded cities; the Distribution of Industry Act of 1945 cut the proportion of new factory building going to the South-east from about 50 per cent, the pre-War figure, to 12·3 per cent. Office-building was not controlled, and the Tories in 1954 abolished all building licensing. It was thus possible for the phenomenon of Central London to develop. From the middle of the fifties office buildings began to shoot up, and land prices soared; as bombed sites were reclaimed more buildings, generally offices, appeared, and the Metropolis began to take on the role of a monster devouring its thousands of workers by day and spewing them out at night. In all the large old-established towns it was the same—the working population for the most part deserting the city centres at night, leaving them to the shut-up shops, perhaps a factory doing night-work, but, generally speaking, to the hundreds of empty offices which by day had been dealing with the paper work of the expanding economy. In Central London—"the paper Metropolis"—there were 114 million square feet of office accommodation in November 1964, with the likelihood of expansion to 140 million square feet, manned by a labour force which had grown by 200,000 since 1951 and was still grow-ing at an annual rate of more than 40,000.[1]

The bulk of this labour force comes from suburbs and outlying towns, the dense streams of slowly moving traffic on the roads, the overcrowd-ed railways outside the city, and the packed Underground trains within it filling London above and below ground with those who serve the Wel-fare State during the day and hurry away as best they can to claim the privileges she grants for a few hours each evening. Commuting—the very word, used in this sense, has only recently become current in Britain—is an accepted feature of British life. The short haul becomes the long haul, the numbers travelling in to central London from outside increased by some 100,000 in the fifties and are expected to increase by 300,000 or more before 1971. Peak commuter travel of all kinds on public transport was 1·2 million daily in 1964. Longer journeys each way are accepted, and a journey of ninety minutes each way by train, not including travel from home to station or London terminal to place of work, is acceptable.

Many prefer to come by car. The rush-hour congestion on the roads almost defeats this end, and the parking in central London of commu-ters' cars slows up traffic, adds to the hazards of drivers and pedestrians, and destroys any attraction that the London streets and squares still

[1] *Offices.* A Statement by Her Majesty's Government, November 4, 1964 (H.M.S.O.).

have. Suggestions ranging from high parking charges to a complete ban on private cars in Central London must wait upon a better commuter service to the capital or big car-parks at the periphery and a minibus service of some kind within.

At the root of the regional problem lies a shifting of the economic nerve centre of the country. Once, the population moved in to the coalfields; now, with the old-established heavy industries declining, the old dependence upon coal and iron partly gone, the old industrial centres are in danger of becoming distressed areas while industry moves to the Midlands and the South-east, drawn negatively because they no longer are dependent upon coal and iron, positively by a mass market, by labour, a useful proximity to science and technology, by London and all a capital city has to offer, by good communications with Europe and the world.

The urgency of the situation was revealed in the depression of the winter 1962–63 and the accompanying high unemployment figures for Scotland, Wales, and the North of England. The Government appointed a Secretary of State for Industry, Trade and Regional Development and set on foot a series of local Inquiries. All the reports from the relatively declining areas stressed that the symptoms were not inherent, but that the areas needed more general spending, not only directly upon industries but upon all the expanding facilities of post-War life that were offered more generously in the South. The reclamation of derelict sites, better health and welfare services, improved roads and communications, including facilities for travel to work from the more attractively sited suburbs, better schools and special industrial training courses, a more vigorous artistic life, were all mentioned, for example, by the Report on the North-east.[1] The Government responded by offering increases in public-service investment—in Central Scotland from £100 million to £140 million in two years, in the North-east from £55 million in 1962–63 to £80 million in 1963–64. The Industrial Training Act of 1964 provided £50 million to set up industrial training boards to provide training in new skills for labour seeking new employment and for young people. Grants were promised to help town-centre development and other amenities, more money was promised from the Arts Council. Even more helpful, perhaps, were the positive approaches made by some of the towns themselves to attract firms and the example of the Civil Service in moving some of its departments to the North. *North to Elizabetha!* proclaimed an article in *The Economist* advocating this policy. The Government is committed to settling 19,000 civil servants out of London

[1] *The North-East; A programme for regional development and growth*, Cmnd. 2206.

by 1970, and probably some 50,000 will be involved finally. But there are difficulties in moving Government departments far from Whitehall, and it is likely that many of the moves will not involve more than transfer from Central London to the Home Counties—which will ease congestion at the centre but not help the problem as a whole.

In March 1964 the Government published its complementary plans for the South-east, defined as being south-east of a line from the Wash to Dorset. "There are expected to be at least three and a half million more people living in South East England by 1981; it might prove to be more. Such an increase will present formidable problems for what is already the most rapidly growing part of the United Kingdom." Nearly 2·5 million of these would be due to natural increase of births over deaths and just over 1 million to net inward migration from all sources. Though jobs in London would go on rising, the actual population of the conurbation would be kept at its existing level of about 8 million, and the majority of the new population would have to be housed outside. While it was hoped to preserve London's green belt some of this might have to be used, but the bulk of the growing population would be housed in new cities and by the expansion of existing ones. There would be new cities in the Southampton–Portsmouth, in the Bletchley, and in the Newbury areas; big new expansions in six districts ranging from Northampton and Ipswich to Ashford in Kent and Swindon in Wiltshire; extensions to some dozen towns from Banbury to the Medway towns, from Maidstone to Poole.[1]

Overall, there was considerable confusion as to whether it was better to build new towns or expand existing ones, and some difference of opinion as to whether it was wise to encourage more growth in the South at all. The Labour Government began by announcing that it would discourage growth and would scrap the previous Government's plan, but by the beginning of 1965 had agreed to follow-up schemes for building more houses for the existing population of greater London at the old Croydon airport, on Erith marshes, at Kidbrooke, on Woolwich Arsenal ground, and at the old Hendon airfield. It also continued the regional planning schemes, naming seven economic planning zones for England, each with its own Board, with separate economic planning boards for Scotland and Wales.[2]

---

[1] *The South-East Study* (H.M.S.O.); *South-East England*, Cmnd. 2308. The two were published simultaneously in March 1964.

[2] George Brown, Secretary of State for Economic Affairs, House of Commons, December 10, 1964 (Hansard, fifth series, vol. 703, cc. 1829 ff.). The Boards would be expected to work within the framework of a national plan for economic development.

Scotland remained a special problem, the net loss of about 300,000 people between 1955 and 1965 showing little signs of halting: in 1964 and 1965 alone 40,000 people each year emigrated from Scotland, which just about offset the natural increase in population. A new Government White Paper, *The Scottish Economy 1965 to 1970*, published at the beginning of 1966, was directed both to showing how Scotland fitted into *The National Plan* and to assessing the measures being taken to counteract the decline of her traditional heavy industries and bring fresh life to the Highlands.[1]

The recession gave way to a new period of prosperity by the end of 1963, and as attention left the 'at risk' areas it more sharply outlined the obverse of that problem: the overcrowding of the great towns, particularly in the Midlands and the South-east, and the traffic problem on nearly all of Britain's roads, in all of her towns, large and small.

Prosperity has meant more consumer goods, and consumer goods have meant, above all, motor-cars. Never, at any time, has mankind been universally moved by the passion of acquisition to such an extent as he now is to own and drive his own car. The growth of the desire and the ability to acquire a car have been far more rapid than any thinking on the question. There were millions of cars on the roads before anyone stopped to think of their effect on towns built for quite different forms of transport and a countryside quite unprepared for the onslaught. In 1963 for the first time the number of cars newly registered exceeded a million, and there were over 11 million mechanical vehicles on the roads. Traffic was growing at the rate of $6\frac{1}{2}$ per cent per annum, and was likely to do so until 1970, after which growth was expected to be at a rather lower rate. The total growth shown by a 1962 census at a hundred points on trunk and class I ('A') roads during a week in August showed a total increase of 67 per cent over 1954. Cars accounted for most of the growth, motor-cycles grew more slowly, lorries and vans grew substantially, while public transport buses declined by 7 per cent. In 1954 there were eight cars to two lorries; in 1962 there were eighteen cars to three lorries. A Report of a Group on the transport needs of Great Britain in the next twenty years estimated that motor-cycles would decline before 1970 and that the buses would continue their decline.[2] The number of vehicles with licences current increased in the ten years 1953–63 as follows:

[1] Cmnd. 2864.
[2] *The Transport Needs of Great Britain in the Next Twenty Years.* Report of a Group under Sir Robert Hall, October 1963.

	1953	1963
	Thousands	*Thousands*
Cars	2,762	7,375
Motor-bicycles	1,009	1,755
Tricycles and pedestrian-controlled vehicles	28	92
Hackney vehicles and tramcars	119	96
Agricultural and general goods vehicles	996	1,529
Agricultural and general haulage tractors, etc.	332	472
Exempt vehicles	40	66
	5,286	11,385[1]

Noise increased unbearably, and a Committee tried, without much success, to assess its effects, its measurability, and its amenability to legislation.[2] Fumes polluted the atmosphere. Again, although it was demonstrable that plants and trees wilted at the sides of traffic-congested roads, it was difficult to measure the extent of the danger to human beings and still more difficult to reduce risk by legislation. As the number of diesel-driven vehicles increased, however, alarm became more vocal. What, asked a *Times* correspondent, is being done to assess the carcinogenic properties of exhaust fumes from diesel engines? "Almost certainly they contain large quantities of unsaturated hydro-carbons, which as far as organic chemicals are concerned, have few rivals as producers of cancer."[3]

More easily demonstrable was the fact that traffic congestion often defeated the ends of the car-drivers who caused it. So far from getting from one place to another more quickly, more cheaply, and with less fatigue, the result was often the opposite. The Annual Reports of the Ministry of Transport showed increasing alarm. New roads were built between towns, round towns, in towns. On the whole the only effect was to bring more motorists on to the roads and into the cities, a period of improvement consequent upon each new stretch of road being followed by a building up of traffic upon it. Generally speaking, the only roads which maintained their usefulness were the big fast motorways, and these were not being built quickly enough. From the first 8½-mile stretch built in 1958 Britain had 345 miles by March 1965, with 115 miles in progress and 1000 miles planned for the nineteen-seventies. Germany by the mid-sixties had over 2000 miles of *Autobahnen*, Italy nearly 1000;

[1] *Highway Statistics*: Ministry of Transport Statistical Paper, No. 3.
[2] *Committee on the Problem of Noise*, Final Report, July 1963, Cmnd. 2056.
[3] *The Times*, November 1, 1963.

Britain had more vehicles to each mile of motorway than any other country in the world.[1]

It was clear that the problem was building up even as a solution was being sought and that more people meant more cars and required a constantly larger area of the country for roads. Since they were also requiring a constantly increasing area of the country for homes, for schools, for factories, for offices, and, with greater leisure and more money, a constantly increasing area for recreation, it became cumulatively more difficult to know where to give the priority. Cars also mean garages and parking space. Few new houses are built without a garage, and 'houses of the future' boast two garages. Meantime homeless cars are left in streets, byways and corners, wherever they can find space. If that is the problem by night, the problem by day, when the cars are in use, is equally difficult. In most cities and towns there is insufficient parking space, and while plans are being made for new parking lots or multi-storey car-parks on the edges of towns, motorists leave their cars in residential streets, in market-places, in public squares, in church and cathedral approaches. It is common for heavy traffic, already slow and congested, to be confined to a trickle because of cars parked on each side of the road. It is common for a city of charm and historic interest to be obscured by vehicles to almost a man's height from the ground. Half a century ago people were building garden cities, planting trees in their streets, making grass verges to their roads Now it is commonplace for private houses to look upon a street full of parked cars. Proposals have been made to ban garaging in streets, to make high charges for kerb-side parking, but on the whole public opinion is with the cars. Only when a stranger oversteps the mark by obscuring access to a householder's own car is resentment expressed; meanwhile thousands of people have no other vista from their front windows than other people's parked cars.

With few to raise their voices for the preservation of the old towns, for the beauty of city squares, for the peace of a suburban street, with few to recognize the dangers of incessant noise and of noxious fumes, the problem of traffic has been seen primarily as one of keeping vehicles on the move—hence increasing sums of money spent on road programmes, both national and local. The five-year road programme which the Ministry of Transport announced in 1962 was intended to transform the most important inter-urban roads over a decade. It would cost £865 million for Great Britain, the bulk being spent on motorways and trunk roads for which the Ministry of Transport was responsible, the rest as grants to local highway authorities. The local authorities

[1] *Roads in England and Wales*, Report by the Minister of Transport for the year ended 31st March, 1965.

themselves would spend some £115 million in addition. The plan included the building of a thousand miles of motorway and trunk roads with numerous improvements to existing stretches; with maintenance, minor improvements, and work on unclassified roads, the total cost would be around £1700 million. For technical reasons there would be no large-scale use of disused railway tracks, but the Ministry felt confident that its rate of building would comfortably take all the traffic expected in 1980, including that abandoned by the railways.

Not until 1963 did a report appear that showed a recognition of the deeper problems created by the motor-car. The Buchanan working group had been appointed by the Ministry of Transport to study the long-term problems of traffic in urban areas, and its report was sincere, deeply aware of the problems created by the motor-car, yet diffident in stating its conclusion in sufficiently striking manner. The motor-vehicle, or something like it, is here to stay. Its numbers may increase three or four times by the end of the century; and half the total increase is likely to come within ten years. This implies dangers to life, health, and civilized life itself, and the greater part of the country could degenerate by the end of the century "into a wilderness of sprawled-out, unco-ordinated development".

The Buchanan approach to the problem was indicated by its postulate that "traffic is seen as part of the comprehensive problem of town planning" and by its practical studies of a small town (Newbury), a large town (Leeds), a historic town (Norwich), and a central metropolitan block in London. As opposed to the studies which had already been made and which were directed to facilitating the passage of vehicles, it turned attention first "to the environment, to delineating the areas within which life is led and activities conducted". Traffic, as a consequence, was seen as part of the wider problem of town-planning. The Buchanan Committee concluded "that the motor vehicle (or some equivalent machine) is a beneficial invention with an assured future, largely on account of the great advantages it offers for door-to-door travel and transport" but that, nevertheless, "there are absolute limits to the amount of traffic that can be accepted in towns", and "it will not be sensible, nor indeed for long be possible, for society to go on investing apparently unlimited sums in the purchase and running of motor vehicles without investing equivalent sums in the proper accommodation of the traffic that results". "It is true", the Report continued, "that there are many other claims on material resources, but it is a weak argument to say the needs of traffic cannot be met, seeing that it is a problem we are continuously creating by our extreme readiness to invest in motor vehicles. There seems to be

an issue here which society must face, for at present the two investments are getting further and further apart. All the indications are that
to deal adequately with traffic in towns will require works and expenditure on a scale not yet contemplated."

The Buchanan Report was pessimistic in its conclusions in the sense
that it believed that the magnitude of the problem of traffic in relation
to life in towns had not yet been grasped. "The best use is not being made
of the motor vehicle in urban areas at present because of grossly inefficient circulations and the adverse effects of traffic on human life and
surroundings. The first is costing the community great sums annually,
the second is building up to a major social problem with a deeply tragic
aspect . . . the motor vehicle has put our urban arrangements based on
streets completely out of date." It believed, nevertheless—and believed
that its Report demonstrated—"that the concept, and indeed the whole
subject of traffic in towns, is capable of being put on a rational and
quantitative basis". More work is required, substantial physical changes
will be necessary, but by what the Report called "the canalisation of
longer movements onto properly designed networks serving areas within
which, by appropriate measures, environments suitable for a civilised
urban life can be developed" it should be possible to preserve the city
as living space without harsh restrictions on motor traffic.

But the Report doubted whether people had faced up, or would face
up, to the fact that very large sums of money would be involved in creating the environment for the motor-car. "Our studies suggest that very
few of the statutory development plans really face up to the future problems of traffic and transport. Most of them seem to have been stultified
by a feeling of hopelessness that funds would ever be available on anything like the scale required. Many contain proposals of a palliative
nature which, if persisted in, can do irreparable harm and prejudice
more constructive measures. We think the plans need re-examining,
with a more optimistic view on the financial side, with the objectives
and values clearly stated, and above all with a determined effort to get
them onto a sound quantitative basis."[1]

The big question left by the Buchanan Report is whether we are prepared, as the Report urged, to subordinate cars to men, to put civilized
life before motor-cars, whether we are prepared to plan cities for
citizens and regard the car as subordinate to that end—or whether we
are going to take the easy way of putting money into roads, allowing

[1] *Traffic in Towns*, A study of the long-term problems of traffic in urban areas.
A report of the Working Group appointed by the Minister of Transport under the
chairmanship of Colin Buchanan (H.M.S.O., 1963).

ad hoc parking, and accepting traffic congestion. There is yet no indication of progress on a national scale, and the Buchanan Report may well
be filed away with those other excellent Blue Books which our Governments, since the nineteenth century, have been so willing to sponsor.
So far action has been confined to individual cities; there are pedestrian
precincts at the newly rebuilt Coventry Centre, at the Cowley Centre in
Oxford, at Birmingham, Leicester, and several other towns. Suggestions
have been made that privately owned vehicles should be charged for the
use of all town roads at the rate of perhaps 1*d.* a mile in the suburbs, 3*d.*
a mile in the centre, twice as much in rush hours, with a parking fee of
5*s.* a day.[1] The most favoured solution is the multi-storey car-park at
the town's periphery, with a ban on private cars in the town itself and
transport provided by light forms of vehicles. The Leicester traffic plan
is interesting in trying to put this into effect and suggesting buses, monorail services, rickshaw-type taxis, and moving pavements to carry the
passenger within the town; its cost is estimated at £135 million spread
over thirty years.[2] Buckinghamshire County Council is planning a new
town, also based on traffic-free residential and shopping streets, served
and linked to the centre by monorail.

But in the welter of discussion on traffic and its problems no national
plan has yet emerged, and the number of cities which have taken town-
planning action is a small minority. Most are still building bypasses or
relief roads and opening their streets to an ever-widening radius to the
passage and parking of cars. At the moment it is still considered good
business to let the driver go where he will, and Chambers of Commerce
are afraid of restraining him. But the restriction on all enterprise which
will shortly result when we grind, physically, to a standstill will be even
greater. All that is at stake, in most cases, is asking the motorist to drive
an extra mile or so to avoid a city or asking him to walk or take public
transport within its boundaries. It is a curious commentary upon our
society that many people would regard this as an attack upon the freedom of the individual, whereas the parking of a car outside someone's
sitting-room window is not felt to impinge upon the freedom or privacy
of the occupant.

The bypassing of towns, or parking at their periphery, will help for
the time being, but the number of cars is expected to treble within the
next twenty years. Not only towns and cities but the whole countryside,
except for farmland, is in danger of being given over to the motor-car.

---

[1] See, *e.g.*, article by Alan Day, Reader in Economics at London University,
in *The Observer*, December 1, 1963.
[2] *The Leicester Traffic Plan*, November 1964.

Already it takes to the ancient Ridgeway over the Downs, it plunges through National Parks, it is promised picnic laybys away from main roads. Every such amenity offered to the car-owner will destroy in the end the pleasure it intends as the 9 million cars of 1966 become the 26 million of 1980. For England and Wales the Government proposes a Countryside Commission, working under the general guidance of the Ministry of Land and National Resources and the Secretary of State for Wales, to plan amenities for car-owners that will at the same time preserve some of the country's natural resources.[1] But nothing will stretch the acreage of land.

People need homes as well as cars: replanned city centres and new highways are not alternatives to houses. House-building was one of the most urgent of the post-War tasks, a deficiency compounded of past neglect, ordinary depreciation, and bomb damage. As the men came back from the War and increased the pressure on houses, families of 'squatters' appeared overnight and took possession of anything with a roof—an empty house if such could be found, otherwise huts or war-time buildings. Prefabricated houses of various types were hastily run up, and the building industry collected building materials and building labour demobilized from the forces under A1 priority. In eighteen months homes had been provided over the whole country, by new building and repair, for nearly 300,000 families, and 58,000 permanent and 92,000 temporary houses had been completed. But it was necessary to keep up with a growing population, earlier marriage, larger families, and a longer expectation of life, all of which spelt more houses. So did higher incomes and increased consumer spending: an appetite for consumer goods necessitated somewhere to put them. In 1951 there were still 750,000 fewer houses than households and severe shortages everywhere. By 1956 some $2\frac{1}{2}$ million houses had been built, the numbers employed in the building industry had grown from 520,000 in June 1945 to 943,000 in December 1946 and $1\frac{1}{2}$ million in 1956. The Government then embarked upon a vigorous slum-clearance programme, and by 1963 half a million slum houses had been replaced. By then more than $4\frac{1}{4}$ million houses had been built in Great Britain since the War. But the population had risen between 1951 and 1963 by $3\frac{1}{2}$ million, the number of households by 2 million, and older houses were continually falling into disrepair. Development plans and house-building often conflicted, and building never caught up with need. At the end of 1965 there were still some 3 million families in Great Britain living in slums, in near slums, or in

[1] *Leisure in the Countryside in England and Wales*, February 1966, Cmnd. 2928.

grossly overcrowded conditions: the worst areas were in the North of England and on Clydeside.

In the early post-War years the trouble was largely in the allocation of scarce resources. Then it became apparent that the building industry was not quick enough to adapt itself to the use of new materials or to new methods of speedier and cheaper construction, and that building labour was not easy to organize or to control. The Ministry of Public Buildings and Works set up a Directorate General of Research and Development to help the building industry to increase its output by using more widely the most up-to-date methods and techniques. It hoped, for example, by co-ordinating the selection and size of building components, by interchangeability and flexibility in their use, by the standardization of parts, by prefabrication in the factory, to minimize the work done on the actual site. Pre-cast concrete, bricks of standard sizes, uniform electrical and plumbing fitments, are all easy to achieve and both time- and money-savers. The Ministry itself is advised by a Central Housing Committee, and is developing a system of light steel and timber construction, with a variety of cladding materials, which is suitable for ordinary house-building and both quick and comparatively cheap to erect because it is based upon a uniform planning grid. Both private builders and public corporations began building more flats of two, three, four storeys, and even higher, from pre-cast concrete blocks; others were experimenting with steel foundations. But the greater the standardization the more difficult it is to achieve diversity; cheapness and speed remain the prime aims, but unless they are accompanied by flexibility and originality of design towns and cities will be very dull places; and unless a reasonable standard of quality in building materials is adhered to they will look very shoddy in a few years' time. All these considerations make the task of building a difficult one. There are many other considerations also: How far should private building, as opposed to public-authority building, be encouraged? What should be the relationship of houses built to let and those built for sale? What should be the proportion of houses to flats?[1]

The Conservative Government in 1957 by the Rent Act removed from control some 800,000 houses whose rent was controlled under war-time legislation,[2] believing that the removal of restrictions would encourage more letting of existing houses, a higher standard of repair, and the

---

[1] Annual Reports of the Ministry of Housing and Local Government; *Housing* May 1963 (Cmnd. 2050); *The Housing Programme 1965 to 1970* (Cmnd. 2838).

[2] The Act also allowed certain increases in the rent of 4·3 million houses which remained controlled.

building of more houses to let, while rents would find their economic level. In fact, there was no spectacular rise of either accommodation offered at rent or of the rents themselves. The problem as it presented itself became rather different. By the middle of the sixties houses and apartment blocks in the big cities, particularly where coloured immigration was pressing upon the housing supply, were becoming more and more crowded, and landlords were drawing more and higher rents from subdividing flats and apartments and encouraging immigrants to bring in more people. Sitting tenants were discouraged by various means from protesting and virtually forced to leave by the deliberate creation of nuisances. "Rachmanism", so-called after one of the most notorious of the rack-renters in London, is difficult to eradicate while there is a housing shortage; while it continues slums are being reproduced as quickly as they are replaced. The Housing Act of 1963 was intended to strengthen the hands of local authorities in dealing with houses in multiple occupation and to assist the growth of Housing Societies.[1] But in March 1965 the Report of a Committee on Housing in Greater London under the Chairmanship of Sir Milner Holland shocked the public by its revelations of gross ill-treatment of tenants, overcrowding, multiple family occupation, lack of amenities, absence of bathrooms, the sharing of W.C.'s. The photographs of slum conditions seemed to come from some nineteenth-century Blue Book and to have no relevance to the Welfare State.[2]

A month after the publication of the Milner Holland Report the Government, in accord with its Election promises but partly as a consequence of the conditions revealed, introduced a new Rent Act. This restored much of the control which the 1957 Rent Act had abolished, giving security of tenure and freezing rents at their existing levels subject to appeal. The Act applied to property of up to £400 reateable value in London and £200 elsewhere; it contained clauses making it a crime to evict without court order or to harass the tenant or anybody in occupation in an attempt to get rid of him or force him into higher rent, and it applied to furnished as well as unfurnished lettings.[3] The Government estimated that it would protect some 800,000 tenants in England and Wales, of whom 300,000 lived in London. There was complaint that there was not enough stimulation in the Act to new private building— the reverse side of the coin—particularly nothing to accelerate the building of new dwellings to rent, not enough to stimulate the improvement

[1] Their object was to help would-be owner-occupiers by borrowing on collective credit, spreading repayment over as long as forty years, and giving security of tenure.

[2] Cmnd. 2605.   [3] The Rent Act, 1965.

or retard the decay of the existing stock of rented dwellings. The Government, both in its housing programme for 1965–70[1] and in *The National Plan*, spoke of increasing the annual rate of house-building to 500,000 by 1970, and it agreed that the accent should be on houses and flats to let rather than to buy; it preferred, however, to encourage local authorities and not private builders to do this and offered them a new, and advantageous, form of general subsidy in place of the existing flat-rate subsidy.

But beyond the houses, beyond the towns, there remains the question of land. We come back to the question, how are we to accommodate the constantly rising population? As land becomes scarcer its price goes up; the Government is talking of compulsory acquisition, but there is an end even to this. And it is not only in terms of building that we need to think. Green belts are required as lungs to towns. Beyond this the population is taking its increased leisure in the countryside and by the sea, and enough open space must be preserved for recreation and the enjoyment of space and beauty. With a further 2 million acres probably needed over the next fifty years for urban development, with further acres slashed by motorways, more gouged by increased quarrying for brick-clay, cement, gravel, and sand,[2] with 45 million acres necessarily kept for farmland, the area for National Parks or wild open spaces is limited. With some 26½ million people spending holidays in Britain, without counting the week-enders and the day trippers, and the 2¼ million who come from abroad, there is also a squeeze at the most popular holiday resorts. "The pressure increased leisure puts on Britain's Coastline" ran the heading to a table which showed growing numbers of people spending holidays on the coast, and the National Trust launched an appeal to save 900 miles of coastline from unsuitable development. "Unsuitable development" covered not only ugly urbanization but all that was implied by the people who were beginning to talk of amusement parks, pleasure centres and "organized leisure", as well as the rash of tea-houses, caravans, and the rest that cater for the holidaymaker.

Fortunately, the motor-car confers this great boon on society, that it can still take the town dweller far away from "unsuitable" developments —if he wishes it to. "It is now perfectly feasible for a well-paid Coventry car factory worker to haul his family and one of those two-berth twin-keel jobs from his home to Windermere, enjoy a day's sailing, and get

[1] *The Housing Programme 1965 to 1970* (Cmnd. 2838).
[2] Michael Dower of the Civic Trust at a meeting of the Town Planning Institute, March 10, 1964, reported in *The Times*, March 11, 1964, and *The Observer*, March 15, 1964.

home again the same night."[1] Unfortunately, there is now a substantial waiting-list for boat moorings on Windermere and parking places for more than 4000 cars!

With the population spilling out of the towns in cars on fine summer days the question of leisure occupies the minds of many people. "The leisure boom is upon us," announced a newspaper.[2] People had little organized knowledge about the recreational boom that was upon them, commented a lecturer[3]; "Ministry of Leisure Needed," said a newspaper columnist[4]; "Leisure—the new problem for Unions," announced another.[5]

That the termination of the long-fought struggle for a shorter working week should present such problems would amaze and sadden the men who used each hard-won hour for 'self-betterment', who, in hours snatched from sleep and family, organized the working-man to match his power to the moment when it came. Leisure presented no problems to them. Nor, indeed, can centrally organized leisure fulfil the need of man for rest from toil. The increasing use of the motor-car has at least the superlative advantage that it can take the population away from its highly organized town life and into the freedom of uncluttered country; but to organize leisure, create amusement parks or pleasure centres, is simply to reproduce urban conditions in another place. Already there are enough man-made devices to 'pass the time' in towns and organized holiday resorts. To let time pass without harrying it with artificial devices is an inestimable refreshment too little remembered in the modern world. It costs little and confers much: it is worth preserving against the onslaughts of the leisure speculators.

[1] *The Times*, April 15, 1964, article by Our Northern Correspondent.
[2] *The Observer*, March 15, 1964.   [3] Michael Dower, *ibid*.
[4] Kenneth Tynan, *The Observer*, March 8, 1964.
[5] Granville Eastwood, *The Observer*, July 8, 1962.

CHAPTER XVI

The Affluent Society

"But . . . wealth is the relentless enemy of understanding . . .
The rich man . . . until he learns to live with his wealth . . .
will have a well-observed tendency to put it to the wrong
purposes."

J. K. Galbraith,
The Affluent Society

ALTHOUGH THERE were dangers not far below the surface at the
end of 1964 no-one would compare the economy with twenty or even
ten years earlier without satisfaction. Growth rate was comparatively
slow, but the country had been off to a good start, and indices of real
gross national product per head of population showed that her standard of living was one of the highest in the world. Others might be
catching up, but in Europe only Germany had passed her.

Few of the citizens of the United Kingdom would contemplate their
own material conditions with anything but pleasure when they looked
back over two decades. A working-man's average weekly earnings had
more than doubled between 1950 and 1961, while retail prices had risen
by about 50 per cent.[1] Between 1955 and 1964 most workers had
increased their pay packets by about 50 per cent, while retail prices had
risen by 28 per cent. Moreover, the wage- and lower-salary earner was
taking home a bigger share of the national income than he had before
the War, the redistribution of earned income that had occurred having
been in his favour. Taking account of the incidence of taxation, of
social-service benefits, including education, and of subsidized housing,
there was an even more decided redistribution of real income in favour
of the lower sections of society. With teenage members of the family or
lodgers also earning good money and contributing to housekeeping, the

[1] *Statistics on Incomes, Prices, Employment and Production* (Ministry of
Labour), April 1962.

family purse was heavier than it had ever been before. At the same time conditions of work had improved, and welfare services, canteens, rest- and recreation-rooms, sports grounds, and social clubs added to the amenities of the working-man's life. His working week was becoming shorter, with hours about 42 a week, but with the prospect of a speedy reduction to 40, and overtime at increased rates of pay was generally there to be had. On the whole, arbitration or some form of strike action in cases of dispute would end in the men's favour. At either end of this comfortable middle section of society were extremes; over 2 million people received an income of less than £250 a year, while at the other end of the scale 25,000 people had incomes of over £10,000 a year.[1] But not much was said about them, and "we're all middle class now" seemed, in general, a fair enough description of society.

Most of the increased incomes were spent.[2] In 1964 consumers in the United Kingdom spent at current prices over £21,000 million on a large variety of goods and services, happily disposing of their increasing incomes in accordance with a fairly general pattern. They spent over £5500 million on food, over £2000 million on housing, nearly £2000 million on clothing and footwear, well over £1500 million on buying cars and motor-cycles and running them. Next largest items, and biggest surprises, perhaps, were the £1300 million spent on tobacco and the £1300 million spent on alcohol. No other single item reached the thousand million mark, but fuel and light came near it, and household goods, furniture and floor coverings, radio, electrical and other durables taken together were well over the thousand million mark. On the 1954 figures all these purchases were up, but cars showed the most spectacular increase.

After the rush to eat and drink after the War people decreased the proportion of their incomes that they spent on food, though the quantities they took of most items continued to expand. Of total retail sales in 1957 food accounted for 48 per cent; it was 46 per cent in 1961, and the annual rate of increase, which had been 2 per cent between 1954 and 1960, was 1·6 per cent between 1960 and 1964 and declined to 1·3 per cent after 1964.[3] Not only is expenditure on food not in- definitely expandable but, with greater affluence, people's eating habits change. Within the food category the nation decreased its expenditure

[1] "Classification of income by size before tax, 1962–63", Table 71 of *Report o the Commissioners of H. M. Inland Revenue for the year ended 31st March, 1964*, Cmnd. 2572.

[2] Expenditure figures are based largely upon *National Income and Expenditure*.

[3] *The Growth of the Economy* (NEDC), and see *infra*, Appendix B XIV(e).

on bread and cereals, but increased it on meat and bacon, sugar, dairy produce, fruit and vegetables, beverages, and manufactured goods. It not only drank more beer but more wine and spirits, sherry (with roasting chicken and fish fingers) for the first time appearing on the cost-of-living index in 1962. On an average in 1964 a Britisher spent 32s. 3d. a week on food. He drank 2·7 oz. of tea, 5·2 oz. of milk and cream, ate nearly 2 lb. of meat, 5¼ oz. of bacon and ham, over ½ lb. of fish, nearly ¼ lb. of cheese, just under 2 lb. of fruit, over 3½ lb. of potatoes, 2 lb. of other vegetables, 2¾ lb. of bread, over ¾ lb. of cake, over 18 oz. of sugar, and 4½ eggs.

The rest of the £21,000 million spent in a year in the United Kingdom goes on items which, unlike food, are indefinitely expandable. It goes to make life warmer and brighter, provide more and better living space: the housing bill is straining to grow still more. It goes to buy more consumer durables to make life easier and pleasanter. The range of purchases is constantly widening, and with electric mixers for the kitchen, electric blankets for the bed, central-heating systems for the house, and a variety of furnishings of many kinds, the line between utility and prestige-buying becomes somewhat thin. We all buy more clothes, particularly more women's clothes, and the turnover of women's wardrobes is larger and faster than it has ever been before. Men buy more clothes also, but they have increased their purchases more modestly—by a mere 25 per cent, compared with women's 74 per cent, since 1948. Women also buy more cosmetics and beauty preparations. The whole population is more medicine-conscious than it was, and, apart from doctors' prescriptions, 'do-it-yourself' medicine swells the sales of chemists' shops. People write more letters, though they are changing over to the telephone. At current prices the public increased its spending on postal services from £46 million in 1954 to £81 million in 1964, and on the telephone and telegraph services from £34 million to £98 million. More money is spent on holidays, and many people take two holidays in the year; many have adopted the week-end habit; more still spend a Saturday or Sunday away from home. Consumers' expenditure abroad in 1964 at current prices was £364 million. People are not so interested now in newspapers and magazines, and the sales of these barely hold their own. Books do rather better by the criterion of money spent, and cheaper paperbacks increase the numbers sold.

Cinema-going declined, average weekly attendances dropping from 17·6 million in 1957 to 6 million in 1964—total box-office takings from £95 million to £63 million at current prices. The sale of records and record-players grew spectacularly—78¼ million discs were produced in

1957 and nearly 85½ million in 1963. Their home sales brought in £14 million and £21¾ million respectively.

But, above all, the population is now putting its money into the two undeniable signs and symbols of affluence—the television set and the motor-car. The television set arrived before the car. With a combined sound and viewing licence costing only £4 a year until August 1965, when it was raised to £5, with sets available either on hire-purchase or simply on hire, more than 80 per cent of households contribute to the 13 million television aerials which, with the garage, are the insignia of the Affluent Society.[1] The only trouble, so far as the manufacturers are concerned, is that television sets do not wear out fast enough, and there is strong propaganda to get people to change them for other reasons. The advent of colour television is awaited as a major break-through to larger sales.

Sales of cars topped the million mark in 1963. There were then 7,375,000 of them on the road as well as 1,755,000 motor-bicycles, whose numbers were diminishing as the number of cars increased. From £234 million in 1954 at current prices the public spent over £837 million on motor-cars and motor-cycles, new and second-hand, in 1964; running costs increased from £191 million to over £768 million during the same period. More than the television set the motor-car brings other expenditure in its train. Not only is the car-owner more likely to change his car and buy another but motoring entails much subsidiary spending. There is the car radio, there are picnic baskets, rugs, camping chairs and tables. There is extra trade for public houses, hotels, and catering establishments of all kinds; work for the garage and for service and petrol stations; there is the sudden boom of the motel in Britain which brought the 26 motels of 1962 to 60 by the end of 1964; there is the increase in the takings of National Trust buildings and of private houses open to the public. In spite of taxes and other curbs, in spite of exhortation and warning, the spending on all fronts reached new heights by the autumn of 1965. Christmas 1965 was a bumper spending spree; for the 'sales' in the New Year more money was found, and the first quarter of 1966 gave no indication of any voluntary curtailment.[2]

In addition to the money spent actually buying things more money than ever before is mortgaged under the system of hire-purchase, which is simply a method of gaining immediate possession of an article by the

---

[1] *Viewing Licences:* England, 11,153,739; Scotland, 1,224,696; Wales, 650,790; Northern Ireland, 223,820. Total, 13,253,045. And see *infra*, Appendix B XV.

[2] For consumers' expenditure see Appendix B XIII(*b*), (*c*).

payment of a proportion of its cost and paying the rest, plus an interest charge, by instalments. The growth of the hire-purchase debt has been one of the outstanding features of the post-War economy. With production high and sellers anxious to sell, terms have been made attractive to buyers, whose acquisitive instincts and standards of living have been raised but whose incomes are not yet high enough to buy all they want. In 1964 the total hire-purchase debt outstanding was well over £1000 million; two years previously it had been £890 million, having grown from £442 million in the middle of 1957. At the end of 1965 it reached the record sum of £1386 million.[1] Household goods of all kinds are taken on the H.P., many a young couple's home containing more articles on hire-purchase than purchased outright. If there are disadvantages in sometimes having bitten off more than can be chewed, in the heavy burden in any economic recession, in the drain of still paying for goods which have lost their bloom if not their utility, in the knowledge that more is paid in the end than the market price, there is the advantage of years of use to set against years of making do while the full price is saved. The greatest dangers lie in the too pressing salesman, the too impulsive housewife, the over-optimistic husband, and a prosperity which is founded upon future effort and reward yet to come. But industry favours and encourages the system, and retail shops, manufacturers, and finance houses are all prepared to give credit. The Government not only accepts hire-purchase as a fact but uses it to manipulate the economy, restricting or loosening the terms of credit as it thinks necessary.

Consumers' expenditure, although rising in a spectacular way, is circumscribed by the increasingly large proportion of consumers' income taken by Government and local authorities in the form of taxes, rates, and insurance contributions. In 1964–65 the public paid over £3000 million in customs and excise duties, some £4000 million in income tax and other direct taxation, £1500 million in National Insurance and Health Service contributions. Of customs and excise duties the largest returns are yielded by the excise duties on tobacco and on hydrocarbon oils, by purchase tax, and by the duty on alcoholic liquors—in that order. Purchase tax alone, payable on a wide range of goods, including road vehicles, clothing and footwear, household goods, radio and television and gramophone sets, toilet goods, confectionery, matches, mechanical lighters, amounted to over £633 million in 1964–65. The

---

[1] *Annual Abstract of Statistics; Monthly Digest of Statistics;* the figures are for Great Britain except for those from members of the Finance Houses Association, which are for the United Kingdom. See *infra,* Appendix B XIII(*e*).

motor-vehicle duty was £187 million. Income tax has been steeply increased since the War, standing at 7s. 9d. in the pound standard rate from 1959–60 to 1964–65, when it was raised to 8s. 3d. by the Finance Act of 1964. The sum of these taxes constitutes the greater part of the Government's income, as rates and Government Aid comprise the local authorities'. Like the income of the individual consumer, Government and local-authority income is spent on an increasing diversity of goods and services, and is becoming larger year by year. As the social services have expanded the public money spent on them has increased; so has expenditure on all the other services, large and small, which appear in no private balance sheet yet are taken for granted—defence, police and prisons, libraries and museums, parks and pleasure-grounds, Government-sponsored research, the Civil Service, education, the water supply, the salaries of local-government officers. In 1964 total public expenditure amounted to some £12,000 million. Expenditure on the public social services was about £5000 million of which Education (£1400 million), the National Health Service (£1125 million), and National Insurance (£2000 million) were the largest items. Military defence, costing nearly £2000 million, was the only other single item of comparable size.[1] Roads and lighting took nearly £400 million, police and the prison service cost over £200 million, research £136 million, parks and pleasure-grounds £60 million.[2]

The incidence of taxation can be varied to affect the contributions of various sections of the community. A low standard rate of income tax, for example, with a steeply upgraded rate of surtax will penalize the higher-income groups; taxes on luxury goods will hit the rich more than the poorer members of the community; higher interest rates on hire-purchase or house mortgages will usually bear more heavily on the lower-income groups; so also will increases in tax on items of common use. Conversely, if the Government uses part of its income to subsidize any form of production the benefit is spread over those who gain as producers and those who gain as consumers: agriculture is here a case in point. As with the social services, if the poor or middle ranges of society take greater advantage than the rich of subsidized goods to which all have contributed equally in the form of taxation, then a redistribution of income equivalent in favour of the lower-income groups will have been effected. If the incidence of taxation also favours the lower-income groups they have reaped a double benefit.

[1] In the estimates for the year 1966–67 what would have been a much higher total was cut by one-third.
[2] *National Income and Expenditure*. See *infra*, Appendix B VI(*b*), (*c*).

What is left of incomes after taxation, insurance, current expenses, hire-purchase, and mortgage payments have been met is saved. In 1964, with total personal incomes of some £28,000 million, with £21,000 million spent and £5000 million taken in direct taxation and insurance contributions, personal savings in the United Kingdom were about £2000 million.[1] Savings of this kind return to industry, to Government, and to local authorities as investment and development capital; they are savings over which the consumer has control both as to amount and direction, but their size and scope is influenced directly by the interest rates offered and indirectly by prices, taxation, the quantity and variety of goods offered for sale, and by Government policy, which can, for example, by raising Bank rate make saving more attractive all down the scale. In an expanding economy, with prices and incomes rising rapidly all round, one of the major difficulties of policy is to keep saving to a level sufficient to provide for depreciation and capital development, and the present level is not high enough for this.[2] But until consumer expenditure takes the rub it is hard to convince the man in the street that there is any danger inherent in his spending-saving ratio.

The wheels of this still expanding economy are turned by less than half of the total population. Of the 54 million persons in the United Kingdom about 25·7 million were working in some form or another in 1964. Less than half a million were in the forces or auxiliary services, leaving a total in civil employment which varied during the year around the 25 million mark.

There were 9 million people making goods of some kind, including food and drink, heavy-engineering products, ships, and motor-cars; 5·6 million people were working in other basic industries—agriculture, mining, building and engineering, gas and electricity, transport and communication—a total of 14·6 million persons. The figure includes the manufacture of frivolous, ephemeral items, the use of power and transport for non-essential purposes, but by and large it covers the basic production of the country. It has been decreasing proportionately since the War, although the total population, and the total working population, has been growing: in 1954, with total working population only 23·8 million, the number engaged on directly productive work was about the same as in 1964.

Some of the old basic industries of the country have shown a steady decline in numbers since the War. Mining and quarrying employed 661,000 persons in 1964 against 865,000 in 1954, the textile industry

---

[1] *National Income and Expenditure.*   [2] *Supra*, pp. 110–111.

840,000 against 986,000. The biggest employer of labour on the productive side is the group classed by the Ministry of Labour as "Engineering and Electrical Goods", whose numbers have grown steadily from 2,020,000 in 1954 to 2,234,000 in 1964. Also large, and growing, is Construction, employing 1,802,000 persons, and Transport and Communications, employing 1,736,000.

But to find the biggest employer of labour it is necessary to look outside the basic or the manufacturing industries to a group which employs more than all those engaged in manufacturing taken together —the group which covers services of all kinds. This group has been leaping upward since the War—from 6·4 million just before the War, 5·5 million just after it, to over 10 million in 1964. It includes doctors, teachers, national and local-government employees, financial and lega workers, those engaged in catering and running hotels, and the distributive workers. The accelerated increase in the service industries over the last ten years, and particularly in the sixties, is shown in Table B II(c). Taking away the Education and Health Services, which are in a different category from the rest, the figures are none the less striking: 8 million people, 32 per cent of the working population, are engaged in occupations, for which they are paid, which are at varying degrees of remove from the production process.

As society becomes larger and more complex the machinery of production and distribution involves more people to plan, to co-ordinate, to engage labour, to advertise, to provide welfare services and canteen services, to review methods of production, to pack, warehouse, and dispatch, to give legal, financial, accounting, and banking services. Each of these breeds its own specialties, offers its own careers, gathers its own momentum, and comes to be regarded as essential in its own right. The distributive trades alone in 1964 employed 3·5 million people —1·8 million more than all the transport services, four times as many people as engaged in agriculture and fishing, five times as many as worked in the mines and quarries, more than twice as many as were employed on all the nation's building enterprises. They had grown by more than 1·2 millions—54·5 per cent—since 1950, and their total was exceeded only by the grand total of all the other services. In particular, retail distribution expanded as consumer spending grew, increasing by 3·5 per cent in terms of value of sales between 1957 and 1961, expected to increase by another 3·7 per cent between 1961 and 1966, and in terms of labour expanding from 1·97 millions in 1959 to 2·13 millions in 1964.

Not so spectacular, but also significant, are some of the other increases in the service professions. The 61,000 accountants of 1950 grew to

89,000 by 1964; the 72,000 employed in some branch of the legal profession to over 99,000; insurance agents, bankers, financiers together grew from about 439,000 to over 637,000, the Civil Service from 600,000 to 800,000. Entirely new professions of people calling themselves 'consultants' of all kinds—on business in general, on retailing, on distribution, on sales—came into being; the advertising industry grew; something called 'consumer research' created new employment.

But growing affluence also demands, and can pay for, more personal services. One of the fastest-growing occupations in the United Kingdom has been hairdressing and manicuring, employing some 53,000 persons in 1950 and in 1964 well over double that number (111,000); garages, filling-stations, motor-repairers and -distributors employ a constantly growing number of people—over 423,000 in 1964—exceeded on the plane of personal service only by the catering and hotels group, which employed over 633,000 persons. Against this, in 1964, 1,094,000 men and women served society as teachers and educationists, 883,000 as medical and dental practitioners. Taken together, they were not much more than a third of the number employed on distribution.[1]

The general picture shows that about 32 per cent of the working population make all the goods the country uses and exports, from frying-pans to television sets, to motor-cars and clothes, from food and drink to iron and steel and tools and machinery; about the same number serve the rest and themselves as lawyers, civil servants, shop assistants, hoteliers, waiters, cooks, hairdressers, entertainers, clerks, advertising agents, and the rest; 7 per cent house the people, build their schools, shops, factories, hospitals and universities, laboratories and public buildings; 6 per cent carry the others about their daily work and on journeys for business and pleasure; 4 per cent act as teachers of all kinds; 3·5 per cent till the land, fish the rivers and seas, tend the animals, and look after the forests; 3·4 per cent provide medical and dental treatment; 3 per cent are occupied in mining and quarrying the earth. When it is considered that less than half the population work at all, it is seen that only about 17 per cent of the whole community is engaged on direct production, 3 per cent on building, less than 3 per cent on transport services, 1·7 per cent on agricultural pursuits, and 1·2 per cent on mining and quarrying.

But the picture is still not complete. In each industry the number of white-collar workers increases out of proportion to the number directly engaged upon production. In all manufacturing industries in 1959, 21·1 per cent were non-manufacturing, in 1963, 22·8 per cent. The

[1] *Annual Abstract of Statistics*, 1965, Tables 127, 130.

chemical and allied industries had the highest proportion of technical, administrative, and clerical staff—32·3 per cent in 1959, 34·5 per cent in 1963. Clothing and footwear had the lowest—11 per cent and 11·6 at the two dates. But this does not mean that the rest are engaged directly upon the production process. In the chemical and allied industries just over one quarter could so rank in 1964. If skilled maintenance men were included the total was still less than one third of the whole, the rest comprising the less experienced, the casual labour, the warehouse-men, packers, dispatch and road-transport staff, the cleaners, the canteen workers—126,000 in all, between one quarter and one third of the whole.

In the food, drink, and tobacco industries, of a total of 705,000 some 186,000—with varying degrees of skill and experience—baked the pies, brewed the beer, moulded the confectionery, mixed the dough, rolled the cigarettes. If maintenance workers—electricians, carpenters, joiners, bricklayers, and others who tended their machines—are in-cluded the total number is still only about 234,000, one-third of the whole, while a quarter were occupied as white-collar workers in one way or another and two-fifths carried on as packers, canteen staff, and the rest. The proportions can be repeated with small variation over the whole of production.

A breakdown of employment figures also emphasizes the fact that the proportion of highly skilled labour used in production is small. In the chemical and allied industries only 7890 out of a total of 465,720 rank as skilled production workers, although there are nearly 45,000 skilled maintenance workers and 19,000 who have acquired skill by experience. In engineering and the manufacture of electrical goods the really skilled men in both production and maintenance number 581,000, not much more than a quarter of the whole labour force, while white-collar, canteen, packing, transport staff account for a half.

But even this is not the full story. The role of the scientist or tech-nologist is becoming increasingly important, yet his numbers remain small. Taking those on the technical side with a university degree or its equivalent—and these include far more than the real controlling technologists—the numbers are 17,000 out of 466,000 (3·6 per cent) in the chemical and allied industries, 5000 out of 590,000 in metal manu-facture (0·85 per cent), 33,000 out of 2 millions in the engineering and electrical industries (1·5 per cent), 3000 out of 705,000 in food, drink, and tobacco production (0·4 per cent).

Finally, if one adds the highly skilled in production, maintenance, and technology the result is that in chemicals and allied industries about

9+

one-seventh, in metal manufacture about one-fifth, in engineering and electrical work about one-third, in food, drink, and tobacco about one-twelfth of the labour employed requires a high degree of training and skill.

So we have a final picture of British production balanced on a pyramid point of highly trained labour of various kinds, supporting an increasingly wide and high superstructure composed partly of the less skilled, but mainly of those employed in auxiliary services of one kind and another. As automation increases the less skilled workers are likely to disappear, and many of the skilled with them, while service industries of all kinds, from those serving production directly to those having nothing to do with it, will continue to grow.[1]

Increasing consumer spending is bringing with it an expansion of retail distribution and the building up of 'retailing' into a career of its own. As the National Economic Development Council said in 1964 when it begged retailers "to expand research, to improve the layout of shops, and to increase the use of mechanical and electronic aids", "retailing can offer a challenging and rewarding career and . . . may quickly change from being a Cinderella to becoming a leader in efficiency and development".[2] Turnover rose from just over £5000 million in 1950 to over £9000 million in 1961, but new forms of organization were reflected in the fact that while the number of persons engaged in retail trading also increased, the number of establishments decreased, and the independent retailer was yielding ground to the multiple store.[3] Increasing prosperity was reflected in the fact that the share of food shops was slowly declining, while the sales of non-food shops were rising.[4] Increasing turnover and a static labour force are associated with the self-service store, most common in food shops, although spreading to almost every type of retailing, and it is here that change in retail technique is most apparent.

'Retailing', while it must continue to include bulk-buying, the knowledge of products, the weighing of quality and price, implies equally the management behind the shop, the organization that puts emphasis on efficiency, reduces overheads and other costs, improves lay-out, knows which forms of packaging sell, devises baits for customers, builds up sales potential, breaks down sales resistance, knows at which point

[1] *Ministry of Labour Gazette*, December 1964, and *cf.* January 1965 and January 1966; *Annual Abstract of Statistics*. And see *infra*, Appendix B II.

[2] *The Growth of the Economy*, March 1964, p. 126.

[3] *Census of Distribution*, 1961, Part I, Table 1. And see *infra*, Appendix B XIV(*c*).

[4] *Growth of the Economy*, Table 88, p. 122; *Census of Distribution*. And see *infra*, Appendix B XIV(*e*).

increased sales compensate for a price cut. All this is helped by canning, prepackaging, and by the post-War boom in freezing foodstuffs from fish to vegetables, from meat to prepared meals, which resulted in a sales increase of about 500 per cent between 1955 and 1960 and accounts for annual sales of about £100 million. Freezing at, or near, the point of production has, for example, revolutionized parts of Lincolnshire and East Anglia, with the growing of peas and beans expressly for freezing; the fishing industry, with about 30 per cent of its catch going into the freezers in 1962, and most of its product needing some kind of preservation before it reached the distant housewife, was a natural candidate for an expansion of deep freezing. Not only does the deep-freeze cabinet give a new dimension to shopping, but it alters the forecasting and shapes the plans of the retailer. The deep-freeze cabinet as a normal appendage to every household will shift again the relationship of salesman and purchaser. In either case the role of the shop-assistant in a supermarket food store becomes almost negligible. He used to know his products, their qualities, origins, suitability—was, indeed, trained to know them and advise the purchaser. Now a school-leaver can be quickly taught to price-mark the goods, stack the shelves, weigh and pre-pack the products that require it, stock the deep freeze, and work the adding-machine at the check-out.

Why the impersonal self-service store sprang to popularity over the more intimate and personal grocer's shop was not always clear. Some shoppers, it is said, prefer the impersonal note in shopping; it makes it easy to buy cheap lines and to weigh up various buys more carefully. Some found it quicker, the wait at the check-out point being shorter than possibly several queues at the counter. Many enjoyed the vistas of stacked shelves, others found a chat with neighbours was easy in the cosy confines of the store, and there was generally the price-cut; few noticed that they were themselves doing the work of locating, reaching, and carting which had previously been done by the shop-assistant.

In the sixties supermarkets multiplied. There were 4000 self-service stores in 1957, by the beginning of 1963 there were 11,000, and they were growing all the time at a rate of something like 100 a month. Competition accented what had always been one of their attractions— the cut-price article—and the slashed prices of baits, which the supermarket could often afford to cut to below cost price, the so-called 'loss leaders', drew customers in increasing numbers from the little shops. Only a firmly established store offering quality or service or convenience, or itself cutting prices while maintaining quality, could compete. Then trading stamps joined the battle. The stamps, given in proportion to the amount of money spent, were generally to the value of 6*d*. in the pound and could be exchanged for goods provided by the stamp company.

Battle was soon joined up and down the shopping streets of Britain— cutting and under-cutting, green stamps, pink stamps, trolleys to pile the goods in, seats to push the children in. Some firms concentrated on price-cutting with the maxim 'Value for money'; others traded chiefly on the something-for-nothing principle that seemed to lie behind the stamps. The housewife was courted as never before, and could enjoy her appraisal of one market after another. "The battle of Coventry Road stopped traffic in Small Heath today," reported *The Times* correspondent from Birmingham in the autumn of 1963. "A crowd of smiling women swept across the roadway as Mr. Tommy Trinder arrived to open the third supermarket in the Small Heath shopping centre. Now three giants of the British shopping world stand poised in perilous confrontation, and no doubt the Small Heath women had something to smile about." Tesco (green stamps), Fine Fare (pink stamps), and Pearks ("We give value, we do not give stamps") were competing. At Tesco's there were "two free bread rolls with every packet of four frankfurters; there was a free pork pie with every pound of proprietary sausages. . . . There was free mint sauce with every joint of lamb, and a saucepan set for each of the first 100 customers to spend £5. The store was filled everywhere with the sound of piano music. . . . Fine Fare was offering four fabulous prizes every day in its Christmas competition. Customers could have an 8*s*. chicken at half-price for every £1 spent in the store (excluding cigarettes). There was the piped music of a dance band."[1]

Some of the giants of the retail trade now weighed in. Sainsbury's, a leading grocery chain, self-service in some districts only, came out against trading stamps. Garfield Weston, for the Fine Fair chain, met them squarely on. Sainsbury's banned all Weston products from their shops. They were joined by other stores of various kinds in denouncing trading stamps as a poor alternative to keen value; someone must pay for the 'gift' of the stamps: who should it be in the end but the consumer? The stamp enthusiasts retorted that the customer could check the prices she was paying and take the stamp into the bargain. 'Little men' meanwhile looked sadly on at both price-cutting and stamp trading. If they had hoped for help from the Government they were disappointed, for the Government, so far from checking competitive price-cutting, was contemplating a move that would extend it and break down any monopolistic restrictions that were hampering any part of the retail trade.

[1] *The Times*, October, 30, 1963.

The Restrictive Practices Act of 1956 had banned the *collective* enforcement by manufacturers of the retail prices of their goods, but it allowed an individual manufacturer to enforce his price on a retailer. Not many individual manufacturers in the food and grocery trades had exerted their right to do this—the chocolate and sweet firms and the cereal manufacturers were two notable exceptions—and the door had been left open for the widespread price-slashing which was giving the housewife such a good time. But although resale price maintenance (R.P.M.) had broken down over almost the whole of the grocery and food trade it was practised by most other manufacturers of branded goods in such commodities as hardware, electrical goods, records, pharmaceuticals, and accounted for some 40 per cent of total consumer spending. The Government, at the beginning of 1964, proposed its complete abolition over the whole retail field, subject only to appeal to a tribunal, on the grounds that R.P.M. was incompatible with Britain's economic objective of encouraging effective competition and keeping down costs and prices. "We are now making great demands upon our industry," said Edward Heath[1] in introducing the Government's Bill in March 1964. "It is only right that we should also look to the distributive services for a similar response. It is just as essential to have increasing productivity and a high degree of efficiency in distribution as it is in production." Hampered by the necessity of a fixed selling price, the shopkeeper could not pass on to his customer through the price mechanism the benefits of efficiency, and the incentive to improvement was absent. The only exception to be allowed was 'loss leaders', goods offered at so low a price that they entailed a loss. This kind of trading was not fair competition, for the losses could be carried only by big firms who could afford to balance them against increased profits on other items.[2]

There was concern for the small shopkeeper on both sides of the House and in all parts of the country—for the man who could not reduce his overheads or who did not trade on a scale sufficiently large to make price-cutting possible. But, generally speaking, it was felt that he could offer a form of service which other shops could not and that he would successfully stand up to the abolition of R.P.M. Among manufacturers themselves there was some division of opinion between the advocates of the mass market at cut prices and the firms who believed that a fair fixed price would preserve a higher standard of

[1] Secretary of State for Industry, Trade and Regional Development and President of the Board of Trade.
[2] Hansard, fifth series, vol. 687, c. 257.

quality and bring in equally high returns. In the event, the Resale Prices Bill received support from the Opposition, its second reading was carried on March 10, 1964, by 287 votes to 20, and it became law in July. There were preliminary skirmishes in March when the Distillers' Company and others announced in advance of the Act that they were not enforcing retail prices and the supermarkets entered into a cut-price war with spirits and wines. Cadbury's, on the other side, threatened to cut off supplies of their goods from any shop which undercut their fixed price and gave notice of appeal for exemption from the Act.

On trading stamps, meanwhile, the Government had acted in the small man's favour. The Trading Stamps Act became law at the end of July, when it was enacted that only a Company or an Industrial and Provident Society should carry on business as promoter of trading-stamp schemes, that trading stamps should bear on their face a value expressed in coin of the realm, and that they should be redeemable, if required, in cash, provided the sum concerned was not less than 5s. So the trading stamps, which in 1963 and 1964 had aroused such intense partisanship, in the course of the year began to find their own level; several shops discontinued them, but they remained part of the retail scene. On the whole the housewife goes her way, making the best buys she can, deciding herself which combination of price, stamp, quality, service, and location best suits her. But the supermarket is not only here to stay, it is bent on expansion along American lines. As car shopping increases and shopping areas become more congested the all-embracing supermarket on the edge of the town with a large car-park will offer the quickest and simplest form of shopping. If the abolition of resale price maintenance turns the supermarket into the discount store, offering under the same roof not only household goods but everything from clothes to cutlery, from records to refrigerators, at cut prices the British way of shopping will have gone all the way with the American.

A blow will also have been struck at the postal or mail-order shopping, which has shown a remarkable expansion since the fifties. Concerned mainly with textiles, hardware, household goods, clothing and foot-wear, but extending to other articles, the mail-order houses' total sales amounted to £227 million in Great Britain in 1961. They had increased their turnover by 87 per cent since 1957, and sales were £300 million in 1962, when they accounted for 3 per cent of all retail sales. Between 1961 and 1964 they grew by about 42 per cent, and in 1965 were about £400 million for the year. Strongest in the North and among the working classes, postal shopping is spreading to the South and to the middle classes. It is a specialized service depending upon speed of dispatch as well as a reasonable standard of quality, style, and price, and upon the advantage of what amounts to credit, since goods are paid for, entirely or in part, after receipt. Some five firms at present control 80 per cent of the trade, obtaining customers by the direct mailing of catalogues or by the use of agents who contact friends and get a commission on each order resulting.[1] Whatever its advantages, it will be difficult for mail-order shopping to compete with discount houses who offer similar goods at cut prices—particularly since the motor-car is all the time extending the range of more people and limiting the advantages of postal supply. The National Plan, however, has assumed that mail-order trading is likely to achieve the most rapid increase in sales of the whole retail sector.[2]

Part of the general retail complex, yet congenitally different and a strange paradox in the contemporary economy, are the 30,000 shops, kiosks, and other retail outlets of the 801 retail Co-operative Societies of the United Kingdom. A century and a quarter ago the Co-ops offered at their inception a dividend on purchases and participation in running their stores. Business participation now offers little attraction. The 'divi' has to compete with price reductions (though the Co-ops sometimes offer them too), stamps, other 'offers', and increased affluence. As a result the Co-operative store has not kept up with retail trading in general. Between 1957 and 1961 multiple shops as a whole increased their business by 37 per cent, the Co-ops by 6 per cent; in food, multiples increased their trade by 42 per cent, Co-ops by 3 per cent.[3] It is, nevertheless, an impressive total of retail trade which they still control. With a membership in Great Britain of over 13 million people, one quarter of the population, representing about half the nation's households, their total receipts in 1962 were well over £1000 million.[4]

Bound up with retailing is advertising. But while the retail store has become a kind of practical essay in advertising, advertising itself has spread right through our society, and in newspapers and journals, on television, and on hoardings, has become an accepted part of the contemporary scene; the amount of money spent on it at current prices has doubled since 1956 and grown more than fivefold since just before the War, jumping from £98 million in 1938 to £309 million in 1956,

---

[1] *Annual Abstract of Statistics;* Articles in *Board of Trade Journal*, May 31, 1963; *The Times*, June 1, 1965.

[2] Part II, p. 226.　　　　[3] *Census of Distribution*, 1961.

[4] *British Co-operatives* (Research Institute for Consumer Affairs), 1964.

to £517 million in 1963 and £590 million in 1965.[1] Press advertising still constitutes the largest item—£282 million in 1965—but, while the BBC bans all advertisement, the amount spent on Independent Television and on independent radio advertising is rising. Expenditure on television advertising rose from £72 million in 1960 to £106 million in 1965; radio advertising, helped by the growth of 'pirate' stations, rose from a mere million in 1960 to £2 million in 1965.[2] All other forms of advertisement—poster, outdoor, cinema, transport—have fallen far behind.

Few firms undertake their own advertising, nearly 60 per cent of the total expenditure on advertising in Great Britain being handled by some 700 advertising agencies employing staff ranging from a mere handful to several hundreds. Some 260 of these agencies belong to the Institute of Practitioners in Advertising, which was founded in 1927, and together handle about 85 per cent of the total advertising turnover. These firms employ not only copywriters, draughtsmen, and artists, but a research staff and sampling staff to study the constituents and make-up of the commodity to be advertised, to compare it with others on the market, to weigh up possible consumer reactions, and to assess the best possible approach to the public.

The best advertising draws attention to the good in an article, and descriptions are required by law to be reasonably accurate. The advertiser is also circumscribed by the general law relating to copyright, contract, noise, blasphemy, obscenity, and so on. Advertisers themselves in 1926 created the Advertising Association, consisting of advertisers, agencies, and media owners "to promote public confidence in advertising and advertised goods through the correction or suppression of abuses". The Association has its own journal, and in January 1962 published a Code of Advertising Practice "to ensure that all advertising in all media should be legal, clean, honest and truthful". There exist also a Code of Advertising Practice Committee and an Advertising Standards Authority whose task is to promote and enforce throughout the United Kingdom the highest standards of advertising in all media and to ensure that no advertising contravenes or offends against these standards.

While insisting that his advertisement should be "legal, clean, honest and truthful", the advertiser also claims that it imparts information to the public, that publicity ensures that the shoddy is driven out and only the best remains—"advertised goods are reliable goods", "look for the

---

[1] *Advertising Expenditure*, Supplement to *The Advertising Quarterly*, summer 1966. And see *infra*, Appendix B XVIII.

[2] *Ibid.* And see *infra*, Appendix B XVIII (*b*).

brand name"—and that the high standards of art and caption employed in the best advertisements are a pleasant addition to the contemporary scene. But, beyond this, and whatever the merits of any particular advertisement, selling remains its primary function, and because of this the advertiser is concerned not merely to describe but to persuade. It is the introduction of this element that makes an advertisement potentially dangerous where a description is not. For it follows that it is not necessarily the best that sells best, but that which has the best persuaders working for it. Persuasion is an attribute which is irrelevant to the quality of the article or to the satisfaction of the consumer, and, while not implying an absence of value or an abrogation of the standards of the profession, yet, by relying on an element that is not intrinsic to the subject, it constitutes an immoral element in all advertising.

Moreover, while still keeping to the standards imposed by the Advertising Association, an advertisement may mislead by half-truths, by the insinuation or implication which is easy in pictorial advertisement, by what has been called the "spurious presentation of technical data", by the misleading use of omnibus and meaningless terms like "best ingredients only" or with the partial description, like "contains pure butter".

Of the media used for advertising, none intrudes more than Independent Television. Here the advertisement is presented, not of its own right, but as an adjunct to an entertainment. Newspaper and magazine advertising, while more adult and therefore in many ways more insidious, is less of an intruder and can more easily be avoided. There are other dangers, however, in Press advertisement. Advertising revenue varies from about 45 per cent to 73 per cent of total Press revenue: as the advertisers themselves have pointed out, the newspapers are dependent upon it. This is the safeguard of a free Press in the sense that it relieves it from other, less desirable and more immediate forms of control and keeps its price low. Yet there is sufficient truth in the dictum that money is power for a feeling of unease. The real danger would lie in any effect upon editorial policy of advertisement revenue, but already there is an unwelcome intrusion in the Press of many kinds of veiled advertisement or 'puffery' under the guise of features. Women's magazines and the Women's pages of the weekly and daily Press are the worst offenders— and the reason may be as much that they lack original material as any other. There is a scale from the full advertisement, clearly intended to be such, through the veiled advertisement which begins as a newspaper report or feature but ends as a straight advertisement and which is now legally required to carry the word 'Advertisement', to the 'puff', which, being written by a member of the newspaper staff, purporting to give

9*

information, probably referring to several products and not necessarily mentioning a name, does not rank as advertisement; 'fashion' articles are often veiled advertisement in this way.

The question is often asked whether money spent on advertising is not loaded into the price of the goods and whether it would not be better spent on reducing their cost? The answer of the advertiser himself is clearly that advertising pays—otherwise he would not be doing it. It is not so clear whether this is also the answer of the consumer. The biggest advertisers are the richest and biggest firms who, by keeping up their advertisements, maintain their sales and keep out of the market smaller or newer firms with little money to spend on advertisement. In this way the big advertisers tend to become monopolists, and, so far from advertising encouraging and making known a wide choice of goods, it encourages concentration on the big and the rich and the well-advertised ones.

As well as advertising, many big firms undertake allied activities which go by the names of 'market research', 'consumer sales', or 'sales research', which are directed towards discovering customers' preferences and reactions, and a great deal of skilled and high-quality labour is used in this way. So specialized has this kind of work become that firms have also come into existence with the sole purpose of undertaking consumer research for a principal. Taken with straight advertising in all media, with 'puffery' of all kinds, and all the activity that lies behind advertising in all its forms, there has come to be an inverted pyramid of effort and endeavour, expense and vested interest upon every article that is marketed, the services section of industry is swollen, and the production-for-use equation becomes less and less real.

Conspicuous is the amount of advertising and the degree of 'sales promotion' and door-to-door canvassing that are indulged in by the big soap and detergent firms. Their products were the subject of the fourth Report of the National Board for Prices and Incomes, published on October 11, 1965,[1] the Minister having referred to the Board price increases of from 8 to $12\frac{1}{2}$ per cent in soap products in the previous year. The Report brought right into the open much that had previously been known to too small a circle. Two major companies dominated the industry—Lever Bros. and their associates, and Procter and Gamble, Ltd—supplying between them over 85 per cent of the market for hard soap and more than 95 per cent for soap flakes, powders, and synthetic powders. These two companies together spent £9·25 million a year on

---

[1] *Report No. 4, National Board for Prices and Incomes. Prices of household and toilet soaps, soap powders and soap flakes, and soapless detergents*, Cmnd. 2791.

advertising of which £8 million went in television advertising. This did not include 'sales promotion'. Advertisement and 'promotion' together ranged normally between 12 and 25 per cent of the net selling price of the goods, but in some cases was as high as 35 per cent. The function of this outlay was ostensibly to inform and persuade the consumer and improve the competitive power of the producer. With only two effective competitors the cost was high and smacked also of keeping others out. As for informing the customer there was "no doubt", concluded the Report, "that expenditure on advertising goes beyond the level needed for simply informing the consuming public of the choices open to it". "Each company's advertising Budget may be determined as much by the action of its competitors as by the needs of the consumer."

A group of people, while not condemning advertising as such, became sufficiently alarmed at some of its manifestations to form in 1959 the Advertising Enquiry Council, whose aim was to ensure, so far as possible, that the function of advertising was performed without damage to the legitimate interests of consumers and the wellbeing of society as a whole. It recommended that a body with powers similar to those of the Federal Trade Commission in the United States should be established to control the use of "the false, the misleading and the meaningless" in all types of advertisements and in all media and that the burden of substantiating all claims should rest with the advertisers. It wanted the Monopolies Commission to investigate the relationship between advertising and control of the market, and also the relationship of the advertising industry itself to trading. Of the products advertised, the AEC would ban completely any which, by generally accepted standards, were a hazard to the public interest. Such terms are themselves open to abuse, but the AEC named only one commodity—cigarettes—which it would ban in all media "in view of the generally-accepted claims that cigarette-smoking involves hazards to the health of the nation." It won a signal victory in February 1965, when cigarette-advertising was banned by Government order from the television screen.

All trading relies upon some form of self-advertisement, and none is more important than the agent or travelling salesman. While his importance to the export drive is recognized and training courses in salesmanship, business schools and classes at all levels are directed to him, it might be remembered that as long ago as 1934 Alfred Tack started sending out little daily articles to his sales executives on the general principles and virtues of salesmanship, and with his brother started the Tack Sales Training Courses. In due course the axioms were

published as *Sell Better—Live Better*,[1] and Alfred Tack was revealed
as a kind of latter-day Samuel Smiles, substituting for the virtues of
thrift and self-help the virtues of salesmanship and self-help. "Weigh
Up Your Day!" is one exhortation, and there follows the picture of a
balance where work is light in the scale compared with various time-
consumers. "The scales will always be in your favour if you cut out all
time-wasters!" read the caption.

Alfred Tack also popularized the widely used advertisement gambit
"Never, Never sell *things*—sell love . . . sentiment . . . happiness . . .
pictures . . . profit . . . health . . . security . . . and the admiration of
others. . . ."[2] Just so the beauticians never sell soap or face cream; they
sell beauty, glamour, social life, admiration. A full-scale trade was built
up on a similar principle by an American, Elmer Wheeler, whose
little book *Tested Sentences That Sell* embodied much of his research.
"For the past ten years it has been the sole business of Mr Wheeler
and his staff of word consultants to survey and analyse selling words
and techniques . . . to date they have tested over 105,000 words
and word combinations on upwards of 19,000,000 people" stated the
preface to the American edition of his book, published in 1954. One of
his most successful gambits, which typifies the rest, occurred when the
Cunningham Drug Stores of Detroit found itself overstocked with
products for the feet and came to what the author calls his "laboratory"
for help in selling them. Fifty-five customer approaches were tabulated,
one after another different sentences were tried, "until", we are told,
"this subtle, indirect, harmless, split-second attention-getter was
successfully created: 'Are you on your feet much?'" Result, he records,
a sell out! No reference to the quality or nature of what was being
offered for sale was needed; it was sufficient simply to set in train a
reaction starting from a simple question to which most people would
answer 'Yes'.[3] *Tested Sentences That Sell* was launched on the British
market in 1963.

The advertisers' own code of advertising, consumers' protection
councils, a fondness for certain advertisements—even a feeling that art,
history, and wit combine to enliven newspapers, magazines, and streets
—all deal with the overtones of advertising, with a positive advertisement that may be true or false, which may or may not offend morals or
religion or good taste. But beneath this there are uncharted seas upon
which the public and its spokesmen are at present merely drifting. The
"tested sentences that sell", the formula for selling attributes and

---

[1] In 1958.   [2] *Sell Better—Live Better*, p. 206.
[3] English edition, p. 106.

images rather than things, are but part of the advertisers' stock-in-trade. He will play with a man's daydreams, promise him romance or success; he will use sex to further the sales of anything from tobacco to motor-cars; he will play on fear by talk of hidden handicaps and social blemishes: already the psychiatrist has been called in to aid the advertiser. And, deeper than this, there has appeared in America a form of per-suasion so insidious that the eye is at the time of its operation unaware of it. 'Subliminal' advertising consists in flashing a message or exhorta-tion across a screen in such small print and so rapidly that it is not consciously perceived. Yet, it is claimed, it will have made its mark upon the subconscious and will result in higher sales for the goods advertised. Britain has banned such advertising. We might be bam-boozled, bludgeoned, or besought, but we must know that we are being worked upon.

Actually we do not always know as much as we think we do, and are often no more aware of what is being done to us than the subject of a subliminal advertisement. The advertisement value of window-dressing, of 'sales', is well known as leading to much impulse buying. The dressing of well-known women, of fashion shows, are advertisements for clothes. There is always less resistance to buying when the subject is unaware of the pressures being exerted. An example of this was given recently by a Director of Hartmann Fibre, Ltd, writing in *New Horizons*, a supple-ment to *Self-Service and Supermarket*, under the heading "A Fresh Food Philosophy".[1] The spirit of the title was marred in the first place by the author's talk of the Fresh Food Image. 'Image' has become a euphemism which pretends at truth without necessarily being the whole truth. A politician's 'image' is not so much what he is but what the public believes he is, and particularly what his party wants the public to believe he is; the 'image' of a product is not necessarily a reflection of itself but how its producer believes the public would like it to be. Both politicians and manufacturers rely upon advertisers to build up the image they jointly arrive at as being most acceptable to the public. So the supermarket was out to create an 'image' of freshness, and the writer concluded his article: "Whenever time permits we also like to say a few words about eggs. These too can contribute considerably to the FRESH FOOD image of the store, but only if they are displayed with imagination. It is not generally realised what a useful addition can be made to the store's profit by having a bold display of pre-packed eggs augmented by a small quantity of loose eggs on straw or green matting, the whole backed by a farmyard scene." If, by playing on suppressed

[1] December 1964.

memories of earlier associations, he thus hopes to increase the supermarket sales of battery-produced eggs many would say he is creating a
false impression; he is also doing a disservice to the exponents of the
battery system, who labour to prove that it is as welcome and produces
as good eggs as free-range poultry. Only if these are, in fact, free-range
eggs is the lay-out accurate. And if this were the case, why not say so?

"Consumption is the sole end of all production," said Adam Smith.
The implication is that production waits upon the consumer's need as
the harvest is for the hungry man, the house for the homeless. But
today the position is reversed. Consumption must be built up to serve
production; production serves not need but the producer. The whole
machinery of advertising and salesmanship, of new models only
fractionally different from existing ones, the constant production of
something new, is geared to this end. A saner society would produce
what it needed and then take time off. Instead we are short of goods
and houses while shops are cluttered with shoddy knick-knacks, the old
must be disposed of to make way for the new, and 'expendable' becomes
the operative term, strangely inconsistent with some of the durable
qualities advertised. But since 'expendability' dispenses with mending
and patching and making do, and since incomes are high enough for
something to be 'expendable' to nearly every section of society, from
the wealthy who discard their fur coats to the poor who discard their
stockings, the sense of intrinsic value declines. With mass production
perhaps there is insufficient difference in possessions to make any one of
them a treasure to be preserved: the expendable age buys its goods from
the same stores, collects the same knick-knacks, builds its furniture and
its houses from the same components, follows the same trends in
fashion and design.

This does not mean that people do not need to be protected against
the urge to spend and against bad buys. It is all too easy for the
bludgeoned, ill-informed consumer to buy badly. How should he know
the faults of a complex washing-machine or television-set or motor-car?
How should he assess the quality of even simple everyday articles like
cooking utensils, clothes, furniture, carpets, footwear, in face of the
wide new range of materials and processes that are constantly coming
into use? How should he weigh the quality and goodness of the food
he buys when it is frozen, dehydrated, pre-packed, added to by artificial
colouring and synthetic flavouring, by preservatives and vitamins?
When animals, both dead and alive, are treated with tenderizers, bled
to make them white, injected to make them red; when fruit and veget-

ables are treated at the roots with chemical fertilizers, above ground with chemical sprays? The most elaborate labelling injunctions cannot meet all contingencies; the recommendations of the Food Standards Committee, by tightening up labelling requirements, improve the position within the present framework, but make no recommendations which will remove food additives or stop chemical treatment. Advertising, which, if it lived up to its claims, could help the consumer, only succeeds in making all articles sound the best, all foods the most beneficial. A Consumer Protection Committee, after surveying the field widely, recommended the creation of a Consumer Council "to ascertain and review the problems experienced by the consumer, and to devise and advance the means of resolving them"[1]. The Government accepted the Committee's recommendations, and a national Consumer Council came into being in 1963, which works in co-operation with Citizens' Advice Bureaux and local consumer associations to report on goods and services and investigate complaints. Consumers had already been helping themselves in various ways, notably by means of the magazines *Shopper's Guide* and *Which?*, both founded in 1957 with the object of reporting upon the quality, efficiency, and value of various articles on sale. *Which?*, in particular, goes further than the Consumer Council in actually carrying out laboratory and other tests on the articles under examination. A new Bill for consumer protection, published at the beginning of 1966, laid down severe penalties of unlimited fine or up to two years' imprisonment for false trade descriptions or misleading indications about the price of goods.

[1] *Final Report of the Consumer Protection Committee*, July 1962 (the Molony Committee), Cmnd. 1781.

PART THREE

CARE AND CULTURE

"... if any are lost from want of care and culture, there is a
sin of omission in the society to which they belong."
Robert Southey, *Colloquies on the Progress and
Prospects of Society*, I, p. 110

CHAPTER XVII

Care

"... increasing attention has been given in recent years to training in the art of 'human relations' ... these developments have taken place against a background of increased public understanding of the varied problems of the less fortunate people in the community and of the causes and symptoms of social deprivation."

*Report of the National Assistance Board
for the year ended December 31, 1965*, p. vi

THE SOCIAL-SECURITY system which is an integral part of the Welfare State spreads a safety-net beneath most of its citizens. But the net extends not quite far enough, and its meshes are not quite small enough, to secure everyone who needs its support; nor is it held quite high enough to keep them from falling below the standard of life which is now the accepted minimum. This is in spite of the fact that insurance benefits have risen and that the total bill for national insurance, at over £2000 million, is the largest item on the national balance sheet, with the exception of military defence, which costs about the same; it is larger even than the National Health Service, whose cost has received far more publicity. The mounting expense has not been borne entirely by the State, and contributions from both employers and employed have been stepped up several times,[1] but the State's contribution remains by far the biggest, and the 'insured' man's 'insurance' payments by no means cover the benefits paid out. Family allowances and war pensions, indeed, do not pretend to any insurance principle but are straight payments from the Exchequer.

Little alteration had been made in the structure of National Insurance since its inception, except that in 1952 the Ministry of Pensions was amalgamated with the Ministry of National Insurance. As the population grew the number of records kept had multiplied, covering some

[1] See Appendix B X.

24 million contributors, but automation had kept the process of checking, recording, and amending speedy and streamlined. By 1964 the Ministry of Pensions and National Insurance was responsible for the payment each week of some 12½ million benefits and allowances. Over 633,000 war pensions were being paid, over 6 million retirement pensions, 624,000 widows' benefits and guardian allowances, 195,000 industrial-disablement pensions, and 992,000 maternity grants. Family allowances (the age at which a child could be included was raised to nineteen in 1964) were being paid to 3¾ million families containing 10 million children, an average of 955,000 people were currently claiming sickness benefit, 199,000 unemployment benefit, and 66,000 benefit for industrial injury. In all, some 16 million claims for benefits and allowances are received each year, including about 9 million for sickness benefit and 2½ million for unemployment. The staff who deal with these benefits number nearly 40,000, of whom nearly 9000 are employed at the Newcastle Central office. There are in addition the Post Office clerks at the 25,000 post-offices who actually pay out the pensions and allowances, the staffs of the labour exchanges who pay unemployment benefit and help place the unemployed in jobs, and the offices of the 900 local branches of the Ministry where all questions relating to insurance are dealt with.[1]

It could almost be said that Beveridge had provided better than he knew. Certainly the child placed on the doorstep by Lloyd George had been nurtured so effectively and had grown to such a size that Lloyd George at least would have had difficulty in recognizing it. Beveridge died in 1963, having lived long enough for his death to create far less stir than the publication of his Report twenty years earlier. The new generation took for granted the benefits that created such excitement when propounded in his Report. The old people who spoke of drawing their "Lloyd George" had died, and no-one now spoke of drawing his "Beveridge".

According to the Beveridge principle, payment of benefit is made without test of means in the same way that the Health Service is free to all irrespective of income, the only proviso being a stated number of insurance contributions. The payment, also according to the Beveridge principle, constitutes a minimum to keep a person or a family from destitution, and is intended to be a temporary expedient to tide over bad times; it is not intended to replace individual effort or take the place of private thrift. With affluence spreading through society to a degree not contemplated when the post-War legislation was drawn up, and with

[1] *Report of the Ministry of Pensions and National Insurance for the year 1964.*

unemployment low and temporary rather than chronic, the principle has not been seriously challenged, and the rates of sickness, accident, and unemployment pay have, generally speaking, been accepted for what they are—subsistence payments to help tide over a temporary crisis. War pensions and industrial-injury pensions are in a different category in that they may have to last for life and may be the only foreseeable means of income. War pensions are now paid in respect of war wounds incurred in either of the two world wars or disabilities incurred in the armed services since the last war. It is recognized that they may need to be more than a temporary subsistence payment, and pensions for either war or industrial injury can reach £20 a week, free of income tax, the actual amount depending upon both medical and economic evidence of need as well as size of family; where necessary the pension will be paid to a widow or dependent.

At the end of 1965 and the beginning of 1966 two aspects of the social-insurance provisions were being questioned by the Labour Government. In a new National Insurance Bill published in January 1966 it put forward proposals for wage-related unemployment and sickness benefits, so departing from the Beveridge principle of subsistence payments to be supplemented by private savings. At the same time the Government was talking of merging the Public Assistance Board into a Ministry or Department of Social Security. In view of the debate in the House of Commons nearly twenty years earlier[1] the latter suggestion would have made Beveridge smile. He would not have been so pleased with the first. One of the principles upon which he had built his Plan was that "The State in organising security should not stifle incentive, opportunity, responsibility; in establishing a national minimum, it should leave room and encouragement for voluntary action by each individual to provide more than that minimum for himself and his family." It should give "in return for contributions benefits up to subsistence level, as of right and without means test, so that individuals may build freely upon it".[2] The need to save for a rainy day, he would have argued, not only made thrifty and responsible citizens but reduced irresponsible spending on consumer goods, helped industry, and stemmed the price rise.

The principle of making, by and large, equal payments for the same symptoms without questioning the means of the recipient implies that benefits are sometimes paid to the wealthy, who do not need them, while the help given to those who remain outside affluence may be inadequate. There is, moreover, the danger of too completely abandoning the

[1] *Supra*, p. 27.   [2] *Social Insurance and Allied Services*, pp. 6–7.

philosophy of Samuel Smiles.[1] Thrift and self-help were bitter precepts to preach to a class whose weekly wage no more than kept it miserably alive; State aid granted indiscriminately in an affluent society may prove to be as lacking in perception as the derided Victorian doctrine. The principles have become inverted in time. The Victorian working-man needed State aid; to-day self-help and thrift are possible on a scale unknown to Samuel Smiles. And that they should supplement State aid is precisely what Beveridge advocated. By paying all benefits irrespective of means we emphasize the rights of all citizens on the one hand, but, on the other, run the danger of dulling the impetus to self-help and giving aid where aid is not really needed. At the same time there are some who cannot, and cannot be expected to, supplement the State payment by thrift or abstinence or self-help—those who through age or sickness or disability cannot help themselves; those who fail through faults of character or circumstance to take their places in society. Whether or not there is a means test for any of the social-security benefits, these people need help outside and beyond the scope of National Insurance.

There are the old. The retirement pension has risen with the rising cost of living, and reached £4 a week at the end of March 1965—still a bare subsistence rate—but while with full employment and higher wages it can be expected that people in employment will save out of income to supplement the basic pension, those too old to to have known the higher wages that make this possible are not well off. Still worse off are those whose pension is paid under the Insurance Acts already in force in 1948— who at the time of the new legislation were already receiving pensions and had never paid into the insurance fund. These pensioners received only 10*s.* a week until March 1965, when their pension was raised to £1 10*s.* Yet, inadequate as the provision is for those who are dependent upon it, retirement pensions constitute the greatest and the most rapidly growing payment of the Ministry of Pensions and National Insurance. In 1963–64 they cost nearly £960 million, compared with £65 million for unemployment benefit, £191 million for sickness, £110 million for war pensions, and £140 million for family allowances. Retirement pensions are a strain upon the National Insurance Fund, not only because of the numbers concerned, but because no-one now drawing a pension has contributed for his whole working life, nor at rates compatible with the rising benefits: the pension fund had always lagged behind payments, and always will, since increased benefits are always one step ahead of increased contributions. At the same time, those over pensionable age are increasing both in numbers and in proportion to the rest of the popula-

[1] *Self-help*, 1859; *Thrift*, 1875.

tion.[1] Two suggestions have been made to meet the problem: one is to make retirement pensions a straight charge upon the Exchequer, like family allowances, when they would be met squarely by taxation[2]; the other is to institute a means test for pension payments. The size of total pension payments is an argument against the former scheme; the latter is open to the grave injustice of reducing a State pension because of personal thrift and careful living. On the whole, with the continuing increase in wages and salaries, income-tax contributions to old age are not inequitable.

Others whose needs are not met by National Insurance are those chronically unemployed through some deficiency or run of bad luck; these include the handicapped, the mentally retarded, those suffering from some disability since childhood, those simply unable to cope with a job. There are those who have temporarily run out of National Insurance benefits and need to be 'tided over'. There are also those who for some reason other than age have not contributed to the social-insurance scheme. These include people who have remained at home looking after parents or relatives; they include separated or divorced wives and unmarried mothers, often with dependent children; they include also those persons described as 'without a settled way of life'—people who, often through bad luck, often of their own volition, sometimes through force of some strange circumstance, have remained outside the structure of welfare.

A second safety net, designed to help all these people, was provided by the National Assistance Board, which, under the National Assistance Act of 1948, was given the duty to help in money or kind families whose resources were inadequate, and to promote welfare generally. The NAB paid each week about a million weekly allowances and about a million single payments for temporary need, mostly supplementing National Insurance benefits. It still suffered from the disadvantage of being associated with Public Assistance and the pre-War means test and with all that these implied of shame to the recipient. This feeling was particularly strong with the old, who remembered the days before Beveridge, but younger people for the most part accepted the NAB as they accepted the Health Service and National Insurance.

In 1964 the Board helped some 72,000 non-contributory old-age pensioners, nearly 90 per cent of the total, and some 127,000 others over pensionable age also received supplements. The Board helped even more

---

[1] See *Report of the Committee on the Economic and Financial Problems of the Provision for Old Age* (the Phillips Committee) December 1954, Cmnd. 9333, but also *supra*, p. 216 *and n.*

[2] By, notably, R. M. Titmuss.

people under pensionable age—some 245,000 in 1964. These included 95,000 women with dependent children, mostly separated or divorced wives and unmarried mothers; 12,000 persons who had spent their adult lives at home looking after relatives, 135,000 people who were unfit for work, and others whose unemployment pay under the National Insurance scheme had run out.

The scale rate to which the NAB was authorized to make up a weekly allowance was, from the spring of 1964, 76s. for a single person, 125s. 6d. for a husband and wife, and amounts for young people or dependants varying from 23s. to 67s. 6d. a week. These sums were in addition to rent payments. The Board also made in 1963 repayments of National Health Service charges amounting to £2·75 million in respect of prescriptions, just under £1 million in respect of spectacles, half a million for dentures and dental treatment, £60,000 for surgical appliances.[1]

For the chronically unemployed and handicapped there are also rehabilitation and re-establishment centres, both residential and non-residential. These do excellent work, and there are many examples of people finding confidence and self-respect through the skills they acquire and so taking their places in the wider community and contributing to the common pool. But there are others—the 'tramps', the solitaries of society, often basically fit but sometimes suffering from some mental or physical handicap that has kept them from regular work. These people frequently sleep out during the summer, but in the winter gravitate to the reception centres administered by the State, by local authorities on behalf of the State, or by some charitable organization. The reception centres vary greatly in amenity and cleanliness as well as in the types of people who use them. While many of these could find jobs if they were really keen, the unfit could, if willing to be helped, be sent by an officer of the Ministry to a residential rehabilitation course. Often, however, the man found at the reception centre really prefers to be 'without a settled way of life'. In the summer he can be found sleeping rough on London's embankment; often he is found on railway-station benches; he frequents all-night coffee-houses. The situation contains many elements which it should be possible to sort out—the gipsy, freelance temperament which will not be shackled by a conventional job with conventional social benefits, which does well in youth but builds no security for old age; those suffering from disability of mind or body; those dogged by bad luck who yield to the pressure of circumstance. The problem is not big in numbers: in London in November 1963 only 115 men and 14 women were discovered sleeping rough; the nightly

[1] Reports of the National Assistance Board.

average of persons in local-authority reception centres is a thousand or so men and some sixty women—though others are found in voluntary hostels like those run by the Salvation Army. Moreover, there is a changing population in these centres, and the number of different people who use them is greater than those present at any particular time.[1] Since, theoretically at least, the people accommodated receive a pension or benefit of some kind a charge is made by the reception centre of about 5s. for bed and breakfast, but no-one without means is turned away.

The people dealt with by the National Assistance Board—and there were others who for some reason did not come before it—constituted an element outside affluence, outside welfare, which needed to be brought within the scope of the welfare society. The problem is not always so simple as giving them money; in most cases it is teaching a new self-assurance or self-respect. Individual officers of the National Assistance Board did excellent work in this connection; and in cases of long unemployment, of inability to hold a job, of some congenital defect, a great deal depends upon an individual officer's ability to make a bridge that the applicant can cross. An extension of this kind of social work by enlarging the staffs and the scope of those concerned and by catching the misfits or the maladjusted at some other point—at the employment exchange or at a social-service centre—is vitally necessary.

Generally speaking, as Beveridge noted in 1962, the problem is no longer chiefly one of unemployment; the hard core who remain unemployed for more than a year, including many with physical and mental handicaps, number only some 50,000 and for much of the time—for example, from April to September 1965—vacancies exceeded the numbers unemployed. But if large-scale unemployment should return, the social services of the Welfare State would be strained to an extent not yet realized, and a great deal of rethinking and re-evaluation would be necessary. For the time being—again as Beveridge noted—the problem has changed from one of unemployment to one of old age. If people now in full earning capacity realize that their retirement pension will be a supplement, not a full living wage, and save or insure for a higher income in old age the problem should be soluble. An immediate difficulty concerns housing of a kind suitable to the old and to the infirm where they can maintain independence, have their own furniture if they wish, cook and otherwise provide for themselves while they are able, and yet have companionship and help at hand when needed. The National Insurance Act of 1948 placed a duty on local authorities to provide residential accommodation for persons who, by reason of age, infirmity, or

[1] Reports of the National Assistance Board.

other handicap, require attention not otherwise available and to provide temporary accommodation in an emergency. The NAB and the local authorities work closely together in these respects, and besides the remedial and rehabilitation centres and the reception centres local authorities are making progress with some excellent building schemes, both in residential homes for the old and in flatlets which are part of general rehousing schemes. A great improvement would be made if residential homes contained more single rooms and more unfurnished rooms; there needs, in fact, to be great variety of accommodation to deal with varying types and circumstance—from the old people who can do for themselves and want their own things around them with the maximum of independence to those who want the comfort of being looked after with or without their own furniture and effects.[1]

It was no discredit to the work of the National Assistance Board that the Government introduced a Bill that dissolved the NAB and the Ministry of Pensions and National Insurance and provided for the appointment of a Minister who would embrace the functions of assistance as well as of pensions and national insurance. Every person over sixteen whose resources were insufficient to meet his requirements would be entitled to benefit, and payment would be made together with insurance benefits. The Ministry of Social Security Act became law in July 1966. Who remembered the debate in the Commons at the end of 1944?[2] The Welfare State was still in debt to Beveridge, down to a tardy adoption of the name he had suggested twenty years earlier!

In a different category, requiring specialized forms of assistance, are the children who have no homes or who come from broken families, children who are uncontrollable or who are guilty of some misdemeanour or crime, children whose parents are permanently or temporarily unable or unfit to look after them. These children are taken 'in care' by local authorities acting under the jurisdiction of the Home Office.[3] There are some 65,000 of them in England and Wales, making five children 'in care' for every 1000 of the population under eighteen. In 1963 over 31,000 were boarded out with private families, about 52 per cent of the total; nearly 20,000 were in local-authority children's homes, nearly 4000 in homes run by voluntary organizations, and the rest were in lodgings, in residential employment, in hostels, or in homes or boarding-schools for handicapped children. The cost to the local authority

---

[1] See Peter Townsend, *The Last Refuge.*
[2] *Supra*, p. 27.
[3] And of the Scottish Home and Health Department and the Ministry of Home Affairs for Northern Ireland.

was nearly £7 a week for each child—over £21·5 million a year all told—and parental contribution averaged about 6s. a week. But the cost in money to the nation is the least part of the tragedy that lies behind the figures. The most fortunate of the children are the 27,000 or so who are in care for only a short while because of some temporary incapacity of a parent or guardian—perhaps because of illness or childbirth or a passing family upset. But nearly 4000 came into local-authority care in the twelve months ending in March 1962 because of desertion by their mother, a further 716 because of the death of their mother, the father not being able to manage both the children and his work. In the course of the year some 325 were found abandoned or lost, 235 had no parent or guardian or near friend or relative; some 4000 or more were brought into care because their parent or guardian was considered unfit to be in charge of a child; other children had been before the courts for stealing or uncontrollable behaviour and were in care as part of the remedial treatment; others were difficult children whom their families were unable to control.[1]

The largest age group of those coming into care are those of school age, the smallest those above school age; these latter are often found a job or apprenticed to a trade, meanwhile living in a hostel or lodgings or sometimes in one of the smaller family homes like the elder child of a family: one imaginative house parent provided a caravan in the garden where two older boys lived independently after they had started work, taking meals with the rest and watching television as they pleased. Many of the homes are kindly and imaginatively run by house parents who have their own children living with them and create a genuinely home-like atmosphere. But most children feel the difference between a real parent and a house mother, however kind and sympathetic; most understand that, simply by being there, they are placed in a category apart from others, and a group of mixed children and young people is frequently full of tensions; one difficult or unbalanced or over-demanding child can create frustrations and unsettlement in the rest.

The problem of children in care had been brought sharply to people's notice, even through the clouds of war, when a little boy was so badly treated by the foster-parents who were boarding him for the local authority that he died. The foster-father was imprisoned for six months, and Committees were set up by the Caretaker Government in March 1945 to examine the question of "providing for children who from loss of parents or from any other cause whatever are deprived of a normal

[1] *Children in Care: England and Wales*, 1962; *Report of the Work of the Children's Department*, 1961–1963.

home life". The Curtis Committee *Report on the Care of Children and Young Persons in England and Wales* was published in September 1946,[1] a deeply sincere and humanitarian document which shocked the country by its revelations of life in local-authority 'homes', carrying the reader back to the old mixed workhouse of the nineteenth century. There was the same indiscriminate mixing of the well, the sick, and the mentally deficient, of the senile and the young, the expectant and nursing mothers, and the families fallen on bad times. Inspection of these institutions was perfunctory, recommendations for improvement were either not carried out at all or dealt with tardily and partially. The homes where children were boarded, like the home where little Dennis O'Neill had died, were not only given no careful inspection but were subject to two sets of rules —those under the Poor Law Act of 1930 and those under the Children and Young Persons Act of 1933.

The Children's Act of 1948, following the two Reports, dealt directly with this situation. It was an Act "to make further provision for the care or welfare, up to the age of eighteen, and, in certain cases, for further periods, of boys and girls when they are without parents or have been lost or abandoned by, or are living away from, their parents, or when their parents are unfit or unable to take care of them, and in certain other circumstances". The Government had decided that "the task of providing a home background for children deprived of a normal home life should be brought under the supervision of a single central department", and chose the Home Office, with a new and enlarged Children's Branch and an expanded Inspectorate organized on a regional basis, as their chief instrument. A Standing Advisory Committee, widely representative of the many interests involved and including representatives of the Ministry of Education, the Ministry of Health, and the Ministry of Labour, was to assist the Home Office in its administration. In Scotland the Secretary of State was already responsible for all aspects of child care, and he was to assign to the Scottish Home Department functions broadly similar to those which would be given to the Children's Branch of the Home Office and would appoint a Scottish Standing Advisory Committee. County Councils, County Borough Councils in England and Wales, and County Councils and Town Councils of large burgs in Scotland would be the local authorities responsible for the children concerned. Each authority was to appoint a Children's Committee on the lines suggested by the Curtis and Clyde Reports and a

---

[1] Cmd. 6922. The Scottish Committee was under the chairmanship of J. L. Clyde and reported in the same year under the title *The Committee on Homeless Children (Scotland) Report*, Cmd. 6911.

special Children's Officer in general charge of the children's wellbeing. The Children's Bill was given its second reading on May 7, 1948, and became law shortly after, it being then the duty of a local authority to receive into care any child under seventeen who had neither parent nor guardian, who was abandoned or lost, or whose parent or guardian was unable to provide for him.[1]

The Children's Act was reinforced by a section of the National Assistance Act which laid it as a duty upon the local authority to provide residential accommodation for persons who, by reason of age, infirmity, or other circumstance, require care and attention not otherwise available, to provide temporary accommodation for persons in urgent need, and to give help in money or kind to families whose resources are inadequate. Though applying to many kinds of person it was clear that any help given to a family, as such, would help to maintain it as a unit and prevent children from coming into care. The National Health Act similarly, in laying upon the local authority the duty to make arrangements for the care of expectant and nursing mothers and of children up to school age, including the provision of day nurseries and recuperative holidays for mothers with young children, was helping to preserve family unity. The Education Acts also impinge upon the problem of family preservation and child care. The local education authorities have a duty to provide for medical inspection of pupils and to see that free medical attention is given where necessary; they are also empowered to arrange that pupils be examined for cleanliness, that school nurses or qualified health visitors follow up cases of neglect, that education welfare officers visit homes to make inquiries concerning children absent from school without a reasonable excuse.[2] The Housing Acts place upon the local authority the responsibility for seeing that houses are fit for human habitation and that there is no undue overcrowding; probation officers follow up cases of court conviction or imprisonment; reception centres will receive mothers and children temporarily homeless for any reason, and local-authority family reception centres for the homeless are open in London.

In practice the services are not always as efficient as the intention, and reception centres can be bleak and inhospitable. But administratively at least a fairly fine web has been woven, of which the local authority is the centre, functioning as children's authority, health authority, welfare authority, education authority, housing authority, and with general powers of assistance and guidance. It could seem that there are too

---

[1] The Children's Act, 1948.   [2] And see *supra*, p. 206.

many powers, that initiative is too dispersed, and this feeling is emphasized by the many voluntary organizations whose efforts are directed to the same ends of helping those outside welfare and preventing family breakdown. There are the Family Service Units, primarily concerned with 'problem families' and giving help in practical, immediate ways; the Women's Voluntary Service, covering a wide range of practical help to people and families of all kinds; the Salvation Army; the National Society for the Prevention of Cruelty to Children, with its own inspectors and visitors; Dr Barnardo's Homes; the Marriage Guidance Council; the National Council of Social Service; the British Red Cross Society; the National Old People's Welfare Council; the St John Ambulance Association and Brigade; and others. A working party of officials from the Home Office, the Ministry of Health, the Ministry of Education, and the corresponding Scottish Departments issued in 1949 a report on the activities of these voluntary organizations, and the Government, concluding that the immediate need was for some co-ordination of the existing statutory and voluntary services, secured the appointment of "designated officers" in the localities for this purpose. But ten years later the Ingleby Committee felt it necessary again to draw attention to the many voluntary organizations concerned with welfare, and the Children and Young Persons Act of 1963 empowered local authorities to make use of voluntary agencies in a more direct way than they had previously done, in particular by making them money grants for such purposes, for example, as the improvement of voluntary children's homes.

The Departmental Committee on Children and Young Persons under the chairmanship of Viscount Ingleby had been appointed in October 1956 and reported four years later, having covered wide ground, including not only children in care but juvenile delinquents and their families. It laid much stress upon the family as a social unit and the need to preserve it. Medical practitioners, ministers of religion, teachers, social workers—all those, professional and voluntary, paid and unpaid, who came into contact with people in their homes—should be able to recognize the inadequate family or the maladjusted family and know how, and from what source, help would be available. And families themselves must be left in no doubt as to where help is to be found; they must be shown "the door on which to knock". And because the Committee believed that a family was more likely to survive a crisis if it could be preserved intact, it recommended that local authorities should have power to help families directly with money in their own homes before they became destitute—in such ways, for example, as paying arrears of rent or the travelling expenses of a relative to assist in a crisis. The Children and Young Persons Act of 1963 followed the Ingleby Report in this respect also, and help became more positive and realistic than it had been before.[1]

In the piecemeal development of welfare work, in the multiple strands of voluntary and local-authority effort, of various departments and many officials, some services are naturally better than others. On the whole, those that deal with normal conditions, like the maternity and child-care services, are excellent; those that deal with breakdown, emergency, and crisis work less well, partly because the subjective side is here to the fore and the social worker has to start afresh on each problem. How should he deal with a child so difficult that its parents are unable to control it? How should he restore the faith of children whose mother has left them or help their father to make a home as well as keep a job? And, most difficult of all, perhaps, how does he tackle one of the most disturbing problems of our society—the increase of crime generally and of juvenile delinquency in particular?

Between 1958 and 1962 the total number of indictable offences recorded by the police in England and Wales increased by 43 per cent. In 1963 there was a further 9 per cent increase over the figure of the previous year, in 1964 yet a further increase of over 9 per cent. In that year well over 1 million indictable offences became known to the police in England and Wales; in Scotland, where the figures were similarly growing, there were 352,000.[2] About one-third of all those found guilty of indictable offences each year are under the age of seventeen, one half are under the age of twenty-one; two-thirds of those found guilty of breaking and entering are under twenty-one years of age; just under half are under seventeen. Far more boys and men are guilty of indictable offences than women and girls, but the figures of the latter are showing a sharp increase. Among males the biggest rise is in the seventeen-to-twenty-one-year-old group, which between 1938 and 1964 grew more than threefold; those under seventeen meanwhile more than doubled, and those over twenty-one grew some two and a half times.[3] Among females the seventeen-to-twenty-one-year-old group grew nearly

[1] *Report of the Committee on Children and Young Persons*, October 1960 (the Ingleby Report), Cmnd. 1191.

[2] *Annual Reports of Her Majesty's Chief Inspector of Constabulary for England and Wales and for Scotland.*

[3] *The War Against Crime in England and Wales*, 1959–1964, Cmnd. 2296; *Criminal Statistics.*

threefold, the under seventeens more than quadrupled, and the over twenty-ones nearly trebled over the same period.[1]

Of the total increase in crime in England and Wales between 1963 and 1964 robbery and violence together comprised 40 per cent. Cases of violence against the person have increased consistently and rapidly, amounting to over 14,000 in 1964. The upsurge of crime involving the use of firearms, causing injury and death to policemen and others, led to the Firearms Act of 1965, which laid down severe penalties for improperly possessing and carrying firearms and gave the police powers of search. Larceny, with breaking and entering, remains the most widespread crime—nearly 160,000 of the total of 205,000 indictable offences in 1964; sexual offences, which have been fluctuating between 5000 and 6000 a year, were 5571 in 1964.[2]

Fundamentally crime is a sign of sickness in the individual and sickness in the society that breeds him—"It is no good condemning plants for not growing and blossoming as they should, if the soil is sour"[3]— but while the individual and society are being reformed rising crime figures need to be tackled on four levels: the police force needs to be strengthened, the prison system needs to be organized so as to give security to society, administration needs to be co-ordinated, and the criminal law itself needs to be kept under review in order to remain closely related to the current issues. A low recruiting rate of constables and a general unease about the service led to the appointment of a Royal Commission which issued its first Report in 1960, advocating, among other reforms, an increase in the pay of police constables[4]; its Final Report in 1962 rejected the idea of a national police force (which was put forward, however, in a minority report) but called for greater powers of co-ordination to be vested in the Secretary of State.[5] Both recommendations were carried into effect. Wages were raised, though inadequately, and the Police Force Act of 1964, while maintaining the traditional partnership of the Secretary of State, the Police authorities, and the service itself, gave greater overall powers to the Home Secretary. Improved training for police officers was provided, with better equipment and technical aids, and there were all-round improvements in staff facilities.

---

[1] *Criminal Statistics*.

[2] *Ibid.*

[3] Henry Brooke, Foreword to *Report of the Work of the Children's Department, 1961–1963*.

[4] *Royal Commission on the Police* (the Willink Report) Interim Report.

[5] *Ibid.* Final Report, May 1962, Cmnd. 1728.

By 1964 there were 80,000 policemen and policewomen in England and Wales and 10,000 in Scotland. The majority of the provincial forces were up to strength; but in London and the large cities where other employment was attractive numbers were still not adequate. In February 1965 the Home Office estimated an overall deficiency of about 15,000 men.[1] The reasons for this were not far to seek. Pay was still not comparable to that in many other occupations—£700 a year at nineteen, £1000 at thirty, and the maximum of £1100 not reached until after twenty-two years of service.[2] Hours were long, often 46 to 48 a standard week, and more in emergency; they were irregular, and included much shift work and night work. Conditions on the beat, much of which was still lonely patrol work, were far from attractive and frequently highly dangerous. Good pensions, a free house or help towards acquiring a house, improved conditions at the station, and personal radio on the beat help to recruit, and to keep, an adequate police force, but perhaps the strongest factor in maintaining a force of the right size and the right morale is its relationship with the public. Greater delinquency rapidly develops into less respect for the policeman; a fear of involvement or of victimization hampers public co-operation; a growing defence tactic on the part of those apprehended is to lodge counter-claims against the police—and a few genuine cases of police corruption or intimidation can make the position of the average policeman extremely difficult. By and large he works in conditions which, as *The Times* said, "would provoke strike action in an industry with a militant trade union".[3] Much of this cannot be avoided, but it is at least possible to make the job compare in material terms with other occupations.

The rebuilding and expansion of prisons lagged for some time behind the growth of crime—the total prison population numbered nearly 21,000 in 1956, 30,000 in 1964, an increase of 43 per cent—but in face of what *The Times* called "the gathering gloom of prison officers"[4] and a general change in policy, which in 1963 transferred the building functions of the Prison Commissioners to the Home Secretary, a massive building programme was planned which stepped up the amount spent in England and Wales from £822,000 in 1958–59 to nearly £7 million in 1964–65. New building was put in hand, including the construction of more open prisons, at least one psychiatric prison, and re-equipment and conversion provided better facilities all round, the accent being removed from the uncomfortable prison cell which would restrain and

1 Hansard, February 4, 1965.
2 See three articles in *The Times* beginning February 3, 1965.
3 Leading article, February 6, 1965.   4 Leading article, June 18, 1962.

10+

deter to a place of constructive work with entertainment provided by films and concerts and by the prisoners themselves, which, it was hoped, would reform and rehabilitate. A similar programme was planned for Scotland. At the same time a Committee, reporting in 1960,[1] pronounced against the reintroduction of corporal punishment which had been abolished in 1948. Was the change to better prison conditions going a little too far? Was the prison officer's job being made more difficult? Occasional Press stories of prison rioting, of brawls developing from social evenings, of complaints about food, gave cause for some disquiet. When a prisoner was stabbed to death by two of his fellow-prisoners in a prison said by the prosecuting council to be "more like a club than a prison", the men were walking about freely, visiting each other, playing guitars in each other's cells, watching or playing football, watching television, playing darts.[2] But increases in pay and improved conditions increased the number of prison staff in Great Britain from under 7000 in 1958 to over 10,000 in 1964. In August 1963 imprisonment for offenders under seventeen was abolished, and it was intended that eventually detention in a detention centre should replace short sentences of imprisonment for the seventeen-to-twenty-one age group. But while this liberalizing policy was developing, public confidence was shaken by the escapes at different times and from different prisons of two long-term prisoners gaoled for the notorious mail-train robbery of 1963. The prisoners were not caught, and the escapes were obviously carefully planned from outside with, in one case at least, the co-operation of a group of prisoners inside. The murder of a young Borstal officer by escaping youths at the end of 1965 further shook public faith in official policy.

While the emphasis throughout was increasingly on prevention, on reformation, on rehabilitation, on seeking to cure rather than to punish, it was at the same time necessary to give society adequate protection from wrongdoers: "A grave responsibility is placed upon those who pass sentence on criminal offenders. It is their duty to protect the public and to see that there are effective deterrents to crime, but at the very same time they must never lose sight of the personal needs and problems of the individual offenders who come before them. . . . The interests of the public and the offender need not be in conflict; both can be served by matching the treatment to the offender as well as to the offence."[3] It is a principle which is easier to follow with the young offender, partly because reformation would then seem to be easier, but partly because there

---

[1] Cmnd. 1213.   [2] Henry Scott, Q.C., prosecuting at Leeds.
[3] Henry Brooke, Foreword to *The Sentence of the Court, A Handbook for Courts on the Treatment of Offenders*, April 1964.

is a greater variety of treatment suited to his age and misdemeanour—the remand home, the detention centre, the approved school, the Borstal— all of which emphasize creative and worth-while work within a routine which is intentionally tough. Its most difficult application concerns the abolition of the death penalty for murder, over which considerable feeling was growing both in Parliament and outside. A step towards abolition was made by the Homicide Act of 1957, which altered the definition of murder and introduced the special defence of diminished responsibility. Seven years later, at the end of 1964, a private Member's Bill for the abolition of the death penalty was introduced, but while it was being considered several crimes of great brutality, including the murder of a policeman and the severe wounding of another, were weakening the case of the abolitionists. Would abolition not involve the corollary of arming the police and encouraging vicious armed conflicts on a scale not known before in Britain, it was asked. There were 142 murders of persons aged one year and over in 1963, 152 in 1964.[1]

There were also those who spoke for the victims of murder: the obligation to the victim of crime rests primarily on the society which has failed to protect him and which alone can effectively compensate him, said Miss Margery Fry. "The assumption that the claims of the victim are sufficiently satisfied if the offender is punished by society becomes less persuasive as society in its dealings with offenders increasingly emphasises the reformative aspects of punishment. Indeed in the public mind the interests of the offender may not infrequently seem to be placed before those of his victim," remarked a Government Report on penal practice.[2] A working party, appointed to consider the question of compensation for victims of crimes of violence, reported in June 1961, and in March 1964 Government proposals for lump-sum monetary compensation became law.[3] Not until sixteen months later did the House of Lords, at the third time of asking, and after considerable amendment had been made, give a majority to the second reading of the Abolition of Hanging Bill, but merely for a trial period of five years.[4]

For bringing the criminal law up to date a Criminal Law Revision Committee, to work alongside a general Law Reform Committee, was set up, while a Home Office Research Unit was formed for criminological research, and an Institute of Criminology was established at Cambridge with its own chair in Criminology.

[1] *Criminal Statistics, England and Wales*, 1965.
[2] *Penal Practice in a Changing Society*, February 1959, Cmnd. 645.
[3] Compensation of Victims of Violence Act.
[4] On July 20, 1965. The Bill became law as the Murder (Abolition of Death Penalty) Act, 1965.

Meanwhile persons are continuing to be discharged from penal establishments at the rate of 5000–6000 annually, with some 6000 more from detention centres,[1] and society must ask to what extent they have been reformed? A White Paper on the record of approved schools, published in March 1964, was not reassuring, judging by the frequency with which a young person reappeared in the courts within three years of his discharge. But since such reappearances could be for any offence, even for riding a bicycle without a light, the statistics were not very revealing.

Among the present tasks of the Home Office is a far more realistic statistical approach to the whole question, and until the results of this are produced no convincing conclusion can be drawn. Meanwhile most of those who leave prison or detention need to be helped to take their places again in society. They are offered financial aid, given help in finding work and lodgings if they need it by one of the After Care Services or the National Association of Discharged Prisoners' Aid Societies; in the case of juveniles they are helped by probation officers, the managers of approved schools, or other social workers.[2]

As 1965 opened the Home Office summed up the position thus: "a study has been initiated of the criminal statistics—the means whereby the incidence and gravity of crime are measured. Research into the causes of crime and the effectiveness of the means of dealing with criminals is going ahead. The modernisation of the criminal law . . . is being pressed onward. The police service has been greatly strengthened and the enlarged Inspectorate and the new Police Research and Planning Branch at the Home Office will enhance police efficiency for the dual task of preventing crime and detecting offenders."[3] Yet there were more prison escapes, including a spy who should have been under maximum security; the 152 murders of 1964 grew to 161 in 1965, and many of them were unsolved. In 1966 three police officers were savagely shot dead while on duty in broad daylight in London. Police and prison officers asked for the tightening of detention, and the reimposition of capital punishment for the murder of policemen. Voices were asking whether the abolition of the death penalty had been wise. A fresh vote in the House of Commons in November 1966 still decided that it had.

While the war against crime proper continues there is a great deal of delinquency, largely on the part of the young, which is both vicious in itself and likely to lead to more serious crime. Trouble ranges from

---

[1] *The Organisation of After-Care*, 1963 (H.M.S.O.).   [2] *Ibid.*
[3] *The War Against Crime*, p. 14.

window-smashing to sex, from drunkenness to drugs; it includes wilful damage, brawling, gang fighting, sometimes the use of dangerous weapons. Apart from gang warfare, sexual promiscuity and the birth of illegitimate children has focused more attention than any other aberration. The number of illegitimate births in England and Wales grew from 34,000 (4·8 per cent of the total number of live births) in 1956 to 63,000 (7·2 per cent of the total) in 1964. The figures for Scotland were 4100 (4·3 per cent) and 5600 (5·4 per cent); and for Northern Ireland 800 (2·7 per cent) and 1000 (3 per cent).[1] This means that 1 in 14 babies born in the United Kingdom is illegitimate.

For mothers under twenty years the figures are far higher—some 1 in 4 of babies born are illegitimate, some 2 out of 3 were conceived out of wedlock.[2] A particularly disturbing aspect of the situation is the youth of the girls who are conceiving outside marriage. Some of these marry before their children are born, and for those who marry in their teens the divorce rate is twice as high as for those who marry between twenty-one and twenty-four. In 1961, 2534 children were born to unmarried mothers between eleven and sixteen years old; over 41,000 children were born to unmarried mothers under twenty or conceived by them out of wedlock; and the number of illegal abortions was possibly some 50,000. In 1958 there was one known unmarried mother of eleven years old; in 1959 there were four of twelve years old.[3]

Highly disturbing in itself, this situation is the more dangerous because of the spread of the venereal diseases which accompanies it. Gonorrhoea has increased steadily since 1954, syphilis since 1958. The actual figures are not large, but the venereal diseases are rarely transmitted outside sexual contact, and both the ages of those contracting the diseases and its rapid growth are alarming. In 1963, 179 girls and 46 boys under sixteen years of age attended clinics for the treatment of gonorrhoea, one girl and one boy under sixteen for syphilis, out of a total of 32,646 of all ages and both sexes attending clinics for these two diseases; there were a further 3856 cases of these diseases in young people between sixteen and twenty. In all, there were some 150,000 new cases of sexually transmitted diseases seen at clinics in 1963—which means that the number treated was far higher, and the total number, including those treated privately or not at all, higher still.[4] The consultant

[1] *Annual Abstract of Statistics.*
[2] *Venereal Disease and Young People* (British Medical Association Report, March 1964).
[3] *Ibid.*
[4] *On the State of the Public Health*, Annual Report of the Chief Medical Officer of the Ministry of Health for the year 1963, pp. 64–67, and Table C.1, p. 213.

venereologist at Holloway Prison reported that, of 415 prostitutes admitted in 1963, 85 were between fifteen years old and twenty and that 19 of them were found to have gonorrhoea. The Chief Medical Officer of the Ministry of Health regards it as a sign of profound social malaise whose cure lies not so much in medical as in social factors. Nor is it peculiar to Britain alone, the rise of the venereal diseases by 73·5 per cent in Britain between 1951 and 1962 being matched by world figures. A Committee appointed by the British Medical Association which reported in March 1964 heard evidence from teachers, social workers, parents, nurses and from teenagers themselves. In so far as it was possible to draw any conclusion it seemed that sexual intercourse outside marriage developed partly as a group phenomenon; it was a way of being accepted into a group and was a sign of being wanted. It also contained a certain element of revolt from tradition and marked the attainment of a new freedom. But, above all, it developed because there was no moral, or any other, deterrent that the teenager could or would accept.[1]

Drunkenness is sometimes held to be an accompaniment or a contributory cause of promiscuity. Between 1938 and 1962, in England and Wales, there was a big increase in male drunkenness, the number of convictions rising from 47,000 to nearly 80,000, but the number of women convicted fell from 7600 to under 5000. By far the heaviest drinkers are males between thirty and sixty years old—and among women who drink this is the heaviest drinking period. But this does not coincide with the growth of promiscuity in young people; in the eighteen-to-twenty-one age group there was, indeed, a decrease in drunkenness, and in 1963 the convictions for drunkenness decreased all round. Convictions, however, could not take account of private drinking nor of amounts that merely broke down inhibitions.

Drug-taking is another alarming aspect of modern society. Used in the wide sense that covers everything from the omnipresent Aspirin to anything that the doctor might prescribe, drugs are used, at some time, by everyone. It is not this but a growing reliance upon drugs which causes concern: "For every deviation from health, great or small, a specific chemical corrective is sought and, if possible, applied, and it is also widely believed that health may be positively enhanced by the use of drugs." Advertising and the stress of modern life encourage the illusion, and there is a growing tendency to look for a drug as the way

---

[1] *Venereal Disease and Young People.* A Report by a Committee of the British Medical Association (B.M.A., March 1964).

out of a crisis, real or imagined. But the drug-addiction that causes the real alarm is due to drugs like marihuana and the more vicious, habit-forming drugs, ranging from the 'purple hearts' that gained such notoriety in 1963 to the illegal narcotics, particularly heroin, which are smuggled into the country to an extent difficult to estimate, but sufficient to alert the police of many nations. Many police officers relate drug addiction of this type and the rise in crime. Many doctors relate drug addiction to deep-seated psychological disturbance. A Committee appointed to investigate the matter published some alarming figures at the end of 1965 showing that the number of heroin and cocaine addicts had increased five- and six-fold over the previous six years. The Committee laid some of the blame on a few doctors who prescribed excessively for addicts under their care, so releasing more supplies than were necessary. It recommended that no doctor other than a member of a clinic dealing with addicts should be allowed to prescribe, and that clinics be set up with powers of compulsory detention of addicts if they considered this necessary.[1] To keep supplies of harmful drugs from getting into general circulation through normal channels; to stop smuggling; to track down sources of illegal distribution are three of the main tasks of the police. The search for distribution centres leads them to dance-halls, clubs, cafés, restaurants. But the dope-pedlar plays for high stakes and is highly organized. The police have a job that is both difficult and dangerous.

Gambling, forced off the streets by the Betting and Gaming Act of 1960,[2] is booming. There were by 1965 some 15,000 or more betting shops, 2000 more than in 1963. Betting can lead to abuses like those revealed by footballers rigging the game, the doping of greyhounds and of racehorses; it detracts from the excitement of sport, as such, and focuses upon the football pool or the amount of money at stake. There is nothing essentially vicious in this, yet the values are false; the Church condemns it, and in London councillors urged a sociological survey of the effects of betting. Gambling and games of chance come within the same category, from the 16·5 millions who indulge in casino-type and other gaming at one extreme to the 14·3 million members of Bingo clubs at the other.

These are not the pastimes of the young. The children, meantime, get their own exploits—particularly the more culpable kind—well publicized.

---

[1] *Drug Addiction.* Second Report of the Interdepartmental Committee, November 1965.
[2] An Act based partly on the recommendations of the Royal Commission on Betting, Lotteries, and Gaming, 1949–51, Cmnd. 8190.

Four hundred teenagers started a riot against a ban on the Twist at a local dance-hall after complaints about hooliganism, pouring into the little fishing-port of Brixham, Devon, on motor-cycles and buses, some carrying banners, others blocking traffic by lying down in the road. Shop-windows were smashed at Glasgow by groups of young people from a new housing estate, apparently without cause. Two rival groups rioted in a London teashop, throwing about crockery and other articles. A gang of youths, armed with knives, iron bars, and bottles, raided a church hall in Finchley, North London, while a dance was in progress. According to the judge who tried them, they behaved in a way that would have brought discredit on a pack of wolves—without even the excuse of being hungry. At another London dance-hall a fight resulted in the death of a young man by stabbing. In a street brawl a newspaper reporter, going to the rescue of an older man, was killed by a teenager. Disturbances at seaside towns in the spring and summer of 1964 caused considerable trouble as gangs fought with bottles, deck-chairs, stones, and rubbish-baskets. Seventy-five young people were arrested at Brighton, forty at Margate, as many more at Clacton where a thousand youths were said to have been involved. "Mentally unstable hooligans" they were called; "petty little sawdust Caesars", finding courage "like rats, by hunting only in packs".

On many occasions trains were damaged by young passengers. On May 18, 1964, for example, an excursion train from Tenby to Swansea arrived at Swansea 110 minutes late with six of its ten coaches damaged. Six windows, twenty-two light bulbs, a door, and two lavatory mirrors had been smashed, and a luggage rack had been pulled away from its fittings. This kind of conduct caused the railway companies to cancel many football excursion trains. In the spring of 1965 a train was de-railed south of London, killing the driver and a passenger and injuring many more: children or young people were held responsible for putting objects on the line, and this whole stretch of railway was feared by drivers as "hooligan mile"; there were many more cases of children either tampering with railway lines or throwing stones or bottles at passing trains, smashing windows and causing other damage. In June 1965 two boys were convicted of putting on a railway line a bar which would have derailed the oncoming train; a month earlier an eleven-year-old boy had admitted trying to wreck an electric train with another eleven-year-old by placing a steel drawer filled with stones, a large porcelain insulator, and some timber on the track at Gospel Oak, near Kentish Town, London. "We wanted to cause an accident", he said.

Punishment ranged from big terms of imprisonment where lives were taken to fines or periods at detention centres. Glasgow authorities decided that an outbreak of window-smashing was due to lack of recreational facilities on new housing estates and decided to build more dance- and concert-halls. The Chief Constable of Southend dealt with rival groups who were disturbing the peace by confiscating the leather belts, generally somewhat prized, of those participating. "They complain", he said, "that they cannot keep their trousers up, but that is their problem entirely." An eighteen-year-old dock-labourer making a nuisance of himself at a football game was put on probation for a year at Glasgow Sheriff Court and made to report each Saturday afternoon at 3.30—so missing the weekly game—but he could be excused if he were going to play football himself on any particular Saturday: a sensible punishment. On a slightly different level, a group of twelve, tough, antisocial council-house tenants were removed to a new estate built in a lonely country area by Richmond Rural District Council, Yorkshire, where the houses were so designed that fittings could not easily be torn out and smashed. "We must do something about this group of families who upset everyone," said a Councillor; "they smash everything possible in a normal house, They are dirty and noisy and give their neighbours no peace. Once they are all together it will be easier to help them. Welfare workers will try to teach them decent habits and any family which improves will be welcomed back to a normal house."

While its resources are taxed to deal with crime and delinquency, society is still left with its unsolved problem: why is crime increasing? Why is juvenile crime in particular increasing? Why, contrary to the previous assumption that poverty is a chief cause of crime, is the affluent society resulting in more crime than ever before? What lies behind the change in moral values? At first the War was held responsible—families broken up, men in the forces, children evacuated, homes bombed. Until the sixties it could be held that the delinquents were the war babies, inheriting their parents' anxieties, suffering from underfeeding in babyhood; then National Service, taking the young men away from the core of life at a critical time, was a cause; then "the bomb" was blamed. Insufficient schooling, too much money, parents away at work, over-indulgent parents, uninterested parents, lack of parental authority, television, "fundamental insecurity", the lack of purpose, have all been cited. The Ingleby Committee remarked that "more desirable objects, greater opportunities for acquiring them illegally, and considerable chances of immunity from the undesirable consequences of so doing"

10*

were a factor.[1] Besides, it pointed out, "it is not always so clearly recognised what a complete change there has been in social and personal relationships (between classes, between the sexes and between individuals) and also in the basic assumptions which regulate behaviour."[2] In other words, uncertainty, lack of continuity, the shifting sands of an expanding and rapidly changing society that not only stimulated but bewildered the young people growing up in it resulted in maladjustment and crime: they needed help, but felt that the guidance they were offered was neither sufficient nor relevant. "Is it that, in the upheaval of social change, the mechanism by which one generation communicates its beliefs and values to the next has broken down? Or is it that we have been a generation without beliefs and values which we thought worth communication?"[3] It is all too likely to be a case of visiting the sins of the fathers upon the children; for what was in their parents' time a beginning of doubt and uncertainty has now become a gigantic question-mark that can obscure all values but the most immediate. The parents can hardly be blamed, for the writing on the wall was far from clear; and there still remained many good causes to support—the status of the trade union, a living wage, socialism, education, missionary work at home and abroad. One of the tragedies of the young is that, at one and the same time, there appear to be fewer causes at hand worth fighting for and greater emphasis on personal acquisition. The young, as Mr Edelman said in the House of Commons, were growing up in a climate of opinion in which acquisition was admitted to be the ultimate goal and acquisitiveness the ultimate virtue. Young people tended to imitate take-over bidders and tycoons, and if they could not achieve their aims legally they turned to delinquency and crime.[4] Our very attempt to be liberal may be defeating its own end. As society sees the causes of crime less in the guilty person and more in his upbringing and circumstances it becomes increasingly difficult to punish, increasingly difficult to focus guilt, and this, in turn, makes it increasingly difficult to know which sanctions operate in society. There are many who would be helped by a sterner code of crime and punishment to keep clear of wrongdoing; many who slip into a life of crime under cover of the feeling that not they, but society, or parents, or circumstance or some psychological aberration is responsible.

And this is true not only of the young. What are their parents' standards and values? Ask any man what he lives by. Not many will go further than being decent to his friends and neighbours, doing a good

1 P. 7.   2 *Ibid.*
3 *Moral Welfare*, editorial, July 1961.   4 April 27, 1964.

turn when he can. Most people do this. And the majority, parents and children, will rise to a crisis with courage and determination. Meanwhile they are too willing to follow the cult of acquisition, the cult of the consumer, the cult of the bigger penny. The bombardment of young people by advertisements of all kinds urging them to buy, the building up of a 'teenage ego' for this sole purpose, is bad in giving them a sense of importance for quite the wrong reasons; they are not asked to do things but to buy things—not to give but to acquire. The spirit of idealism, the desire to help, the thirst for adventure, is strong in all young people, as many spontaneous reactions in schools and homes will testify. That it should be damped down, or diverted, by the immediate ends of an acquisitive society is tragic no less for the young people themselves than for society as a whole. It is ironic that in many respects it is the virtues of the past, turning in on themselves, which have created the present situation; the trade unions' struggle for a better life becomes the cult of acquisition and, as it does so, discards or overrides the very virtues that made this possible.

The cult of acquisition, or the cult of the consumer, easily becomes the pursuit of the vulgar, and "vulgarity, blatant and unashamed, is undeniably a hall-mark of our age".[1] All organs of public opinion help to make this so; they all strive more for effect, and as familiarity dulls the edge of each new gambit the search for means to make an impact exploits new aspects of sex, adventure, crime, and violence. This is true not only of advertisements but of films, plays, novels, the Press, and television. Not only are imaginary situations exploited but privacy is shattered in the glare of television lights or the exposure of newspaper columns. Situations, real and imaginary, are built up with such wealth of superlative that words lose their meaning and the commonplace is vested with such importance that nothing remains with which to describe the truly significant.

> "All words like peace and love,
> All sane affirmative speech
> Has been soiled, profaned, debased,
> To a horrid mechanical screech."[2]

The only answer is to come to terms with affluence by using it to create a counterweight to its own defects. Knowledge, 'learning' in its fullest sense, depends upon wealth and leisure—wealth to provide the tools, leisure the opportunity. In other ages which have been fortunate enough

[1] *The Times*, leading article, May 18, 1964.
[2] W. H. Auden, "Dedication", in *Nones*.

to combine the two a small section of society alone has benefited. An affluent society for the first time gives the opportunity of spreading the benefits of 'culture', which covers the sciences as well as the arts, at the feet of all the people. Unfortunately, distorted by many of the mass media, this wider culture is not always acceptable. Naturally, each generation will make its own choice of values and taste, but a common heritage, freshened by new contributions, provides the stable background to all education. 'Education' is a word often misunderstood, sometimes derided, frequently used in too narrow a context. But it is education, for which the foundation is laid in childhood and youth, but which continues throughout a man's whole life, which is one of the most pressing needs of the affluent society.

CHAPTER XVIII

Culture

"Upon the education of the people of this country the fate of this country depends."

Educational Reconstruction, 1943

". . . the things outside the schools matter even more than the things inside the schools, and govern and interpret the things inside."

Sir Michael Sadler 1900

IN EVERY age there is a general complex of wisdom, learning, understanding, and means of expression that constitutes a way of life, which is the culture of the age. Culture is the outcome of inherited standards, of responses to life, of accumulated knowledge and newly discovered ways of living. It is also a method of passing on standards and ways of life from one generation to the next. In the sense that 'to culture' means to make grow, to cause to develop, or to train in a desired way, so the culture of an age is the chief formative instrument of the age. The culture of an age is what it is, how it thinks, works, plays, how it instructs its citizens, what code of religion or morals it adheres to. There is the unconscious culture that results from the ordinary contacts of daily life and the accepted way of living; there is the consciously imparted culture of the educational system.[1] The two interlock and are interdependent, but the second is influenced by conscious decision more often than the first, which is the outcome of more unknown, unestimated, and unpredictable factors.

One of our greatest educationists believed that "the things outside the schools matter even more than the things inside the schools, and govern and interpret the things inside".[2] In this sense a country, or an age, can

[1] Education is "an instrument for conserving, transmitting, and renewing culture". (M. V. C. Jeffreys, *Glaucon*).

[2] Sir Michael Sadler, *How Far Can We Learn Anything of Practical Value from the Study of Foreign Systems of Education?* (Guildford, 1900), quoted by Vernon Mallinson in *Comparative Education*, p. 1.

only have the education it deserves, and the formative factors in the wider society are as important as anything that is taught in school. For centuries Christianity has been one of the most important of these influences, laying down a code of ethics and setting a standard of conduct that were generally accepted. There were periods of aberration, but the Victorians set Christianity firmly in place as a determinant of morals and arbiter of conduct. Later in the century its tenets appeared to be challenged by advancing science; two world wars shook the Christian Church profoundly, and since the Second War Christianity has become weaker as a moral and social influence. Britain is nominally a Christian country, prayers are said in her Parliament, her monarch rules "by the grace of God" and is expected to be a practising Christian; State schools are required to conduct morning prayer and to instruct such pupils as do not contract out in the rudiments of the Christian religion. Yet, though the country possesses many honoured Christians, churchgoing all over the land has declined; young people, particularly, have deserted church and chapel, and in the ordinary give and take of human relationships there is little public recognition of Christianity as a belief, a creed, or an ethical code. With the decline in churchgoing has come a loosening of some of the standards prescribed by the Christian doctrine. Cause and effect is not easy to determine, but it is at least possible that as "the fathers rejected the doctrine, the children have abandoned the morals"[1]—the fathers and grandfathers who interpreted Darwin and Huxley as giving the lie to the Scriptures have bred children who project the lack of a faith into their whole way of life. Chastity, honesty, truthfulness, integrity, are not the preserves of the Christian way of life but are nevertheless at the core of Christian moral teaching, and it is not far-fetched to see a connection between the growth of crime and sexual promiscuity and the weakening of the formerly accepted standards of the Christian religion.

The Church is aware of its waning influence and in many ways tries to arrest it. A vigorous preacher, a persuasive vicar, can still draw a large congregation; some device particularly attuned to their way of life can bring in young people for a while: a great deal of thought and writing by churchmen tries to sound the national pulse, to make the contact that will be permanent. A small paperback book by a Bishop dealing generally with the problem of Christianity today went into four impressions in less than twelve months,[2] but this showed general interest rather than growing belief, and still the barriers were not down

1 John A. T. Robinson, Bishop of Woolwich, *Honest to God*, p. 106.
2 The Bishop of Woolwich, *Honest to God*.

between the organized Church and the majority of the population. Young people, particularly, remained aloof; the Christian language was not theirs, the ritual was not theirs, there was too much that was unreal, if not hypocritical, in the Church's teaching. Nor was the approach to their fathers any more convincing. Praise for the poor and lowly, the assertion that only the poor can achieve Christian salvation, is not an easy doctrine to convey to a generation many of whom, not without struggle, are for the first time savouring the joys of escape from poverty.

There are, of course, moral codes apart from the Christian that proscribe dishonesty, theft, and violence: many of the atheist or agnostic leaders of the Labour Movement in the nineteenth century expected that the end of class warfare and the recognition of the working-man as a decently paid, respected member of society would automatically open the doors of the New Moral World. That it has not been so may be due to the speed of developing affluence and to society's failure to gear its pattern of culture sufficiently rapidly or with sufficient pertinence to the new conditions.

The organs of public opinion that could help are frequently committed in other directions, or just not equal to their task. The popular Press, in particular, is too concerned with the size of its circulation and its revenue from advertisements to provide a continuing background to the New Moral World. Broadcast and television news, talks, and news programmes are far more suited to a mature society; but radio services are on the air for 20 hours a day, television for 14, and it is not only news and talks that are influential. The quality of much light entertainment is very low, and though some of the drama presented is good some is of poor quality, and in a great deal there is an emphasis upon sex, violence, and perversion. Since it is largely presented at peak listening periods its impact is likely to be large.

The BBC defends itself stoutly against criticism, especially concerning drama. It is part of its policy to present new plays written specially for television by younger British writers "on themes of contemporary relevance" and other plays for the "specialized" viewer of television drama. Criticism, it says, "will not make the BBC abandon its policy of presenting established plays by established playwrights about the problems of sex and violence in human relations, which have been the very stuff of drama since it was first written. Nor will it change the BBC's belief that the serious writers of to-day must be allowed to say freely what they feel about the society in which they live." The BBC concedes, however, that "if, by accident or inadequate planning, it allows plays of a certain type to be bunched together so as to create an impression of nihilism and ugliness in its own approach to life, then that is a fault which can and must be remedied. If at any time there is too gross or too intimate a presentation of sex on the screen this too is something which should be corrected. This is not the same thing as ignoring the realities of sex and violence."[1]

If the axe were wielded too drastically television drama would become merely an emasculated version of the real-life stuff performed in the live theatre. Yet the effects of crime and violence in general, and particularly in programmes which children are likely to see, are open to considerations other than those of literary merit. There might well be a case for cutting down sex and violence on the television screen on the grounds that it is better contained in a theatre, which is consciously sought by its patrons, than projected into a family circle.

With almost 90 per cent of the population having television in their homes and possibly 75 per cent using their sets each day for one or more of the BBC or ITA programmes,[2] television is bound to be influential in determining values and impressing beliefs as much in what is taken for granted as in what is projected. At the same time it inculcates certain attitudes of life. Viewing, particularly, helps to emphasize the vicarious, already a marked feature of modern life: in place of activity on the games field the seat at the stadium; in place of the journey to the ground the seat before the small screen; in place of the rough-and-tumble of the hustings the close-up of the politician, in place of the political meeting or the WEA class the recorded discussion of experts. In pretended real-life serials that continue week after week the characters become confounded with reality, and television 'personalities' in their real or assumed roles become national figures. The viewer participates only as he watches and listens. He cannot interrupt or ask a question, nor will his emotional reactions be heard. It is a passive participation, a one-way relationship stimulating or refreshing in small doses but not food to build up a complete man. At the same time repeated emotional stimulants dull the appreciation of the real and the ordinary and lend to sensationalism a false merit. A fantasy world is easy to slip into, particularly if work is monotonous and undemanding and when there is no preparation in training or education to encourage reflection. In all that has been said about the British people and their failure to wake up to the urgency of the economic situation, in the repeated failure of politicians of all parties, or of

---

[1] *Annual Report of the British Broadcasting Corporation*, 1963–64, pp. 22–23.
[2] *Annual Report of the British Broadcasting Corporation*, 1963–64, p. 44. And see *infra*, Appendix B XV.

leaders in any sphere, to strike fire from what was, after all, very good tinder a decade or two ago, it might be well to ask what dampening effect, what sapping of energy and initiative, is attributable to the fantasy world of the television set?

Rather different is the role of the BBC as direct teaching adjunct: some 8000 schools were equipped with television sets in 1964, and 70 sound programmes a week were listened to by about 30,000 schools. There are excellent further-education programmes on both television and radio and talk of "a University of the Air" which will take viewers forward to a full university degree.[1] Broadcast or televised aids to lessons actively conducted by a teacher, and still under the control of a teacher, who remains the projector, the giver of the lesson, are of great value. But once the teacher takes a passive role, if he throws his whole lesson into the ambit of the small screen or the microphone, then something intrinsically valuable has gone from the teaching function. The same applies to a University of the Air. It can with advantage be a temporary expedient or a clearly defined adjunct to the real process of learning which goes on in an institution where real people rub shoulders and strike sparks from themselves and their tutors. The trouble is that what starts as an aid too quickly becomes the master. How far are we prepared to substitute the individuality, the idiosyncrasy, the driving force, the affection for their work and for their pupils of hundreds of thousands of teachers of all grades from primary schools to post-graduate institutions for the ministrations of the disembodied voice, the face on the screen? A shortage of teachers of all grades, a shortage of buildings, of libraries, of equipment, makes the answer not quite certain.[2]

The State influences the arts indirectly through its ultimate control of broadcasting and television, through its use of the official censorship, and through laws relating to slander and libel, blasphemy, obscenity, and indecency. It has also felt it necessary to take a more positive interest in the fine arts in particular, and in 1946 the Arts Council was given a Royal Charter for developing "a greater knowledge, under-standing and practice of the fine arts". Small sums of money were dispersed through it to help the Covent Garden Opera and Ballet, Sadler's Wells theatre, the Welsh and Scottish National Opera Com-panies, several orchestras and picture galleries, the Royal Shakespeare Company, the Edinburgh Festival, and other bodies. The grant has been increased from time to time, and in 1964 the Labour Government appointed a junior Minister to take charge of its Arts and Culture policy

---

[1] *A University of the Air*, February 1966, Cmnd. 2922.
[2] See Appendix B XV, for analysis of programme output, BBC and ITV.

and to spread benefits more widely, particularly in the provinces, than previously. A National Theatre has been founded, with a site earmarked on London's south bank, but Britain is still behind many Continental cities and countries who more fully subsidize their opera, ballet, and theatre.

A fundamental, if not more immediate, influence on culture is provided by the schools.

The right to organized education has been one of the most keenly fought and most cherished prizes of the working classes; every section of the British working-class movement since the Industrial Revolution has claimed the right to education, and has ascribed to it a remedial quality that would help the worker to better his own material condition, raise his class socially, and introduce justice and humanity over the land. Before the State provided education for all its children the ranks of the working class were brightened by men like Francis Place, William Lovett, Thomas Cooper, who, after days of incredible toil, educated themselves to an extent not always equalled by a university student a hundred years later. The belief in education as a philosopher's stone was naïve, at times pathetic, and could be profoundly humiliating to those to whom formal education came as a right, and yet it has proved a mighty warrior for the working classes, and as a social leveller is matched only by wealth.

Before the Industrial Revolution swamped them there existed grammar schools in some parts of the country that had been founded centuries earlier by private benefaction for the education in Latin and Greek grammar of the poor boys of the district. By the beginning of the nineteenth century most of these had become fee-paying schools, a few had become known as the public schools and were the preserve of the rich. Because they still specialized in Latin and Greek there were shortly to rise by their side new foundations endowed by the newly rich middle classes who required for their sons an education less strictly based upon the classics.

None of these schools were for the children of the poor. But by the end of the eighteenth century many factors—a growing population, the rise of industrialism, humanitarianism, the desire to instruct the poor in the principles of religion, and a degree of common sense—had resulted also in various kinds of private school for the poor. There were schools run by religious societies, schools run cheaply by profit-making concerns (also closely associated with religious teaching), and simple little 'dame' schools—a valuable legacy of earlier times.

The pressures of the growing population, a perception of the benefits of a rudimentary education in its citizens, together with the exhortations of religious bodies, Radicals, and Utilitarians, as well as the need of the private education societies for more money than their pupils could afford to pay, at last led the Government to provide in 1833 a grant of £20,000 towards education. It was for building purposes only, and could be given only to a school which had itself raised 50 per cent of such expenses. From this small beginning, a century and a half ago, began the progress towards the expenditure in 1953–54 of £470 million on education and in 1965 of £1567 million. Progress was slow until the First World War. Not until 1880 was universal, compulsory, whole-time education achieved, and then it covered only children from five years old to thirteen. The First World War was a liberalizing factor, as it was with all the social services, and in 1918 the school-leaving age was raised to fourteen. There was much educational discussion between the Wars, and the school-leaving age was to have been further raised to fifteen from September 1, 1939. The outbreak of war prevented this, but committees were considering education throughout the War. Reports on *The Curriculum and Examinations in Secondary Schools*[1] and on *The Public Schools and the General Education System*[2] were produced before the War was over, and the Coalition Government, as part of its reconstruction policy, in 1943 published *Educational Reconstruction*.[3] Upon this was built an Education Act which, with the support of all parties, became law in 1944, a year before the German war was over; it was the first of the Government's measures of social reform.

The Education Act of 1944 replaced the old Board of Education by a Ministry of Education, the Minister's duties being "to promote the education of the people of England and Wales and the progressive development of institutions devoted to that purpose, and to secure the effective execution by local authorities, under his control and direction, of the national policy for providing a varied and comprehensive educational service in every area". It re-enacted the compulsion to keep a child at school until it was fifteen years old and spoke of the desirability of extending the school-leaving age to sixteen. The "varied and comprehensive educational service" which the local education authorities were expected to supply was to cover the whole period from five to fifteen or sixteen, with extensions downward in the form of nursery schools and upward in the form of county colleges which would provide part-time education until eighteen. "The statutory system of public education",

[1] The Norwood Committee, 1943.   [2] The Fleming Committee, 1944.
[3] Cmd. 6458.

ran the Act, "shall be organised in three progressive stages to be known as primary education, secondary education, and further education; and it shall be the duty of the local education authority for every area, so far as their powers extend, to contribute towards the spiritual, moral, mental, and physical development of the community by securing that efficient education throughout those stages shall be available to meet the needs of the population of their area." It was a liberal conception of education.

Of the three stages of education, primary was to continue until the age of eleven, and thereafter there was to be a division of education according to the abilities, aptitudes, and leanings of the child. Support for such a division at the secondary school stage came from many well-known educationists and teachers. A Committee under the charmanship of Sir Henry Hadow had published reports on *The Education of the Adolescent* in 1926.[1] After weighing much evidence they had come to the conclusion that a break in the educational process at the age of eleven was to be recommended and that children of that age should be drafted to new schools which might be a grammar-school type or such combination of the academic and the technical as suited those who were not so academically minded. The recommendations of the Hadow Report were only partly put into operation, but a Committee under Mr Will Spens, which reported in 1938,[2] gave further thought to the matter, and so did the Norwood Committee.[3] Both Reports agreed with the Hadow break at eleven plus and a threefold division thereafter. Those who drew up the White Paper on *Educational Reconstruction* and those who drafted the Education Act of 1944 were not, therefore, innovators when they decided upon a tripartite division of secondary education.

The division was to take the form of grammar, modern[4] (or secondary modern), and technical schools; the grammar school was to continue in the best tradition of the grammar schools and leading secondary schools of the country in providing the best possible form of academic instruction; the technical schools were to combine a general education with instruction of a practical kind; the secondary moderns were to provide an education which, although not technical, was more general than that of the grammar schools. Each was thought to have its value;

---

[1] *Report of the Consultative Committee of the Board of Education on the Education of the Adolescent*, December 1926 (H.M.S.O.).

[2] *Report of the Consultative Committee of the Board of Education on Secondary Education* (H.M.S.O.).

[3] *Supra*, p. 295.   [4] The term used by the Hadow Report.

it was a question of choice and ability; a "parity of esteem" was intended and expected.

It was clear that there would have to be some method of selection, apart from the unlikely possibility of all children wanting to do that course of study where their aptitudes lay and where school places permitted. But the degree of friction, worry, and unhappiness with which the whole process of transition was accompanied could hardly have been foreseen. A simple examination was instituted to try to separate at the age of eleven the children academically brightest from the rest. It was not always so difficult to find out which children were technically minded, and these went to the technical schools. But there developed a rising competition for the grammar school, and the secondary modern came to be regarded as a very much less than second best not only in itself but because it marked the children who attended it as less able and because it became increasingly clear that it led to a poorer career: the intended "parity of esteem", in short, never existed. Dissatisfaction with the secondary modern was accompanied by a growing dissatisfaction with the method of selection. So, regardless of the fact that secondary moderns have sometimes been developing sufficiently to give their best pupils the equivalent of a grammar-school education, the 'eleven-plus' has become increasingly the villain of the educational scene. To grade a child at eleven, runs the argument, is unreal, impossible, and will always result in many misplacements; there may be 'good' years and 'bad' years affecting the quality of the intake to the grammar schools; some counties are better placed for providing grammar-school places than others; and, above all, a child's potential ability changes from eleven to thirteen, from thirteen to fifteen; there are slow developers right up to university age; there are bright children, good examinees, who never afterwards make real solid progress.

Not many people spoke for the actual eleven-plus method of testing, even of those who supported the tripartite division of secondary education, and there were several attempts to amend it. The original written examination, comprising simple papers in English and arithmetic, did not take account of a child's 'intelligence', as opposed to what it had learned, and involved the possibility of luck in the questions, and it was therefore supplemented by the 'intelligence test'. But methods of answering intelligence-test questions, it was found, could be learned and developed into a technique imparted by primary schools anxious to get the best results; so primary-school education in its final stages could be warped by the shadow of the intelligence test. School reports were then added to the sorting media, but had many obvious disadvantages besides adding considerably to the work of the primary-school staff. Some people preferred a test and a break in the educational process at thirteen, but were faced with the same difficulties of selection. But, whatever sorting method was devised, it was clear that many parents would continue to feel themselves and their children cheated out of the best possible education by the results of little more than one day's testing. There was, in addition, a widely held belief that more children from middle-class homes were likely to have the background that made them good examinees at eleven than children from working-class homes. And so—in spite of the hope of *Educational Reconstruction* that diversifying education would not "impair the social unity within the educational system but would open the way to a more closely knit society"—it did, in fact, appear to create a class division of society based upon the schools, and the 'eleven-plus' came into the political arena as a weapon of 'left' against 'right'.

If the eleven-plus remained a bad method of selection and no better could be devised, it was still possible to make adjustments to the secondary schools themselves to improve matters. Many hoped that the secondary modern would take bright pupils into sixth-form work and send an increasing number on to the universities, while a fluidity between grammar school and secondary modern would correct wrong drafting and make adjustments according to a child's development. *Educational Reconstruction* had hoped that this would happen—"it would be wrong to suppose they will necessarily remain separate and apart"—and by the sixties it appeared that good progress was being made in both these directions, except that it was far more difficult to correct a too high grading than to upgrade a too low one. At the same time a process known as 'streaming' was combining in one school more than one type of pupil. So, besides grammar, secondary modern, and technical schools there were coming into existence bilateral schools, which provided two of the main types of education in separate streams, and multilateral schools, which provided three of the main types in separate streams.

There was also developing the comprehensive school. Its distinguishing feature was that it collected all the secondary pupils in a district, regardless of their ability and without qualifying examination, and classified or 'streamed' them within the same school into a varying number of groups. There were variations upon this theme. The comprehensive school could cater in one unit for the whole ability range and the whole age range of a district from eleven to eighteen; it could split at fourteen into upper and lower schools, the upper only becoming selective; it could rely on a kind of district sixth-form college to cater for pupils staying on beyond sixteen, and itself concentrate upon the younger children; and various other permutations were possible on the main theme that education should not divide at the age of eleven-plus into self-contained units.

The comprehensive school has been accepted as the alternative to the tripartite division at eleven-plus, and has focused all the dissatisfaction felt over secondary education since the War—with the examination, the schools, or selection at eleven. The Labour Party's Election Manifesto of 1964 made it clear that they stood for the comprehensive system. The Labour Government, calling the existing system 'separatism', announced at the end of 1964 that "we ought now to accept that the reorganisation of secondary education on comprehensive lines should be national policy".[1] "It is the Government's policy", said the Secretary of State for Education and Science at the end of 1964, "to reorganise secondary education on comprehensive lines."[2] Many education authorities were already abolishing the eleven-plus and establishing comprehensive schools or preparing to do so. In 1964 there were some 189 comprehensives in England and Wales, and 39 local education authorities had some secondary-school provision of a comprehensive type.[3] The Secretary of State claimed that nearly two-thirds of the secondary-school population was already living in the areas of authorities who were either implementing or making plans for such reorganization.[4] In general, he said, entry to grammar schools would no longer be restricted to certain selected children at the age of eleven plus, and the range of studies would be greatly expanded. It would be the aim of Government policy, he added, to preserve what was valued in grammar-school education for those who now received it and to make it available for more children.[5]

The establishment of a comprehensive school generally means the merging of local grammar and modern schools into the new unit. The new school has to show, therefore, both that it is able to give the apparently less bright children the chance of achieving the best, and that it can cater for the full development of those who are brighter or quicker. The process of streaming usually divides children into blocks

[1] November 27, 1964, House of Commons (Hansard, fifth series, vol. 702, c. 1785).

[2] November 12, 1964, House of Commons (*ibid,,* vol. 701, c. 1177).

[3] Michael Stewart, November 12, 1964 (*ibid.,* vol. 701, c. 1180).

[4] November 27, 1964 (*ibid.,* vol. 702, c. 1784).

[5] November 12, 1964, *ibid.*

of varying ability. The division is still in some cases made on the basis of an eleven-plus examination, sometimes in accordance with school reports; in other cases testing within the comprehensive school occurs on entry, or after one, two, or three years without streaming. The practice of 'setting' is also growing, which streams a child not according to his general intelligence but according to his ability in various subjects. Streaming is the more static conception, for while children can and do change from one group to another there is likely to remain a core who do not move and who give stability to the whole stream. The danger that in this way a group loyalty might develop is being met by systems of 'houses', which will bring children together on a different basis. Setting would almost seem to go to the opposite extreme of too much restless change between group and group, and the more efficient the setting process the more unsettling it is likely to be, the fewer firm contacts a child is likely to make with pupils or staff. But, at bottom, streaming and setting will achieve their ends only if there is sufficient fluidity between streams and if there is sufficient incentive to make for the top stream. An easier option may well be preferred by a child in a comprehensive school who would have given his best in a grammar school.

There is also the question of size. For the administrator large units of 2000 or more are very tempting. Financially they are economic and can afford superior equipment; but to maintain personal relations between staff and pupils and to evolve sufficiently flexible timetables requires very considerable skills. The Headmaster perforce has to become primarily an administrator, teaching becomes more difficult and more involved with other problems and the pupil is bound to suffer. Some Education Authorities, realizing the danger, have put a limit on size, but protagonists of the comprehensive system are not afraid of schools of 2000.[1] The question of buildings alone should impose a brake. A comprehensive school consisting of three separate buildings widely separated is merely paying lip-service to comprehensiveness. The true comprehensive will be purpose-built, and as a physical background to school life the large buildings necessary for large numbers are likely, on grounds of cost, to be uniform; and large, uniform buildings are not the best containers of young school life. Meanwhile, among the staff, administration will proliferate, and the sheer difficulty of controlling a large unit will tend to stereotype instruction and standardize the school framework, leaving too little opportunity for individuality or idiosyncrasy. These are trends already too apparent in the whole educational process, exacerbated by the exami-

[1] See Robin Pedley, *The Comprehensive School*, pp. 82–84 and 201–208.

nations system and by the increasing use of broadcasting and television in school curricula. In 1964 a working party of the newly formed Schools Council was considering broadly the question of the school syllabus and of school teaching. They reported that the schools, and particularly the secondary schools, were finding that "the opportunity for independent initiative and experiment is being reduced by a complex of decisions and pressures which they cannot sufficiently control or influence. They consider . . . that the underlying trend is towards an excessive standardization of their work, and away from that variety of syllabus content and teaching method which is desirable if our educational system is to be in any real sense alive."[1] A new type of school must mitigate, not exaggerate, these weaknesses in the educational system, and it still remains for the comprehensive school to make a case for something better than diversity in diverse institutions.

Meanwhile, however, the Secretary of State for Education issued a general request to local authorities in July 1965 to prepare in twelve months a general statement of long-term proposals and by September 1967 a detailed statement of plans for the following three years. "The request was made in accordance with the Government's declared objective of ending selection at the age of eleven-plus and of abolishing separatism in secondary education" it was stated.[2] It is not surprising that the prospect of such a radical revolution caused considerable concern in the grammar schools. Among them were old-established schools like Manchester and Bristol Grammar Schools, who had among the finest academic records in the country. Submerged in the new comprehensives they would lose their identity. Could their academic standards be maintained when they were merged in larger and more amorphous units? Were the best educational interests of the country being sacrificed to political interests? Impressive protest meetings were held by parents' associations, massive petitions were submitted. Educationists were divided; but in some areas at least politics seemed to dominate the issue.

It was not unreasonable to maintain that the Labour Government was attempting to go too far too fast. What was needed was a thorough-going report analysing mistakes and successes. More also needed to be known about the various forms that the comprehensive school could take. Strong arguments could be made, for instance, both for and against the sixth-form college which would concentrate the sixteens to eighteens of a whole district. But the arguments needed to be tested in practice,

[1] *Report of the Working Party under Sir John Lockwood*, March 1964.
[2] Circular 10/65; *Education in 1965, Report of the Department of Education and Science.*

and as yet there had been virtually no practice and nothing to disprove what a Committee of the Ministry of Education said in 1958: "whatever the local pattern may be, not even a comprehensive school is likely to be able to satisfy all the varied demands which may properly be made by seventeen-year-old boys and girls. Nor, if it could, is it . . . wise to have only one place in which a seventeen-year-old can get full time education. Freedom to choose the institution as well as freedom to choose a course is important to teenagers and their parents."[1] Freedom of choice supposes parity of esteem, because otherwise there is no choice. It also supposes a method of selection combined with the choice, and it leaves open the question of age—at which point in a child's life the choice is to be made. There are, indeed, many problems still to consider; and, in spite of the increasing pressure of economic considerations upon the question of choice, it remains true that children are "individual human beings and the primary concern of the schools should not be with the living they will earn but with the life they will lead".[2]

In general, we are faced with one of the most important educational issues of the century. Already it is apparent that there are several alternatives to the system established by the Education Act of 1944. Some of these are to be found in trends already developing, others in experiments in existing schools. Yet, without waiting for a sufficient number of reports to come in, before the results of existing comprehensive schools have been determined, and in the absence of any major Report on the whole subject, not only are local education authorities making widespread changes that jeopardize the position of grammar schools which provide an education comparable with the best in any country, but the Government has made a statement of official support. In an age which proliferates committees such precipitate action is difficult to understand and lays the Government open to the charge of political expediency rather than of sober educational reform.

The Education Act of 1944 made little difference to the position of the independent and fee-paying schools, and they still remain within the system, from public schools to small prep schools and covering a wide range of educational establishments of varying size, fee, efficiency, denomination, and endowment. All are now subject to inspection of one kind or another. In the drive towards a classless educational system the public schools in particular remain an embarrassment. Following the report of the Fleming Committee, they offered 25 per cent of their

---

[1] *Report of the Crowther Committee, of the Central Advisory Council for Education*, H.M.S.O., 1959.
[2] *Ibid.*

places to local authorities, hoping to achieve a wider social mixture, but the local authorities have been unwilling to pay high fees when a perfectly good education was available at their own grammar schools. The public schools have therefore remained a class institution, producing a privileged class separated from the main stream of national education. If their standards were as unsatisfactory as their more bitter opponents would like to believe there would be no serious problem. But many of them have outstanding academic records, and in general they command a hard-working loyalty from their staff which is not easily matched.

The school population is growing rapidly. In 1962 there were over 2 million more children on the registers of maintained schools in England and Wales than there were when the 1944 Act was passed, and by 1964 there was a total of 7 million. In Scotland there were 893,000, in Northern Ireland 300,000. The supply of teachers does not keep pace. To help meet the immediate post-War shortage teachers were recruited by a scheme of shortened post-War training courses; but industry and other professions were attractive and, generally speaking, offered higher monetary reward than teaching, especially to the more highly trained graduate. Various campaigns to persuade married women to return to teaching helped, particularly in the graduate section, but in 1964 the total of 280,000 teachers in maintained primary and secondary schools in England and Wales was not adequate; nor the 40,000 in Scotland nor 11,000 in Northern Ireland. As with teachers, so with school buildings: since the War there has been a constant struggle to keep up the supply against competing demand. A shortage of teachers spells oversize classes; this, with inadequate buildings, affects the quality of work done. At the same time increasing pressures from outside are affecting the content of school teaching and subjecting the syllabus to constant strain. On the one hand is the continuing plea for a liberal education, on the other for the science, mathematics, and economics that society needs immediately. The requirements of University Entrance Examinations encourage specialization in sixth forms, and the course of study that produces the 'full man' often runs counter to that which will make a university man. Questions of syllabus, teaching methods, and examinations are constantly under review—for example, by a Curriculum Studies Group of the Ministry of Education—while a Secondary Schools Examination Council, which in 1964 became the Schools Council, has conducted many inquiries on various aspects of teaching.

Consideration was meanwhile being given to two unfulfilled provisions of the 1944 Act: the raising of the school-leaving age to sixteen and the provision of county colleges for compulsory part-time education to the age of eighteen. A Committee of the Central Advisory Council for Education, which reported in 1959, advocated the immediate implementation of both provisions,[1] and the raising of the school-leaving age was again recommended by a similar committee which reported in 1963.[2] In 1964 the year 1970 was given as the date for raising the school-leaving age, but the provision of county colleges still lagged. So, while the country was becoming increasingly concerned with the teenager, and in particular with the young delinquent, one of the possible antidotes was lacking. A hopeful sign was the rising popularity of technical colleges, which in many ways took the place of county colleges, except that attendance was not obligatory. Young people leaving school at fifteen or sixteen are finding in 'the tech' their own people's university, all the more valued because they found it, and are creating it, themselves. With its own common-rooms, societies, and corporate life it creates a kind of non-residential university that has the two facets of day and evening life, courses of work that range from dressmaking to preparation for external university degrees and a wide age-range. It takes full-time students, part-time students, day students, evening students, students released from industry under the Industrial Training Act of 1964 for vocational courses, students sent under day-release schemes to add to an education cut short at the earliest possible age, students taking 'sandwich courses' of possibly a year's duration in the course of a working career. The adult education classes sponsored by the Workers' Educational Association and the extramural departments of universities also continue to increase, the 137,000 students in England and Wales in 1953 rising to 212,000 in 1964. The increase, however, was mainly in yearly and terminal courses, the more ambitious three-year tutorial courses dropping in number from 936 to 697.

With the State increasingly willing to give grants for higher education, with a constantly rising demand from industry and the professions for more highly trained recruits, the pressure upon university places was greater than the existing institutions could stand. Older universities expanded, took in more students; by 1960 eight new universities had been established, seven of them since the War.[3] But still Britain was not keeping pace either with the advances in learning or with the

[1] *The Crowther Report*, 1959.
[2] *The Newsome Report: Half our Future*, 1963.

[3]

Name	Founded	Full univ.	Name	Founded	Full univ.
Reading	1902	1926	Exeter	1922	1955
Nottingham	1881	1948	Leicester	1918	1957
Southampton	1902	1952	Keele	1949	1962
Hull	1927	1954			

Sussex was founded as a full university in 1961.

progress of other countries. In particular she lagged in the training that affected her production and her exports. To examine the situation a committee was appointed in December 1960, under the chairmanship of Lord Robbins, with the particular task of reviewing the pattern of full-time higher education in Great Britain. The emphasis by this time was increasingly upon education as a national asset, and the Robbins Report, published in October 1963, was outspoken: "Both in general cultural standards and in competitive intellectual power, vigorous action is needed to avert the danger of a serious relative decline in this country's standing." The first essential was an expansion far greater than hitherto. By 1980–81 there should be 560,000 students in full-time higher education in Great Britain; in the short run there should be a short-term, emergency programme which would increase existing plans by 10 per cent and provide about 390,000 places in 1973–74. To this end the foundation of six additional new universities was recommended, besides the six already in process of formation,[1] and as well as the further expansion of existing ones, and the promotion to technological universities of four of the most important Colleges of Advanced Technology and the establishment of one new one. It was an ambitious programme, which perhaps erred on the side of piping too much training into a university mould and not encouraging a parity of esteem in other institutions of higher training, and it involved heavy expenditure which might mean spending less on other forms of education. The Newsome Report, for example, eloquently pleading for the children in the secondary modern schools—*Half Our Future* in the words of the title of the Report—had asked for more money to be spent on building and equipment for the teaching of these thirteen-to-sixteen-year-olds at almost the same time as Robbins was asking for more money for university education. The Robbins proposals were also likely to bring about a drain of teachers, particularly the urgently needed sixth-form specialists and the scientists, from the schools to the universities. The stocking of libraries would be difficult and costly. The plans would, in short, be a heavy strain upon the expanding economy and one impossible to bear if a recession set in. Yet a recession was one of the very things that university expansion would guard against. With curricula directed more to the sciences and to technology, with more students receiving a broader education for their first degrees, with technical and scientific subjects linked to a related social subject, and with more students proceeding to post-graduate work, it was expected that a pool of intellect would be provided that might avert the danger foreseen by the

[1] Sited at Canterbury, Colchester, Coventry, Lancaster, Norwich, York. *Higher Education* (the Robbins Report), Table 3, p. 15, Cmnd. 2154.

Report "of a serious relative decline" in the country's standing. The Government was in no two minds, and in the very month that the Robbins Report was published agreed with its principle that courses of higher education should be available for all those who wished to pursue them and were qualified by ability and attainment to do so, and accepted its specific proposals.[1]

The business world was meanwhile calling for people better equipped in business management, in salesmanship, in retailing. Never before had Britain taken the problem of education so seriously, nor interpreted the word so widely. The first Report of the National Economic Development Council had advocated business schools.[2] Now, following the report of a Committee under Lord Franks[3] and a further report by a working party to examine the cost,[4] the Secretary of State for Education announced in May 1964 that the Government was prepared to share with business the provision of the capital and recurrent expenditure on two new business schools within the framework of future university programmes. One was to be associated with the London School of Economics and the Imperial College of Science and Technology, the other with Manchester University.

The University Grants Committee, meantime, had appointed a committee under Sir Edward Hale to examine university teaching in relation to the pressures being put upon it by the all-round expansion. If the standard of teaching were to be maintained, it reported, "with no more than legitimate claims on national revenue and on the limited pool of ability, ways will have to be found of making better use of university buildings and plant and of the time of university teachers".[5] The universities, in short, had to face teaching problems similar to those of the schools and complicated by even heavier administrative duties; the older universities had to decide how they could continue the highly prized tutorial method of teaching with its close contact between teacher and taught and its heavy demands on teaching time.

Nursery and primary schools, the education of the very young, has—as the Report of the Education Department for 1964 pointed out—for many years had its educationists, its books, its theories, and its precepts. Now, it seems, higher education is to have its turn. The needs of industry, new technological and scientific knowledge, must be assessed, the old teaching revalued, the relationship between specialization and a general education affirmed, a new synthesis produced. While economic

---

[1] Cmnd. 2165.   [2] *Conditions Favourable to Further Growth*, April 1963.

[3] *British Business Schools* (British Institute of Management, November 1963).

[4] Lord Normanbrook, *British Business Schools: The Cost* (British Institute of Management, March 1964).

[5] *Report of the Committee on University Teaching Methods* (H.M.S.O., 1964).

demands must seem more immediately urgent than the content of a poem, doing more vital than contemplating, the man of action more useful than the man of consideration, and while it may seem that we are on the verge of a reversal of our traditional values, it must clearly remain a duty of the educational process to carry on the best traditions of a liberal education as well as to instruct in the sciences. But there comes a point when any load becomes too heavy—whether it is the straw that breaks the camel's back or the extra subject pushed into the curriculum. The weight of many centuries' accumulated knowledge is itself heavy; combined with the rapidly growing bulk of scientific learning and increased specialization, one person's life becomes too short to carry it all.

Education was formerly shaped by an aristocratic society; it was taken over by a middle class which, as well as using the traditional aristocratic forms, founded its own schools, and now it becomes, in the true sense of the word, popular. The right to vote presupposes the ability to judge an argument, to weigh conflicting statements, and democracy and education have gone together. Twice, at least, education has become associated with the national balance sheet and industrial prosperity—at the time of the Great Depression a hundred years ago, and in our own day. In the sixties of the nineteenth century Great Britain was accused of failing to use the trained chemist and the scientist, of falling behind her Continental competitors through a neglect of technical education, and the same solutions were offered, and accepted, as now—more commercial, technical, and scientific education. Then the Technical Instruction Act of 1889 authorized the levy of a penny rate to aid technical education under the supervision of the Science and Art Department founded in 1851; now, besides sanctioning the expansion envisaged by the Robbins Report and the raising of the school-leaving age to sixteen, the Government, in April 1964, adapted the administrative framework of the educational system to meet the new requirements. The Minister of Education became the Secretary of State for Education and Science with two distinct administrative units under his unifying authority—one for the schools of England and Wales, one for civil science and the universities over the whole of Great Britain, the Secretary of State for Scotland retaining separate control of Scottish schools. In the Labour Government of October 1964 there was created, in addition, a separate Ministry of Technology. With machinery adapted to the new age and, it would seem, the determination to implement the new decisions, it only remains to ask: have we, now that we have the resources at our command, the ability to propound a continuing formula for the Good Education?

CHAPTER XIX

Conclusion?

"The merging of opposites is completion".
James Stephens, *The Crock*
of Gold

THAT WE stand on the threshold of another industrial revolution has so often been said that the significance of the words tends to be lost. Yet undoubtedly we are at the beginning of a major break-through into new fields where cybernetics, nuclear power, and the conquest of space will give an entirely new aspect to man's relationship to his material resources and to his environment. Far-reaching social changes and an unparalleled growth in the size and complexity of the economic system multiply the problems to be solved. The Labour Government returned in March 1966 had a large enough majority to give it five clear years of power in which to try.

When Labour came to power in 1945 it was still an Opposition Government, a revolutionary Government, in spite of a wide area of agreement with other Parties, marching to office with the Red Flag flying over the ranks of the poor and dispossessed. In the years ahead the area of difference will be much smaller, the Government's margin of choice will be narrower, and the Labour Government will find itself in the position of doing what, by and large, any other Government would be bound to do. What it has to show is that it can do it better.

A major problem for any Government is size. Leviathan has never more aptly portrayed our society than now, and never before has the difficulty of propelling him one way been more apparent. Delegation in the form of a proliferation of committees, deputation in the form of regional and advisory bodies, the calling for reports—too many to be digested or acted upon—the inability to find Parliamentary time to discuss Bills adequately or to get through the increasing number that modern government requires are signs of overburdened government. To maintain the forms of democracy in these circumstances is increasingly difficult. The raising of the M.P.'s salary by the Labour Government enables him to make a full-time career of Parliament. But, with Governments anxious to get through as much business as possible and the Party whips constantly vigilant, his accountability for his trust can become little more than following his Party machine, and the exercise of democracy a somewhat infrequent exercise of putting a X on a ballot paper.

A common feature of the Western world is the emergence of the working classes as a powerful group, still distinguishable, yet not sharply defined from the rest of society. In Britain a parallel can be made with the rise of the middle classes in the nineteenth century. But there are many differences in development. The middle classes used economic strength to achieve political power. The working classes had already won the forms of political democracy when they began to rise in the economic scale, and, using the two together, they are achieving political and economic power simultaneously. This comes about through no forcible overthrow of either the aristocratic or the middle-class state, but rather as a general fusion of the three classes that comprise it, helped by the media of mass culture, universal education, and a spreading affluence. So the working classes come to power as Britain becomes increasingly one society. And as other groups have given their names to other periods of history because they are characteristic of it, so might the working classes give their name as subtitle to the era we shall know as the Welfare State—except that the working classes are changing their nature even as we think of appending their signature to an Age. If present trends continue the old classes will merge and the old dichotomy will have no meaning as the rise of the working classes is followed, not by the Age of the Working Classes, but by the classless society.

In politics such fusion is apparent in the underlying agreement on most issues of all three political parties as well as in the mixed-class membership shown particularly in the Labour Party. While government tends to become a changing amalgam of all the talents, and changes of name make little difference in fundamental policy, in economic affairs the mixed membership of the Boards of nationalized industries, in private industry an increasing infiltration of working-class directors, and a wider spread of shareholding among all classes diffuse real power.

In a society where sharp differences of income, of status, or of power become less pronounced the role of working-class organization, which for two centuries has been a thread running through social and economic history, is bound to change. Co-operation and the Co-operative store are less important in saving money, less vital as a means of replacing

11+

capitalist ownership by ownership of the people. The local Labour Party still serves its purpose of proposing and returning Members to Parliament, but has lost the impetus the poor man gave it of an organization of social justice. It exists rather as a party-political machine no different from the other two party-political machines, spending money as freely, using the same 'capitalist' tools to achieve its ends. The national Labour Party, the object of these exertions, has grown through two world wars and a century of devoted service from its members to become Her Majesty's Government, still carrying in its constitution the objective of common ownership of the means of production but making use of no fundamentally new concept in the government of the country.

The trade unions remain the most immediately class-conscious of the working-class organizations, but suffer from a disrupting dichotomy. They can see that their interest lies with the developing economy and wish to identify themselves with the Welfare State, particularly when a Labour Government is in office. At the same time they still feel the worker-employer conflict as the reality of the situation, whoever holds the political reins and whatever form the State may take. One of the grave question-marks which hang over the Affluent Society is whether, and for how long, and on what terms, the trade unions will agree to subordinate this issue. The failure of the voluntary incomes policy was a blow to the Government. The six months' compulsory prices and incomes standstill from July 1966 was followed by a "period of severe restraint" for the first six months of 1967.[1] Together with the Selective Employment Tax, "the freeze" led to short time, redundancy, and unemployment. Redundancy and unemployment pay helped to soften the impact, and politicians promised that a better distribution of the labour force would result, but to avoid disaster the Government needed the full collaboration of the trade unions. The role of these bodies in the changing society was meanwhile still being considered by the Royal Commission, and amalgamations and take-over bids were changing the nature of ownership, at one and the same time spreading it more widely and yet concentrating enormous economic power, and very big fortunes, in fewer hands.

If post-War Britain is to be called, even by way of subtitle, the Age of the Working Classes, we may well ask what distinguishing mark it is likely to leave upon its time. It is too early to make a full assessment. The

---

[1] *Prices and Incomes Standstill*, July 1966 (Cmnd. 3073). *Prices and Incomes Standstill, Period of Severe Restraint*, November 1966 (Cmnd. 3150).

Age will certainly be remembered for its social legislation, for a continued breaking down of class divisions and the spread of equality. It will be remembered for a growing affluence. It will be remembered, perhaps, as the age when the pound stood at a fraction of its pre-War value and the housewife shopped first with £5 notes and then with £10 notes. It could be remembered for the universal adoption of the motor-car and the television set or for the coming of the supermarket. It could be remembered as the time when central heating swept the country and reduced the normal hardihood of the population. It might bear the mark of James Bond, "Britain's best-loved spy" of fiction, whose books and films made fortunes for author, producer, actor, and all concerned to market his exploits. The 'pop' groups might claim to have left a more indelible mark than anyone else upon the Age. The teenager, courted by all who have goods to sell, might well be the symbol of affluent welfare.

Others, looking for a more continuing culture, might note the development of drama from the pre-War intellectual protests of Shaw, the sharp class criticism of Galsworthy in *Strife* and *The Silver Box*, the straight bitterness of *Love on the Dole*, to the post-War angry young men typified by John Osborne's Jimmy Porter in *Look Back in Anger*; and then the merging of the angry men into the helpless, non-contact nihilists whom the BBC speaks of as dominating the plays sent to it. Becket's *Waiting for Godot* or Pinter's *The Caretaker*, in their unfocused uncertainty, certain only in their lack of contact, are centuries away from the straightforward issues propounded by Galsworthy and a very long way from Jimmy Porter's anger. It might be considered, also, that we have moved to a very much smaller stage in all our literature. Osborne's Luther does not rake the world with his anger nor rouse a century with his protest: he complains of his digestion. Great characters are brought within the span of a homely man's mind, rather than rousing the mind to new horizons.

What age can say which of its novels will survive? Many novels of the contemporary scene will be read for their historical value; the twist of horror, or bitterness, or perversion in many will be noted. In painting, 'pop' art and amateur art and serious professional art often merge in a frenzy of experiment with new forms and new materials, new colours and new juxtapositions. Yet, beside this, stand some of the world's greatest sculptors. As two of the greatest musicians, William Walton and Benjamin Britten, stand side by side with 'pop' music, so Henry Moore and Barbara Hepworth stand side by side with 'pop' art. Perhaps the age, on its cultural side, will be pleased to stand or fall by this, that it can produce such diversity.

Meanwhile the breaking down of taboos of the body, of sex, of religion, and the continued search for sensation and sensationalism have failed to produce a continuing standard, or ethic, or yardstick of conduct. No philosophy, moral code, or religion has taken the place of what has been abandoned, and many founder for want of a lifeline. The value of national stock-taking and of assessing Britain's role in the world is vitiated by this same inability to focus attention upon the larger issue, but a letter to *The Times* in August 1966 came near to putting it in generally acceptable terms: "It is merely masochistic to remind us that Britain is no longer and never again can be a great power. It is more important to realize that we can still be a first class people, a more exciting objective."[1] It is a well-known tradition of the fairy-tale that virtue is found more often in poverty than in affluence. Though that is no reason for perpetuating want, it is nevertheless a warning, borne out in many ways by the Affluent Society, that virtues tend to become lost in a society geared to high consumption. To become, and to remain, a first-class people we must control, not be controlled by, the affluence we create.

To examine the present is like peering into the waters of a stream which has come from the past and flows to the future. The future is dim and barely discerned; of the past we know a little and can assess the rest but imperfectly. The present, for all our probing, is difficult enough to understand. Even when all is calm the moment cannot be caught. The water that laps my hand was—is—will be—and is different at one and the same time. The wind whips up ripples that give false impressions of the water's movement, the current is disturbed by boulders, a thrown stone causes ever-widening circles that beat the farther bank. The onlooker can only record what he sees and try to estimate the effect of such action as dredging the stream to make it flow more clearly, removing the boulder to prevent diversion, or stopping the bystanders from throwing stones. But, for all our difficulties of assessment and interpretation, we can be certain that the present channel is well and deeply cut. Accident or diversion may stem the flow or divert the current, but nothing can stem or divert the main movement to welfare within a society of equals which was begun a quarter of a century ago when Britain arose out of the devastation of war to build again.

[1] Russell Meiggs, August 16.

APPENDIX A

I. ECONOMIC PLANNING AND SOCIAL SECURITY OUTSIDE THE UNITED KINGDOM

(a) GENERAL

BEFORE THE Second World War economic planning was confined almost solely to Soviet Russia, and its supporters were mainly those of the political 'left'. Social security, as a State responsibility, was becoming more generally accepted, and, notably, New Zealand and Sweden had gone farther than either Germany or Britain in establishing national insurance systems. Not until after the War did the intellectual climate change sufficiently to remove the stigma of communism from economic planning and to bring it, publicly and openly, to the forefront of national policies. At the same time, with varying degrees of emphasis, the nation states of the Western world were shouldering varying amounts of responsibility for social misfortune.

Britain, therefore, is not exceptional in what she is doing, and though in social security she stands well in the van she has been slower than some other countries to plan her economic development.

Norway, for example, makes a special feature of controlling her economy through her national budget, which annually sets out her investment targets, consumption, imports and exports, manpower and materials, licences, quotas, price-controls, and subsidies in accordance with a longer-term programme.[1] She has an advanced social-security system: 75 per cent of the population now receive medical and pecuniary benefits in illness, there are old-age pensions for all citizens over seventy years of age, accident insurance schemes, unemployment insurance, family allowances, and three weeks' holiday with pay for all workers. In Sweden, where compulsory health insurance for the whole nation was initiated at the beginning of 1955, there are accident and unemployment insurance schemes, maternity grants, child allowances, old-age pensions, and other benefits; Sweden is now preparing a plan for a compulsory provident and pensions scheme whereby old people will be guaranteed an income corresponding to two-thirds of their earnings during the best fifteen years of their working lives. In both Norway and Sweden Labour Governments have been in power since the War. In both countries central or municipal control or ownership of public utilities or amenities is a feature of the economy.

New Zealand is an outstanding example of minimum economic control and maximum social-service benefits. Under a Labour Government she had built her Welfare State before the War, and now, by the index of wealth per head, she is one of the wealthiest countries in the world. Her Government controls

---

[1] *The Norwegian Long-term Programme 1962–1965* (Royal Norwegian Ministry of Finance, April 19, 1961), *The Norwegian Long-term Programme 1966–1969* (*ibid.*, 1965).

the marketing of her agricultural produce through guaranteed prices; by central-bank policy it controls the foreign exchanges; it controls imports by a system of licensing. Meanwhile a high income tax and extensive social-security benefits, including a National Health Service, universal retirement pensions without means test, children's allowances, and other benefits, coupled with some price-control, give her a social system with a high degree of equality, few poor and no very rich.

Even the U.S.A., though social security is here less emphasized, has not been untouched by the prevailing trends. The Fair Deal of President Truman after the War extended social-security benefits, gave higher minimum wages, initiated slum-clearance and building projects; an attempt to institute a National Health Service was, however, defeated by the American Medical Association. More important in America was the Government's price support to agriculture and its conscious policy of full employment. The Employment Act of 1946 created a clear legal obligation on the Government to use all practicable measures to promote employment and maintain purchasing power in times of crisis. Under the Act the Council of Economic Advisers has instituted swift action from the centre to hold recession in check, and its policy has, in fact, been remarkably successful.

It is more remarkable that in France the emphasis since the War has been upon planning, and four consecutive Plans have resulted in outstanding growth and development. Banking and insurance, railways, and such big public utilities as gas, electricity, and coal are publicly owned, but steel remains under private enterprise, and Air France is a mixed concern. A system of social insurance covers family allowances, pensions and industrial accident; unemployment benefit is administered separately, while the health service is based upon a system of rebates made to poorer patients. But the State makes very little contribution to social-security benefits, which are expected to be self-financing, and depend largely upon employers' contributions, which form about three-quarters of the whole.

(b) THE NORWEGIAN LONG-TERM PROGRAMME, 1962–1965
(from abridgment published by the Royal Norwegian Ministry of Finance, April 19, 1961)

"Economic outlook and trends in the 1960's

"With a reasonable development in world economy it should be possible for Norway to double her national product within less than 20 years. But the considerable possibilities of economic growth and improved living conditions can only be realised if an objective and active economic policy is pursued.

"Technical progress and new production methods will raise productivity in the various sectors of the economy. Parallel with this, technical gains and the marketing of new commodity types will influence consumer developments. Higher incomes will lead to big shifts in demand which will, to an increasing extent, be directed towards commodities which are not now produced in Norway. Higher productivity will also justify shorter working hours and more spare time.

"Rapid economic expansion will go hand in hand with important structural changes and adjustments in the economy. These latter will be further encouraged by the changing composition of the population during the 1960's and through altered competitive conditions in the foreign economy.

"Economic planning and the effectiveness of the tools of economic policy will determine how rapid the change-over is to be and the degree of increase in production. It is therefore of decisive importance that the economic policy is built on as strong a foundation as possible and that the objectives set by the Government each form part of a co-ordinated plan covering the whole economy.

"Private consumption

"Parallel with the growth in private consumption, there are important changes in its composition. Expenditure on food and beverages, clothing and shoes gradually occupies a less dominating position in the consumer's budget. An increasing share of income goes to housing, new equipment in the home, and to provide the basis for better utilization of spare time. Furniture, electric household equipment and other home equipment, radio and television, sports equipment and private cars occupy a more and more important place on the consumer market. A general tendency towards easing housework shows itself in the choice of furniture and fittings, in the change-over to new heating methods, and in the purchase of electrical aids, and the consumer prefers commodities which need little or no further preparation—ready-made clothes, prepared foods, etc."

[*Chapter I in original document, p. 3 in translation.*]

II. GLOSSARY OF NEW TERMS AND
THE NEW LETTER-ACY

The Sterling Area. Comprises countries, mostly members of the Commonwealth, whose currencies are linked to sterling and who hold their reserves in the form of sterling balances with the Bank of England. Originally known as the Sterling Bloc, it emerged after the United Kingdom abandoned the gold standard in 1931.

The Sterling Bloc. See above.

IMF. The International Monetary Fund. Developed from the Bretton Woods Conference of 1944. Holds funds of gold and of members' currencies which members may draw upon. Started operating in 1947.

The World Bank. The International Bank for Reconstruction and Development, set up at Bretton Woods, 1944. Provides long-term loans to Governments or to private businesses backed by Government guarantee for specific objects of financial soundness.

GATT. General Agreement on Tariffs and Trade, 1947; has forty-four signatories agreed to enter into "reciprocal and mutually advantageous agreements directed to the substantial reduction of tariffs and trade". Any concessions between GATT countries automatically extend to the rest.

The "Kennedy Round". Visits of GATT countries instigated by President Kennedy in an attempt to secure tariff reductions; there have been several 'Rounds'.

The Marshall Plan. American dollar aid to Europe after the War; began in 1947.

ERP. European Recovery Programme; proposals presented to U.S.A., September 1947, by European countries in implementation of the Marshall Plan.

OEEC. Organization for European Economic Co-operation. Set up in 1948 by sixteen European nations, including the United Kingdom, to co-ordinate economic activity and co-operate in the distribution of Marshall Aid. Became

OECD. Organization for Economic Co-operation and Development, 1961, bringing in U.S.A. and Canada and later Japan and Australia. Its objects were to extend its work beyond Europe, to co-ordinate aid to developing countries, to give mutual economic help in various ways.

NATO. North Atlantic Treaty Organization, set up by treaty April 1949—links America and Canada with Europe; members will regard an attack on one as an attack on all. Most European countries belong.

Council of Europe. Set up May 1949 to discuss all matters of common concern, except defence. Most European countries belong.

EPU. European Payments Union, 1950, for convertibility of European currencies. Wound up 1958.

ECSC. European Coal and Steel Community, based on the Schuman Plan, began to operate 1953 with the object of closer co-operation and integration of production and distribution.

Euratom. European Atomic Energy Committee, 1957.

EEC. European Economic Community, 1958, based on the Treaty of Rome of 1957 for closer economic and political integration. The six member countries—France, West Germany, Italy, Belgium, Holland, Luxembourg—aim at a uniform external trade tariff and free intra-community trade.

The Common Market. Another name for the EEC.

EFTA. European Free Trade Association, 1959, based on the Treaty of Stockholm; for greater freedom of trade within the Association. Members are Britain, Sweden, Denmark, Norway, Finland, Switzerland, Austria, Portugal. Agriculture is excluded from the agreement.

Neddy. National Economic Development Council, created by the United Kingdom with the purpose of achieving the maximum sound economic development of the U.K. economy. Started operations in 1962.

Little Neddies. Similar organizations for various industries.

ESRO. European Space Research Organization, founded 1962, formally established 1964.

ELDO. European Space Vehicle Launcher Development Organization, founded 1962, formally established 1964.

The National Plan. United Kingdom attempt to plan the economy up to 1970.

III. POST-WAR GENERAL ELECTIONS IN THE UNITED KINGDOM

(a) SEATS

Year	1945	1950	1951	1955	1959	1964	1966
Conservative	213	298	321	345	365	304	253
Labour	393	315	295	277	258	317	363
Liberal	12	9	6	6	6	9	12
Other	22	3	3	2	1	0	2
Total	640	625	625	630	630	630	630

The reduction in the total number of seats between 1945 and 1950 was due to the Representation of the People Act, 1949, which abolished plural voting—both the 'business premises' vote and the 'University' vote—abolished two-Member constituencies by breaking them into single-Member seats; and redistributed seats in accordance with population movements since the previous distribution in 1918. Five more constituencies were added between 1951 and 1955 to accord with electoral requirements.

(b) VOTES CAST

Year	1945	1950	1951	1955	1959	1964	1966
Conservative	9,577,667	12,502,567	13,717,538	13,311,936	13,749,830	12,001,396	11,418,433
Labour	11,632,891	13,266,592	13,948,605	12,404,970	12,215,538	12,205,814	13,064,951
Liberal	2,197,191	2,621,548	730,556	722,405	1,638,571	3,092,878	2,327,533
Other	674,863	381,964	198,969	321,182	275,304	348,914	452,689

The results are conveniently tabulated in the British General Election books. These are taken from the latest: D. E. Butler and Anthony King, *The British General Election of 1966*, p. 296.

IV. THE DEVELOPMENT OF NATIONALIZATION IN BRITAIN

Name of Act	Purpose	Passage of Second Reading	Date of becoming law	Vesting or Appointed day
The British Overseas Airways Act	to provide for the establishment of BOAC and "to make further and better provision for the operation of air transport services" adapted and amended by	July 10, 1939	1939	Appointed Day April 1, 1940
The Civil Aviation Act	to establish a British European Airways Corporation.	May 6, 1946	1946	Vesting Day August 1, 1946
The Bank of England Act	"to bring the capital stock of the Bank of England into public ownership and bring the Bank under public control".	October 29, 1945	1946	Appointed Day March 1, 1946
The Coal Industry Nationalization Act	"to establish public ownership and control of the coal-mining industry and certain allied activities".	January 30, 1946	1946	Vesting Day January 1, 1947
The Atomic Energy Act	"to provide for the development of atomic energy and the control of such development and for purposes connected therewith".	October 8, 1946	1946	—
The Atomic Energy Authority Act	"to provide for the setting up of an Atomic Energy Authority for the United Kingdom".	March 1, 1954	1954	Appointed Day August 1, 1954

Name of Act	Purpose	Passage of Second Reading	Date of becoming law	Vesting or Appointed day
The Transport Act	"to provide or promote an efficient, adequate, economical and properly integrated system of public inland transport and port facilities within Great Britain for passengers and goods".	December 18, 1946	1947	Date of transfer January 1, 1948
The Electricity Act	"to provide for the establishment of a British Electricity Authority and ... for the transfer to the said Authority ... of property ... and liabilities of electricity undertakers and other bodies".	February 4, 1947	1947	Vesting Day April 1, 1948
The Gas Act	"to provide for the establishment of Area Gas Boards and a Gas Council".	February 11, 1948	1948	Vesting Day May 1, 1949
The Iron and Steel Act	"to provide for the establishment of an Iron and Steel Corporation of Great Britain". (nationalization).	November 17, 1948	1949	General date of transfer February 15, 1951
The Iron and Steel Act	to restore "independence, initiative and enterprise in the iron and steel industry" (de-nationalization).	November 27, 1952	1953	Appointed Day July 13, 1953
The Iron and Steel Act	(renationalization).	July 25, 1966		

Name of Act	Purpose	Passage of Second Reading	Date of becoming law	Vesting or Appointed day
The Post Office Act	"designed to give practical recognition to the commercial character of the Post Office" partial (nationalization).	January 25, 1961	1961	Date of operation April 1, 1961
THE BROADCASTING AND TELEVISION SERVICES				
The Television Act	to provide television broadcasting services in addition to those provided by the BBC.	March 25, 1954	1964	Date of operation July 30, 1954
The Television Act	to give the Independent Television Authority increased powers over programmes and advertising and "to ensure that the programmes broadcast ... maintain a high general standard in all respects".	March 9, 1964	1964	Date of operation July 31, 1964

The British Broadcasting Corporation owes its existence not to Act of Parliament but to incorporation by Royal Charter. Originally the British Broadcasting Company, inaugurated in 1922, it received its first Charter in 1927. The Charter is generally for a prescribed period of ten years, but can be extended. The BBC's fifth Charter was granted to run from July 30, 1964.

V. REMUNERATION OF HEALTH SERVICE DOCTORS

(a) G.P.'s: THE CENTRAL POOL

The juggling with a central pool which Spens, Danckwerts, and the doctors themselves accepted was due partly to the fact that most doctors derived some of their income from sources other than panel patients—from maternity work for the local authorities, for giving anaesthetics, for emergency and accident work, for attending visitors not on the panel and patients from other districts. There were also expenses like mileage payments made to country doctors and others with largely spread practices for which they needed to be reimbursed. All these payments and expenses were taken first from the pool, and doctors then drew on it at the agreed capitation rate in accordance with the numbers of their registered patients, any residue being finally divided between them. Specific expenses like mileage payments had been drawn from the pool by those entitled to them, but general expenses were merged in the general pool, and what a doctor drew out depended solely upon the number of his patients and the size of the residue in the pool—not upon any expenses he incurred in running his surgery; there was consequently no direct inducement to modernize equipment or improve premises. The whole method of payment was a cumbersome way of circumventing a series of straight payments on a capitation basis augmented by any expenses or additional fees deemed proper; nor did it disguise the fact that the National Health doctor received his salary from the State.

The Spens Committee had suggested that the doctor's salary be worked out on the basis of a capitation fee for each patient on a doctor's list—15s. was proposed. Later it was considered that 18s. on 95 per cent of the estimated population was a better method of calculation since it would allow for a 20 per cent increase in prices since 1939. Danckwerts, however, judged that the central pool should be calculated on the basis of the number of medical practitioners and not of patients. The size of the pool should then be the Spens estimate of the average income of G.P.'s (£1111) increased by 100 per cent (£2222) multiplied by the number of general practitioners and increased by something like 38·7 per cent for expenses. Payments to the doctors should be retrospective. The matter was refined on by a joint working party, as a result of which a general capitation fee of 17s. was agreed upon, augmented by a loading fee of 10s. for each patient on a doctor's list from 501 to 1500. The maximum number of National Health patients allowed to a doctor was reduced from 4000 to 3500 for a single practitioner or as the share of a partnership, and for an assistant was reduced from 2400 to 2000. The £300 basic allowance for starting practice was abolished, but instead, in designated areas, an initial practice allowance, starting at £600 and reducing annually to £200, was payable in the first three years of practice.

(b) CONSULTANTS: THE MERIT AWARDS

The distinction, or merit, award was additional to salary and was paid to a given number of consultants in various groupings, the number in each group being published but not the names. Selection was made by the Minister on the advice of an Advisory Committee under the chairmanship of an eminent medical man whose terms of reference were simply to recommend which specialists engaged in National Health Service work should receive awards for professional distinction. The chairman consulted professional opinion widely, visited hospitals in many parts of the country, and finally put names to his Committee for final choice; other things being equal, there was an assumption that merit awards should be geographically spread. Actual payments were made by the Boards of Governors and Regional Hospital Boards. In addition to a salary increase Pilkington recommended that the value of these merit awards should be advanced and their grading slightly changed, and there was a further stepping up in 1963. There were then 88 of the highest A+ awards of £4550 a year, 265 A awards of £3425 a year, 707 of the B awards of £2000, and 1413 of the C awards of £850 a year. Pilkington advanced a similar idea for general practitioners, but they rejected it.[1]

VI. FLOWERS ON COMPUTERS

In January 1966 the *Report of a Joint Working Group on Computers for Research* under the chairmanship of Professor B. H. Flowers[2] made revealing comparisons between Britain's total computer establishment and that of the United States. In July 1964 there were about 15,000 computers in the U.S.A., increasing by about 25 per cent per annum, with a value of some $4000 million. To be comparable (in terms of spending related to gross national product) Britain should have some 2125 computers, for all purposes, to the value of some £180,000,000. In fact she had about a thousand computers—only half of what she should have to achieve parity. The size and range of American machines compared with British made the comparison even more damaging. The Flowers Committee urged that "the British Government should take a strong positive initiative in furthering all imaginative and realistic applications of computing, instead of simply assessing applications for grants as they arise". But though advising, wherever possible, the use of British computers, the Committee was compelled to state that "the cheapest way of meeting the shortage of national computer power would undoubtedly be to take advantage of recent American developments by installing a relatively small number of large American machines".

[1] *Report of the Royal Commission on Doctors' and Dentists' Remuneration* (the Pilkington Report), February 1960, Cmnd. 939, *passim*.
[2] Cmnd. 2883.

VII. WAGES AND SALARIES

(a) Average Weekly Earnings of Men Manual Workers in Some Occupations[1]

Occupation	October 1948		April 1966		Percentage increase
	s.	d.	s.	d.	
Vehicles	161	8	474	11	193·8
Motor vehicles	—		488	11	—
Textiles	129	1	370	0	186·6
Paper, printing, publishing	146	8	477	8	225·7
Newspaper and periodical	—		566	1	—
Chemicals and allied	137	9	426	9	209·8
Construction	131	3	399	9	204·6
Food, drink, tobacco	127	6	390	6	206·3
Metal manufacture	156	10	430	5	174·4
Engineering and electricity	144	8	411	5	184·4
Shipbuilding and marine engineering	150	0	433	0	188·7
Clothing, footwear	136	1	352	4	158·9
Bricks, pottery, glass, cement	139	2	411	5	195·6
Timber, furniture	132	6	382	0	188·3
	April 1956				
Coal-mining	294	11	432	0	
Dock labour	269	7	447	5	
			April 1965		
Agriculture	174	2	279	5	
Railways other than workshop	218	10	369	0	
workshop	238	11	392	0	

(b) Average Weekly Earnings of Men Salaried Employees in Some Occupations[2]

Occupation	October 1955			October 1965		
Average all male salaried employees	£14	0	8	£25	10	1
Male clerical	£10	4	5	£16	3	1
National and local-government employees, including teachers and National Health Service workers	£14	1	3	£25	15	7
Workers in nationalized industries	£12	14	6	£24	11	6
Banking and insurance	£16	3	2	£25	13	5

[1] *Statistics on Incomes, Prices, Employment and Production*, September 1966, Table B.8.

[2] *Ibid.*, Table B.17.

APPENDIX B

I. THE POPULATION OF THE UNITED KINGDOM[1]

(a) TOTALS

Year	England and Wales	Scotland	Northern Ireland	Total
1931 (census)	39,952,000	4,843,000	1,243,000	46,038,000
1951 (census)	43,758,000	5,096,000	1,371,000	50,225,000
1961 (census)	46,105,000	5,179,000	1,425,000	52,709,000
1963 (mid-year estimate)	47,028,000	5,205,000	1,446,000	53,678,000
1964 (mid-year estimate)	47,401,000	5,206,000	1,458,000	54,066,000
2000 (projection)				74,660,000

(b) AGE DISTRIBUTION OF TOTAL POPULATION[2]

	1961 (census)	1963 (mid-year estimate)
Under 15	12,336,000	12,399,000
15–19	3,695,000	4,195,000
20–64	30,487,000	30,763,000
65–74	3,972,000	4,054,000
75–79	1,201,000	1,221,000
80 and over	1,017,000	1,047,000

[1] *Annual Abstract of Statistics*, 1965, Tables 6, 7, 12.

[2] The Government Actuary estimated in December 1966 that the percentage of dependants would increase from 38·2 in 1965 to a peak of over 42 about 1980 and then tend to fall.

II. DISTRIBUTION OF MANPOWER
IN THE UNITED KINGDOM

(a) TOTALS[1]

(June each year; in thousands)

	1961	1962	1963	1964
Total working population	25,285	25,554	25,652	25,780
Armed forces, etc.	474	442	427	424
Total in civil employment	24,528	24,706	24,728	25,007
Unemployed (wholly)	283	406	497	349
Agriculture, forestry, and fishing	1,021	993	977	947
Mining and quarrying	735	716	688	661
Manufacturing	9,109	9,029	8,889	9,017
Construction (building and civil engineering)	1,660	1,697	1,727	1,802
Gas, electricity, water	386	394	404	409
Transport and communications	1,777	1,785	1,755	1,736
Distributive trades	3,384	3,439	3,475	3,495
Service industries	5,155	5,327	5,439	5,634

(b) MANUFACTURING[2]

(June each year; in thousands)

	1961	1962	1963	1964
Food, drink, tobacco	860	857	848	845
Chemical and allied industries	534	520	516	511
Metal manufacture	631	596	593	622
Engineering and electrical goods	2,168	2,205	2,174	2,234
Shipbuilding and marine engineering	261	251	224	216
Vehicles	905	891	881	885
Metal goods not elsewhere specified	571	563	560	580
Textiles	899	859	838	840
Leather, leather goods, and fur	68	67	67	67
Clothing and footwear	611	607	588	582
Bricks, pottery, glass, cement, etc.	350	355	344	357
Timber, furniture, etc.	313	311	307	314
Paper, printing, and publishing	627	636	635	637
Other manufacturing	311	311	314	327
Total manufacturing	9,109	9,029	8,889	9,017

[1] Source: *Annual Abstract of Statistics*, 1965, Table 127; analysis based on Standard Industrial Classification, 1958.

[2] *Ibid.*

(c) THE SERVICE TRADES[1]

(in thousands)

	1960	1961	1962	1963	1964
Distributive Trades	2,870	2,892	2,975	3,023	3,026
Wholesale	542	542	567	580	574
Retail	2,033	2,053	2,101	2,131	2,134
Insurance, Banking, Finance	550	568	589	617	637
Professional and Scientific Services	2,025	2,103	2,203	2,276	2,362
Accountancy	79	82	86	87	89
Educational	910	951	997	1,042	1,094
Legal	88	90	95	96	99
Medical, dental	774	795	832	851	883
Religious organizations	21	21	22	23	22
Other professional and scientific	153	164	172	177	175
Miscellaneous Services	2,036	2,047	2,130	2,157	2,230
Cinemas, theatres, radio	136	138	139	141	135
Sport and other recreations	53	55	57	60	67
Betting	39	42	45	46	50
Catering, hotels	592	583	614	605	633
Dry cleaning, etc.	46	47	48	49	48
Laundries	130	129	130	129	124
Motor repairs, motor distribution, garages, filling stations	361	375	390	408	423
Boot and shoe repairs	18	17	17	17	16
Hairdressing and manicure	87	95	101	110	111
Private domestic service	287	264	256	250	237
Other services	287	302	333	342	387
Public Administration	1,294	1,313	1,346	1,398	1,325
National Government service	534	540	551	570	550
Local Government service	760	773	795	828	775

[1] *Annual Abstract of Statistics*, 1964, Table 132, and 1965, Table 130; based on the Standard Industrial Classification, 1958.

(d) Administrative, Technical, and Clerical Workers in Manufacturing Industries in Great Britain[1]

(expressed as percentage of total number of employees in employment in each industry at October in each year)

	1959	1960	1961	1962	1963	1964
All Manufacturing Industries	21·1	21·3	22·1	22·6	22·8	23·1
Food, drink, tobacco	18·8	18·7	18·8	19·2	19·3	20·0
Chemical and allied	32·3	32·2	34·0	34·8	34·5	35·5
Metal manufacture	18·4	18·8	19·0	21·0	20·7	20·9
Engineering and electrical	28·2	28·2	28·9	29·5	29·8	29·6
Shipbuilding and marine engineering	14·8	15·8	16·0	16·6	17·7	17·4
Vehicles	24·1	24·8	26·2	25·1	25·2	26·8
Metal goods	17·4	17·3	18·2	19·0	18·7	18·8
Textiles	12·1	12·3	13·2	13·4	13·6	13·5
Leather, leather goods, fur	13·8	14·6	14·3	14·3	15·4	15·0
Clothing and footwear	11·0	11·0	11·1	11·6	11·6	11·6
Bricks, pottery, glass, cement	16·0	16·3	17·0	17·9	18·2	18·4
Timber, furniture, etc.	15·7	16·6	17·0	17·1	18·1	17·7
Paper, printing, publishing	23·0	22·9	24·0	24·7	25·1	25·2

III. POWER PROVISION IN THE UNITED KINGDOM

(a) Total Inland Fuel Consumption[2]

(million tons of coal or coal equivalent)

Year	Nuclear Electricity	Hydro Electricity	Natural Gas	Oil	Coal
1957	0·2	1·5	—	36·7	207·6
1963	2·5	1·8	0·2	85·3	193·8
1964	3·2	1·9	0·3	93·3	186·6

(b) Comparative Unit Power Costs in New Stations[3]

per kWh base-load electricity

Coal-fired stations planned or under construction		Oil-fired station under construction	Nuclear Power station under construction
Drax	Cottam	Pembroke	Dungeness B
0·52d.	0·54d.	0·41d.–0·52d.	0·38d.–0·46d.

[1] *Annual Abstract of Statistics*, 1965, Table 138.
[2] *Ministry of Power Statistical Digest*, 1964, Table 9.
[3] *Fuel Policy*, Cmnd. 2798, pp. 23–24.

(c) MINISTRY OF POWER'S SECTOR ANALYSIS OF
INTERNAL ENERGY DEMAND[1]

Million tons of coal equivalent

	1960 (actual)	1964 (actual)	1970 (estimated)
Iron and Steel	34·8	36·1	37
General industry	77·2	83·8	98
Railways	11·0	7·2	4·5
Other transport	22·5	29·1	38·5
Domestic	71·5	78·7	86
Other inland	46·7	50·4	59
TOTAL	263·7	285·3	323

(d) ACTUAL AND ESTIMATED INDUSTRIAL FUEL DEMAND
IN THE UNITED KINGDOM[2]

Million tons of coal equivalent

	1960 actual	1964 actual	1970 estimate
Coal			
For power-stations	51·9	68·0	84
For gasworks	22·6	20·5	10
For other purposes	122·2	98·7	81
TOTAL	196·7	187·2	175
Oil (including petroleum gases)			
For power-stations	9·2	9·7	14
For gasworks	1·9	5·0	14·5
For other purposes (including road and air transport and refinery fuel)	54·4	78·6	115·5
TOTAL	65·5	93·3	144
Natural gas	0·1	0·3	1·5
Nuclear power and hydro-electricity	2·6	5·1	16·5
Total inland demand for energy	264·9	285·9	337
Electricity (thousand million kilowatt hours)	104·9	143·4	241
Gas (million therms)	2,636	3,014	4,635

[1] *Fuel Policy*, Appendix, p. 35.
[2] *Fuel Policy, Ibid.* Table 4, p. 11.

IV. NATIONAL INCOME

(a) Gross National Product, National Income, and Consumers' Expenditure, 1958-65[1]

£M

	1958	1960	1962	1963	1964	1965
Gross national product (at factor cost)	20,385	22,767	25,457	27,033	29,062	30,904
Capital consumption	1,791	1,933	2,198	2,323	2,469	2,625
National income	18,594	20,834	23,259	24,710	26,593	28,279
Consumers' expenditure	15,365	16,963	18,893	20,049	21,380	22,708

(b) The Ingredients of National Income, 1965[2]

	£M
Income from employment	20,965
Income from self-employment	2,503
Gross trading profits of companies	4,834
Gross trading surpluses of public corporations	996
Gross profits of other public enterprises	97
Rent	1,733
Total domestic income before providing for depreciation and stock appreciation	31,128
less stock appreciation	−365
Residual error	−332
Gross national product at factor cost	30,431
Net property income from abroad	473
Gross national product	30,904
Capital consumption	2,625
National income	28,279

[1] *National Income and Expenditure, 1966,* Table I.   [2] *Ibid.*

V. THE UNITED KINGDOM BALANCE OF PAYMENTS

(a) SUMMARY BALANCE OF PAYMENTS[1]

	£M Year	£M Year
	1964	1965
Imports (f.o.b.)	5,006	5,044
Exports and re-exports (f.o.b.)	4,471	4,779
Visible balance	−535	−265
Government (net):		
military	−268	−278
other	−166	−176
Interest, profits and dividends (net)	+406	+454
Private services and transfers (net)	+157	+129
Invisible balance	+129	+129
Current balance	−406	−136

(b) VALUE OF THE EXPORTS OF THE PRODUCE AND MANUFACTURES OF THE UNITED KINGDOM

some important items for the year 1964[2]

Commodity	£M	£M
Total food and live animals		159·2
of which		
sugar, sugar preparations and honey	43·5	
live animals	32·4	
Textile fibres, not manufactured and their waste		98·0
Total mineral fuels, lubricants, etc.		138·8
of which		
coal, coke, briquettes	36·9	
petroleum and petroleum products	101·0	
Chemicals		412·2
Total manufactured goods and articles		1,298·8
of which		
textile yarn, fabrics and articles	275·4	
iron and steel	217·7	
non-ferrous metals	138·4	
manufactures of metal	144·0	
clothing	43·8	
Professional, scientific and controlling instruments, photographic and optical goods, watches and clocks		88·7
Machinery and transport equipment		1,825·9
Value of total exports		4,254·1

[1] *Economic Trends*, March 1966.
[2] *Annual Abstract of Statistics*, 1965, Table 267.

(c) VALUE OF UNITED KINGDOM IMPORTS FROM ALL SOURCES
some important items for the year 1964[1]

Commodity	£M	£M
Total food and live animals		1,624·6
of which		
meat and meat preparations	368·9	
dairy produce, eggs	214·5	
cereals and cereal preparations	219·2	
fruit and vegetables	283·7	
sugar and sugar preparations and honey	144·2	
coffee, tea, cocoa, spices and preparations		
thereof	168·9	
Tobacco		91·1
Total crude materials		1,065·6
of which		
wood, lumber, cork	218·2	
pulp and waste paper	137·4	
textile fibres not manufactured and their		
waste	277·2	
metalliferous ores and metal scrap	185·1	
Petrol and petrol products		583·1
Chemicals		252·5
Total manufactured goods		920·6
of which		
non-ferrous metals	328·5	
textile yarn, fabrics and articles	177·0	
paper, paperboard and manufactures thereof	132·5	
iron and steel	106·1	
Machinery and transport equipment		545·0
Miscellaneous manufactured articles		293·1
Value of total imports		5,513·5

[1] *Annual Abstract of Statistics*, 1965, Table 266.

(d) THE NATIONAL PLAN
(i) British Imports, *Actual and Intended*[1]

	£M 1964 *prices*		*Average annual percentage increase*
	1964	1970	1964–70
Food, drink, tobacco	1,774	1,860	0·8
Basic materials	1,119	1,210	1·3
Fuels	585	790	5·1
Semi-manufactures	1,325	1,820	5·4
Finished manufactures	899	1,515	9·1
TOTAL (c.i.f.)	5,702	7,195	4·0

(ii) British Exports, *Actual and Intended*[2]

	£M 1964 *prices*		*Average annual percentage increase in vol.*
	1964	1970	1964–70
Agriculture, forestry, fishing	64	70	1·5
Mining and quarrying	46	39	−2·8
Food, drink, tobacco	235	319	5·3
Chemicals and allied industries	528	773	6·6
Metal manufacture	315	312	−0·2
Mechanical engineering	823	1,293	7·8
Electrical engineering	319	499	7·7
Shipbuilding	45	55	3·7
Vehicles	817	1,110	5·2
Textiles	389	472	3·3
Leather, clothing, footwear	72	112	7·5
Bricks, pottery, glass, cement, etc.	70	94	4·9
Timber, paper, printing, publishing	115	165	6·2
Other manufacturing industries	107	146	5·3

[1] *The National Plan*, Part I, p. 79, Table 7.1.
[2] *Ibid.*, Part I, p. 81, Table 7.2.

VI. PUBLIC EXPENDITURE AND RECEIPTS IN THE UNITED KINGDOM

(a) TOTAL EXPENDITURE AND SOME OF THE MORE IMPORTANT ITEMS CENTRAL AND LOCAL[1]

				£M		
	1958	1960	1962	1963	1964	1965
Grand Total	7,257	8,273	9,763	10,389	11,372	12,598
Military Defence	1,543	1,630	1,839	1,892	1,988	2,095
National Insurance, Pensions, Assistance	1,345	1,488	1,744	1,988	2,097	2,413
Education	779	916	1,172	1,281	1,410	1,567
National Health Service	728	861	971	1,035	1,126	1,269
Housing	420	496	540	601	808	934
Transport and communication	333	498	464	469	505	577
Agriculture, forestry, and food	327	324	411	378	334	336
Water, sewage, refuse disposal	141	165	209	217	242	255
Police and prisons	130	150	190	209	225	247
Roads and public lighting	197	239	319	362	413	428
Local welfare services, including child care, school meals, milk, welfare foods, and other services	129	144	174	187	207	230
Research	64	97	127	130	132	154
Parks and pleasure grounds	35	43	54	57	62	68
Libraries, museums, and arts	25	30	38	41	45	50
Fire services	29	33	42	45	48	53
Parliament and Law Courts	21	24	34	38	42	48
Public Health	18	21	26	28	31	34

[1] *National Income and Expenditure*, 1966, Table 53.

(b) CURRENT ACCOUNT OF CENTRAL GOVERNMENT: RECEIPTS
MAIN ITEMS AND TOTAL[1]

Rents, Dividends, Interest			Taxes on Income			Taxes on Expenditure		
£M			£M			£M		
1962	1963	1965	1962	1963	1965	1962	1963	1965
611	576	684	3,455	3,385	4,023	2,980	3,034	3,766

National Insurance Contributions			National Health Contributions			Total		
£M			£M			£M		
1962	1963	1965	1962	1963	1965	1962	1963	1965
1,034	1,138	1,511	163	165	169	8,260	8,315	10,177

(c) CURRENT ACCOUNT OF CENTRAL GOVERNMENT: EXPENDITURE
MAIN HOME ITEMS AND TOTAL[2]

£M

Military Defence			National Health Service			Subsidies		
1962	1963	1965	1962	1963	1965	1962	1963	1965
1,804	1,849	2,060	823	875	1,053	576	537	513

National Insurance Benefits			Grants to local authorities			Debt interest		
1962	1963	1965	1962	1963	1965	1962	1963	1965
1,213	1,413	1,774	926	1,031	1,248	887	949	988

Total Expenditure		
1962	1963	1965
8,260	8,315	10,177

[1] *Economic Trends*, July 1966, Table F.   [2] *Ibid.*

(d) EXPENDITURE OF CENTRAL GOVERNMENT: OVERSEAS, 1965[1]

	£M
Military	279
Administrative and diplomatic	47
Economic grants	88
Military grants	20
Subscriptions and contributions to international organizations	52
Other transfers	14
TOTAL	500

(e) CURRENT ACCOUNT OF LOCAL AUTHORITIES[2]: RECEIPTS (£M)

Gross trading income			Rent, Dividend, Interest			Rates		
1962	1963	1965	1962	1963	1965	1962	1963	1965
56	64	73	430	471	577	930	1,012	1,214

Current Grants from Central Govt.			Total Receipts		
1962	1963	1965	1962	1963	1965
926	1,031	1,248	2,328	2,575	3,131

(f) CURRENT ACCOUNT OF LOCAL AUTHORITIES: EXPENDITURE (£M) (Main Items and Total)

Education			Housing Subsidies			Current Grants to Persons			Goods and Services		
1962	1963	1965	1962	1963	1965	1962	1963	1965	1962	1963	1965
799	874	1,044	39	37	44	122	135	166	789	867	1,014

Debt Interest			Total Expenditure		
1962	1963	1965	1962	1963	1965
364	392	457	2,328	2,575	3,131

[1] *Economic Trends*, March 1966.   [2] *Ibid.*, July 1966, Table G.

VII. CENTRAL GOVERNMENT SOURCES OF FINANCE

(a) UNITED KINGDOM TOTAL TAX REVENUE, 1938–65[1]

Year	Total Tax Revenue		Inland Revenue		Customs and Excise Revenue		Motor Vehicle Duties	
	%	£M	%	£M	%	£M	%	£M
1938–39	100	896·9	58·1	520·8	38·0	340·6	4	35·6
1946–47	100	3,160·6	61·0	1,928·0	37·4	1,182·9	1·6	49·7
1954–55	100	4,478·3	56·5	2,528·3	41·8	1,870·5	1·8	79·5
1955–56	100	4,639·1	54·8	2,542·9	43·3	2,008·5	1·9	87·7
1956–57	100	4,920·3	55·3	2,720·9	42·9	2,108·4	1·9	91·0
1957–58	100	5,126·5	56·1	2,874·7	42·0	2,152·2	1·9	99·6
1958–59	100	5,307·6	56·8	3,012·8	41·2	2,188·5	2·0	106·4
1959–60	100	5,377·4	55·5	2,985·0	42·4	2,282·6	2·0	109·9
1960–61	100	5,722·0	56·1	3,208·9	41·8	2,389·1	2·2	123·9
1961–62	100	6,363·0	57·1	3,636·2	40·6	2,581·9	2·3	144·8
1962–63	100	6,578·8	57·0	3,752·5	40·6	2,670·4	2·4	155·9
1963–64	100	6,657·8	55·9	3,719·3	41·5	2,766·1	2·6	172·4
1964–65	100	7,431·4	54·5	4,071·2	42·7	3,173·5	2·7	186·8

(b) TOTAL AND PRINCIPAL INLAND REVENUE DUTIES IN THE UNITED KINGDOM, 1964–65[2]

	£M
Total	4,072·0
Income tax	3,088·3
Surtax	184·4
Profits tax	421·5
Death duties	296·5
Stamp duties	80·0

[1] *Report of the Commissioners of H.M. Inland Revenue for the year ended 31st March, 1965*, Tables 2A and 2B, p. 5.

[2] *Ibid.*, Table 5, p. 8.

(c) The Yield of Customs and Excise Duties
in the United Kingdom, 1964–65[1]

	£M	Percentage of total
Tobacco	983·7	31
Hydrocarbon oils	674·2	21·25
Purchase tax	633·1	20
Alcoholic liquors	574·7	18
Protective duties	179·0	5·75
Temporary charge on imports	77·1	2·5
Other duties	49·6	1·5
	3,171·4	100

(d) Purchase Tax in the United Kingdom:
Approximate Yields of Some Items in 1964–65[2]
(Rates of tax vary between 10 and 25 per cent)

	£M
Cars	147·9
Apparel (excluding footwear)	91·3
Stationery and office requisites, greeting cards	46·4
Domestic gas, electric, and other appliances	39·6
Confectionery	36·5
Radio, television sets, and valves	29·3
Perfume, cosmetics, toilet preparations	26·8
Furniture, mirrors	22·4
Floor coverings	19·3
Toys and sports equipment	18·7
Footwear	17·9
Soft drinks	16·8
Domestic hardware and ironmongery	14·5
Drugs and medicines	11·0
Light fittings, bulbs, torches, etc.	10·6
Toilet requisites and hairdressing goods	10·4
Jewellery and imitation jewellery	8·3
Trunks, bags, etc.	8·2
Clocks and watches	7·2
Cameras and photographic goods	6·0
Gramophone records	5·8
Ice cream	5·4
Motorcycles, mopeds, etc.	4·5
Gramophones and radio-gramophones	4·4
Pedal cycles	2·3

[1] *Report of the Commissioners of H.M. Customs and Excise for the year ended 31st March, 1965*, p. 9.
[2] *Ibid.*, p. 103.

(e) YIELD OF BETTING DUTIES IN THE UNITED KINGDOM, 1964–65[1]

	£M
TOTAL	32·4
From totalisators on dog race courses, net receipts	3·9
Football and similar pools, net receipts	23·6
Betting by coupon at fixed odds	3·9
Bookmakers' licence duty	1·0

VIII. CONSOLIDATED CURRENT AND CAPITAL ACCOUNT EXPENDITURE ON SOCIAL SERVICES AND HOUSING BY THE PUBLIC SECTOR IN THE UNITED KINGDOM[2]

	£M	
Service	1964–65	1965–66
Education	1,437·5	1,613·4
National Health Service	1,172·5	1,314·5
Local welfare services	54·7	59·7
Child care	40·6	46·2
School meals and milk	93·2	107·0
Welfare foods	38·7	42·1
National Insurance and industrial injuries	1,590·5	1,929·1
War pensions	115·4	127·2
Non-contributory old-age pensions	6·3	5·2
National Assistance	248·5	274·0
Family allowances	154·3	158·7
Housing	754·2	832·2
TOTAL	5,706·4	6,509·3

[1] *Report of the Commissioners of H.M. Customs and Excise for the year ended 31st March, 1965*, Table 54, p. 108.

[2] Monthly Digest of Statistics, May 1966, Table A.

IX. THE NATIONAL HEALTH SERVICE

(a) Cost[1]: ENGLAND AND WALES

	Year			
	1962–63		1964–65	
	Amount (£M)	*Percentage*	*Amount* (£M)	*Percentage*
Central administration	4	½	6	½
Hospitals (current account)	493	52	567	50½
Hospitals (capital account)	37	4	65	5¾
Council services (administrative)	6	½	6	½
General medical	77	8¼	82	7¼
Pharmaceutical	89	9¼	116	10¼
General dental	57	6¼	60	5½
Supplementary ophthalmic	15	1½	17	1½
Welfare foods	28	3	35	3¼
Local health authorities	85	9	102	9
Local welfare	43	4½	52	4¾
Other	13	1¼	14	1¼
	947	100	1,122	100

(b) SOURCES OF FINANCE[2]: ENGLAND AND WALES

Source	Year			
	1962–63		1964–65	
	Amount (£M)	*Percentage*	*Amount* (£M)	*Percentage*
Exchequer	629	66½	769	68½
N.H.S. contributions	143	15	146	13
Payments by persons using the Health Service	63	6¾	71	6¼
Rates and Exchequer grants to local authorities	110	11½	132	11¾
Other income	2	¼	4	½
	947	100	1,122	100

[1] Annual Reports of the Ministry of Health, 1963, 1965.   [2] *Idem.*

(*c*) PRINCIPALS PROVIDING FULL GENERAL MEDICAL SERVICE
IN ENGLAND AND WALES[1]

July 1, 1960	19,914
October 1, 1961	20,175
October 1, 1962	20,312
October 1, 1963	20,335
October 1, 1964	20,232
January 1, 1965	20,194
April 1, 1965	20,190
July 1, 1965	20,144
October 1, 1965	20,014

(*d*) PRINCIPALS PROVIDING UNRESTRICTED MEDICAL
SERVICES IN SCOTLAND[2]

July 1, 1960	2,628
July 1, 1961	2,654
July 1, 1962	2,663
July 1, 1963	2,666
July 1, 1964	2,662
January 1, 1965	2,652
April 1, 1965	2,643
July 1, 1965	2,625
October 1, 1965	2,611

(*e*) COST: SCOTLAND[3]

	1962–63 £,000	Percentage of whole	1964–65 £,000	Percentage of whole
Hospital, specialist, and ancillary services	68·7	61·0	80·3	61·5
General medical	9·3	8·0	9·9	7·5
Pharmaceutical	10·1	9·0	11·9	9·0
General dental	5·7	5·0	6·0	4·5
Supplementary ophthalmic	1·6	1·5	1·7	2·0
Local health authority	7·5	7	8·8	6·5
Local-authority welfare	4·0	3·5	3·7	3·0
Other services	5·7	5·0	8·0	6·0
	112·6	100·0	130·3	100·0

[1] Written answer, House of Commons, November 22, 1965 (Hansard, fifth series, vol. 721, c. 7).

[2] *Ibid.*, vol. 721, cc. 15–16.

[3] *Health and Welfare Services in Scotland—Reports for 1963 and 1965.*

(f) Sources of Finance: Scotland[1]				
	1962–63 £,000	Percentage of whole	1964–65 £,000	Percentage of whole
Exchequer	80·5	72	96·5	74
N.H.S. contributions	15·8	14	16·3	12·5
Part Exchequer and part rate-borne	9·3	8	10·5	8·0
Patients' payments	7·0	6	7·0	5·5
	112·6	100	130·3	100

X. NATIONAL INSURANCE

(a) Contributions from Employers and Employees from March 29, 1965								
	National Insurance		Industrial Injuries		National Health Service		Total	
	s.	d.	s.	d.	s.	d.	s.	d.
Employee (men over eighteen)	10	2½	0	9	2	8½	13	8
Employer	11	5½	0	10		7½	12	11
	£1 1	8	1	7	3	4	£1 6	7

For women, girls, and boys the contributions are lower for both employee and employer in respect of each item.

Additional Graduated Contributions payable since April 6, 1961, by both employer and employee. Stepped up from June 1, 1963, to be payable on that part of employee's pay which exceeds £9 a week or £39 a month.
Examples:

Wage	Contribution (by both employee and employer)
£18 weekly or over	7s. 8d. weekly
£15 weekly or over	5s. 2d. weekly
£10 weekly or over	11d. weekly
£78 monthly or over	£1 13s. 2d. monthly

Further increased from October 1966 to meet cost of earnings-related supplementary benefit.

From September 5, 1966, the Employers Selective Employment Tax became payable. The rates of tax, payable by employers only, are 25s. a week for each man employed; 12s. 6d. for each woman employed; 12s. 6d. for each boy under the age of eighteen; and 8s. for each girl under the age of eighteen. The tax is paid with the flat-rate insurance contribution in one combined stamp, and steps up the employer's contribution by the specified amount. In certain cases—generally speaking in all productive industries—a refund of the tax is made. From December 6, 1965, the employer was also liable for redundancy tax.

[1] *Health and Welfare Services in Scotland—Reports for 1963 and 1965.*

(*b*) MAIN BENEFIT RATES, 1965

Unemployment benefit, Retirement pension, Sickness benefit*
Single man: £4 weekly
Married couple: £6 10*s*. weekly
First child: £1 2*s*. 6*d*. weekly
Each other child: 14*s*. 6*d*. weekly
Family allowances: 8*s*. weekly for the second child and 10*s*. a week for
the third and subsequent children. Basic age limit fifteen, but nine-
teen for children at school or college or serving apprenticeship, etc.
Maternity benefit: £22
Maternity allowance: £4 a week for 14 weeks, with increases for depen-
dants where applicable.
Widow's benefit: £5 12*s*. 6*d*. a week for first thirteen weeks of widow-
hood (extended to 26 weeks from October 1966).
Widow's pension: £4 weekly.

The earnings rule for widows was abolished by the National Insurance Act of 1964 and ceased to operate from December 21, 1964.

* From the first week in October 1966 an earnings-related supplement to
unemployment and to sickness benefit was also paid.

XI. EDUCATIONAL FINANCE
Summary of public authorities' educational expenditure, 1964–65[1]

	(£M)		
England and Wales	*Current*	*Capital*	*Total*
Local education authorities	942·2	146·7	1,088·9
Department of Education and Science	42·5	24·1	66·6
Scotland			
Education authorities	108·8	23·0	131·8
Education Department	15·7	3·1	18·8
University Grants Committee			
In England and Wales	73·9	50·2	124·1
In Scotland	13·0	6·0	19·0
Total			
England and Wales	1,058·6	221·0	1,279·6
Scotland	137·5	32·1	169·6
TOTAL Great Britain	1,196·1	253·1	1,449·2

[1] *Education in 1965, Report of the Department of Education and Science,* Table 17.

XII. AGRICULTURE IN THE UNITED KINGDOM

(a) AGRICULTURAL HOLDINGS[1]

Size range— acres of crops and grass	No. of Holdings '000	Proportion of Holdings per cent	Total Area '000 acres	Proportion of Total Area per cent
Up to 50	305	64	4,738	15
50 to 150	115	24	10,135	31
150 to 300	41	9	8,387	27
Over 300	17	3	8,372	27
Total	478	100	31,632	100

(b) AGRICULTURAL PRODUCTION: CROP ACREAGES[2] (at June) '000 acres

Crop	Pre-War averages	1964
Wheat	1,856	2,206
Rye	16	21
Barley	929	5,032
Oats	2,403	1,125
Mixed corn	97	80
Potatoes	723	778
Sugar beet	335	443
All tillage	8,908	11,496
Temporary grass	4,180	6,886
Total arable	13,088	18,382

[1] N.E.D.C. *Growth of the United Kingdom Economy, 1961–1966*, Table 32, p. 61.
[2] *Annual Review and Determination of Guarantees, 1965*, Appendix I, p. 19.

(c) AGRICULTURAL PRODUCTION: CROP YIELDS
Totals ('000 tons)[1]

Crop	Pre-war average	1963–64
Wheat	1,651	2,998
Rye	10	22
Barley	765	6,599
Oats	1,940	1,438
Mixed corn	76	118
Potatoes	4,873	6,577
Sugar	415	778
Total cereals	4,442	11,175

Livestock Products[2]

Commodity		
Milk (million gallons—all purposes)	1,556	2,478
Eggs (million dozen)	545	1,155
Beef and veal (1,000 tons)	578	903
Mutton and lamb (1,000 tons)	191	252
Pigmeat (1,000 tons)	368	752
Poultry meat (1,000 tons)	89	349

(d) FARM SALES AND NET AGRICULTURAL OUTPUT IN THE UNITED KINGDOM AT 1961 PRICES[3]

Farm Sales	1956 (actual) £M	1961 (actual) £M	1966 (forecast) £M	1956–61 actual % change	1961–66 forecast % change
Milk and milk products	320	360	407	+12	+13
Fatstock	413	462	527	+12	+14
Eggs and poultry	167	246	288	+47	+17
Farm crops	248	275	317	+11	+15
Horticultural products	149	154	172	+3	+12
Other	47	54	58	+15	+7
Total sales	1,344	1,551	1,769	+15	+14
Index of net output	85	100	118	+17	+18

[1] *Annual Review and Determination of Guarantees, 1965*, Appendix I, p. 26.
[2] *Ibid.*, pp. 20, 25.
[3] N.E.D.C. *The Growth of the United Kingdom Economy, 1961–1966*, Table 33.

(e) ESTIMATED COST OF EXCHEQUER SUPPORT TO AGRICULTURE[1] (£M)	1961-62	1962-63	1963-64
Implementation of price guarantees	225·5	190·1	178·9
of which cereals	73·3	63·9	77·1
eggs, hen and duck	16·2	21·5	20·2
cattle	46·4	30·5	40·8
sheep	30·7	18·9	13·3
pigs	36·2	51·7	26·5
Farming grants and subsidies	107·5	109·4	104·1
TOTALS, including administrative and other services	342·6	309·6	293·9

XIII. THE CONSUMER

(a) CLASSIFICATION OF INCOME BY SIZE[2]
(All incomes which were reviewed by the Inland Revenue for tax purposes)

For the year 1963–64

Annual Income before Tax		*Annual Income after Tax*	
Range of income lower limit £	*Numbers* ('000)	*Range of income* lower limit £	*Numbers* ('000)
275–	430	275–	5,037
300–	1,933	500–	5,611
400–	1,951	750–	4,997
500–	1,958	1,000–	4,504
600–	2,063	2,000–	433
700–	1,977	4,000–	74·6
800–	3,774	6,000–	15·9
1,000–	4,727		
1,500–	1,029		
2,000–	469		
3,000–	228		
5,000–	106		
10,000–	22		
20,000–	4·9		

[1] *Annual Review and Determination of Guarantees, 1965,* Appendix V, Table A, p. 38.

[2] *Report of the Commissioners of H.M. Inland Revenue for the Year ended 31st March, 1965,* Tables 59, 60.

(*b*) CONSUMERS' EXPENDITURE IN THE UNITED KINGDOM
AT 1958 PRICES (£M)[1]

The figures for 1948, immediate post-War, inserted for rough comparison but at 1954 prices and therefore lower than would be at 1958 prices.

Commodity	1948	1955	1960	1962	1963	1964
Food						
Bread and cereals	538	565	551	555	564	559
Meat and bacon	602	1,017	1,115	1,185	1,198	1,186
Fish	143	125	143	145	143	154
Oils and fats	177	183	194	204	200	204
Sugar, preserves, confectionery	233	401	405	411	402	397
Dairy products	481	591	650	676	685	709
Fruit	191	254	283	288	290	302
Potatoes and vegetables	333	425	479	481	496	515
Beverages	167	237	271	275	284	292
Other manufactured food	91	104	135	127	134	138
Other personal expenditure	381	465	521	548	565	581
TOTAL	3,337	4,367	4,747	4,895	4,961	5,037
Alcoholic drink						
Beer	597	571	625	655	658	690
Wines, spirits, cider	235	308	390	429	457	500
TOTAL	832	879	1,015	1,084	1,115	1,190
Tobacco	890	973	1,087	1,055	1,084	1,058
Housing	1,199	1,377	1,529	1,605	1,661	1,688
Fuel and light						
Coal and coke	269	313	307	300	301	271
Electricity	97	148	246	333	381	381
Gas	142	142	133	145	159	167
Other	54	34	56	59	65	57
TOTAL	562	637	742	837	906	876

[1] *National Income and Expenditure*, 1965, Table 19, pp. 27, 28.

CONSUMERS' EXPENDITURE AT 1958 PRICES (£M) (*contd.*)						
Commodity	1948	1955	1960	1962	1963	1964
Clothing						
Footwear	228	229	275	274	281	290
Men's and boys' wear	369	405	456	453	467	480
Women's, girls' and infants' wear	559	725	903	927	964	996
TOTAL	1,156	1,359	1,634	1,654	1,712	1,766
Consumer durables						
Motor-cars and motor-cycles	71	354	600	614	869	1,045
Household						
Furniture and floor coverings	246	319	402	397	398	417
Radio, electric and other durables	152	345	463	484	544	552
Household textiles, soft furnishings, hardware	225	289	332	340	347	368
Matches, soap, and other cleaning goods	131	171	175	181	184	177
Books, etc.						
Books	44	44	54	52	56	58
Newspapers	134	141	133	132	131	134
Magazines	47	50	50	47	45	43
Chemists' goods	146	193	246	255	270	282
Communication						
Post	55	60	72	67	68	68
Telegraph and Telephone	43	56	68	78	83	92
Running costs of motor vehicles	77	259	446	559	603	696
Travel (not independent private transport)	527	540	524	524	529	541
Cinema	178	130	63	52	49	47
Miscellaneous recreational goods	169	265	352	368	374	398
Expenditure abroad	170	219	274	287	310	327

Total Consumers' Expenditure, 1964 at 1958 prices	£18,943,000,000
Total Consumers' Expenditure, 1964 at current prices	£21,334,000,000
Total Personal Current Expenditure, 1964 (including taxes, insurance, etc.)	£25,553,000,000
Saving, 1964	£1,841,000,000
Total personal incomes, 1964	£27,394,000,000

(c) CONSUMERS' EXPENDITURE (1965) AT CURRENT PRICES[1]	
Commodity	*Amount* (£M)
Food	
Bread and cereals	677
Meat and bacon	1,387
Fish	191
Oils and fats	249
Sugar, preserves, confectionery	492
Dairy products	791
Fruit	307
Potatoes and vegetables	553
Beverages	309
Other manufactured food	156
Other personal expenditure	653
TOTAL Food	5,765
Alcoholic drink	
Beer	837
Wines, spirits, cider, etc.	580
TOTAL	1,417
Tobacco	1,428
Housing	2,479
Fuel and light	
Coal and coke	351
Electricity	472
Gas	206
Other	68
Clothing	
Footwear	348
Men's and boys' wear	559
Women's, girls', and infants' wear	1,127
TOTAL	2,034
Consumer Durables	
Motor-cars and motor-cycles	791
Household	
Furniture and floor coverings	510
Radio, electric and other durables	528
Household textiles, soft furnishings, hardware	412
Matches, soap, and other cleaning materials, etc.	228

[1] *National Income and Expenditure*, 1966, Table 27, pp. 34–35.

CONSUMERS' EXPENDITURE (1965) AT CURRENT PRICES (*contd.*)	
Books, etc.	
Books	76
Newspapers	196
Magazines	67
Chemists' goods	321
Running costs of motor vehicles	917
Travel (not independent private transport)	728
Communication services	
Postal	95
Telephone and telegraph	110
Cinema	63
Other recreational and entertainment services	292
Expenditure abroad	394
Total consumers' expenditure, 1965	£22,708,000,000

(*d*) THE RISE IN PRICES: CONSUMER PRICE INDEX
PERCENTAGE INCREASE OVER PREVIOUS YEAR[1]

Year	Percentage increase	Year	Percentage increase
1946	—	1956	4·6
1947	6·8	1957	3·3
1948	7·3	1958	2·8
1949	2·3	1959	0·5
1950	2·6	1960	0·9
1951	9·6	1961	3·0
1952	5·9	1962	3·6
1953	1·9	1963	1·3
1954	1·9	1964	2·8
1955	3·6	1965	4·6
		1966	2·4

[1] Written answers, House of Commons, February 25, 1966 (Hansard, fifth series, vol. 725, cc. 159, 168).

(e) HIRE-PURCHASE AND OTHER INSTALMENT CREDIT
OUTSTANDING IN GREAT BRITAIN[1]

At end of Period
(£'000)

1958	1959	1960	1961	1962	1963	1964
556	849	935	934	887	959	1,115

XIV. TOTAL RETAIL TRADE IN THE UNITED KINGDOM

(a) SUMMARY[2]

	1950	1961
No. of establishments	583,132	577,307
Turnover	£5,000,000,000	£9,000,000,000
Persons engaged	2,392,226	2,524,084

(b) GENERAL ANALYSIS OF TURNOVER[3]

Retailer	Turnover	
	1950 £	1961 £
Food	2,220,128,000	4,137,405,000
Clothing and footwear	929,921,000	1,339,129,000
Household durables, electric, radio, cycles, etc.	536,892,000	1,039,107,000
Confectioners, tobacconists, newsagents	502,661,000	799,622,000
Booksellers, stationers	67,359,000	84,008,000
Chemists, photographic dealers	167,037,000	347,423,000
General stores, including department stores	436,115,000	929,687,000

[1] *Annual Abstract of Statistics*, 1964, Table 356, 1965, Table 354.
[2] *Ibid.*, 1965, Table 225.
[3] *Report on the Census of Distribution and other Services, 1961*, Part I, Table I, p. 17.

(c) NUMBER OF RETAIL ESTABLISHMENTS[1]

	1950	1961
Total	583,132	577,307
Co-ops	25,544	29,396
Retail establishments of organizations other than Co-ops having 1–9 branches	503,639	480,612
Retail establishments of organizations other than Co-ops having more than 10 branches	53,949	67,299

(d) TOTAL SALES: PAST, PRESENT, AND FUTURE (£M) 1961 PRICES[2]

			Increase percentage per year	
1957	1961	1966 (est.)	1957–61	1961–66
7,929	9,095	10,900	3·5	3·7

(e) THE CHANGING PATTERN OF SALES (at 1961 prices) [3]

(Percentages)

	1957	1961	1966 (est.)
All shops	100	100	100
Food shops	48	46	44
of which			
Co-op Societies	9	8	7
Independent retailers	29	26	24
Multiple retailers	10	12	14
Non-food shops	52	54	56
of which			
Co-op Societies	2·2	2·2	2·2
Independent retailers	29	28	26
Multiple retailers	14	17	20
Department stores	5	5	5
Mail order business	1·6	2·5	3

[1] *Report on the Census of Distribution and other Services, 1961*, Part I, Table 3, pp. 20–21.

[2] N.E.D.C. *The Growth of the Economy*, March 1964, Table 87, p. 121.

[3] *Ibid.*, Table 88, p. 122.

(*f*) Types of Retail Organization[1]

	1950	1961
Departmental stores	529	784
General stores	1,112	2,966

(*g*) Numbers of Establishments for the Sale of Various Types of Goods[2]

	1950	1961
Total retail trade	583,132	577,307
Grocers and provision dealers	143,692	149,548
Other food, including:	139,884	128,910
Dairymen	10,231	6,580
Butchers	41,799	44,248
Fishmongers, poulterers	9,511	7,857
Greengrocers, fruiterers	43,948	42,070
Bread and flour confectioners	24,181	17,549
Off-licences	8,197	9,000
Confectioners, tobacconists, newsagents	74,606	70,662
Clothing and footwear	97,162	92,426
Household goods	65,795	73,319
Booksellers, stationers	10,388	6,284
Chemists, photographic goods	18,205	18,392
Jewellery, leather, sports goods	18,896	19,277

[1] *Report on the Census of Distribution and other Services, 1961*, Part I, Table I, p. 17.

[2] *Ibid.*, Table 3, p. 20.

XV. RADIO AND TELEVISION

(a) LICENCES[1]

United Kingdom

Year	Sound	Sound and Television	Free	Total
1927	2,263,894		5,750	2,269,644
1939	8,915,717		52,621	8,968,338
1945	9,663,369		46,861	9,710,230
1947	10,713,298	14,560	49,846	10,777,704
1950	11,819,190	343,882	56,376	12,219,448
1955	9,414,224	4,503,766	62,506	13,980,496
1960	4,480,300	10,469,753	54,958	15,005,011
1963	3,212,814	12,442,806	43,371	15,698,991
1964	2,959,011	12,885,331	40,337	15,884,679
1965	2,759,203	13,253,045	34,355	16,046,603

(b) SOUND BROADCASTING: ANALYSIS OF PROGRAMME OUTPUT[2]
British Broadcasting Corporation—All Services
(53 weeks ended April 2, 1965)

Type of Programme	Number of hours	Percentage of total
Serious music	3,014	18
Entertainment music	5,246	31
General light entertainment	618	4
Outside broadcasts	443	3
Features	513	3
Drama	1,153	7
News	1,722	10
Talks	1,739	10
Religious broadcasts	461	3
Broadcasts for schools	410	2
Other educational broadcasts	240	1
Programmes for special minorities	913	6
Miscellaneous	268	2
	16,740	100

[1] *Annual Report of the British Broadcasting Corporation, 1964–65*, Appendix I.
[2] *Ibid.*, Appendix III.

(*c*) TELEVISION NETWORK HOURS: ANALYSIS OF PROGRAMME OUTPUT[1]
British Broadcasting Corporation—Both Services (BBC 1 and BBC 2)
(53 weeks ended April 2, 1965)

Type of Programme	Number of hours	Percentage of total
Outside broadcasts	897	16·5
Talks, documentaries and other information programmes	787	14·4
British and foreign feature films and series	710	13·0
Drama	631	11·6
School broadcasts	359	6·6
Children's programmes	454	8·3
Light entertainment	372	6·8
News, weather and other news programmes	353	6·5
Presentation material	369	6·8
Religious programmes	139	2·5
Adult Education programmes	135	2·5
Further Education	54	1·0
Music	152	2·8
Sports news and reports	39	0·7
	5,451	100

(*d*) ITA PROGRAMME OUTPUT[2]
Weekly average in London, thirteen weeks ended March 28, 1965

Type of Programme	Length of Time Hrs.	Mins.	Percentage
News and news magazines	5	01	8
Talks, discussions, documentaries	6	21	10
Religion	3	16	5
Adult education	1	51	3
School programmes (including repeats)	4	49	7
Other children's programmes			
(*a*) information	1	20	2
(*b*) entertainment	5	30	8
Plays and serials	10	26	16
Entertainment and music	6	46	10
Films	12	42	19
Quizzes and panel games	2	00	3
Sport	5	41	9
Other outside broadcasts		27	—
	60	10	100

[1] *Annual Report of the British Broadcasting Corporation, 1964–65*, Appendix III.
[2] *Annual Report of the Independent Television Authority, 1964–65*, p. 13.

(e) LISTENING SCHOOLS AND VIEWING SCHOOLS IN THE UNITED KINGDOM[1]

	Listening Schools		Viewing Schools
1938–39	11,170		
1959–60	29,195	1959	2,017
1963–64	31,085	1964	8,467

(f) VIEWING NUMBERS[2]

Programme	Authority	Numbers
Coronation Street	ITA	21 million
Emergency Ward 10	ITA	15 million
Dr Who	BBC	13 million
Dr Finlay's Case Book	BBC	12 million
Z Cars	BBC	12 million

XVI. THE POST OFFICE

(a) POST OFFICE AND TELECOMMUNICATIONS ACCOUNTS FOR THE YEAR 1965–66[3]

Postal Services	£M
Income	318·8
Expenditure	317·9
Profit	0·9

Telecommunications	
Income	404·0
Expenditure	364·7
Profit	39·3

[1] *Annual Report of the British Broadcasting Corporation, 1964–65*, Appendix VII.
[2] *Ibid.*, p. 24; *Annual Report of the Independent Television Authority, 1964–65*, p. 7.
[3] *Post Office Report and Accounts for the year 1965–66*, pp. 8, 27.

(b) POST OFFICE STATISTICS FOR THE YEAR 1965–66[1]

	Numbers—million
Correspondence posted	11,300
Parcels handled	235
Correspondence sent abroad by air	328
Parcels sent abroad by air	1·9

	£M
Total transactions	7,610
Remittances made	1,320
Savings under management (end of year)	6,065

	Number
Post-offices open	25,025

XVII. THE ORGANIZATION OF LABOUR IN THE UNITED KINGDOM

Year	Trade Unions[2]	Membership in Millions Co-operative Societies[3]	Labour Party[4]
1900	2·0	1·7	0·4
1914	4·1	3·1	1·6
1945	7·8	9·4	3·0
1954	9·5	11·5	6·5
1964	10·1	13·1	6·4

[1] *Post Office Report and Accounts for the year 1965–66.*
[2] *Ministry of Labour Gazette.*
[3] Annual Reports of the Co-operative Congress.
[4] Annual Reports of the Labour Party Conference.

XVIII. ADVERTISING

(a) Total Advertising and Sales Promotion Expenditure in the United Kingdom related to Consumers' Expenditure, National Income, and Gross National Product[1]

Year	Total Expenditure (£M)	Total Expenditure as a Percentage of		
		Consumers' Expenditure	National Income	Gross National Product
1938	98	2·2	2·0	1·9
1956	309	2·2	1·8	1·7
1960	457	2·7	2·2	2·0
1961	475	2·7	2·1	2·0
1962	488	2·6	2·1	2·0
1963	517	2·6	2·1	2·0
1964	568	2·7	2·1	2·0
1965	590	2·6	2·1	1·9

(b) Total Advertising and Sales Promotion Expenditure in the United Kingdom by Media[2]

Media	1956	1960	1964	1965	1956	1960	1964	1965
	£M				Percentage of Total			
Press								
National newspapers	39	64	84	87	13	14	15	15
Regional newspapers	51	66	81	87	16	14	14	15
Magazines and periodicals	32	40	46	48	10	9	8	8
Trade and technical journals	22	31	37	39	7	6	6	7
Other publications	2	2	3	3	1	—	1	—
Press production costs	13	15	18	18	4	3	3	3
Total Press	159	218	269	282	51	47	47	48

[Continued overleaf

1 "Advertising Expenditure 1960–65", Special Statistical Supplement to *The Advertising Quarterly*, No. 8, Summer 1966, Table 1, p. 70.

2 *Ibid*, Table 2, p. 71.

(*b*) TOTAL ADVERTISING AND SALES PROMOTION EXPENDITURE
IN THE UNITED KINGDOM BY MEDIA (*continued*)

Media	1956	1960	1964	1965	1956	1960	1964	1965
	£M				*Percentage of Total*			
Television	11	72	102	106	3	16	18	18
Poster and transport	15	16	18	18	5	4	3	3
Outdoor signs	11	13	15	15	4	3	3	3
Cinema	6	5	6	6	2	1	1	1
Radio	1	1	2	2	—	—	1	—
Catalogues, leaflets, calendars, etc.	35	39	44	45	11	9	8	8
Window and interior display	22	29	35	36	7	6	6	6
Exhibitions	11	16	19	20	4	4	3	3
Free samples and gift schemes	12	15	19	20	4	3	3	3
Miscellaneous	5	7	10	10	2	1	2	2
Administration	21	26	29	30	7	6	5	5
TOTAL	309	457	568	590	100	100	100	100

XIX. BRITAIN AND THE WORLD

(*a*) VOLUME INDICES OF GROSS NATIONAL PRODUCT[1]
AT MARKET PRICES (1958 = 100)

	1955	1964
OECD member countries combined	94	134
European OECD member countries combined	90	136
EEC member countries combined	88	139
Austria	86	131
Belgium	96	131
Canada	90	129
Denmark	91	141
France	87	137
Germany (Federal Republic)	86	141
Greece	83	153
Italy	87	143
Netherlands	94	137
Norway	93	135
Sweden	92	135
United Kingdom	95	126
U.S.A.	98	129

[1] *Statistics of National Accounts* (OECD), 1955-1964, p. 4.

(b) Volume Indices of per Capita Gross National Product[1]
(1958 = 100)

	1955	1964
OECD member countries combined	98	124
European OECD member countries combined	92	127
EEC member countries combined	90	130
Austria	87	127
Belgium	98	127
Canada	98	115
Denmark	92	135
France	90	126
Germany (Federal Republic)	89	131
Greece	86	147
Italy	88	138
Netherlands	98	127
Norway	96	128
Sweden	94	130
United Kingdom	96	120
U.S.A.	103	117

(c) Indices of Total Agricultural Production[2]
(Average 1952–53—1956–57 = 100)

Country	1952–53	1963–64 (prelim.)
Western Europe	94	126
N.W. Europe	95	126
Austria	91	134
Belgium Luxembourg	93	122
Denmark	100	118
Finland	98	130
France	91	126
Germany (Federal Republic)	95	127
Greece	79	146
Italy	93	118
Netherlands	100	118
Norway	97	105
Portugal	87	108
Spain	100	134
Sweden	104	99
Switzerland	101	107
United Kingdom	97	132
Canada	111	126
U.S.A.	98	118

[1] *Statistics of National Accounts* (OECD), 1955–1964, p. 4.
[2] *The State of Food and Agriculture, 1965* (Food and Agriculture Organization of the United Nations), Annex Table 1A, p. 210.

(*d*) INDICES OF PER CAPITA AGRICULTURAL PRODUCTION[1]
(Average 1952–53—1956–57 = 100)

Country	1952–53	1963–64 (*prelim.*)
Western Europe	95	117
N.W. Europe	96	116
Austria	91	130
Belgium Luxembourg	94	116
Denmark	101	111
Finland	100	120
France	93	113
Germany (Federal Republic)	97	114
Greece	81	136
Italy	94	112
Netherlands	102	105
Norway	99	97
Portugal	87	102
Spain	101	125
Sweden	105	94
Switzerland	103	90
United Kingdom	97	125
Canada	117	103
U.S.A.	102	102

[1] *The State of Food and Agriculture, 1965* (Food and Agriculture Organization of the United Nations), Annex Table 1B, p. 212.

XX. CRIME AND THE CRIMINAL

(a) TOTAL INDICTABLE OFFENCES KNOWN TO THE POLICE: ENGLAND AND WALES[1]

Year	Known to the Police	Percentage cleared up
1938	283,220	50·1
1957	545,562	47·2
1958	626,509	45·6
1959	675,626	44·7
1960	743,713	44·4
1961	806,900	44·8
1962	896,424	43·9
1963	978,076	43·1
1964	1,067,963	39·6
1965	1,133,882	39·2

(b) SOME CATEGORIES OF INDICTABLE OFFENCES KNOWN TO THE POLICE, 1964, 1965, IN ENGLAND AND WALES[2]

	1964	1965	Percentage increase
Violence against the person	23,470	25,549	8·9
Breaking and entering	233,930	252,733	8·0
Robbery	3,066	3,736	21·9
Sexual offences	19,903	20,155	1·3
Larceny	704,116	744,155	5·7
Receiving	17,663	19,406	9·9
Malicious injuries against property	7,891	8,520	8·0
Forgery	8,589	9,719	13·1

[1] *Report of H.M. Chief Inspector of Constabulary for the Year 1965*, p. 41.
[2] *Criminal Statistics, England and Wales*, 1965, p. x.

(c) NUMBER OF PERSONS, WITH AGE AND SEX, FOUND GUILTY OF INDICTABLE OFFENCES IN ALL COURTS IN ENGLAND AND WALES IN 1965[1]

	Total	Under 14	14 and under 17	17 and under 21
Male	187,424	22,376	32,818	40,486
Female	31,011	2,697	4,979	4,318

	21 and under 25	25 and under 30	30 and under 40
Male	25,258	21,841	23,605
Female	2,535	2,740	4,452

	40 and under 50	50 and under 60	60 and over
Male	12,923	5,804	2,313
Female	4,163	3,301	1,826

(d) NUMBER OF PERSONS IN ENGLAND AND WALES FOUND GUILTY OF NON-INDICTABLE OFFENCES[2]

	Motoring offences	Other
1964	805,353	317,034
1965	839,008	310,605

(e) POLICE FORCE: ACTUAL STRENGTH[3]

Year	England and Wales[4]	Scotland
1956	49,568	8,108
1958	52,051	8,354
1960	53,126	8,669
1961	55,476	9,015
1962	57,953	9,527
1963	59,065	9,738
1964	59,862	9,859
1965	62,119	10,175

[1] *Criminal Statistics, England and Wales,* 1965, Table IV.
[2] *Criminal Statistics, England and Wales,* 1964, 1965.
[3] *Reports of H.M. Chief Inspector of Constabulary and of H.M. Inspector of Constabulary for Scotland.*
[4] Including City of London but excluding the Metropolitan Police.

(*f*) CRIMES AND OFFENCES MADE KNOWN TO THE POLICE: SCOTLAND[1]

	1964	1965	1964	1965
			Percentage cleared up	
Total	352,358	364,401	72·2	71·9
of which				
Crimes	*133,654*	*140,141*		
Against the person	5,517	6,345		
Against property with violence	60,869	64,232		
Against property without violence	63,535	65,155		
Malicious injury to property	1,013	1,496		
Forgery and crimes against currency	804	1,016		
Other crimes	1,916	1,897		

(*g*) ALL CRIMES AND OFFENCES AGAINST WHOM CHARGE PROVED, 1964: SCOTLAND[2]

	Total	8–16	*Age* 17–20	21–24	25–29
Male	161,695	20,445	27,399	20,320	20,324
Female	14,876	1,635	1,445	1,401	1,690

	30–39	40–49	50–59	60+
Male	34,918	21,263	12,306	4,720
Female	3,960	2,545	1,469	731

[1] *Criminal Statistics, Scotland*, 1964, Table 5; 1965, Table 5.
[2] *Ibid.*, 1964, Table 7.

Production and Incomes Since 1950

Gross Domestic Incomes and Gross Domestic Product
(at 1958 constant prices)   (1950=100)

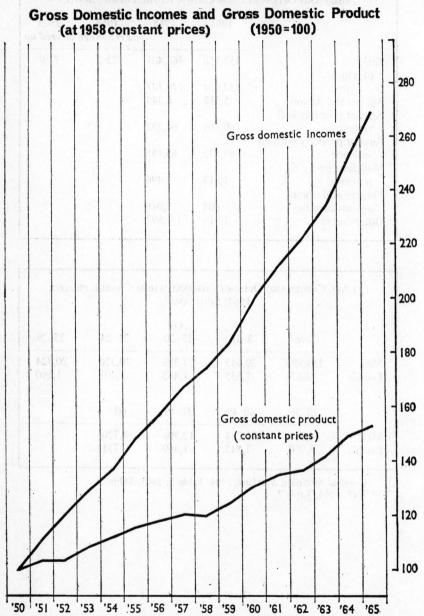

From *Statistics on Incomes, Prices, Employment and Production* (Ministry of Labour), No. 18, September 1966.

INCOMES — 1950 AND 1965

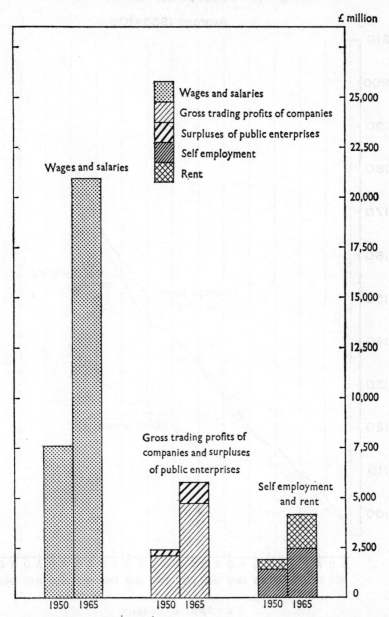

From *Statistics on Incomes, Prices, Employment and Production* (Ministry of Labour), No. 18, September 1966.

12*

Wages, Salaries, and Prices 1955-66

Average 1955=100

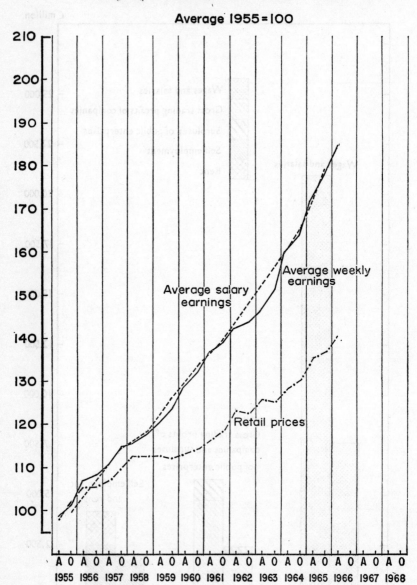

A = April   O = October

From *Statistics on Incomes, Prices, Employment and Production* (Ministry of Labour), No. 18, September 1966.

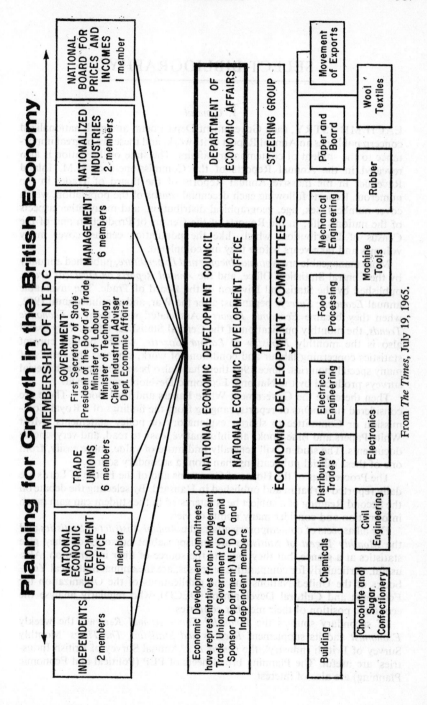

Planning for Growth in the British Economy

MEMBERSHIP OF NEDC

INDEPENDENTS
2 members

NATIONAL ECONOMIC DEVELOPMENT OFFICE
1 member

TRADE UNIONS
6 members

MANAGEMENT
6 members

NATIONALIZED INDUSTRIES
2 members

NATIONAL BOARD FOR PRICES AND INCOMES
1 member

GOVERNMENT
First Secretary of State
President of the Board of Trade
Minister of Labour
Minister of Technology
Chief Industrial Adviser
Dept. Economic Affairs

DEPARTMENT OF ECONOMIC AFFAIRS

NATIONAL ECONOMIC DEVELOPMENT COUNCIL
NATIONAL ECONOMIC DEVELOPMENT OFFICE

STEERING GROUP

ECONOMIC DEVELOPMENT COMMITTEES

Building

Chocolate and Sugar Confectionery

Chemicals

Civil Engineering

Distributive Trades

Electronics

Electrical Engineering

Food Processing

Machine Tools

Mechanical Engineering

Rubber

Paper and Board

Wool Textiles

Movement of Exports

Economic Development Committees have representatives from: Management Trade Unions Government (D E A and Sponsor Department) N E D O and Independent members

From *The Times*, July 19, 1965.

SELECT BIBLIOGRAPHY

1. *General*

EACH MINISTRY, each Government Department, and each nationalized concern publishes an Annual Report of its work, and these are of great importance to the student of contemporary affairs. The state of the nation is also revealed in the Annual Reports of the Commissioners of H.M. Inland Revenue; in the massive Annual Reports of the Board of Trade; in the numerous Reports following each decennial census of the population, which cover numbers, sex, age, geographical distribution, and many other aspects of the nation's life; in the Reports of the Census of Production and of the Census of Distribution, which, like the population census, cover many volumes and take years before they are completed.

More manageable are *National Income and Expenditure*, published annually by the Central Statistical Office, and the *Annual Reports on Overseas Trade*, published by the Statistical Division of the Board of Trade. The invaluable annual *Economic Surveys* began just after the War, and continued until 1962, when they became *Economic Reports*. Associated with them is *Economic Trends*, the monthly publication of the Central Statistical Office. Very useful also is the monthly *Ministry of Labour Gazette*, which, besides current statistics concerning labour and conditions of work, contains the results of many special inquiries. Since 1963 there have also been the important special surveys produced by the National Economic Development Council.

Then there are the Government White Papers and Blue Books. These are considered statements or reports, ranging from the findings of a Royal Commission or Committee to shorter explanatory or policy statements. Most White Papers and Blue Books are informative, easy to read, and very sincere documents. The student will generally find more of value, more easily, from one of these official publications than from a secondary source.

The Proceedings of the House of Commons and of the House of Lords are daily reported verbatim and published in Hansard. By selecting the debate on the Second Reading of a subject he is interested in the student can gain much information and consider many points of view.

For all aspects of contemporary affairs the *Annual Abstract of Statistics* and the *Monthly Digest of Statistics* are indispensable: not only do they give statistics at a glance, but they indicate the source of their information. Also useful, particularly for comparative purposes, are the annual Statistical Yearbooks of the United Nations and the publications of the Organization for Economic and Cultural Development (OECD), who regularly analyse the economic position of their member countries.

Of secondary sources the *Financial Times Annual Reviews*, the weekly *Economist* and its supplement *Records and Statistics*, *The Times* 'Monthly Survey of British Industry', the *Guardian*'s 'Annual Survey of British Industries' are useful. The Planning broadsheets of PEP (Political and Economic Planning) are also of interest.

2. *General Secondary Sources Useful to a Study of the Welfare State*

ABEL-SMITH, B.: *Freedom and the Welfare State*, in the series "Socialism in the Sixties" (Fabian Society, 1965).

BRUCE, MAURICE: *The Coming of the Welfare State* (Batsford, 1961).

GALBRAITH, J. K.: *The Affluent Society* (Hamish Hamilton, 1958).

ROBERTS, DAVID: *Victorian Origins of the British Welfare State* (Yale University Press, 1960).

SAMPSON, ANTHONY: *Anatomy of Britain To-day* (revised edition, Hodder and Stoughton, 1965).

TITMUSS, RICHARD M.: *Essays on the Welfare State* (Allen and Unwin, 1958).

WEYMOUTH, A.: *This Century of Change, 1853–1952* (Harrap, 1953).

3. *Secondary Sources Useful for the Early Years of the Welfare State*

ATTLEE, CLEMENT: *As It Happened* (Odhams Press, 1956).

—— *A Prime Minister Remembers*, conversations with Francis Williams (Heinemann, 1961).

BEVAN, ANEURIN: *In Place of Fear* (Heinemann, 1952 and 1961).

BROME, VINCENT: *Aneurin Bevan: A Biography* (Longmans, 1951).

CHURCHILL, WINSTON: *The Second World War*, vols. IV, VI, *passim* (Cassell, 1951, 1954).

DALTON, HUGH: *The Fateful Years*, being vol. 2 of *Memoirs* (Frederick Muller, 1957).

—— *High Tide and After*, being vol. 3 of *Memoirs* (Frederick Muller, 1962).

MORRISON, HERBERT: *An Autobiography* (Odhams Press, 1960).

4. *Official Publications and Secondary Sources Useful for the Social Services before the Welfare State*

Report of the Royal Commission on the Poor Laws, 1909 (Cd. 4499) (Majority and Minority Reports published in the same volume, and Minority Report also published separately).

First Report of the Royal Commission on Unemployment Insurance, June 1931 (Cmd. 3872).

Final Report and Minority Report of the Royal Commission on Unemployment Insurance, 1932 (Cmd. 4185).

Secondary Sources

Rev. William Lewery Blackley, Rector of North Waltham, Hants, Vicar of King's Somborne, Honorary Canon of Winchester, and finally Vicar of St James the Less, London, wrote many articles in favour of his scheme of national insurance. Most of them are collected in two books:

Collected Essays on the Prevention of Pauperism (Kegan Paul, 1880);

Thrift and National Insurance as a Security against Pauperism, papers collected by his wife, M. J. J. Blackley (Kegan Paul, 1906).

BROCKINGTON, C. FRASER: *A Short History of Public Health* (Churchill, 1956).

COHEN, PERCY: *The British System of Social Insurance* (Philip Allan, 1932).

EVANS, A. DELBERT, and HOWARD, L. G. REDMOND, *The Romance of the British Voluntary Hospital Movement* (Hutchinson, 1930).

JONES, THOMAS: *Lloyd George* (Oxford University Press, 1951).

Lloyd George's Ambulance Wagon, the Memoirs of W. J. Braithwaite, edited by Sir Henry Bunbury (Methuen, 1957).

OWEN, FRANK: *Tempestuous Journey: Lloyd George, His Life and Times* (Hutchinson, 1954).

WEBB, S. and B.: *The State and the Doctor* (Longmans, 1910).

5. *Care and Social Security*

Social Insurance and Allied Services (the Beveridge Report), November 1942 (Cmd. 6404).

Employment Policy, May 1944 (Cmd. 6527).

Social Insurance, Part I, September 1944 (Cmd. 6550).

Social Insurance, Part II (Industrial Injuries), September 1944 (Cmd. 6551).

Annual Reports of the Ministry of Pensions and National Insurance.

Annual Reports of the National Assistance Board.

Ministry of Social Security Bill, 1966, Explanatory Memorandum, May 1966 (Cmnd. 2997).

Reports of the Work of the Children's Department, particularly for 1961–63.

Report of the Committee on the Care of Children and Young Persons in England and Wales (the Curtis Report), September 1946 (Cmd. 6922).

Report of the Working Party on Social Workers in the Local Authority Health and Welfare Services (the Younghusband Report), 1959 (Cmnd. 1191).

Report of the Committee on Children and Young Persons (the Ingleby Report), October 1960 (Cmnd. 1191).

Report of the Committee on the Youth Service in England and Wales (the Albemarle Report), 1960.

Public Social Services (National Council of Social Service, eleventh edition, 1961).

Secondary Sources

BEVERIDGE, JANET: *Beveridge and His Plan* (Hodder and Stoughton, 1954).

HALL, M. P.: *The Social Services of Modern England* (Routledge, sixth edition, 1963).

KING, GEOFFREY S.: *The Ministry of Pensions and National Insurance* (Allen and Unwin, 1958).

TITMUSS, R. M.: *Problems of Social Policy* (History of the Second World War, H.M.S.O. and Longmans, 1950).

TOWNSEND, PETER: *Family Life of Old People* (Routledge, 1957).

—— *The Last Refuge: A Survey of Residential Institutions and Homes for the Aged in England and Wales* (Routledge, 1957).

YOUNGHUSBAND, EILEEN L.: *Social Work in Britain* (T. and A. Constable, 1951).

6. *The Health Service*

A National Health Service, February 1944 (Cmd. 6502).

Annual Reports of the Ministry of Health for England and Wales.

Health and Welfare Services in Scotland, Annual Reports.

Report of the Committee of Enquiry into the Cost of the National Health Service (the Guillebaud Report), 1956 (Cmnd. 9663).

Report of the Royal Commission on Doctors' and Dentists' Remuneration (the Pilkington Commission), 1957–60 (Cmnd. 939).

A Hospital Plan for England and Wales, 1962 (Cmnd. 1604).

A Hospital Plan for Scotland, 1962 (Cmnd. 1602).
Health and Welfare: The Development of Community Care, 1963 (Cmnd. 1973).
Report of the Joint Working Party on the Medical Staffing Structure in the Hospital Service, Chairman Sir Robert Platt (H.M.S.O., 1961).
Report of the Gillie Committee on General Practice, Central Health Services Council (H.M.S.O., 1963).

Secondary Sources

ABEL-SMITH, BRIAN, and TITMUSS, R. M.: *The Cost of the National Health Service* (The National Institute of Economic and Social Research, Occasional Papers, XVIII, 1956).
COX, ALFRED: *Among the Doctors* (Christopher Johnson, 1950).
ECKSTEIN, HARRY: *The English Health Service* (O.U.P., 1959).
JEWKES, JOHN and SYLVIA: *The Genesis of the British National Health Service* (Basil Blackwell, 1962).
LINDSEY, ALMONT: *Socialised Medicine in England and Wales* (O.U.P., 1962).
PERROTT, ROY: "The Drug Makers", in *The Twentieth Century*, autumn 1962.
PLATT, ROBERT: *Doctor and Patient: Ethics, Morale, Government* (Nuffield Provincial Hospitals Trust, 1963).
ROSS, JAMES STIRLING: *The National Health Service in Great Britain* (O.U.P., 1952).

7. *Economic Affairs*

Besides the general material mentioned in section 1 the following are of special interest:
Statistical Material presented during the Washington Negotiations, December 1945 (Cmd. 6707).
Financial Agreement between the Governments of the United States and the United Kingdom, December 1945 (Cmd. 6708).
Economic Implications of Full Employment, March 1956 (Cmnd. 9725).
Control of Public Expenditure, July 1961 (Cmnd. 1432).
The Economic Situation: A Statement by Her Majesty's Government, October 1964 (H.M.S.O.).
The National Plan, September 1965 (Cmnd. 2764).

Publications of the National Economic Development Council
  Growth of the United Kingdom Economy, 1961 to 1966 (H.M.S.O., February 1963).
  Conditions Favourable to Further Growth (H.M.S.O., April 1963).
  Growth in the United Kingdom Economy (H.M.S.O., 1964).

Incomes Policy
Incomes Policy: The Next Step, February 1962 (Cmnd. 1626).
Machinery of a Prices and Incomes Policy, February 1965 (Cmnd. 2577).
Prices and Incomes Policy, April 1965 (Cmnd. 2639).
Prices and Incomes Policy: An 'Early Warning' System, November 1965 (Cmnd. 2808).
Prices and Incomes Standstill, July 1966 (Cmnd. 3073).
Prices and Incomes Standstill: Period of Severe Restraint, November 1966 (Cmnd. 3150).

Final Report of the Committee on Consumer Protection (the Molony Committee), July 1962 (Cmnd. 1781).

Secondary Sources

BAGRIT, LEON: *The Age of Automation, the Reith Lectures*, 1964 (Weidenfeld and Nicolson, 1965).
BECKERMAN, W.: "Projecting Economic Growth", in *Economic Journal*, December 1962.
DONALDSON, PETER: *Guide to the British Economy* (Pelican Original, 1965).
LAMFULASSY, A.: *The United Kingdom and the Six* (Macmillan, 1963).
LIVINGSTONE, J. M.: *Britain and the World Economy* (Pelican Original, 1966).
MADDISON, A.: *Economic Growth in the West* (New York, 1964).
MALIK, R.: *What's Wrong with British Industry?* (Penguin Special, 1964).
PEARSEY, J., and TURNER, G.: *The Persuasion Industry* (Eyre and Spottiswoode, 1965).
SCHONFIELD, A.: *British Economic Policy since the War* (Penguin Special, 1960).
WELLS, S. J.: *British Export Performance: A Comparative Study* (Cambridge University Press, 1964).
WORSWICK, G. D. N., and ADY, P. H.: *The British Economy 1945–1950* (Clarendon Press, 1952).
—— *The British Economy in the Nineteen-fifties* (Clarendon Press, 1962).
YOUNGSON, A. J.: *The British Economy 1920–1957* (Allen and Unwin, 1960).
The Common Market: A Survey by *The Times*.
Colour in Britain (British Broadcasting Corporation, 1965).

8. *Agriculture and Forestry*

Annual Review and Determination of Guarantees (published by H.M.S.O. jointly for the Secretary of State for the Home Department, the Secretary of State for Scotland, and the Minister of Agriculture, Fisheries and Food).
Agricultural Statistics (Ministry of Agriculture, Fisheries and Food).
Agriculture in Scotland (Department of Agriculture and Fisheries for Scotland).
Post War Forest Policy: Report by H.M. Forestry Commissioners 1943 (Cmd. 6447).
The Dedication of Woodlands, Principles and Procedure: H.M. Forestry Commission Booklet No. 2 (H.M.S.O., 1948).
Seventh Report of the Estimates Committee, Session 1963–64; H.M. Forestry Commission.

Secondary Sources

HOUSE, FRANK H.: *An Account of the Activities of the Timber Control*, 1939–1945 (Ernest Benn, 1965).
McCRONE, GAVIN: *The Economics of Subsidising Agriculture* (Allen and Unwin, 1962).
MEIGGS, RUSSELL: *Home Timber Production, 1939–1945* (Crosby Lockwood, 1949).
WHITLOCK, RALPH: *A Short History of Farming* (John Baker, 1965).

9. Nationalization: General

Efficiency in the Nationalised Industries (Institute of Public Administration, 1952).

Interim Report of a Court of Inquiry into a Dispute between the British Transport Commission and the National Union of Railwaymen presided over by Sir John (later Lord) Cameron, January 1955 (Cmd. 9352).

Final Report, January 1955 (Cmd. 9372).

Report of the Committee of Inquiry into the Electricity Supply Industry (the Herbert Committee), 1956.

The Financial and Economic Obligations of the Nationalised Industries, April 1961 (Cmnd. 1337).

Secondary Sources

CHESTER, D. N.: *The Nationalised Industries, a Statutory Analysis* (Allen and Unwin, second edition, 1961).

GROVE, J. W.: *Government and Industry in Britain* (Longmans, 1962).

KELF-COHEN, R.: *Nationalisation in Britain* (Macmillan, 1961).

ROBSON, W. A.: *Nationalised Industry and Public Ownership* (Allen and Unwin, 1960).

10. Iron and Steel

White Paper on Iron and Steel, July 1952 (Cmd. 8619).

The Iron and Steel Industry in 1962 and Trends in 1963, a Study by the Iron and Steel Special Committee of the Organisation for Economic Co-operation and Development (OECD, 1963).

The Iron and Steel Industry in 1963 and Trends in 1964 (OECD, 1964).

Research in the Iron and Steel Industry, Special Report, 1963 (H.M.S.O.).

Development in the Iron and Steel Industry, Special Reports, 1957, 1961, 1964 (H.M.S.O.).

Steel Nationalisation, April 1965 (Cmnd. 2651).

The Iron and Steel Board: Annual Reports.

Annual Reports of the British Iron and Steel Corporation, 1951, 1951-52.

Iron and Steel Board and British Iron and Steel Federation Monthly Statistics (Statistics Department of the Board and Federation).

Secondary Sources

CARR, H. C., and TAPLIN, W.: *History of the British Steel Industry* (Basil Blackwell, 1962).

KEELING, B. S., and WRIGHT, A. E. G.: *The Development of the Modern British Steel Industry* (Longmans, 1964).

11. Transport and Communications

Annual Reports of the British Transport Commission (1958–1962).

Annual Reports of the British Railways Board.

Annual Reports of the British Overseas Airways Corporation.

Annual Reports of British European Airways.

Annual Reports of the British Broadcasting Corporation.

Annual Reports of the Independent Television Authority.

Annual Reports of the Post Office (Post Office and Telecommunications).

Post Office Prospects (annual Statistics).
The Re-organisation of the Nationalised Transport Undertaking, December 1960 (Cmnd. 1248).
Transport Policy, July 1966 (Cmnd. 3057).
The Re-shaping of British Railways (the Beeching Report), 1963.
The Development of the Major Railway Trunk Routes, February 1965 (the second Beeching Report).
The Financial Problems of the British Overseas Airways Corporation, November 20, 1963 (Ministry of Aviation).
Report of the Committee on Broadcasting (the Beveridge Committee), December 1950 (Cmd. 8116).
Report of the Committee on Broadcasting, 1960 (the Pilkington Committee) (Cmnd. 1753).
The Inland Telephone Service in an Expanding Economy, November 1963 (Cmnd. 2211).

Secondary Source

CALVERT, ROGER: *The Future of Britain's Railways* (George Allen and Unwin, 1965).

12. *Fuel and Power*

Annual Statistical Digest of Ministry of Fuel and Power.
Fuel Policy, October 1965 (Cmnd. 2798).

Coal

Coal Mining: Report of the Technical Advisory Committee (the Reid Committee) March 1945 (Cmd. 6610).
Annual Reports of the National Coal Board.
Report of the Committee on Air Pollution, 1954 (Cmd. 9322).
Investing in Coal, April 1956.
Revised Plan for Coal, 1959.
Finances of the Coal Industry (Cmnd. 2805).

Gas

Annual Reports of the Gas Council.
Annual Reports of the Scottish Gas Board.

Electricity

Annual Reports of the British Electricity Authority (until 1955).
Annual Reports of the Central Electricity Authority (1955–1957).
Annual Reports of the North of Scotland Hydro-electric Board.
Annual Reports of the South of Scotland Electricity Board.
Annual Reports of the Electricity Council (since 1957).

Nuclear Power

Annual Reports of the United Kingdom Atomic Energy Authority.
A Programme for Nuclear Power, 1955 (Cmnd. 9389).
The Nuclear Power Programme, June 1960 (Cmnd. 1083).
The Second Nuclear Power Programme, April 1964 (Cmd. 2335).

Report on the United Nations Conference on the Peaceful Uses of Atomic Energy, 1964.

13. Population, Housing, Towns, Traffic, and Regional Development

Report of the Royal Commission on Population, June 1949 (Cmd. 7695).
Annual Reports of the Ministry of Housing and Local Government.
White Paper on Housing, 1963 (Cmnd. 1952).
The Report of the Committee on Housing in Greater London (the Milner Holland Report), March 1965 (Cmnd. 2605).
The North-East; A Programme for Regional Development and Growth (November 1963, Cmnd. 2206).
Central Scotland: A Programme for Development and Growth, November 1963, Cmnd. 2188).
Annual Reports of the Scottish Development Department.
The South East Study, H.M.S.O. 1964.
South East England, 1964 (Cmnd. 2308).
The West Midlands—a Regional Study (H.M.S.O., August 1965).
The North-West—a Regional Study (H.M.S.O., 1965).
Final Report of the Committee on the Problem of Noise, July 1963 (Cmnd. 2056).
Staggered Holidays, July 1963 (Cmnd. 2105).
The Transport Needs of Great Britain in the Next Twenty Years (the Hall Report), October 1963.
Traffic in Towns, A Study of the long-term problems of traffic in urban areas. A report of the Working Group appointed by the Minister of Transport under the chairmanship of Colin Buchanan (the Buchanan Report) (H.M.S.O., 1963).
Leisure in the Countryside: England and Wales, February 1966 (Cmnd. 2928).

Secondary Sources

The Paper Metropolis: A Study of London's Office Growth (Town and Country Planning Association, 1963).
SELF, PETER: *Cities in Flood: The Problems of Urban Growth* (Faber and Faber, second edition 1961).
OSBORN, FREDERIC, and WHITTICK, ARNOLD: *The New Towns, the Answer to Megalopolis* (Leonard Hill, 1963).

14. Law and Order

Annual Reports of Her Majesty's Chief Inspector of Constabulary (England and Wales).
Annual Reports of Her Majesty's Inspector of Constabulary for Scotland.
Annual Home Office Criminal Statistics for England and Wales.
Annual Criminal Statistics (Scotland).
Penal Practice in a Changing Society, February 1959 (Cmnd. 645).
The War against Crime in England and Wales 1959–1964, April 1964 (Cmnd. 2296).
Children and Young Persons (Scotland), April 1964 (Cmnd. 2306).
Report of the Royal Commission on the Police (the Willink Report), Fina Report, May 1962 (Cmnd. 1728).

Corporal Punishment: Report of the Advisory Council on the Treatment of Offenders, November 1961 (Cmnd. 1213).

Compensation for Victims of Crimes of Violence, Report of a Working Party presented June 1961 (Cmnd. 1406).

15. *Education*

Annual Reports of the Ministry of Education for England and Wales (until 1964).

Annual Reports of the Department of Education and Science (from 1964; Schools in England and Wales, Universities in Great Britain).

Education in Scotland: Annual Reports of the Scottish Education Department.

Statistics of Education: England and Wales, published annually.

Report of the Consultative Committee of the Board of Education on Secondary Education (the Spens Committee), 1938.

Educational Reconstruction, July 1943 (Cmd. 6458).

Report of the Committee on the Curriculum and Examinations in Secondary Schools (the Norwood Committee), 1943.

Report of the Committee on Public Schools and the General Educational System (the Fleming Committee), 1944.

Half Our Future: a Report of the Central Advisory Council for Education (England) (The Newsom Report—H.M.S.O., 1963).

Report of the Committee on Higher Education (The Robbins Report), 1963 (Cmnd. 2154).

A University of the Air, February 1966 (Cmnd. 2922).

Secondary Sources

CURTIS, S. J.: *History of Education in Great Britain* (University Tutorial Press, Ltd, fifth edition, 1963).

PEDLEY, R.: *The Comprehensive School* (Penguin, 1963).

Crisis in the Humanities: A Symposium (Penguin, 1964).

16. *The British General Elections since the War*

McCALLUM, R. B., and READMAN, A.: *The British General Election of 1945* (Oxford University Press, 1947).

NICHOLAS, H. G.: *The British General Election of 1950* (Macmillan, 1951).

BUTLER, D. E.: *The British General Election of 1951* (Macmillan, 1952).

BUTLER, D. E.: *The British General Election of 1955* (Macmillan, 1955).

BUTLER, D. E., and ROSE, R.: *The British General Election of 1959* (Macmillan, 1960).

BUTLER, D. E., and KING, A.: *The British General Election of 1964* (Macmillan, 1965).

BUTLER, D. E., and KING, A.: *The British General Election of 1966* (Macmillan, 1966).

Index of Subjects

Hospitals, *contd.*
  Regional Hospital Boards, 53–54;
  Management Committees, 54; teaching hospitals, 54; expenditure, 191,
  199; expansion, 191, 198–200; *Hospital Plan for England and Wales*
  (1962), 199; *Hospital Plan for Scotland* (1962), 199; number of patients
  treated, 200; consultants, 200–201;
  nurses, 201–202; increased pay for
  staff, 208
Hours, weekly working, 109, 119, 237
House of Commons: unrepresentative
  nature of in 1944, 27–28; dissolution
  controversy, 28; Churchill and war-
  time, 27–28
Household goods, expenditure on, 237
Houses, building of: post-War, 231–232;
  1945–50, 80; 1951, 231; 1956, 231;
  1963, 231; 1965, 231–233; *National
  Plan* and, 234
Housing, expenditure on, 237
Housing Societies, 233
Hydro-electric Board, North of Scotland, 73, 171; financial return, 126

ILLEGITIMATE BIRTHS, 214, 281
Immigration, 216–221
Imports, 39, 40, 80, 85, 97, 111; *Tables*,
  331, 332
'In care' children, 270; cost of, 271;
  categories of, 271; accommodation
  for, 271, 272
Income tax, 240, 241; *Table*, 334
Incomes, 87, 93–94, 108, 118, 237, 310;
  Table, 345; *Graphs*, 364–366
Incomes Policy, 88, 310
Independent Labour Party, 65–66
Independent Television Authority, 159–
  160; programmes, 160; advertising,
  252–253; *Tables*, 354, 355
Industrial Revolution, 7
Industry, Trade and Regional Develop-
  ment, Secretary of State for, 223
Institute of Practitioners in Advertising,
  252
Insurance—*see* Health Insurance; Na-
  tional Insurance
Insurance agents, 244
Insurance, Ministry of: Social, 27;
  National, 27, 63; debate on name of,
  27; scope of, 47
International Monetary Fund, 89, 100–
  101
Investment, 110–111

Iron and steel: nationalization, 74–76,
  130; Steel Board, 74; denationalization, 79, 131–132; Tory Party and, 79;
  output, 1948–60, 132–133; 1962–63,
  133–134; world production, 133; exports, 133; imports, 133; development of the industry, 134; renationalization, 134–135
Iron and Steel Board, 131, 132, 134
Iron and Steel Corporation, 130, 131,
  132
Iron and Steel Holding and Realization
  Agency, 131, 132

KOREAN WAR, 80, 130

LABOUR EXCHANGES, 10–11
Labour Governments: 1923, 16; 1929,
  16–17; 1945, 35–36, 40; 1951, 80;
  1964, 97; 1966, 118
Labour mobility, 88
Labour Party: inception, 9, 66; between
  the Wars, 16; in War-time Coalition,
  17; in General Election of 1945, 31–
  36; at time of assuming office in 1945,
  37–38; constitution, 66; and nationalization, 66 *et seq.*, 123–125, 128–129;
  further nationalization proposals in
  1950, 79, 128; and Common Market,
  91; programme in 1964, 95–96; and
  Election of 1964, 96–97; *Tables*, 317,
  356
Labour Representation Committee, 66
Land: and nationalization, 67; pressure
  on, 234
Lawyers, 244
Leisure, 234–235
Lend-Lease, 40
Lever Bros., 254
Liberal Government of 1906, 10
Liberal Party: and Election of 1945, 33,
  35; and Election of 1951, 80; and
  Common Market, 91; and Election of
  1964, 97; *Tables*, 317
'Little Neddies' — *see* Economic De-
  velopment Councils
London Passenger Transport Board,
  66
London Passenger Transport Executive,
  137, 143; composition of Board, 123
London Transport Board, 142

MAIL-ORDER SHOPPING, 250–251
Management studies, 96, 103
Management training, 88

Index of Persons